THE ORIGINS OF

GREEK CIVILIZATION

THE

ORIGINS OF

GREEK CIVILIZATION

1100–650 B.C.

by Chester G. Starr

W · W · NORTON & COMPANY

New York / London

First published as a Norton paperback 1991

Originally published by Alfred A. Knopf, Inc., 1961

L. C. catalog card number: 60-53446

Printed in the United States of America.
Library of Congress Cataloging-in-Publication Data

Starr, Chester G., 1914-
The origins of Greek civilization : 1100-650 B.C. /
by Chester G. Starr
p.   cm.
Reprint. Originally published: New York : A.A. Knopf, 1961.
ISBN 0-393-30779-4 (pbk.)
1. Greece—Civilization—To 146 B.C.   I. Title.
[DF77.S62   1991]
938'.01—dc20   91-6458
                                                                    CIP

ISBN 0-393-30779-4
W. W. Norton & Company, Inc.
500 Fifth Avenue, New York, N.Y. 10110
W. W. Norton & Company Ltd.
10 Coptic Street, London WC1A 1PU

1 2 3 4 5 6 7 8 9 10

TO

KARL R. BOPP

THOMAS A. BRADY

WALTER MILLER

PREFACE

THE SUBJECT of this volume is the formative centuries of Greek civilization. What the term "Greek" will mean in the following pages I had best make clear from the beginning. In the geographical sense ancient Greece included the Aegean basin as a whole, although its focus lay in the mainland districts south of Thessaly. Culturally I shall apply the words "Greek" and "Greece" solely to that coherent structure of thought and art which flowered in the great achievements of classical Hellenism.

This is not an idle precision. Men nowadays are inclined to find Greeks far back in the early history of the Aegean world. Quite often the inhabitants of the Mycenaean age, in the second millennium B.C., are described as Greeks inasmuch as they spoke a Greek tongue. This tendency underlines the undoubted fact that very deep connections linked the successive epochs of Aegean development; yet it also muffles the tremendous cultural gulf which separates Mycenaean and Greek civilization. The latter outlook, the root of Western culture, was essentially a new creation in the centuries just after 1100 B.C.

Virtually all the period considered in this work is prehistory in the sense that datable written documents are not available to guide one's study; but physical evidence is at hand to suggest the tempo and causes of early Greek progress. Thirty years ago this was not true. Historians then could use little beyond the feeble hints of myth and epic, and commonly summed up the long period from 1100 to 650 as an undifferentiated Homeric age. The archaeological evidence for early Greece, fortunately, has grown at a great pace in the past generation. Much is still dark. Much which today seems certain will be overturned by fresh excavations tomorrow. The historical student will inevitably make mistakes in assessing the material we already have, which is not always completely published and which presents a host of complex problems. But it is time to estimate the meaning of this evidence; and a historian, applying soberly the canons of his craft, may hope to make out a pattern of the principal stages in early Greek history.

In an earlier study on the end of classical civilization, *Civilization and the Caesars: The Intellectual Revolution in the Roman Empire,* I had occasion to advance some arguments on the major forces which moved history. In the present investigation there has appeared no reason to change my views, but the evolution of early Greece does lead one to reflect more particularly upon the tempo of historical change. As will be suggested at various points in the text, I have been driven to feel that the common historical view on this matter is faulty. It is time we gave over interpreting human development as a slow evolution of Darwinian type; great changes often occur in veritable jumps, two of which will appear before us in the following story.

The documentation for my argument rests both upon the footnotes and upon the illustrations. The former are designed primarily to suggest the evidence, much of which is new and not yet fully digested into common acquaintance; but I have also indicated the specialized studies, where they exist, on matters which I have perforce treated generally in an effort to clarify the main line of progress. Commonly my references are to the latest works, from which may be derived the earlier literature; in the case of Homer, for instance, a complete bibliography would require a very large volume in itself. The quotation of literary fragments is based for the lyric poets on the edition of Ernest Diehl, *Anthologia lyrica graeca* (3d ed.; Leipzig, 1949–52); for Archilochus on François Lasserre and André Bonnard, *Archiloque: Fragments* (Paris, 1958); for Sappho and Alcaeus on E. Lobel and D. Page, *Poetarum Lesbiorum Fragmenta* (Oxford, 1955); for the pre-Socratic philosophers on H. Diels, *Die Fragmente der Vorsokratiker* (6th ed.; Berlin, 1951–52). Translations are generally from the Loeb Classical Library unless they are my own.

The illustrations furnish representative or important examples of the main body of physical evidence. For permission to reproduce photographs and in most cases for original prints I am much indebted to the sources noted on the plates.

It remains for me to thank those who have aided my researches in a difficult field. More than in any previous work they have been numerous, and I am deeply grateful to the unselfish kindness of museum custodians, librarians, and scholars in many localities. In particular my thanks must go to C. W. Blegen, Mr. and Mrs. J. L. Caskey, J. M. Cook, Paul Courbin, Emil Kunze, S. S. Weinberg, N. M. Verdelis, and Dietrich von Bothmer, the last two of whom opened closed collections respectively at the Argos Museum and at the Metropolitan Museum of Art. I am also obligated to the University of Illinois, both for funds to photograph vases and for a sabbatical leave; and to the renewed assistance of the John Simon Guggenheim Memorial Foundation, which made it possible for me to extend the course of my second stay in the ever fascinating land of Greece over the year 1958–59.

CHESTER G. STARR

Champaign, Illinois

Note to the Paperback Edition

Fascinating archaeological material has turned up in recent years, especially in the Attic countryside, but this new evidence essentially supports the line of argument in the following pages. Since the work has been so well received I am very pleased that W. W. Norton is reissuing it in a paperback edition.

C.G.S.

January 1991

CONTENTS

PART I · THE EARLY AEGEAN

PART II · THE DARK AGES

Contents

ILLUSTRATIONS

MAPS

ABBREVIATIONS

AA *Archäologischer Anzeiger*

AEGEAN AND NEAR EAST *The Aegean and the Near East: Studies Presented to Hetty Goldman* (New York, 1956)

AJA *American Journal of Archaeology*

AJP *American Journal of Philology*

AM *Mitteilungen des deutschen archäologischen Instituts, Athenische Abteilung*

ANATST *Anatolian Studies*

ANNUARIO *Annuario della scuola archeologica di Atene*

ARCH. EPH. ʼΑρχαιολογική ʼΕφημερίς

BCH *Bulletin de correspondance hellénique*

BELLETEN Türk Tarih Kurumu: *Belleten*

BSA *Annual of the British School at Athens*

CP *Classical Philology*

CVA *Corpus Vasorum Antiquorum*

ERGON Τό ἔργον τῆς ʼΑρχαιολογικῆς ʽΕταιρείας

HSCP *Harvard Studies in Classical Philology*

ILN *Illustrated London News*

JDI *Jahrbuch des deutschen archäologischen Instituts*

JHS *Journal of Hellenic Studies*

KERAMEIKOS *Kerameikos: Ergebnisse der Ausgrabungen* (Berlin): I (1939), IV (1943), V. 1 (1954), VI. 1 (1959)

MATZ, GGK Friedrich Matz, *Geschichte der griechischen Kunst,* I (Frankfurt, 1950)

NEUE BEITRÄGE *Neue Beiträge zur klassischen Altertumswissenschaft (Festschrift B. Schweitzer)* (Stuttgart, 1954)

NILSSON, GGR M. P. Nilsson, *Geschichte der griechischen Religion,* I (2d ed.: Munich, 1955)

OPUS. ARCH. *Opuscula archaeologica*

PW Pauly, Wissowa, et al., *Real-Encyklopädie der classischen Altertumswissenschaft*

PRAKTIKA Πρακτικά τῆς ἐν 'Αθήναις 'Αρχαιολογικῆς 'Εταιρείας
RA *Revue archéologique*
REA *Revue des études anciennes*
REG *Revue des études grecques*
RM *Rheinisches Museum*
VENTRIS AND CHADWICK, DOCUMENTS Michael Ventris and John
    Chadwick, *Documents in Mycenaean Greek: Three Hundred
    Selected Tablets from Knossus, Pylos and Mycenae with Com-
    mentary and Vocabulary* (Cambridge, 1956)

PART I

THE EARLY AEGEAN

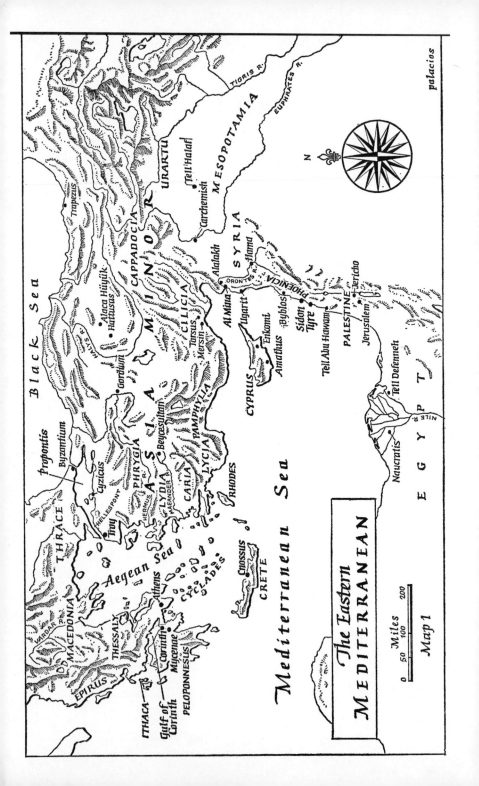

The Eastern
MEDITERRANEAN

Miles
0   50   100   200

Map 1

The AEGEAN BASIN

■ ● (Troy, Eutresis) – SITES PROMINENT BEFORE 1100 B.C.
● ● (Athens, Teos) – SITES OCCUPIED 1100 – 650 B.C.

Map 2

Miles
0   50   100

palacios

CHAPTER 1

THE EARLY AGES

OF GREECE

ⅬⅬⅬⅬⅬⅬⅬⅬⅬⅬⅬⅬⅬⅬⅬⅬⅬⅬⅬⅬⅬⅬⅬⅬⅬ

THE MOUNTAINS OF GREECE have long loomed sharp, beautiful, and barren over narrow valleys. For millennia the blue Aegean has sparkled in vivid sunlight or has roared into sudden, fierce storms against the cliffs and sandy beaches of its many islands. Since the earliest phase of human history, the Paleolithic, men have lived in this area, adapting themselves to the vagaries of its climate while exploiting its resources, and have slowly molded the landscape to their own desires. The pattern of civilization, however, which we call "Greek" and which has directly influenced all subsequent Western history, was evolved only in the centuries between 1100 and 650 B.C.

This was not the first true civilization in the Aegean world, for an earlier phase of development had produced the heights of Minoan and then Mycenaean culture. But catastrophe befell Minoan Cnossus about 1400 B.C., and the lords who thereafter ruled Greece met their fate in turn during the early and middle decades of the twelfth century B.C. The great citadel of Mycenae, then the center of the Aegean world, went up in flames despite its grim rock walls which later, awed generations were to call the work of the Cyclopes. Far off on the west side of the Peloponnesus other invaders gutted the noble palace of Pylos; behind their fury lay fragments of gold leaf and spilled clay tablets on the floor of the royal record room.

More than sudden death and physical destruction took

place in the twelfth century. If royal scribes survived the initial sack, they found thenceforth no call for their ability to set down accounting marks, for the whole structure of Mycenaean kingship had ended. Greece was not to need or to know writing again for centuries. The cunning workers in gold and ivory, in fresco and stone, lost their markets and trained no apprentices to carry on the advanced arts developed up to their time; only the most basic skills, those demanded for survival, continued to be employed. The peasants in the villages round about the Mycenaean fortresses may have watched almost with joy as smoke spiraled up from the gleaming palaces of their fallen masters, but they suffered too. Social, economic, and political organization swiftly sank, and with it fell the level of population.

The catastrophe which lies behind Greek civilization was not an accidental interruption to Aegean development but rather cleared the way for the emergence of the true Hellenic outlook. To understand this important fact more fully we must go back to look at the glittering Mycenaean civilization. This, in turn, can only be understood if it is placed against the background of Minoan Crete and of the Greek mainland during the Neolithic and Bronze ages.

A brief consideration of these preliminary matters has two other advantages as well. Since the Aegean landscape underwent no magical change between the second and the first millennia, the earlier development of the area will help to throw light on the manner in which geographical factors influenced Greek history. We shall, moreover, find very considerable evidence of a basic continuity in patterns of culture and society from early times; though much of the superstructure vanished in the Mycenaean debacle, the men who came thereafter did not totally discard their inheritance. In this Part, Chapter 1 will carry the story across the Neolithic, Early Bronze, and Middle Bronze eras, with a side glance at the amazing phenomenon of Minoan Crete; Chapter 2 will consider the rise and fall of the Mycenaean world.

THE GEOGRAPHICAL POSITION OF GREECE [1]

A MODERN TRAVELER from the great territorial states of western Europe and the Americas feels himself in a different world when he enters the Aegean. The basic cast of civilization here is today European, yet wares in stores are distinguished as "European" or "Greek"; despite decades of philological purification, Greek speech and town names have still their traces of eastern (Turkish) and northern (Albanian) influence; life takes place on a simple plane, materially speaking, and seems almost fatalistic. Some of the characteristics of modern Hellas are the product of its recent history. Some, however, are the fruit of geographical and climatic factors which today affect social and economic institutions, even intellectual attitudes, very much as they did four thousand years ago.

In Greece there are no great plains, nodding with crops to a dim horizon, nor mighty rivers which roll throughout the seasons down to the sea. The land, indeed, is only one part of the geographical framework, for the historic backdrop of Greek civilization is a sea, the Aegean, together with its main islands and its shores in Asia and in Europe (see Map No. 1). The western border of the Aegean, or Greece proper, is a region of limestone mountains which have sunk at their southern end in recent geologic times. Where they meet the main bulk of the Balkans, the mountains still stand tall and are bordered by the major plains of Macedonia and Thessaly. In the south islands abound as the remnants of sunken mountain ranges; and the sea sends long fingers up between the mountain ridges.

Nowhere in southern or central Greece are men more than forty miles, a day or so on foot, from the sea; nowhere on the Aegean, again, will a ship be entirely out of sight of land on a clear day, until it breaks out to the south beyond Crete and

[1] See generally Max Cary, *The Geographic Background of Greek and Roman History* (Oxford, 1949), chap. 1–3; J. L. Myres, *Who Were the Greeks?* (Berkeley, 1930), 1–25; Alfred Philippson and Ernst Kirsten, *Die griechischen Landschaften*, I-II. 1 (Frankfurt, 1950–56); J. Holland Rose, *The Mediterranean in the Ancient World* (Cambridge, 1933). Climate: Philippson, *Das Klima Griechenlands* (Bonn, 1948).

Rhodes into the eastern Mediterranean. These conditions tended
to encourage seafaring, though we must not fall into the error,
common since the days of Thucydides, of interpreting Aegean
history purely as a function of naval activity. The mountains do
not often produce good ship timber, and at times stand so close
to the water's edge as to cut off inland residents from the coast.
The Aegean waters are too clear, too devoid of plant life, to
support large schools of useful fish; nor was overseas trade vital
in an age of economic simplicity and local self-sufficiency. Many
Greeks may have lived and died without ever catching more
than a distant, dimly curious glimpse of salt water; very few
made their living out of the sea. The influences which were
waterborne were important, but they are not all the story.

Though only something over a fifth of the Greek landscape
is cultivable, farming has been the main occupation of the Greek
population since Neolithic days. The agricultural lands, in
southern Greece at least, are small plains, divided from each
other by the hills. The latter were forested with brush and small
trees throughout much of ancient history but were the prey of
charcoal burners and voracious goats; and even by the fourth
century B.C. Plato (*Critias* 111c) described Attica virtually
as it is today, a decayed carcass with the bare bones sticking out
through the skin. The mountains have long had their herders,
who tend to take over the plains in periods of social and political
collapse. Crystalline layers in the hills along the western shores of
the Aegean also provide veins of silver, copper, and other metals;
the rock here is frequently marble; and good clay beds furnish
the raw material of pottery almost but not quite everywhere.
Along the eastern fringe of the Aegean the coastal plains of Asia
Minor are more extensive, and are traversed by rivers such as the
Hermus and Maeander which break down from the central
plateau of Anatolia through rocky ridges.

Greek rural life was never as sure of results or as rich in
returns as that of the river valleys in the ancient Orient. The
population of Mesopotamia and Egypt became large and heavily
packed, while the small resources of Greece supported a relatively thin inhabitation, clustered in groups around the small
agricultural plains wherever never failing springs were available.

Farming techniques in Greece, too, had to follow a somewhat different pattern from their Oriental prototype. There irrigation and drainage required the co-operation of great masses of peasants under common direction; in Greece individual farmers tilled their own plots, for the sharply seasonal rainfall offered few possibilities of harnessing permanent water supplies.

Farming in Greece, nonetheless, was not usually a desperate venture in eras of relative order, once men had learned to tailor their agricultural methods to the seasons. Raising crops by hand was a hard task, yields were low, but the effort was not an unending chore. While "Greece has always had poverty as her companion" (Herodotus VII. 102), the needs of life, including clothes and heat, were far less than in continental Europe. Even today, when life in Greece is much simpler economically than in England or the United States, an outsider feels twinges of envy when he sees how richly its residents manage to savor the non-material aspects of human existence.

The area within which Greek history throbbed is small, about three hundred miles on a side. The significant quality of Greek civilization as a basically uniform pattern which was invigorated by rich local diversity is paralleled in the geographic structure of this area. Of the three main divisions imposed by the sea—i.e., the coast of Asia Minor, the islands, and the Greek mainland—the latter has normally been the most important economic and cultural center; in its turn it falls into several distinct regions. A north-south ridge separates the east and west coasts of Greece, while another ridge from Olympus south to Euboea cuts off Thessaly from the coast; other ridges run roughly east and west to mark the northern and southern limits of Thessaly and Boeotia (see Map No. 2). An even sharper division is that of the Saronic Gulf and the Gulf of Corinth, which separate the Peloponnesus from central Greece. Throughout ancient Aegean development the major cultural and political units accorded with the geographical framework, though only in general terms. It must also be remarked, first, that these districts were not sharply sundered from each other; and, secondly, that they shared in the main a common pattern of hills, small plains, and corresponding agricultural and industrial potentialities.

Climatically as well all of Greece experiences the well-known "Mediterranean" pattern of weather. In the fall, as the Sahara cools, rain-bearing winds can drive in through the Mediterranean from the west and drop their precious contents now in sudden cloudbursts, now for a day or two, down to April. Average temperatures drop markedly in the winter, but the warming influence of the enfolding seas makes outdoor life possible throughout most of the season, at least in the coastal districts. In late May and early June comes the harvest season; thereafter Greece dries up in the cloudless days of a desert-like summer. The heat usually is moderated by the seas, but anyone who has wilted in Athens will comprehend the picture of summer lassitude in Hesiod's *Works and Days* (lines 582–96):

> When the artichoke flowers, and the chirping grasshopper sits in a tree and pours down his shrill song continually from under his wings in the season of wearisome heat, then goats are plumpest and wine sweetest; women are most wanton, but men are feeblest, because Sirius parches head and knees and the skin is dry through heat. But at that time let me have a shady rock and wine of Biblis.

Within the common climatic pattern, however, there is an extraordinary range of variations for so small a land. The western shore of Greece, which first receives the rain-bearing winds, has up to three times as much rain as the eastern coast and enjoys a mild winter. The inland valleys become bitterly cold in winter: the mountains cap themselves with long-lasting snow, and the shepherds pull close their coats. Even Athens knows freezing weather and snow. The opposite range of summer is also more marked along the eastern coast, where the north winds scourge the hot, dusty plain of Attica; farther north, Macedonia and Thrace have almost a continental climate. Yet virtually everywhere the air throughout most of the year is sharp and crisp.

No significant alterations in Greek climate or topography have been detected over recent millennia. One important aspect of Greek geography, however, was subject to change, and to that aspect—the position of Greece relative to other principal centers of population and culture—I shall have constantly to recur in later chapters.

Greece proper is a promontory of Europe thrust out into the eastern Mediterranean. By the islands which prolong the promontory into the Aegean it is closely linked with the sea and with the opposite shore of Asia Minor to form a distinct enclave. In the modern world the area still lies on the border line between Europe and Asia—a factor apparent in the stores and streets of Athens—but the rise of the Atlantic community has markedly reduced the importance and benefits of this position. In ancient times, however, the Aegean was unique in its accessibility to two entirely different reservoirs of peoples and cultures.

On the north lay the great land mass of Europe, the home of barbaric tribes which were bound only tenuously to any one tract of land. Whether self-moving or impelled by the invasions of others, these tribes shifted back and forth in Europe through both the prehistoric and early historic periods; and at times their movements spilled over into the peninsulas which jutted southward into the Mediterranean. On the east lay the seats of the first civilizations in Eurasia, the fertile valleys of Mesopotamia and Egypt with the connecting avenue of Palestine and Syria (the Fertile Crescent). Here migrations of peoples were checked, at least in part, by the emergence of firmly organized states; but movement of trade and ideas was thereby facilitated.

The Aegean enclave, it must be emphasized from the outset, was not completely open to influences from either the north or the east. By that very fact it tended to serve as a terminal point to both currents. With respect to the north, peoples moving down out of the great plains of Hungary and Russia had first to make their way through the Balkans, particularly along the relatively open center of modern Yugoslavia (the Morava and Vardar rivers). Then they had to cross a very decided climatic and topographic frontier, for as men twisted and turned through the broken, at times mountainous reaches of Epirus and Macedonia they passed from the temperate, continental regions of Europe, marked by deciduous forests, into the parched lands of the southern evergreen scrub. Only very powerful movements were to sweep all the way through Greece and still have enough momentum to launch out on the sea.

Men coming from the ancient Orient also traversed perilous distances if they were to reach the Aegean. By sea, the more open route, they made their way from Syria along the dangerous south coast of Asia Minor and entered the Aegean by Rhodes or Crete; by land, travelers plodded interminably along the even more hazardous and physically difficult tracks across the high plateau of Asia Minor. A casual glance at a map has often suggested to students of east-west relations that Asia Minor may be called a bridge between the Aegean and the Fertile Crescent. This concept is almost diametrically opposed to the reality, for down to the very end of the era considered in this volume the peninsula of Asia Minor was commonly a buffer between East and West.[2] Influences tended to work along its coasts or to penetrate its interior either from the southeast or from the western seaboard; they rarely can be shown to have passed directly *across* it. Whether trade and ideas made their way from the east by land or by sea, they tended to exhaust their strength within the Aegean and advanced farther north and west only with difficulty. From this fact arose the otherwise puzzling result that the very regions least favored climatically in the Greek promontory—the southeastern districts of the Peloponnesus, Attica, and Boeotia—were culturally dominant.

Both the basic fact that the Aegean can be reached alike from north and east and the qualification that the access was not easy are deeply significant elements when we place them against the lines of force emanating from prehistoric Europe and the ancient Orient. From as early a point in Greek history as our view can reach, the interplay of eastern and northern factors furnished much of the external stimulus for Aegean development.

[2] Carl W. Blegen, "The Royal Bridge," *The Aegean and the Near East* (New York, 1956), 32–35, is basically sound. On the geographical and early historical division of eastern and western Asia Minor, see also Albrecht Goetze, *Kleinasien* (2d ed.; Munich, 1957), 8, 178. The point of view advanced in the text seems to me valid also with respect to Eurasian incursions across the Caucasus into Asia Minor; only rarely did such onslaughts as those of the Cimmerians carry directly across to the Aegean coast. At this point I am not concerned with *local* movement of ideas westward from the Asiatic shores of the Aegean.

(*a*) *Early Helladic sauceboat from Lerna, in level preceding destruction of the House of the Tiles. Photograph courtesy American School of Classical Studies, Athens.*

(*b*) *Neolithic statuette from Lerna. Photograph by Alison Frantz, courtesy American School of Classical Studies, Athens.*

(a)

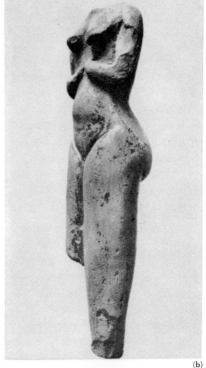

(b)

(c)

(d)

(*c*) *Middle Helladic matt-painted pithos from Eutresis, perhaps made in Aegina. Drawing by Piet de Jong; from Hetty Goldman, Excavations at Eutresis in Boeotia (Cambridge, Mass., 1939), pl. XIII.*

(*d*) *Early Helladic painted jar from Lerna, in level after destruction of the House of the Tiles. Drawing by Piet de Jong, courtesy American School of Classical Studies, Athens.*

PLATE 1 · *The Earliest Ages of Greece*

(a)

(b)

(c)

(a-b) Kamares vases from Phaestus, showing the "all-over" pattern of decoration and torsion (Heraklion Museum). Photographs courtesy YDAP, Athens.

(c) The Harvesters' Vase in steatite from Hagia Triada (Heraklion Museum). Photograph courtesy Bildarchiv Foto Marburg.

PLATE 2 · Minoan Crete

THE FIRST MEN AND CULTURES IN GREECE [3]

HUMAN HISTORY is not simply a mechanical response to geographical factors, important though these may be in determining ultimate limits or in predisposing men in certain directions. In the Aegean basin the activities of its inhabitants have varied widely over many aeons in reflection of external influences and internal innovations. Paleolithic remains have been found in Greece; but the first patterns of human settlement which can be described are those of Neolithic farmers, probably from the fifth millennium B.C. onward.

Neolithic sites have emerged all over Greece in recent years, for the archaeologists have turned their attention more consciously to this era. To keep abreast of the constantly widening picture of the excavations a student must rely not only upon the slow tempo of professional reports but also upon newspaper accounts and oral summaries. Very early layers, in which pottery was not yet used, have just been found in Thessaly near Larisa and at Sesklo; similar pre-pottery levels of settled farmers are known from such Near Eastern sites as Khirokitia in Cyprus and

---

[3] General surveys: Carl W. Blegen, "Preclassical Greece—A Survey," *BSA*, XLVI (1951), 16–24; V. Gordon Childe, *The Dawn of European Civilization* (6th ed.; New York, 1958), and *Prehistoric Migrations in Europe* (Oslo, 1950); Friedrich Matz, *Handbuch der Archäologie*, II (Munich, 1950), 177 ff.; Fritz Schachermeyr, *Die ältesten Kulturen Griechenlands* (Stuttgart, 1955), 37–150, and *s.v.* Prähistorische Kulturen Griechenlands in PW, 1359–1400; A. J. B. Wace, "The Prehistoric Exploration of the Greek Mainland," *BCH*, LXX (1946), 628–38, and "The History of Greece in the Third and Second Millenniums B.C.," *Historia*, II (1953), 74–94.

Thessaly: Chr. Tsountas, 'Αι προϊστορικαὶ ἀκροπόλεισ Διμηνίου καὶ Σέσκλου (Athens, 1908); Hazel D. Hansen, *Early Civilization in Thessaly*

(Baltimore, 1933); Vladimir Milojčić, *AA* 1954, 1–28; *AA* 1955, 157–231; *BCH*, LXXXI (1957), 593–96.

Examples in central and southern Greece: Leslie W. Kosmopoulos, *The Prehistoric Inhabitation of Corinth*, I (Munich, 1948); Emil Kunze, *Orchomenos*, II (Munich, 1931); Doro Levi, "Abitazioni preistoriche sulle pendici meridionali dell'Acropoli," *Annuario*, XIII–XIV (1930–31), 411–98; Hazel D. Hansen, "The Prehistoric Pottery on the North Slope of the Acropolis, 1937," *Hesperia*, VI (1937), 539–70; D. R. Theocharis, "Nea Makri," *AM*, LXXI (1956), 1–29; J. L. Caskey's forthcoming publication of Lerna, the excavation of which is briefly reported in *Hesperia*, XXIII (1954) and following.

Cyclades: Hubert Gallet de Santerre, *Délos primitive et archaïque* (Paris, 1958), 20–23.

Jericho. Then came the more developed strata which we have been accustomed to associate with the word "Neolithic."

One such site which has long been known and so has commonly been used for illustrative purposes is Thessalian Sesklo; for though Thessaly was somewhat isolated and atypical in all eras, early farmers here inhabited the same spots continuously enough to build up little hillocks with some stratification of deposits. In the Sesklo level which Tsountas excavated fifty years ago men lived in houses of clay or stone foundations and rectangular shape; oval huts of more perishable materials occur elsewhere. Among the household wares were pots, often painted or incised in zigzag patterns. Female figurines of clay and stone, which are a hallmark of Neolithic strata, are sometimes of lumpy, abstract proportions, sometimes rather naturalistic and indicative of a keen eye (see Plate 1b). Seals, obsidian from the island of Melos, and other evidences of relatively advanced life occur. The basic economic mode was agriculture, which rested on a variety of crops and was supplemented by some herding and fishing. In Thessaly a remarkably heavy population was supported by these means, and the Neolithic settlements at Corinth and Cnossus were extensive. Shipping was also known; some sites on the sea, such as Nea Makri in Attica, seem to have been chosen with an eye in part to their commercial (or fishing) advantages.

Today it is evident that the Neolithic villages of Thessaly were not the only such settlements in Greece, nor were they even necessarily the first farming communities in the Aegean. Scattered evidence from central Greece betrays much the same patterns with local variations, though the mounds left by the early hamlets have not yet received much attention. The Peloponnesus was also settled, and at Lerna the Neolithic inhabitants left valuable stratified deposits. The Cretan Neolithic level is rich at Cnossus; only in the Aegean islands and on the coast of Asia Minor is direct evidence for settlement at this time still extremely sparse. The importance of the Cyclades, however, at the beginning of the next phase suggests strongly that human inhabitation of the islands went back well into the Neolithic period.

The ultimate source of this way of life lay not in the Aegean but in the ancient Orient. Recent investigations have virtually fixed on the grassy upland hills of the Near and Middle East as the scene where agriculture emerged and whence it radiated to much of Europe and Asia.[4] Here several kinds of wheat and barley grew wild, as well as the ancestors of domesticated goats and sheep. The step to deliberate food-raising seems to have been taken before 6000 B.C.; Jericho was a walled settlement in the seventh millennium. These early farmers molded female figurines, presumably as fertility emblems in connection with agricultural rites and beliefs, and soon developed pottery. Copper, too, quickly came into use, first hammered out cold from chance-found natural lumps and then reduced from ore and cast.

It is universally agreed that agriculture with its companion achievements spread west to the Aegean—this indebtedness to the East is the major point about the Neolithic which we must keep in mind as a pointer for the forces affecting later Greek development. There is still great controversy over many of the details of the passage. One early agricultural settlement has recently been found in southwestern Asia Minor, at Hacilar, which has affinities both with Sesklo and with prehistoric Mersin in Cilicia; but, despite some as yet uncertain connections of Hacilar with other south-central Turkish sites, we do not have any firm testimony for the spread of agricultural techniques by land from the Orient to the Aegean. All that can be said is that throughout all sites so far known in Asia Minor and in Greece the Neolithic advance owed much to direct or indirect impetus from Halafian and other early cultures of Mesopotamia. Mersin and Hacilar, which lay much closer to this nucleus, experienced a wider range of change than did Sesklo.[5]

[4] Useful general studies are Robert J. Braidwood, "Reflections on the Origin of the Village-Farming Community," *Aegean and Near East,* 22–31, and "The Earliest Village Communities of Southwestern Asia," *Journal of World History,* I (1953), 278–310; V. Gordon Childe, *New Light on the Most Ancient East* (4th ed.; New York, 1952), and *What Happened in History* (London, 1942); Kathleen Ken-

yon, *Digging Up Jericho* (London, 1957), 51–76.
[5] John Garstang, *Prehistoric Mersin* (Oxford, 1953), 143–44, by Schachermeyr; Hetty Goldman, *Excavations at Gözlü Kule, Tarsus,* II (Princeton, 1956); James Mellaart, "Excavations at Hacilar," *AnatSt,* VIII (1958), 127–56, who is also much influenced by Schachermeyr. The parallels of Mersin, Sesklo, and Halaf are conveniently il-

On the whole I am inclined to suspect, in the present state of our evidence, that the new techniques came primarily by sea and that they were passed on as ideas rather than as baggage in a large-scale migration of peoples. Such a conclusion, it should be noted, stands in opposition to the views of many archaeologists, who postulate early movements of Oriental farmers; in support of their assumption stands the axiom that cultural transfers in prehistoric eras generally entailed ethnic shifts.

Before considering further the implications of this axiom for Aegean history, it is imperative that I indicate my views as to the historical use of archaeological evidence and assumptions; for these views underlie both the interpretations and the methods of approach which will appear in subsequent pages. Virtually all the centuries of Greek development which will be considered in this volume are prehistoric in the sense that they lack datable written documents, apart from the tantalizing hints of the Mycenaean tablets. In such a period the historian must turn first to the archaeological evidence, which may be mute but is at least relatively sure as to temporal and geographical location. Only after building a solid framework on this material can he hope to employ—and then secondarily—the hints to be derived from literature, chronological and genealogical traditions, and mythology, most of which were long preserved only in oral forms. The dangers of proceeding primarily from this latter type of evidence, which is, alas, the common method, will be illuminated at several points in our story.

The historian thus is deeply indebted to the archaeologist. He must also trust his confrere in the depths of his alien field, as in the detailed application of the ever more skilled techniques of excavation and in the factual interpretation of the discoveries, though even here the historian must keep a wary eye for hidden prejudices, faulty methods of digging, and other dangers. The more the historical student knows of archaeological practices and the more detailed his study can be of the actual evidence at

---

lustrated in Schachermeyr, *Die ältesten Kulturen,* 60–61.

Parallels in figurines are studied by Saul S. Weinberg, "Neolithic Figurines and Aegean Interrelations," *AJA,* LV (1951), 121–33. Early Cyprus, which lay in independent isolation at this time (as often later), is illuminated by Porphyrios Dikaios, *Khirokitia* (London, 1953).

first hand, the better. Beyond this point, the man trained in historical discipline must always be alert to the limitations and the logical problems of the archaeological outlook. He must, in sum, be both grateful and cautious.

To take an example or two, excavators can discover only physical objects, but not all human activity leaves behind it such testimony. Archaeologists tend often—with honorable exceptions —to take a materialistic view of the cultures which they uncover and to overstress the economic and social side of life. This tendency affects particularly their views of religion; it also helps to explain why a historian always has difficulty in adjusting the history of a society which rests on written records to its pre-history, which depends solely on archaeological materials. Archaeologists are, again, naturally hopeful scholars, dedicated to the proposition that everything has significance; but we must not forget, in our sober search for truth, that men in all ages have engaged in whimsey.

And, finally, to return to the issue immediately at hand, cultural change in a primitive society is too often considered to be a mechanical product of outside influences introduced solely via movement of peoples. Complex concepts, such as the practice of agriculture, are not easily discovered afresh and were, for the most part, fairly clearly transmitted from one place of origin. Yet their mode of diffusion need not have been large-scale migration. The historian will call to mind numerous occasions in more recent epochs when considerable innovations have resulted simply from commercial or intellectual intercourse, with at most the passage of a few experts—e.g., the spread of Renaissance art over northern Europe or the transmittal of the Industrial Revolution from England to the continent of Europe and to North America. Less extensive changes can often occur simply through imitation; one must never forget that motifs in pottery and other materials, often heralded as evidence of outside forces, may be independently invented in several areas.[6]

[6] J. D. S. Pendlebury, *Studies Presented to D. M. Robinson*, I (St. Louis, 1951), 185: "Likenesses are great pitfalls, and he would be a rash man who would trace any connection between Neolithic Thessaly and modern Mexico, though the vase shapes and painted patterns are hard to distinguish." Henri Frankfort, *Studies in Early Pottery of the Near East*, II

The important matter in any era is its general cultural outlook. Changes in this pattern may be of local origin; at times in Greek history we can show indebtedness to other societies. In the latter cases, the vehicle of the innovations needs to be sought, but the progress of early Aegean history has been much overcomplicated by the unnecessary assumption of hypothetical invasions, which then become the primary focus of attention. As we shall see in later pages, evidences of migration will occur where no immediate cultural revolution is visible; and, on the other hand, massive changes will take place in Greek culture which are not connected with any major movements—e.g., the Orientalizing wave of the eighth and seventh centuries B.C. Particularly where advanced cultures flourish close to relatively backward areas, the possibility exists of simple imitation and adaptation of ideas by an already existing population in the less developed regions. This condition obviously existed throughout most of the history of the early Aegean, which lay in happy proximity to the Oriental center of early civilization.

The skeletal remains of the earliest population of Greece are too scanty to support any firm conclusion, but suggest that the land then had already a variety of human types. These types were largely but not entirely of Mediterranean nature, and may have entered Greece from the southeast, the south, and the north. When each variety came, we do not know; they may have been on hand in the late Paleolithic period and could have increased rapidly in numbers once settled agricultural life was adopted. Thenceforth, certainly, the inhabitants of Greece were essentially descended from the mixture of stocks visible in Neolithic times. Alpine and other types were added later—at times in small numbers, at other points in more massive quantities—but over the centuries merged into the already existing population.[7]

(London, 1927), 2, thus illustrates three Pueblo vessels which are very similar in patterns to early Aegean and European wares. Within the basically parallel framework of ancient Mediterranean society, moreover, the same principles may independently produce

similar results; see Georg Hanfmann, *Altetruskische Plastik* I (Würzburg, 1936), 91.

[7] Greece: J. Lawrence Angel, "Neolithic Ancestors of the Greeks," *AJA*, XLIX (1945), 252–60, and "Skeletal Material from Attica," *Hesperia*, XIV

Development within the Neolithic age is hazily visible, though this picture is less easily drawn now that we must cope with a broad panorama of finds and can begin to sense the existence of local variations. [8] The period, too, apparently covers a far longer span of time than has generally been assumed. Since the Neolithic settlement at Mersin began by 6000 B.C. and Hacilar in southwestern Asia Minor, which has parallels to Sesklo, was under way in the sixth millennium, the Sesklo level in Thessaly may have to be put back to the early fifth millennium. Recent discoveries in Thessaly would tend to confirm this by their proof that a variety of cultures existed both before and after this level. Some scholars have divided the Neolithic period as a whole in the favorite trinitarian classification of archaeology and essay to demonstrate Early, Middle, and Late phases, based largely on pottery patterns; even more minute subdivisions and cross-currents are sometimes argued.

These changes need not concern us, but the widespread argument must be noted which attributes various somewhat unusual influences to an invasion of northerners. Among these cultures, marked often by the use of spirals and meanders, are those of Rachmani, of the first known settlements in the Aegean islands, and especially of Dimini and its parallels, which reach down into southern Greece. The common source of such cultures, it is argued, is the *Bandkeramik* pattern of spirals and meanders prevalent all across the great European plain in this era. [9]

(1945), 279–363, with articles there cited. Asia Minor: Angel, *Troy: The Human Remains* (Princeton, 1951); Goetze, *Kleinasien*, 8–12; Muzaffer Şenyürek in Seton Lloyd, *Early Anatolia* (London, 1956), 205–09, who summarizes his articles in *Belleten*. See also C. S. Coon, *The Races of Europe* (new ed.; New York, 1948); J. L. Myres, *Geographical History in Greek Lands* (Oxford, 1953), 19–21; and below, Chap. 2, n. 9 (p. 72). Are later changes in body types entirely the result of added elements from outside?

[8] Vladimir Milojčić, *Die Chronologie der jüngeren Steinzeit Mittel-und*

Südosteuropas (Berlin, 1949); Saul S. Weinberg, *Relative Chronologies in Old World Archeology* (Chicago, 1954), 86–88; Fritz Schachermeyr, "Die Abfolge der neolithischen Kulturen in Griechenland," *Geras A. Keramopoulou* (Athens, 1953), 89–104; Mellart, *AnatSt*, VIII (1958), 156; carbon-14 date of 6000 B.C. for Mersin, *ibid.* 33.

[9] Beyond the works listed in n. 3 (p. 13), see also the following: Ch. Delvoye, "Remarques sur la seconde civilisation néolithique du continent grec et des îles avoisinantes," *BCH*, LXXIII (1949), 29–124; Frankfort, *Studies in Early Pottery of the Near*

The problem of northern contacts is not simply a minor archaeological matter, but one which plunges to the heart of the vital forces at work all across Greek history. Those who try to introduce northerners into the Aegean world at every possible opportunity do so, consciously or unconsciously, in an effort to link its progress to Indo-European sources. The ramifications of this Nordic myth will concern us later; here it may be observed that the Neolithic period is perhaps the poorest in which to assume movements from the north. The restlessly surging tribes of Europe quite possibly were already throwing off splinter groups southward; and odd pots which smack of alien origins turn up sporadically in almost any excavation of a prehistoric Aegean site. Yet the evidence that whole cultures of this world, Dimini or any other, before the Middle Helladic era were indebted to northern sources is far from conclusive. Contact between the Balkans and the Aegean existed at this time, but the weight of argument is perhaps heavier that ideas moved mainly northward from the Aegean throughout the Neolithic centuries.[1] Both the difficulties of terrain and the very different ecological conditions in the Balkans, however, always required very extensive changes

---

East, II, 14 ff.; Kimon Grundmann, "Aus neolithischen Siedlungen bei Larisa," *AM*, LVII (1932), 102–23, "Donauländischer Import im steinzeitlichen Thessalien," *AM*, LIX (1934), 123–36, and "Magula Hadzimissiotiki," *AM*, LXII (1937), 56–69; Erik J. Holmberg, "Some Notes about the Ethnical Relations of Prehistoric Greece," *Opus. arch.*, VI (1950), 129–38; Fritz Schachermeyr, "Dimini und die Bandkeramik," *Prähistorische Forschungen* (Anthropologische Gesellschaft in Wien, IV [1954]), Gallet de Santerre, *Délos primitive*, 23 n. 5, on possible Cycladic influence.
[1] V. Gordon Childe, *Prehistoric Migrations*, 48–51, *The Danube in Prehistory* (Oxford, 1929), and "The Relations between Greece and Prehistoric Europe," *Acta congressus Madvigiani*, I (Copenhagen, 1958), 293–315; Miodrag Grbić, "Preclassical Pottery in the

Central Balkans: Connections and Parallels with the Aegea, the Central Danube Area and Anatolia," *AJA*, LXI (1957), 137–49; Wace, *Historia*, II (1953), 78–80; Weinberg, *Relative Chronologies*, 97. On the coupling of spiral and meander with central Europe, note their appearance in early Sicily and Italy: L. Bernabò Brea, *Sicily before the Greeks* (London, 1957), 53, 55.
    The old argument that the rectangular house with foreporch at Dimini, a prototype of the later *megaron*, reflects northern influence is even more doubtful; the type appears even earlier in Thessaly (Milojčić, *AA* 1955, 167) and in the Near East (Schachermeyr, *Die ältesten Kulturen*, 112–14). On the *megaron*, see also A. W. Lawrence, *Greek Architecture* (Harmondsworth, 1957), 67–68.

in those ideas and customs which did pass back and forth between Danubian and Aegean cultures.

The springs of Neolithic development, in sum, can be seen, but not its detailed progress. First, surely, we must put an initial impetus from the Orient, which probably came chiefly by sea; this force made its way beyond the Aegean even more slowly and incompletely. Both facts may warn us against any tendency to treat the Neolithic age in Greece as a straight copy of Oriental prototypes. As the pots of Greek farmers differed markedly from those of Syrian villagers, so too undoubtedly did the ideas in their heads; only in the largest sense was the eastern Mediterranean of Neolithic times one cultural province. Once agricultural life was under way in the Aegean, moreover, there is no compelling archaeological evidence against concluding that it developed essentially on its own for centuries.

THE EARLY BRONZE AGE [2]

FOLLOWING THE NEOLITHIC comes the Bronze age, an era which has different names in the separate parts of the Aegean world. In Greece the very long span from the early third millennium to 1100 B.C. is currently divided into Early Helladic, down

[2] General Surveys: Schachermeyr, *Die ältesten Kulturen,* 153–264, and *s.v.* Prähistorische Kulturen in PW, 1400–47; the other works listed in n. 3 (p. 13), with a bibliography down to 1947 in Saul S. Weinberg, *AJA,* LI (1947), 166–67. Examples in Greece: Hetty Goldman, *Excavations at Eutresis in Boeotia* (Cambridge, Mass., 1931); W. A. Heurtley, *Prehistoric Macedonia* (Cambridge, 1939); Emil Kunze, *Orchomenos,* III (Munich, 1934); Kurt Müller, *Tiryns,* IV (Munich, 1938); the excavations at Lerna.

The Helladic divisions rest initially on Blegen's careful excavation in 1915–16 of *Korakou: A Prehistoric*

Settlement near Corinth (Concord, New Hampshire, 1921), *Zygouries: A Prehistoric Settlement in the Valley of Cleonae* (Cambridge, Mass., 1928), and *Prosymna: The Helladic Settlement Preceding the Argive Heraeum,* 2 vols. (Cambridge, Mass., 1937); and secondly upon the classification of pottery of the Bronze age by A. J. B. Wace and Blegen, "The Pre-Mycenaean Pottery of the Mainland," *BSA,* XXII (1916–18), 175–89.

Cycladic divisions are based primarily on the British excavations of Phylakopi, 1896–1899: T. D. Atkinson and others, *Excavations at Phylakopi in Melos* (Society for the Promotion

to about 1950; Middle Helladic, from about 1950 to 1580; and Late Helladic, from about 1580 to 1100. The development of the Aegean islands, excluding Crete, is marked by a roughly parallel Early, Middle, and Late Cycladic. On the coast of Asia Minor, unfortunately, excavation has thus far been too limited to permit any such divisions; the most suitable relative yardstick of the region is that furnished by the levels of Troy, Troy I–V being Early Bronze, Troy VI Middle Bronze, and Troy VI–VII Late Bronze.

The physical evidence for the period is far greater than for the Neolithic age, and periodic cross-checks can be obtained for some sites through wares imported from other Greek centers, from Minoan Crete, and even from Oriental lands. In the last centuries of the Bronze age, moreover, we can break for a moment the limits implicit in purely archaeological evidence and gain a wider view of men's thoughts and institutions through written documents (and perhaps oral tradition). The great developments of the third and second millennia are three: first, a new, powerful impetus from the east; then an undoubted invasion from the north; and finally that amalgam of influences which we call the Mycenaean age.

The shift from Neolithic to Early Bronze is not a tidy step in Greece itself. Such settlements as Asine appear only in the Early Helladic period; at Athens the pottery typical of this era does not lie with Neolithic ware, yet at some sites about Corinth there is a mixture of old and new; Orchomenos and other points break from the Neolithic rather sharply and late. [3] In most districts Early Helladic pottery differs quite evidently from Neolithic styles, and in its high burnish, monochrome treatment, and

---

of Hellenic Studies, Supp. Paper IV, 1904); R. M. Dawkins and J. P. Droop, "Excavations at Phylakopi in Melos, 1911," *BSA*, XVII (1910–11), 1–22. Other evidence to 1947 is listed in Saul S. Weinberg, *AJA*, LI (1947), 176–77. See also K. Scholes, "The Cyclades in the Later Bronze Age: A Synopsis," *BSA*, LI (1956), 9–40, who gives a useful conspectus of the later stages; Gallet de Santerre, *Délos*

primitive, 24–27; C. Zervos, *L'Art des Cyclades* (Paris, 1957).

Troy and Western Asia Minor: C. W. Blegen et al., *Troy*, I (Princeton, 1950); Goetze, *Kleinasien*, 19–36; Winifred Lamb, *Excavations at Thermi in Lesbos* (Cambridge, 1936); see *ILN*, August 3, 1957, 197–99, on the recent Italian finds at Poliochni.
[3] Weinberg, *AJA*, LI (1947), 171–72.

clean shapes seems to simulate metal wares (see Plate 1a). These patterns have clear connections across the Aegean islands to northwestern Asia Minor, where a generally common culture has been found at Chios, Thermi (on Lesbos), Poliochni (on Lemnos), Troy I, and elsewhere. Somewhat developed Early Helladic vases have turned up in the middle of the Troy I settlement, which has, however, ties to inland Asia Minor also. Influences of this northwestern Asia Minor culture, in turn, have appeared at Mersin in Cilicia in a layer dated about 2900–2800 B.C.[4]

On the basis of these interconnections we should be able to assign an approximate date B.C. to the beginning of the Early Bronze age. Troy I, which is the basic key, is, however, not entirely fixed. Its American excavators extend its duration over about 3000 to 2600, while others essay to lower the foundation to 2700.[5] Fortunately for our purposes this disagreement is not a serious stumbling block; the Early Helladic era was a long one on either basis, and its consecutive stages of development are becoming somewhat clearer, thanks to excavations at Lerna and elsewhere. On the whole, if Early Minoan culture begins in Crete only about 2700, it would seem dangerous to assign really Bronze-age patterns elsewhere in the Aegean to a much earlier date.

More critical is the problem of the events which produced the change to Early Bronze cultures all over this area. This issue must be placed in a wide framework, for the coming of the Bronze age is not just a matter of changing outlooks among the ever more proficient potters or of an increasing frequency of the wares of the metalsmith. Both of these developments can be traced back into the last stages of the Neolithic era;[6] the really significant

[4] Garstang, *Prehistoric Mersin*, 183–84, 188; Goldman, *Tarsus*, II, 61, 347; M. V. Seton-Williams, "Cilician Survey," *AnatSt*, IV (1954), 121–74.

[5] *Troy*, I, 40–41; Goetze, *Kleinasien*, 35–36. For 2700: Milojčić, *Chronologie*, 25–27; Schachermeyr *s.v.* Prähistorische Kulturen, 1357–58; James Mellaart, "Anatolian Chronology in the Early and Middle Bronze Age," *AnatSt*, VII (1957), 55–88, who essays (pp. 79–84) to refute Blegen's

claim that Early Helladic wares appear in Mid-Troy I. F. Matz, "Zur ägäischen Chronologie der frühen Bronzezeit," *Historia*, I (1950), 173–94, reduces Troy I to 2600 and Early Helladic to 2500 on.

[6] Childe, *BSA*, XXXVII (1936–37), 26–35; Frankfort, *Studies in Early Pottery of the Near East*, II, 29 ff.; Schachermeyr, *Die ältesten Kulturen*, 126 ff.

marks of the Bronze age are much more sweeping and generalized. They emerged in the last analysis neither in Asia Minor nor in Greece but in the primary seat of early civilization, the ancient Orient.

By the fourth millennium the upland farmers in this area were moving down into the fertile river valleys of Mesopotamia and Egypt.[7] Equipped with the necessary technical facilities of improved tools and animal power, these men had also evolved the requisite social organization; for settlement of the plains had to be virtually a conscious act by a fairly large number of human beings who were prepared to dam and dike and to dig canals on a large scale. Once this step had been taken, subsequent development was swift. On their surplus of food the villages of the valleys grew rapidly in size and population; before 3500 they had in Mesopotamia the appearance of towns, with markets for the interchange of goods. Then, in the last centuries of the fourth millennium, civilization suddenly crystallized in the Orient. Specialization of economic activity, writing, kingship and military expansion, monumental architecture and art, the working of bronze—all could be found by 3000 in the firmly organized states of Mesopotamia, clustered about the imposing temples of the gods, and in the consolidated kingdom of Egypt.

From these nuclei new forces spread outward. Elsewhere, to be sure, the basic requirement of rich land was not always present, and so only parts of the Mesopotamian and Egyptian achievements appear throughout most of the Orient during the third millennium B.C. The Aegean, still farther off, picked up the new waves in even less degree, but the impetus was enough to set off Early Bronze cultures—Early Minoan in Crete, the northwestern Asia Minor complex about Troy, Early Cycladic in the islands, and Early Helladic in Greece. That this impetus came principally by sea is clearer than for the Neolithic wave. The latest studies of early Asia Minor are beginning to disentangle several cultural areas for the third millennium, but on present

---

[7] See generally Robert J. Braidwood, *The Near East and the Foundations for Civilization* (Eugene, Oregon, 1952); Childe, *The Most Ancient East;* Henri Frankfort, *The Birth of Civilization in the Near East* (Bloomington, Indiana, 1951); Ann L. Perkins, *The Comparative Archeology of Early Mesopotamia* (*Chicago,* 1949).

evidence there was no direct, easy flow of ideas and wares across the heart of the peninsula.[8]

Within the Aegean itself archaeologists seem almost unconsciously to accord priority for the new ways to the area about Troy, for they generally agree in deriving Early Helladic pottery patterns from an extensive migration westward across the Aegean and perhaps also around its northern end by land.[9] The bases of this argument are, first, the apparent imitation in Early Helladic pottery of metal prototypes which seem to have originated in western Asia Minor; then the perceptible influence of Cycladic culture on mainland settlements; and finally the progress of Early Helladic from south to north in Greece. Thessaly, in particular, was late in taking up the new ways. A recent theory suggests that this Aegean migration was in turn a reflex to major invasions of peoples speaking Indo-European languages, who would have pushed from the southeast Balkans into Asia Minor.[1]

Here, certainly, we must be cautious, less we fall into the common tendency of treating early peoples and cultures like billiard balls, bouncing one against another to set a whole table in motion. Movements in western Asia Minor about the middle of the third millennium, while possible, are not absolutely fixed, and

[8] Kurt Bittel, *Grundzüge der Vor- und Frühgeschichte Kleinasiens* (2d ed.; Tübingen, 1950), 16–24; Seton Lloyd, *Early Anatolia*, 62–63; James Mellaart, "Preliminary Report on a Survey of Preclassical Remains in Southern Turkey," *AnatSt*, IV (1954), 175–240; C. A. Burney, "Northern Anatolia before Classical Times," *AnatSt*, VI (1956), 179–203, and "Eastern Anatolia in the Chalcolithic and Early Bronze Age," *AnatSt*, VIII (1958), 157–209. The survey of surface sherds by James Mellaart, "Some Prehistoric Sites in North-Western Anatolia," *Istanbuler Mitteilungen*, VI (1955), 53–88, suggests again that early Troy had inland connections; at this point it seems as probable that forces moved inwards as that they came down toward the coast.

Seafaring in this era: A. Köster, *Schiffahrt und Handelsverkehr des*

östlichen Mittelmeeres im 3. und 2. Jahrtausend v. Chr. (Leipzig, 1924).
[9] E.g., Childe, *Prehistoric Migrations*, 53–55, 58–62. Heurtley's argument that the forces moved primarily by land from Asia Minor via Macedonia must meet the serious objections raised by Weinberg, *AJA*, LI (1947), 169.
[1] Mellaart, *AnatSt*, VII (1957), 55–88, and "The End of the Early Bronze Age in Anatolia and the Aegean," *AJA*, LXII (1958), 9–33. The invaders would belong to the Gumelnitza cultures about 2500 B.C. This argument rests on the assumption that Indo-European Luwians had come to Beycesultan in lower western Asia Minor by 2300 B.C.: Seton Lloyd and James Mellaart, "An Early Bronze Age Shrine at Beycesultan," *AnatSt*, VII (1957), 27–36.

their connections with the appearance of Indo-Europeans on the fringe of the then civilized world remain problematical.[2] In any case these background events, which are rather late to explain the appearance of the Early Bronze age in Greece, are not our main concern; nor need the historian even accept the argument that extensive movement took place from east to west across the Aegean in the early third millennium. The only aspect of the physical evidence in Greece which really points in this direction is the frequent change in sites of settlement at the beginning of the Early Bronze era, and this, as will be noted shortly, may have another explanation.

Is it likely, indeed, that the great Oriental developments found their first major Aegean reaction solely in its most northeastern recess, about Troy? This area may have led in metal techniques and in taking over the potter's wheel; but until sounder evidence is at hand we shall be safer to assume that all parts of the Aegean basin entered on basically independent, parallel, and limited imitations of Oriental progress, the Cyclades perhaps being in the lead chronologically. Within the common flow these districts had each its own peculiarities, and cross-influences accordingly now become more perceptible. Such influences need not have been accompanied by anything more than a most restricted movement of smiths and other new specialists to and fro. And, in passing, it may be commented that there is no direct physical testimony thus far for major incursions from the north during Early Helladic times.[3]

To consider now the characteristics of the Early Helladic period itself, one obvious mark is the change in pottery styles which has already been noted. Metals appear in much greater quantities than in late Neolithic sites and are employed for more

[2] Goetze, *Kleinasien*, 9–10, postulates considerable physical change in the population of Asia Minor, as do many in connection with the arrival of the Hittites. Brachycranes at Alaca Hüyük: Şenyürek, *Early Anatolia*, 207–08. As Angel, *Khirokitia*, 422, warns, however, we do not *know* that shortheads came in the Bronze age.

[3] Contra, Paul Kretschmer, "Die prot-

indogermanische Schicht," *Glotta*, XIV (1925), 300–19; Siegfried Fuchs, *Die griechischen Fundgruppen der frühen Bronzezeit und ihre auswärtigen Beziehungen* (Berlin, 1937). But the efforts to show northern influences at this time are generally rejected even by adherents of the Nordic school.

purposes; excavations at this level have uncovered gold, silver, and electrum ornaments as well as vases, weapons, and other objects in bronze. Many of the latter items, however, are still really copper, for tin was not easily obtainable. In general the metals, difficult to work as they were, were far from ousting stone and wood.

More significant in the development from the Neolithic age to the Early Helladic era is the frequent change in the sites of settlements. Some of the new locations simply reflected a great increase in the population of the Aegean world as tools and techniques improved; by the end of the era most of the major centers of later Greece had been occupied. The new foundations, such as the rabbit warren of Thermi, where the several-roomed huts huddled close-packed on narrow lanes, were often of relatively large dimensions, though we must remember that they were still agricultural villages. The term "city," I may note, will be used in this volume only for complex social and economic agglomerations resting on conscious intellectual outlooks and on specialization of functions; such nuclei could be supported by the richer lands of the Orient but were not to appear in the backward Aegean for a long time to come. Troy, for instance, is often mislabeled as a city, whereas it was no more than a fortress; Troy II occupied less than two acres.

Nevertheless, both industry and trade advanced noticeably in the Aegean during the Early Bronze age, and this increase, together with a tighter social and political organization, helps in part to explain the movement in sites of habitation. The skill of the smiths is visible in much of the metal work, especially the jewelry of the treasure of Priam from Troy II; for both in concept and in execution this hoard far surpasses the roughly contemporary treasure of Alaca Hüyük in central Asia Minor. The pottery, too, was well made, though still by hand; only at Troy II did potters use the rotating wheel, already discovered in the Orient. Such shapes as the sauce boat (Plate 1a) are typical. Painted ware also appears; on Plate 1d I illustrate a vase from the last Early Helladic stages at Lerna, which has a variant of a motif (cross-hatched triangles) that appears now sporadically, now commonly, on down into archaic Greek pottery.

The growth of trade by sea is likewise unmistakable. Even in Neolithic times the wide dispersal of Melian obsidian and the location of seacoast sites attest the existence of shipborne trade. Now new ports emerged, such as Asine; Early Cycladic wares and other items have turned up in isolated examples as far west as southern France and the Balearics and southward in Egypt; boats themselves were sketched on Cycladic vases.[4] The argument that cultural forces came from the Orient largely by sea gains support from this naval evidence, even though the details of the conduct of trade entirely escape us at this early date.

The emergence of a tighter political organization is strongly suggested by the very significant evidence of the ground plans of several Early Bronze sites. Troy II, for instance, was essentially a fortress designed to protect a chieftain's palace, a structure of several rectangular buildings akin to the form which the Greeks later called the *megaron* and grouped about a courtyard. The wealth of its ruler is suggested by the treasure buried within the settlement; another hoard has recently been found at Poliochni. At Lerna the large two-story House of the Tiles, erected of yellow stuccoed mudbrick on stone foundations with terra-cotta tiles for its flat roof, must have been the abode of a powerful ruler, whose seal was stamped on the palace stores.[5] Through mastery over the agricultural population and in minor degree through the riches drawn perhaps from trade and warfare, local lords were growing powerful in Aegean lands.

For many aspects of life, unfortunately, only tantalizingly inconclusive evidence is available. The existence of deliberate burial customs from the Neolithic era on, together with the use of female figurines and other evidence, indicates conscious reli-

[4] Seaports: Otto Frödin and Axel W. Persson, *Asine: Results of the Swedish Excavations, 1922–1930* (Stockholm, 1938), 432–33 (obsidian from Melos, vases from Crete, Cretan seals on wooden and woven containers, Cretan stone vessels, Early Cycladic sherds, etc.); George E. Mylonas, *Aghios Kosmas* (Princeton, 1959); Theocharis, *AM*, LXXI (1956), 1–2.
    Cycladic trade: Bernabò Brea, *Sicily*, 102–03; Frankfort, *Studies in*

Early Pottery of the Near East, II, 110–19; Schachermeyr, *Die ältesten Kulturen*, 174–75; Gallet de Santerre, *Délos primitive*, 48–49.
[5] Caskey, *Hesperia*, XXIII (1954), 23–27; XXIV (1955), 37–41; XXV (1956), 162–65; Lawrence, *Greek Architecture*, 14–18. Asia Minor parallel: Machteld J. Mellink, "The Royal Tombs at Alaca Hüyük and the Aegean World," *Aegean and Near East*, 39–58.

gious views. These are generally associated with a concept of a Great Mother, or fructifying nature; but, as I shall suggest later, theorizing of this type and its ramifications into matriarchal arguments had best be treated with cool reserve. So, too, the survival of place names such as Corinth and Assos which embodied such elements as $s(s)$ and $nd/t(h)$ and the very large percentage of words not of Indo-European root in the later Greek vocabulary do not necessarily mean as much as scholars have often asserted. Whether the place-name elements actually are not Indo-European is now very unsure, and the hypothesis that a primitive Aegean language embodying these materials spread from the southwestern corner of Asia Minor in Early Helladic times is worse than doubtful. The seacoast of Lycia and Caria was virtually unsettled down to the first millennium B.C.; the basic postulate of a great migration westward across the Aegean we have already criticized; and any early, lost tongue of the Aegean world may well have been its basic speech in Neolithic times as well. This language, indeed, might generally have been spoken along the eastern and central European shores of the Mediterranean if place names are actually a sound indication of language distributions.[6]

Though the Neolithic and Early Bronze ages differ in many respects, the ethnic composition of Aegean peoples, as far as we can speculate, remained essentially the same in this long stretch of centuries. Throughout the era the primary influences emanated from the Orient. At times these influences came as sharp waves, but probably they were more often a constant pressure; our evidence is too scanty to show Aegean development century by century, let alone decade by decade. Internal interconnections among the various districts of the Aegean world itself grew steadily throughout these periods, and are quite demonstrable just before the disruption which ended the Early Bronze age.[7]

[6] Schachermeyr, *Die ältesten Kulturen*, 239–263, and *s.v.* Prähistorische Kulturen, 1494–1548, surveys the literature and the evidence; on the risks of using place names, cf. Georges Dumézil, *Naissance de Rome* (Paris, 1944), 141–42. On the elements *ss* and $nd/t(h)$ as possibly Indo-European, see Mellaart, *AJA*, LXII (1958), 21–28; Goetze, *Kleinasien*, 61; Franz Dirlmeier, *Gnomon*, XXVI (1954), 157.

[7] Note the bowls with red cross in the interior and red band about the inside

By the end of the third millennium B.C. men in the Aegean had created an agricultural society of village-dwellers, who used tools both of metal, of stone, and of other materials and were directed to a considerable extent by local lords. This structure was still simple in comparison to the great cities of Mesopotamia and the massive monarchy of Egypt; yet it was firmly rooted and resilient. And if it were simple, Aegean society was nonetheless more advanced than that in any other part of continental Europe.

THE MIDDLE BRONZE AGE [8]

Not all of the factors which were to enter into the background of Greek civilization proper had yet been introduced by 2000 B.C. Off in Crete, the Minoan culture was just beginning to rise; but before this refined civilization cast its glow northward, mainland Greece itself experienced a great shock. Down to this date there is no firm archaeological proof that any major waves of northern invaders had entered Greece, though men of European origin may well have infiltrated in ways too devious to affect markedly our records. The beginning of the Middle Helladic era (*c.* 1950 B.C.), however, was almost surely marked by a great assault of peoples from the north.

---

of the lip, which appear in Greece, Troy IV-V, Anatolia, and Tarsus: Weinberg, *Relative Chronologies*, 89–90; Mellaart, *AnatSt*, VII (1957), 74–75.

[8] The background of Europe and the Indo-Europeans: V. Gordon Childe, *Prehistoric Migrations*, 179 ff., and *The Aryans* (New York, 1926); Albrecht Goetze, *Hethiter, Churriter und Assyrer: Hauptlinien der vorderasiatischen Kulturentwicklung im II. Jahrtausend v. Chr. geb.* (Oslo, 1936); Hugh Hencken, *Indo-European Languages and Archeology* (*American Anthropologist*, Memoir No. 84, 1955); A. Meillet, *Introduction à l'étude comparative des langues*

indo-européennes (8th ed.; Paris, 1937); Richard Pittioni, *Die urgeschichtlichen Grundlagen der europäische Kultur* (Vienna, 1959); E. D. Phillips, "New Light on the Ancient History of the Eurasian Steppe," *AJA*, LXI (1957), 269–80.

The Aegean proper: C. W. Blegen, J. L. Caskey, and M. Rawson, *Troy, III: The Sixth Settlement* (Princeton, 1953); Fritz Schachermeyr *s.v.* Prähistorische Kulturen, 1447–75, 1489–94; Gallet de Santerre, *Délos primitive*, 31–34; and the other works listed in n. 3 (p. 13). Thessalian tardiness: Milojčić, *AA* 1955, 205–06, 219–20.

To understand this significant development we must broaden our gaze to include not only the Near East but also the central reaches of Eurasia. From Neolithic times onward the great plains of eastern Europe and Siberia had been the home of unstable peoples, who became increasingly expert in nomadic ways of life. Only after 1000 B.C. did they progress to the stage of riding on horseback; in the second millennium the patriarchal clans moved on foot, herding cattle and transporting their women and valuables in carpet-hung wagons or on small steppe horses. Whatever their mode of migration, the peoples of the north poured down repeatedly across the more civilized lands of the farming societies which stretched from the Mediterranean to China—the last such invasion took place only five centuries ago under Tamerlane.

These migrations cannot easily be compressed into the strait-jacket of conventional historical causation, which is derived from the pattern of stable, politically integrated agricultural and commercial societies. Sometimes the more advanced cultures virtually invited this attack through being both rich and weak. At rare points a master strategist and statesman, such as Jinghiz Khan, arose to marshal and hurl his tribesmen southward. Mechanical factors—overpopulation, shortage of rainfall, and so on—are often advanced in modern accounts but are rarely susceptible of proof. The tendency to move was always inherent in the society of the plains; on occasion either internal or external factors facilitated this propensity and converted it into a full-scale migration.[9]

The second millennium B.C. experienced two great spillings-out of the northern savages, one at its beginning and one close to its end. In both cases the migrants spoke, at least in part, varieties of Indo-European languages. Their sweep is commonly traced by the appearance of these tongues, though, as investigation has proceeded, it has become ever more difficult to be sure when Indo-European speakers entered various areas. More datable evidence of the actual invasions is afforded by mute marks of

[9] See Owen Lattimore, *Inner Asian Frontiers of China* (2d ed.; New York, 1951); Myres, *Geographical History*, 127–30, 177–78.

extensive physical destruction and by terrified references in those areas which were already using some form of writing.

The earlier wave, which concerns us at the moment, scattered its participants all the way from India across the Middle East to western Europe. In Mesopotamia the Kassites of Babylonia and the Mitanni of the upper Euphrates appeared before the middle of the second millennium; in Asia Minor the Hittites were masters of the central Halys region by at least the early second millennium, if not before. They came perhaps across the Caucasus passes, and soon learned to write their native tongues in cuneiform script.[1]

The evidence that one part of this wave entered Greece is both archaeological and linguistic. The physical record shows that Early Bronze society underwent a very serious disturbance. A decided break in settlement or destruction by fire is clear at Asea, Malthi, Tiryns, Korakou, Zygouries, Aghios Kosmas, Orchomenos, and Eutresis. In other excavation reports similar testimony appears: Corinth was deserted for a time; Asine was badly damaged; Troy VI (c. 1900) obviously had new lords; the middle and northern islands of the Aegean seem almost, but not quite, deserted. Thereafter an evidently new phase of Aegean culture begins, which is labeled Middle Helladic (c. 1950–1580). New styles of pottery, matt-painted or burnished monochrome ware (gray, then red, yellow, and black), became dominant;[2] equally sharp changes are visible in architecture, burial rites, and the general physical patterns of life.

None of this material points clearly to the stages and routes of invasion or to the source of the invaders. Some sites in Asia Minor suffered destruction before the end of the Early Bronze

---

[1] O. S. Gurney, *The Hittites* (London, 1952); Goetze, *Kleinasien*, 82–183, treats the cultural aspects well.

[2] Arne Furumark, *The Mycenaean Pottery: Analysis and Classification* (Stockholm, 1941), 214–35, gives the fullest analysis; see also the clarifying remarks of Childe, *Acta congressus Madvigiani*, I, 300–01; and Wace, *Historia*, II (1953), 83. Frankfort, *Studies in Early Pottery of the Near East*, II, 14–15, 137–44, strove to derive this pottery from Neolithic–Early Helladic roots; Scoles, *BSA*, LI (1956), 23, suggests a Cycladic origin for the matt-painted ware; Mellaart, *AJA*, LXII (1958), 15–18, tries to establish the precedence of Minyan ware in western Anatolia (but cf. Bittel, *Gnomon*, XXVIII [1956], 250–52).

era. The House of the Tiles at Lerna, in Greece itself, fell, and quite a new type of pottery appears here after the evidence of destruction (see Plate 1d). The introduction of new peoples accordingly may have taken place over a considerable period; small bands may have led the way in preliminary raids. But a more massive, sudden sweep seems suggested, for the end of the Early Bronze world is roughly contemporaneous across much of the Middle and Near East as well as in Greece.[3]

The high road for this attack, one might assume, lay through the Balkans and northern Greece, yet the facts do not clearly point in this direction. Macedonia largely lingered in Neolithic styles; the transition to Middle Helladic at some sites in Thessaly seems to have been peaceful. Strong connections, on the other hand, exist in pottery and others matters between western Asia Minor and the Greek mainland, though styles of burial differ between the two.[4]

None of the phenomena, again, can be directly and unequivocally connected with the fashions of temperate Europe north of the Balkans. The burnished monochrome pottery, which is called Minyan after a legendary people of central Greece, turns up both in Greece and in Asia Minor and at Lerna may have begun in Early Helladic times. The matt-painted ware, which comes later, seems to have been of purely local origin (see Plate 1c). Neither type points directly to the Balkans and beyond; nor are the stone battle axes as strong a link between the Aegean and central Europe as has often been stated. Weapons of similar shape appear in Mesopotamia in the fourth millennium B.C. and have been found both in Asia Minor and in Greece during the Early Bronze era. All that we can safely infer is that their greater prominence at the time of the invasions, together with the appearance of the

---

[3] C. F. A. Schaeffer, *Stratigraphie comparée et chronologie de l'Asie occidentale* (*IIIe et IIe millénaires*), I (Oxford, 1948), 539–41, is a useful conspectus, though unfortunate in its choice of explanation; Winifred Lamb, *Iraq*, XI (1949), 199, sums up the evidence in Asia Minor.

[4] Mellaart, *AJA*, LXII (1958), 9–33,

accordingly suggests that the Hittites pushed other Indo-Europeans out of western Asia Minor and across the Aegean. This explains some Anatolian evidence, but does not account for such Aegean facts as the later presence of Greek-speaking peoples as a reservoir in the western Balkans.

horse, *perhaps* refers back to the cultures of the European plain.[5] At the very point at which the first almost certain migration from the north into the Aegean basin took place, the physical material, taken alone, neither proves an entry from outside nor shows its direction of progress.

The main clue lies elsewhere. The Aegean world knew and used writing before its next great upheaval; that writing, on the tablets of Mycenae, Pylos, and elsewhere, can now essentially be read; and the language of the tablets is Indo-European—Greek, in fact. The detailed problems which ensue, such as the dialect of the tablets, will be considered in Chapter 2; for the present point, one of two conclusions follows. Either Greek had been the tongue of Aegean peoples before the Middle Helladic period—and against this conclusion one must place, first, the evidence, already noted, that an earlier language had been spoken in the area; and, secondly, the fairly reliable consensus that the speakers of Indo-European languages intruded elsewhere in the Middle East in the second millennium. Or, as virtually all scholars in my judgment rightly agree, the great disruption at the beginning of the Middle Helladic era reflects the coming of an Indo-European people to the Aegean.

The true significance of this addition must be soberly assessed. To the devotees of the Nordic myth, the entry of the men who spoke Greek gave the vital impetus which, when reinforced by a second wave of invasion at the end of the Mycenaean age, led to the creation of Greek civilization. This argument I shall examine at the close of Chapter 2, but it may be well to state here two basic anthropological and physiological facts. A man who spoke an Indo-European language did not necessarily share with all his comrades one particular structure of body or color of hair and eyes; and his blood stream did not carry any specific outlook on life or aesthetic point of view.

A simple consideration of the physical evidence, on the other hand, may lead one to underestimate the importance of the upheaval. To some extent the rapine with which the Middle Hel-

[5] Caskey, *Hesperia*, XXIV (1955), 36–37; Childe, *Acta congressus Madvigiani*, I, 300, 303–04; Erik J. Holmberg, *The Swedish Excavations at* *Asea in Arcadia* (Lund, 1944), 11 ff.; Mellink, *Aegean and Near East*, 42; N. Valmin, *The Swedish Messenia Expedition* (Lund, 1938), 346–48.

ladic era opened meant a material setback, which is obvious in the subsequent cultural patterns. The invaders were far more barbaric than their subjects and perhaps pushed much of the land back into nomadic ways. It is not surprising that they contributed little of tangible nature which can be marked in the archaeological record; and one may doubt that they brought much of a positive nature in religion, political organization, and other impalpable aspects. Yet they did add something of great weight —namely, an impetus to change. As outsiders, they had a cultural background greatly different from that of the world to which they had come; as masters, they could question and transform old beliefs and standards.

Much of the old structure did endure: economically, in the survival of agriculture in at least some areas; technically, in the ways of the artisans; socially, in the village forms; even politically, in the maintenance of settlement generally on the same sites. Throughout Greek history many of its greatest centers, such as Athens, Thebes, and Corinth, kept pre-Greek names; the sites in which culture was to be focused in Mycenaean times can be shown archaeologically and linguistically to have existed before the Greek-speaking peoples came. The invaders, too, took over into their vocabulary many words from the earlier language, especially terms for seafaring, spices, and other relatively advanced aspects of culture. Yet the new tongue, with its implicit characteristics of logic and outlook on life, eventually supplanted the old speech in most of the Aegean. Here, as in the rise of the new styles of pottery, we can scent the great disturbance of old ways of life and intellectual attitudes; only the break at the end of the Mycenaean age was to approach its magnitude.

In view of the shock with which the Middle Helladic era commenced, it is not surprising that the period was outwardly undistinguished. Time was required to restore order and to knit together the fabric of society; but by the end of the period the earlier growth in population and extension of settlement had resumed. The use of bronze became more common. By the middle of the period pottery was generally turned on a wheel, and displays a number of local variations. While Hellas was a more distinct province in these centuries and its settlements at points retreated inland, trade by sea continued. By 1600 the mainland of Greece had reached an adjustment between the old and new elements, and its lords were ready to reach out and draw on the glory of Middle Minoan culture which had been flowering in Crete, untouched by the invasions.

THE PLACE OF MINOAN CIVILIZATION [6]

FIFTY YEARS AGO scholars were so dazzled by the beauty and freshness of Minoan civilization, which the ruthless drive of Sir Arthur Evans's excavation was restoring to view, that they tended to describe the palace of Cnossus as the culmination of Aegean prehistory. Even now, as one wanders down the corridors of Cnossus, Phaestus, and other Cretan palaces which lead to lovely staircases and the living quarters of their erstwhile lords, one must muse on the gay, polished life passed by the kings and ladies of Crete while Greece was still in barbarism. In the general frame of Aegean development, however, the culture of Crete shrinks to a more modest place. Minoan civilization was highly significant both as an intermediary between the Orient and the Aegean and as a spur to the development of the mainland; but it was essentially an offshoot from the main line of Greek progress.

Basically, Crete illustrates what could happen to the Neolithic–Early Bronze level of the Aegean when this stratum was

[6] Minoan civilization: Helmut Th. Bossert, *Altkreta* (3d ed.; Berlin, 1937); Sir Arthur Evans, *The Palace of Minos*, 4 vols. (London, 1921–36); Friedrich Matz, *Kreta, Mykene, Troja: die minoische und homerische Welt* (2d ed.; Stuttgart, 1956); J. D. S. Pendlebury, *The Archaeology of Crete* (London, 1939); Luigi Pernier, *Il palazzo minoico di Festo*, 2 vols. (Rome, 1935–51). More recent excavations at Phaestus have thrown into some doubt the conventional divisions of the Minoan period (e.g., Doro Levi, *Bollettino dell'Arte*, XXXVI [1951], 341–45, and succeeding volumes).

The arts of Crete: Furumark, *Mycenaean Pottery*, 112–213; H. A. Groenewegen-Frankfort, *Arrest and Movement: An Essay on Space and Time in the Representational Art of the Ancient Near East* (Chicago, 1951), 185–216; Lawrence, *Greek Architecture*, 18–51; Friedrich Matz, *Die frühkretischen Siegel: eine Untersuchung über das Werden des minoischen Stiles* (Berlin, 1928); G. A. S. Snijder, *Kretische Kunst* (Berlin, 1936); C. Zervos, *L'Art de la Crète* (Paris, 1956).

influenced from the outside not by northern invaders but by direct contact with the blossoming High Bronze cultures of the Orient. Down through the Early Minoan era (*c.* 2700–2000) the local cultures in Crete varied greatly and were not, on the whole, markedly different from or superior to the parallel levels in the rest of the Aegean. Movements of ideas into Crete from this side, especially but not exclusively of Cycladic origin, are obvious. By the last centuries of the third millennium, however, Cretan civilization began to coalesce, and in the following Middle Minoan era (*c.* 2000–1580) it skyrocketed into one of the most extraordinary achievements of mankind.

Here, and only here in Aegean history down to the first millennium, true cities appeared beside the palaces of the kings. While the rulers were important, they did not tower over the rest of society as their confreres did in Egypt and Mesopotamia. The citizens of Crete dwelt within several-storied houses and enjoyed a rich urban culture of remarkable grace and polish. More than any other pottery of which I know, the thin, graceful vases of this era must be seen if one is to appreciate their delicate colors and sophisticated patterns, which took the whole vase as a unit (see Plate 2a–b). Besides this Kamares ware there are lithe, nervous figurines in ivory and stone; superb frescoes on the palace walls; and a host of other artistic and practical products.

Minoan civilization is not simply Oriental in its spirit, though it owed much in matters of technique to the Orient. Nor was it at all like the Middle Helladic world; Crete and Greece were moving on quite different paths in the early second millennium. The culture of Crete, polished though it was, was also most certainly not the root from which the later civilization of historic Greece directly drew. Sensitive students of Greek art always feel themselves somewhat puzzled when they turn to Minoan products. The very shapes of the vases lack that solidity which is a hallmark of the Greek world; and their decoration, while elegant, has well been described as intuitive, impressionistic in its rendition of nature rather than analytical and logical in the Greek sense. The human being was rarely the center of attention. Even the figurines of acrobats and the like do not seem to have an inner substance but are rather a "dazzling expression of fugitive movement." The art historian looks to Cretan products in vain for "the innate love of balanced order, the feeling of structural symmetry which are the most essential qualities of Greek art."[7]

Nonetheless the products of this spirit could be widely attractive. Economically, Cretan life continued to be based primarily upon agriculture and the local interchange of wares, which was now fostered by the construction of good roads; but Cretan products moved farther afield. By the last stage of the Middle Minoan period Cretan merchants were active on the Syrian coast and were exporting their wares to Egypt.[8] And before the end of Middle Helladic times the Indo-European lords of the Greek hamlets had become aware of the glamorous, exciting culture which lay to the south.

Cretan traders may have visited Greece, but it is much more likely that first the islanders and then the mainlanders were drawn by the riches of the Minoan world, which they gained either by bartering whatever wares they might be able to sell or by swift piratical raids.[9] Behind their watery barrier the cities and palaces of Crete lay virtually defenseless, a tempting prey for the warlike, semi-barbarous lords of Greece; the common assumption of a Minoan thalassocracy is quite inconsistent with the simple naval and political organization of the era. Shortly after the beginning of Late Minoan times, at least one band of mainlanders swept down on Cnossus, took the palace, and ruled it thenceforth. The evidence for this change is abundant. Mainland

[7] Georg Karo, *Greek Personality in Archaic Sculpture* (Oberlin, 1948), 5.
[8] Helene J. Kantor, *The Aegean and the Orient in the Second Millennium B. C.* (Bloomington, Indiana, 1947), 31–32; J. D. S. Pendlebury, *Aegyptiaca: A Catalogue of Egyptian Objects in the Aegean Area* (Cambridge, 1930), and his brief essay, "Egypt and the Aegean," in *Studies to D. M. Robinson*, I, 184–97; Schaeffer, *Stratigraphie comparée*, I, 32, 65–67, 105, 117–18, 548–49; Jean Vercoutter, *Essai sur les rélations entre Egyptiens et préhellènes* (Paris, 1954).
[9] On the prominence of Cycladic intermediaries, see Scoles, *BSA*, LI (1956), 37–39; Cycladic wares to some degree precede the Minoan at Mycenae (Second Circle).

I have explored the myth of Minoan sea power, which is at once a product of Athenian naval interest in the fifth century B.C. and a reflection of the spirit of nineteenth-century British naval strength in "The Myth of the Minoan Thalassocracy," *Historia*, III (1955), 283–91. Carl W. Blegen, "A Chronological Problem," *Minoica (Festschrift Sundwall)* (Berlin, 1958), 61–66, must, however, be considered carefully with reference to the date when Linear B appeared at Cnossus.

themes were introduced into the pottery of Crete; pottery and fresco thenceforth paid far greater attention to the human figure; war and arms were now depicted, and men were buried with their arms; and the Linear A script, probably used for the tongue of the earlier local lords, was supplanted by Linear B, which we now know to have been Greek. The ensuing Palace style of art, which centered at the palace of Cnossus, was still capable of remarkable vivacity and superb rendition of action, as in a famous steatite vase which depicts drunken harvesters stumbling home amid loud song (see Plate 2c).

Possibly the new lords of Cnossus gained a brief control over the rest of the island, where the other palaces were destroyed one after another in the last half of the fifteenth century. In turn, however, their power fell on a windy day shortly after 1400. A new invasion from the mainland probably took place and sent the palace of Cnossus up in flames. Thenceforth the center of Aegean culture and political strength shifted to Mycenaean sites on the mainland of Greece. Minoan civilization went on, now in a backwater, down to about 1100, and its continuing effects were to mark off Cretan culture even in historic times; but never again did Crete stand in the lead of the Aegean world.

THE EARLY AEGEAN

ANALYZE as we will the factors preceding a specific historical situation, we can never quite explain what actually took place at any moment of time by recounting a list of its inherited ingredients. The eventual emergence of Greek civilization and then its great efflorescence are not to be explained as a simple, mechanical interplay of earlier forces.

The foregoing consideration of the geographical framework of the Aegean and of its earliest history has not been intended as a search for a set of elements which might be tidily assembled as the "causes" of later developments. Neither Neolithic and Early Bronze-age society, nor the wave of northern invaders, nor again the polished civilization of Minoan Crete was a discrete building-

block which persisted unchanged thereafter as a foundation stone
for historic Greece. The historian must always remember that he
deals not with abstract entities which may be combined in accordance with physical laws but with inherited outlooks held by
essentially free-thinking human beings. Nonetheless the reactions of the early peoples of the Aegean to their geographical
position may help to throw light upon the stimuli experienced by
this area in the period which will be our main concern. In any
epoch, moreover, there are elements of continuity from the past
beside new elements of change.

It is from this point of view that I have looked at a very hazy,
remote age, avoiding as far as is proper those detailed problems
which must concern primarily specialists in early Greece. The
conclusions which may be gained can now be summed up. The
geographical position of the Aegean, thus, invited entry of outside influences particularly from the east and from the north. The
first, and greatest, forces toward advancing the culture of the
area came from the east in Neolithic and Early Helladic times
and were reinforced, as will appear shortly, in the Mycenaean
age. Other elements intruded from the north at the beginning of
the Middle Helladic period and perhaps at other times in less
perceptible form. Sometimes people entered the Aegean; more
often, ideas and concepts migrated along the routes of prehistoric trade. These routes did not run across Asia Minor, which
commonly moved independently of the Aegean but along parallel lines.

Periodically the Aegean world had time to digest external
influences into its own unfolding pattern of agricultural village
life under chieftains. While the progress of this area across the
long centuries of the Neolithic and Bronze ages cannot be understood unless we place it within the context at least of the Near
East and of southern Europe, Greece was not at any point simply
a province of foreign-born cultures. Its basic political, economic,
and religious patterns were very similar to those of the Near East,
though less advanced. Intellectually, too, the outlook of early
Aegean men probably had many points in common with that in
the more developed Orient. Yet the archaeological evidence
alone is enough to attest that ways in the Aegean differed signifi-

cantly from those of its neighbors from very early times onward.

The pottery shows this fact. It must also suggest, if one compares Plates 1, 2, and 4, how uncivilized the inhabitants of Greece proper remained until they came into direct contact with Minoan Crete. Down through Middle Helladic times the shapes and the decoration of the pots lack that systematic, conscious elegance which we associate with the presence of true civilization, though their underlying spirit suggests elements of enduring importance. The Mycenaean world, which rose on top of the rather provincial Middle Helladic period, was to adapt the civilized Minoan outlook to this native spirit; it also brought the closest approach of Aegean and Oriental patterns before historic Greek times. Even in this epoch, as we shall now see, Mycenaean lords and craftsmen did not simply ape the East.

CHAPTER 2

THE RISE AND FALL

OF THE MYCENAEAN WORLD

THE EASTERN MEDITERRANEAN experienced an unparalleled prosperity and political development in the middle centuries of the second millennium, down to 1200 B.C. Kings surrounded themselves with the majesty of great palaces. Their governments were based on relatively well-organized bureaucracies of scribes and treasurers. In richly endowed, sumptuously adorned temples such as the mammoth halls of Amon at Karnak, priests invoked the blessings of benign gods for the earthly potentates. Bronze and gold shimmered—and no one thought of the sharp edge of iron which was to end this notable Late Bronze age.

The Minoan world of Crete was only one of the bright stars. Egypt likewise had escaped the worst of the invasions which had swept across the Near and Middle East early in the millennium, and by the sixteenth century had entered the period of expansion which we call the New Kingdom. Culturally and economically it dominated much of the coast of Palestine and Syria; from time to time its pharaohs also exercised political sway over this area. Commercial and cultural interconnections radiated from the Syrian coast westward to the Aegean, eastward to Babylonia and to the thriving upper reaches of Mesopotamia—the lands of the Mitanni and Assyrians—and northward to the Hittite Empire, centered about Hattusas. While these ties were not as intense as those which underlay the Assyrian and Persian empires in the first millennium, the civilized superstructures of the Orient were far more aware of each other in the Late Bronze age than earlier.

To reach the Aegean the new winds had to blow across many miles of open sea; and so the Greek world was linked the most loosely, though yet directly, to the cosmopolitan center of the Near and Middle East. Within the Aegean basin leadership lay on Crete down to 1400, then passed to the mainland, and remained there until the fall of the Mycenaean kingdoms shortly after 1200. Modern excavation has uncovered abundant testimony that the Late Bronze era (c. 1580–1100) was the most advanced which Greece had yet experienced. The lords of Pylos, Orchomenos, Mycenae-Tiryns, and other fortresses lived in many-columned palaces and surrounded themselves with riches of ivory, gold, and bronze, worked by skillful artisans. The heartland of this culture was the area about Mycenae, whence it spread out over southern and central Greece (see Map No. 2).

The Mycenaean age is an absorbing one. In recent years, nonetheless, it has received so much attention that its true place in Aegean prehistory has often been distorted. To deal with all the complexities of the age would carry us far afield from our main topic; what is necessary here is to keep an eye out for those aspects in which the Mycenaean world differed markedly from the subsequent centuries, when Greek civilization proper emerged. Yet we must also not forget that the Late Bronze world paved the way for later developments. The areas in which Mycenaean culture throve correspond very closely to the regions in which historic Greek civilization had its major seats; historical as well as geographical continuity will be found as we proceed. The decline and fall of the Mycenaean world, in particular, deserve careful consideration to determine their causes, their date, and the significance of a new influx of barbarians.

KINGS AND TRADERS IN THE MYCENAEAN AGE [1]

THE MYCENAEAN CENTERS were not true cities, although they are often so called. At Mycenae, which has experienced decades of excavation from the first astounding discoveries of Schliemann

---

[1] Archaeological evidence in general: C. W. Blegen's reports on Pylos, *AJA*, LVII (1953), and following; Georg Karo, *Die Schachtgräber von Mykenai*

down to the recent careful work of Wace, Papademetriou, and others, the citadel itself was clearly a fortress. Below the stronghold appeared, as time went on, a few houses, perhaps of retainers and artisans; but this cluster cannot justly be called a city. The bulk of the population seems to have lived in villages on the hills around about.[2] Though settlement was perhaps more compact at Tiryns and at fortified villages such as Malthi, there was a great difference between these sites and the true urban agglomerations of the Middle East. Greece remained far behind the Oriental level throughout the Late Bronze era.

Yet the wealth of its lords cannot be explained as the product simply of peasant dues. Under the guidance of palace administrators, artisans of Cretan or native origin busily turned out masses of pottery, bronze weapons, and other items in standard

---

(Munich, 1930–33); George E. Mylonas, *Ancient Mycenae: The Capital City of Agamemnon* (Princeton, 1957); A. J. B. Wace, *Mycenae: An Archaeological History and Guide* (Princeton, 1949); and the excavation reports and general studies listed in Chap. 1, nn. 3 (p. 13), 2 (p. 21). See also the bibliographical discussion in Pierre Demargne, *La Crète dédalique: études sur les origines d'une renaissance* (Paris, 1947), 35–45.

Mycenaean pottery: Arne Furumark, *The Mycenaean Pottery: Analysis and Classification* (Stockholm, 1941), and *The Chronology of Mycenaean Pottery* (Stockholm, 1941); qualifications on his views and specialized studies will appear below.

Linear B tablets: Michael Ventris and John Chadwick, "Evidence for Greek Dialects in the Mycenaean Archives," *JHS*, LXXIII (1953), 84–103, and *Documents in Mycenaean Greek: Three Hundred Selected Tablets from Knossos, Pylos and Mycenae with Commentary and Vocabulary* (Cambridge, 1956). Although many of the details are far from clear, the criticism by A. J. Beattie, "Mr. Ventris' Decipherment of the Minoan Linear B Script," *JHS*, LXXVI (1956), 1–17, and elsewhere will not stand.

The basic publications of the texts are, *The Pylos Tablets: Texts of the Inscriptions Found 1939–54*, ed. Emmett L. Bennett, Jr. (Princeton, 1955); *The Olive Oil Tablets of Pylos*, Suppl. *Minos*, II (1958), ed. Bennett; *The Knossos Tablets*, transliterated by Bennett, Chadwick, and Ventris (London, 1956); "The Mycenae Tablets," ed. Bennett, *Proceedings of the American Philosophical Society*, XCVII (1953), 422–70; *The Mycenae Tablets II*, edited by Bennett, with translations and commentary by Chadwick (*Transactions of the American Philosophical Society*, XLVIII. 1 [1958]).

[2] Wace, *Mycenae*, 33, and Mylonas, *Mycenae*, 39, agree with Tsountas's conjecture. The terms coined by Wace for the houses outside the citadel, such as the House of the Oil Merchant, may lend them too private an air; see his comments, "The Discovery of Inscribed Clay Tablets at Mycenae," *Antiquity*, XXVII (1953), 84–86, and in *The Mycenae Tablets II*, 4. Six hands, however, seem visible in the tablets discovered there (Bennett, *The Mycenae Tablets II*, 90–95), a fact which suggests that royal scribes were at work.

(a) The Lion Gate of Mycenae with confronted lionesses protecting the palace, symbolized by the column. Photograph courtesy Alison Frantz.

(b) The Warriors' Vase from Mycenae (National Museum 1426, Athens). Photograph courtesy Bildarchiv Foto Marburg.

PLATE 3 · War Lords of Mycenae

(a) Chariot vase from Enkomi, Cyprus, showing perhaps a lord with his steward. Photograph from M. P. Nilsson, The Minoan-Mycenaean Religion (2d ed.; Lund, 1950), 35, fig. 1.

(a)

(b)

(c)

(b) Ivory carving from Mycenae (National Museum 5897, Athens). Photograph from Christian Zervos, L'Art en Grèce (2d ed.; Paris, 1936), fig. 42.

(c) Cup in III.B style from Markopoulo in Attica (National Museum 3740, Athens). Photograph from AJA, XLII (1938), pl. XXIII. 2.

(d) Vase in III.C "close" style from Mycenae (Nauplia Museum). Photograph from A. J. B. Wace, Mycenae (Princeton, 1949), pl. LXXV. a.

(d)

PLATE 4 · Mycenaean Civilization

patterns; beyond archaeological material we have now the references to smiths in the Pylos tablets, which seem to indicate that in a relatively small area there were 193 active (and 81 inactive) smiths. These men drew bronze in small lots from the palace and returned to it finished weapons.[3] The physical evidence also shows that men of this world were very active on the seas. At suitable junctures they no doubt raided and looted, but at other points they must have engaged in trade and even settlement. From these sources, too, riches poured into the hands of the kings.

While the traders will be considered presently, the first and major aspect which rises to view in Mycenaean organization is its kings. This fact is one of the fundamental differences between the Late Bronze age and the historic Greek world, which was grouped first in tribes under local warleaders and then in city-states. Mycenaean culture itself was very directly connected with the consolidation of powerful kingdoms in Greece, and advanced across the landscape hand in hand with the rise of the great palaces.[4] Much of its pottery may justly be termed a Court style, for the peasants only slowly and incompletely yielded their Middle Helladic ways; the treasures of gold, ivory, and other materials were found in the graves of monarchs.

Politically and socially the chieftains who led the invaders at the beginning of the Middle Helladic era found themselves in a world where local lords were already prominent. When they themselves launched out on the sea and came to Crete, they met an even more advanced centralization; the last step was to make the acquaintance of Oriental monarchy in its homelands. The result was an apparently deliberate effort by the lords of Greece to imitate this model in their homeland. Even though we know nothing directly of the size of the Mycenaean kingdoms, the considerable distances which separate the major palaces thus far identified may suggest that each lord ruled a wide countryside; and certainly the kings could focus large amounts of human

---

[3] Ventris and Chadwick, *Documents,* 123 ff., 352–56.
[4] In this respect the rise of La Tène art among the Celts, a princely art focused on the needs of the great warlords, furnishes a useful parallel: T. G. E. Powell, *The Celts* (London, 1958), 98.

energy, both of captive slaves and of local peasants, on building
their palaces and great false-domed or *tholos* tombs, cut into the
hillsides and elaborately faced with stone.[5]

To fill out our knowledge of the Mycenaean kings and of
their world generally, modern scholars have tended to turn to
the Homeric epics; particularly in recent years the weight of
opinion, it is safe to say, has equated Homeric and Mycenaean
eras to a remarkable degree. This tendency I find overbold in
its assumptions, shaky in its logic, and historically misleading to
a dangerous extent. Nowhere dare we rely upon the *Iliad* and the
Odyssey as independent evidence for conditions in the second
millennium. Between the thirteenth century and the eighth century, in which the epics assumed their present shape, lay virtual
aeons of unrest and even chaos; and, as I shall try to show later,
the basic spirit of the Homeric poems accords chiefly with the
closing stages of the Dark ages.

Beyond this point, which will be justified at its proper place,
there are other serious grounds for rejecting Homeric and mythological evidence for the Late Bronze age. The root of both epic
and myth may go back to this era—names later used for Trojan
heroes and for mythical figures appear in the Mycenaean tablets
as the names of men—but the historian has no valid tool by which
to separate folk memory from later elaboration. In these circumstances, though it may be fascinating to ransack the riches of
myth and epic to enliven an otherwise nameless account based
on broken pots and crumbling stones, the procedure is utterly
unsound historically. For later eras we have at times a legend
and also happen to know the historical situation from which it
rose—e.g., the Nibelungenlied (which concerns the Burgundian
court of the fifth century after Christ); and here we can deter-

---

[5] Note the analyses of Pylos and Cnossus in Ventris and Chadwick, *Documents*, 141–45. Tiryns and Mycenae
were probably alternate dwelling
places of a single ruler; contra, Denys
L. Page, *History and the Homeric
Iliad* (Berkeley, 1959), 129–32. The
catalogues in the *Iliad:* Chap. 4, n. 2
(p. 127). Oriental monarchy: bibliography in Fritz Heichelheim, *Ancient
Economic History*, I (Leiden, 1958),
457–61; Goetze's survey of Hittite
kingship in *Kleinasien*, 86–95; Henri
Frankfort, *Kingship and the Gods*
(Chicago, 1948), on ideological patterns. The practical workings of the
palace economies, as shown in the records of Mari, Ugarit, and elsewhere,
still deserve a full discussion.

mine that, while a major event may long be remembered, its details and even its true shape are distorted in poetic transmission. The common inclination to assume that Homer and myth may be taken as reflecting Mycenaean conditions unless the contrary be proved has much against it. Those scholars who have tried to re-create a detailed historical reality out of this traditional material have wound up with the most gossamer constructions and stand in hopeless disagreement among themselves. Very rarely can Homeric descriptions even of concrete objects be linked to Mycenaean prototypes.[6] Nor, to return to the matter at hand, do the epic references to wide-ruling Agamemnon and other Zeus-born lords fit our knowledge of kingship in the Late Bronze age as well as might appear at first sight. Spiritually the cattle-reeving barons of the Homeric poems are at home in the Dark ages, not the wide world of Mycenaean days; the epic tradition cannot safely be said to show more than a vague memory of Mycenaean political geography.

Today we can more easily forgo quarrying in the Homeric epics on this subject inasmuch as contemporary and consistent evidence is available in the tablets of the palace bureaucracies. Occasional indications that men in Greece knew how to write in the second millennium were long discounted by modern scholars, who pictured the lords of Mycenae as virtually barbarian lords; but this depreciation may no longer endure. Just before and after World War II great bodies of clay tablets in Linear B were dis-

[6] One of the most commonly cited parallels has been discarded by S. N. Marinatos, "Der 'Nestorbecher' aus dem IV. Schachtgrab von Mykenae," *Neue Beiträge zur klassischen Altertumswissenschaft* (*Festschrift B. Schweitzer*) (Stuttgart, 1954), 11–18, and Arne Furumark, "Nestor's Cup and the Mycenaean Dove Goblet," *Eranos*, XLIV (1946), 41–53. Other observations are made by A. Heubeck, *Gnomon*, XXIX (1957), 38–44; D. H. F. Gray, "Metal-Working in Homer," *JHS*, LXXIV (1954), 1–15, and in J. L. Myres, *Homer and His Critics* (London, 1958), 247–48, 268, 288; H. L. Lorimer, *Homer and the Monuments* (London, 1950), passim.

For Mycenaean kingship, Marinatos, "ΔΙΟΓΕΝΕΙΣ ΒΑΣΙΛΗΕΣ," *Studies to D. M. Robinson*, I, 126–34, seeks to use the Homeric evidence.

The most judicious effort to connect Homeric and Mycenaean evidence remains that of M. P. Nilsson, *Homer and Mycenae* (London, 1933). Among the most recent studies, T. B. L. Webster, *From Mycenae to Homer* (London, 1958), is shaky in logic and semantics and rash in historical judgment; Page, *History and the Homeric Iliad*, is more reserved on several important points. On Homer, see below, Chap. 5; on the efforts to find representations of myth in Mycenaean art, see Chap. 5, n. 5 (p. 163).

covered at Pylos; dogged work by many scholars, which was capped by the genius of Michael Ventris, has essentially furnished the key to read the syllabic script of this material. Even though detailed interpretation of the tablets is often hazardous, the language which was written was clearly a form of Greek. As philologists had long surmised, the dialect of the late second millennium (or, at least, its written form) was akin to later Arcadian and Cypriote, but it seems also to have been an ancestor of the East Greek dialects as a whole. Apparently the tongue was the same wherever Linear B was set down—at Cnossus, Pylos, Mycenae; in Attica and Boeotia—and the script shows very little change over the centuries of its employment. While we would do far better simply to call this dialect Mycenaean, the term Achaean has been firmly implanted in historical vocabulary, thanks to the Homeric epics; one may doubt, however, if all the Greek-speaking peoples of the Late Bronze age applied this name to themselves.[7]

The decipherment of Linear B has revealed the Mycenaean world as seen by the palace administrators. The ken of the royal scribes and accountants is narrower than we might like, but their terse fiscal records nonetheless yield great fruit. The general picture is one familiar from Oriental states, where the royal bureaucracy had long pursued centralizing tactics. Artisans and peasants were largely embraced in a palace economy under royal control, though they also had some independent organization within village structures. The gods, who were in the main the divinities of later Greece, seem to have possessed domains of their own with priests and slaves. The class structure rose through serfs or slaves, through the lords and councillors of the villages (*basileis, gerontia,* and the like), to the retainers and agents of the great king, the *wanax.* No less than thirty scribes or secretary-

---

[7] On the Cnossus tablets there is a hint that the Achaeans were a specific people (Ventris and Chadwick, *Documents,* 209 n. 78); Cedric Whitman, *Homer and the Heroic Tradition* (Cambridge, Mass., 1958), 30–33, suggests an Eastern origin for the name, which might fit its appearance in Hittite and Egyptian records (see below). Parenthetically, the common concept that two invasions took place early in the second millennium, first the Ionian, then the Achaean or Aeolian, has virtually no archeological support; see below, Chap. 4, n. 3 (p. 120).

administrators, it is judged, were active at Cnossus and also at Pylos. Land-holding seems in part to have rested on service to the king, also in part upon village organization; but far more has recently been argued on this point than can be proven.[8] In such respects as language and religion the evidence of the Mycenaean tablets proves that much which recurs in the centuries after 1200 was already in existence; the archaeological evidence, too, clearly demonstrates a continuity from the Mycenaean age to the Greek world in many fields. Those aspects of the social and political superstructure, however, which were connected with the ever increasing power of the kings, vigorous in war and in trade, were to be unique to this era.[9]

Abroad, the most significant aspect of the Mycenaean age was the great expansive power of its society, which is quite unlike the conditions prevailing in the subsequent Dark ages. The Greek-speaking peoples of the second millennium were less civilized than those of eastern lands, but once the unrest of the Middle Helladic movements was past they seized their opportunities boldly. In the vigor and speed of the Mycenaean overseas drive the great wave of historic Greek colonization had a notable precursor, and the effects of this earlier outpouring were of considerable weight in setting the background for later centuries. When the Greeks once again turned abroad, they sought virtually the same areas as their predecessors and found the way paved by the remnants of the earlier wave, which at times had deposited lasting settlements.

In the west the Mycenaean explorers themselves followed the trail of Early Cycladic days and probably for the same reasons—in search of the metals which were increasingly consumed

[8] Emmett L. Bennett, Jr., "The Landholders of Pylos," *AJA*, LX (1956), 103–33; W. Edward Brown, "Land Tenure in Mycenaean Pylos," *Historia*, V (1956), 385–400; L. R. Palmer, *Achaeans and Indo-Europeans* (Oxford, 1955), to whose views I return in Chap. 4. Scribes: Ventris and Chadwick, *Documents*, 109–10 (from Bennett); their high position in the Hittite world is well put by Goetze, *Kleinasien*, 172.

[9] In a skeletal analysis, J. Lawrence Angel, "Kings and Commoners," *AJA*, LXI (1957), 181, concludes that the kings of Mycenae were taller and heavier than their subjects (as is quite likely), and led an active life to judge from their bone injuries and the average age of death (36).

by the forges of Late Bronze-age smiths.[1] Mycenaean pottery of the fifteenth through the thirteenth centuries and other objects have turned up in western Greece along the sea lane and on to Sicily and a few spots in southern Italy; Tarentum, it has been argued, was probably a real settlement inasmuch as Mycenaean-type pottery was made locally even after connections were broken about 1200. In the Lipari islands, where Minoan traders had led the way, very extensive Mycenaean deposits have been found, beginning with the sixteenth century. Farther west, in Spain and France, such objects are lacking, though Aegean influences radiated indirectly as far as England. In a house at Mycenae, in return, a stone mold has been found which was used to cast winged axes of a type common in northern Italy and on the upper Danube. The presence of Baltic amber in the tombs of the Mycenaean era also suggests that trade moved between the Aegean and central Europe, here again perhaps in search of metals. The copper mines of the latter region now were much more intensively exploited, and its cultures received stimuli which had great effects on down into the first millennium.

The main drift of Mycenaean days was through the Aegean and eastward toward the principal centers of civilization. In Greece proper, Mycenaean patterns of political organization advanced through Boeotia as far as Thessaly, where a palace has recently been found at Iolkos; pottery and metal products of the age stretch along the north shore of the Aegean from Macedonia across to Troy VI–VII.[2] The latter point was perhaps attacked

[1] Mycenaeans in the west and in Europe: Bernabò Brea, *Sicily*, 102–08, 114–15, V. Gordon Childe, "The Final Bronze Age in the Near East and in Temperate Europe," *Proceedings of the Prehistoric Society*, n. s. XIV (1948), 177–95; T. J. Dunbabin, "Minos and Daidalos in Sicily," *Papers of the British School at Rome*, XVI (1948), 1–18, whose use of myth must be checked by the skeptical observations of Lord William Taylour, *Mycenaean Pottery in Italy and Adjacent Areas* (Cambridge, 1958), 188–89; C. F. C. Hawkes, *The Prehistoric Foundations of Europe* (London, 1940), 351–52; Hencken, *Indo-*

European Languages and Archeology, 18–20; F. H. Stubbings, "A Winged-Ax Mould," *BSA*, XLIX (1954), 297–98. Albin Lesky, *Thalatta: Der Weg der Griechen zum Meer* (Vienna, 1947), is of value chiefly for the historic era.

[2] Thessaly: Milojčić, *AA* 1955, 231; *Ergon* 1956, 43–50. Cyclades: Gallet de Santerre, *Délos primitive*, 62–112. Troy: Blegen, Caskey, and Rawson, *Troy*, III, The Index; the Mycenaean pottery of Troy VI (down to III.B transitional) is well analyzed by Sara A. Immerwahr, *AJA*, LX (1956), 455–56.

Miletus: Carl Weickert, "Graby some of the lords of Greece, more for its own riches than because it dominated the Hellespont or the plains of northwestern Asia Minor; for some kernel of truth probably lies behind the famous Trojan cycle of epics. Thus far there is scattered evidence for Mycenaean trade or settlement at Delos and along the western coast of Asia Minor; especially at Miletus Greek pottery appears above Minoan sherds and continues on across the following centuries. Far off in the center of Asia Minor the Hittite rulers had from the late fourteenth century contacts with the Ahhiyawa (Achaeans) which were at first on friendly terms and then became increasingly uncomfortable; but the Hittite references are far too indefinite to permit precise localization of the Ahhiyawa either on the coast or offshore.

On the sea route eastward men from the Greek mainland were active before Cnossus fell. While contacts with Egypt were perhaps strongest in and before the Amarna age (mid-fourteenth century) and may have passed in part via Crete, Mycenaean connections with Syria were surely direct and became ever more intense down into the thirteenth century.[3] Mycenaean wares turn up along the Syrian coast and even in the hinterland in quantities far beyond those of Minoan origin. Beside its pottery

---

bungen in Milet 1938," *Bericht über den VI. internationalen Kongress für Archäologie* (Berlin, 1940), 325–32, and his surveys of the 1955 campaign in *Istanbuler Mitteilungen*, VII (1957), 102–32, and of the 1957 campaign in *AnatSt*, VIII (1958), 30–31; G. M. A. Hanfmann, *HSCP*, LXI (1953), 4; Frank H. Stubbings, *Mycenaean Pottery from the Levant* (Cambridge, 1951), 21–24. Seton Lloyd, *Early Anatolia*, 152–53, suggests Mycenaean settlement may have been widespread along the coast; but the analysis of James Mellaart, *AnatSt*, V (1955), 80–83, suggests the contrary. Sites such as Colophon (Goetze, *Kleinasien*, 182) have been labeled Mycenaean on far too little evidence. See also F. Cassola, *La Ionia nel mondo Miceneo* (Naples, 1957).

Hittites: Gurney, *The Hittites*, 46–56, gives a good survey of the arguments concerning the Ahhiyawa

from Forrer on; cf. Fritz Schachermeyr, "Zur Frage der Lokalisierung von Achiawa," *Minoica* (Berlin, 1958), 365–80; Page, *History and the Homeric Iliad*, 1–40.
[3] See the works listed in Chap. 1, n. 8 (p. 38); also Furumark, *Opus. arch.*, VI (1950), 203–49, who urges that Mycenaean activity eastward does not begin until c. 1450; Lorimer, *Homer and the Monuments*, 55–64; Stubbings, *Mycenaean Pottery from the Levant*, 53–87; A. J. B. Wace and C. W. Blegen, "Pottery as Evidence for Trade and Colonisation in the Aegean Bronze Age," *Klio*, XXXII (1939), 131–47. Oriental finds in Greece: Pendlebury, *Aegyptiaca*, 43 ff.; Demargne, *La Crète dédalique*, 80–85. Such terms as χρυσός, ἐλέφας, χιτών, βύβλος, which came from the Levant, appeared already in Linear B: Ventris and Chadwick, *Documents*, 135–36.

the Aegean world probably traded oil and wine, metals such as tin and lead gained from Greece and the west, slaves, and the like for ivory, gold, textiles (including linen and purple-dyed wool), ornaments of faïence and niello, papyrus, perfumes and ointments, condiments, and other finished products. If this eastern trade is related to the evidence of Mycenaean activity in the west, the conclusion is perhaps justified that Aegean adventurers had seized the role of prime intermediaries between the Orient and Europe.

The tremendous increase of Mycenaean pottery along the Syrian route, the linguistic evidence of later days, and the hazardous testimony of tradition all suggest that Mycenaean colonies stretched out eastward from Greece.[4] In the Aegean islands pottery of mainland type was being produced locally by the thirteenth century. On the northwest edge of Rhodes, in the accessible plain of Trianda, Mycenaean settlers appear first beside men of Minoan background about 1450 and then supplant the Cretans toward 1400. Cnossus itself fell for the last time about this same date, and the variety of mainland influences in Crete, which include the introduction of the Greek language, betokens beyond doubt settlement from the Greek mainland. Coloniza-

---

[4] Aegean islands: Scholes, *BSA*, LI (1956), 30–35, 39–40, who notes that the change in house plans at Phylakopi and Naxos as well as the Mycenaean ivories at Delos (*BCH*, LXXI-LXXII [1947–48], 148–254), suggest settlement. Rhodes: Arne Furumark, "The Settlement at Ialysos and Aegean History c. 1550–1400 B.C.," *Opus. arch.*, VI (1950), 150–271; Stubbings, *Mycenaean Pottery from the Levant*, 5–20. Cilicia: Garstang, *Prehistoric Mersin*, 253–56; Goldman, *Tarsus*, II, 63, 205–09; and sporadic sherds up onto the plateau, as noted by Mellaart, *AnatSt*, V (1955), 82; Seton-Williams, ibid. IV (1954), 134–35; Nimet Ozguc, *Belleten*, XIX (1955), 303.

Cyprus: Settlement before 1200 is argued by Etienne Coche de la Ferté, *Essai de classification de la céramique mycénienne d'Enkomi* (*Campagnes 1946 et 1947*) (Paris, 1951); J. F. Daniels, as in *AJA*, XLI (1937), 56 ff., XLII (1938), 261 ff., XLVI (1942), 291 ff.; Hanfmann, *AJA*, LV (1951), 428; C. F. A. Schaeffer, as in *Enkomi-Alasia: nouvelles missions en Chypre, 1946–1950* (Paris, 1952); Stubbings, *Mycenaean Pottery from the Levant*, 25–44. For a later date, see especially E. Gjerstad, *Studies on Prehistoric Cyprus* (Uppsala, 1926), 327–28, and "The Colonization of Cyprus in Greek Legend" and "The Initial Date of the Cypriote Iron Age," *Opus. arch.*, III (1944), 73–123; Arne Furumark, "The Mycenaean III C Pottery and Its Relation to Cypriote Fabrics," ibid. 194–265, who notes that III.B was surely made locally on the island but puts the Achaean influx in III.C. The ware he found at Sinda he takes as marking the new settlers, *AJA*, LII (1948), 531; cf. Matz, *Gnomon*, XXII (1950), 122.

tion in Cilicia and in Cyprus has also been asserted, but is more debatable. The appearance of an archaic Greek dialect on Cyprus which was very akin to Arcadian and to "Mycenaean" may reflect settlement in the disturbed days after the Mycenaean age had fallen; yet on the other hand the fact that Mycenaean wares appear in abundance earlier on Cyprus and were locally made might as easily support the assumption that Greek-speaking peoples thrust this far east before 1200.

In trade, in settlement, and in raids, the kings and traders of the Mycenaean age wandered far afield over both the eastern and the western stretches of the Mediterranean. At the time this overseas activity helped to support the luxury of the Mycenaean superstructure and influenced the character of its civilization; in the long run the expansion of the mainland peoples is not totally unconnected with the later Greek outburst in historic times. Between the two waves the chaos of the early Dark ages was to be only a partial setback. Not all of the areas absorbed in the Mycenaean era were to be lost, and contact by sea with Syria was probably never entirely broken.

MYCENAEAN CIVILIZATION

BY THE thirteenth century a very similar tissue of Mycenaean culture extended from a nucleus in southern and central Greece eastward through Crete, Rhodes, and Cyprus. On the basis of its pottery this civilization is now commonly divided into the following phases:

I	*c.* 1550 B.C.
II	*c.* 1500
III.A	*c.* 1425
III.B	*c.* 1300
III.C (including sub-Mycenaean)	*c.* 1230–1050

This division is sound as a scheme of relative sequences, subject to the usual archaeological problems involved in placing any small individual deposit and in defining the transitional

phases (especially from III.B to III.C).[5] No excavation has yet
discovered stratified levels of Mycenaean pottery which extend
across the entire era, but the great masses of ware available from
a host of more limited sites are sufficient to indicate the main
lines of development. Very valuable results ensue. For the first
time in Aegean history we can follow artistic changes century by
century and can even at times hope to spot individual artists;
the uniformity of the pottery, wherever made, permits an inter-
linking of the local districts throughout the Aegean basin; and
many other aspects of this culture, which exhibit the same general forces as the vases, can be ordered in historical perspective.

The absolute dates B.C. which I have included in the table
are quite a different matter. They rest upon discoveries of Mycenaean vases in datable contexts in Egypt and Syria—i.e., upon
Egyptian chronology. This latter scheme is generally secure, and
the links to Aegean materials are enough to suggest the rate of
progress in the Mycenaean world itself; yet the ties are far from
adequate to pin down pottery styles precisely. Every absolute
date assigned to Mycenaean pottery is still subject to serious debate within a range of a half-century or so.[6] Especially in the

[5] Furumark's classifications have not
been universally accepted in detail;
see, e.g., A. J. B. Wace, "Late Helladic III Pottery and Its Division,"
Arch. eph. 1953–54, 137–40. Radio-
carbon dates will be forthcoming from
Pylos, but the margin of error in this
method will probably be too great to
aid us materially in narrowing down
chronological boundaries. My dates
above follow Furumark, *Chronology
of Mycenaean Pottery*, 110–15, except for the end of the sub-Mycenaean
style.

Key points are: (1) the appearance
of III.A at Tell el Amarna, inhabited
only fifteen years and abandoned
c. 1350 at the latest; at Beth Shan not
later than 1400; at Qatna before 1375;
at Gaza together with a ring of Tu-
tankhamon; (2) the appearance of
III.A–B at Gurob, which most scholars place at about 1300, though Wace,
BSA, LII (1957), 222–23, raised this
date for the Mycenaean ware; (3) the

appearance of III.B at Byblos in the
Ahiram tomb in the period of Ramses II.

[6] To give only a few examples, Wace
begins III.B at 1340 and III.C at
1210: *BSA*, XLVIII (1953), 15 n. 22;
Aegean and Near East, 133–34; he
cites the appearance of III.B wares
with a sword bearing the cartouche of
Merneptah at Ras Shamra (C. F. A.
Schaeffer, "A Bronze Sword from
Ugarit with Cartouche of Mineptah,"
Antiquity, XXIX [1955], 226–29). Sir
Leonard Woolley, *Alalakh: An Ac-
count of the Excavations at Tell
Atchana in the Hatay, 1937–1949*
(Oxford, 1955), 369–76, extends
III.B until the attack by the Sea Peo-
ples—i.e., after 1200. Jean Bérard,
"Le mur pelasgique de l'Acropole et
la date de la descente Dorienne,"
Studies to D. M. Robinson, I, 135–59,
raises the beginning of III.C on the
basis of the Tarsus evidence.

stage III.C, when trade between the Orient and the Aegean rapidly declined, correlations virtually disappear—a serious difficulty, as we shall see shortly, in the very important problem of fixing the end of the Mycenaean age. The absolute chronology of the Late Bronze era in the Aegean, accordingly, must be understood as a tentative structure which later finds may render more secure.

In many respects Mycenaean culture was a close adaptation of Minoan civilization; in others, its men copied from the Orient far more baldly than had the artists of Crete. Both of these qualities, together with its relative richness, sharply distinguish the Late Bronze age from the poverty-stricken, localized centuries which were to follow. The differences, moreover, between Mycenaean and historic Greek patterns are patent wherever one turns in the artistic evidence. Pottery shapes in the Mycenaean world had a higher center of gravity (see Plate 4a, c); many forms of vases were totally unlike those of later times; decorative elements, drawn largely from marine and botanical life, were of an alien character, especially in Mycenaean I and II, and reflected in their application to the vase quite another sense of logic and order. The same dissimilarities mark the rare products of Mycenaean sculptors, of the painters of frescoes in the royal palaces, and of smiths in gold and bronze.

This gulf in cultural outlook is admirably illuminated if one travels from classic Athens, standing bold and free in the Attic plain, down to Mycenae, huddled in a safe corner of the rich Argolid (see Plate 3a). The *tholos* tomb called the Treasury of Atreus is the first great architectural monument on the mainland of Europe; but, impressive though its finely fitted stone work may be, the massive dome and noble entryway were created in honor of a king, not the patron god of a city-state. Even more suggestive is the stern, defiant fortress encasing the lovely palace of the Mycenaean kings. The world which expressed itself here was rough and barbarous, though its masters concentrated the energies of their subjects upon their own luxury. Power and strength were available to heap up the amazing structures of Mycenae; their like was not to recur in Greece for centuries. Yet when the Aegean world again reached an advanced level, it directed its renewed social and economic vigor to other ends and harnessed its creations within a more intellectually disciplined pattern. Mycenaean civilization is not a system from which historic Greek culture emerged on a straight line. The importance of this observation must be underlined. The culture of the Late Bronze age, nonetheless, is not to be dismissed forthwith from the Greek background, for the Mycenaean world was not a simple province of Cretan and Oriental inspiration.[7] Much of the structure of Middle Helladic life and thought quite clearly continued throughout the Mycenaean era. Grave styles of earlier days persisted; pottery forms and decoration drew from the Middle Bronze inheritance; beneath the superstructure of the palaces the villagers undoubtedly lived largely as of old— even the sites of their settlements remained the same as in the previous era. Intriguing hints of a hidden line of native development also lie behind the superficial stream of Minoan and Oriental copies. When scholars today occasionally term the grave steles over the shaft graves at Mycenae and the famous Lion Gate the first masterpieces of Greek civilization, they ignore far too much the gulf which I have just emphasized; and yet a first, inchoate struggle to express that outlook which later rose to greatness in historic Greek centuries can be sensed in these works. The emphasis upon the *megaron*, a symmetrical, internally focused unit quite unlike the sprawling palace complexes of Minoan origin, is likewise significant. When we come to the appearance of the first truly Greek pottery, the Protogeometric, we shall have occasion to return to the formal, abstract, even geometric tendency which was rapidly advancing in the last stages of Mycenaean pottery.

[7] Contra, Axel W. Persson, *New Tombs at Dendra near Midea* (Lund, 1942), 176–96, extends very far the indebtedness of Mycenaean culture to Egypt; see also Webster, *From Mycenae to Homer*, 27–36. Furumark, *Opus. arch.*, VI (1950), 221–23, 253–54, is more judicious. Middle Helladic survivals in pottery: Blegen, *Prosymna*, passim; Helen Thomas, "The Acropolis Treasure from Mycenae," *BSA*, XXXIX (1938–39), 65–87; A. J. B. Wace, "Middle and Late Helladic Pottery," *Epitymbion Chr. Tsuntas* (Athens, 1941), 345–50. In sculpture: Karo, *Greek Personality*, 3, 9; Matz, *Kreta, Mykene, Troja*, 140–42; Dirlmeier, *RM*, XCVIII (1955), 36. In architecture: Lawrence, *Greek Architecture*, 65–82.

In sculpture, architecture, and pottery, as also in its social, political, and religious attitudes, the Mycenaean age is an absorbing medley of forces. Human history is never a mechanical, cyclical treadmill, but the Mycenaean experience is nevertheless an intriguing forerunner of the synthesis between local and Oriental influences which marked the great century of revolution 750–650 B.C. The similarity is enough to suggest some of the enduring forces which affected Aegean development across the ages; the differences are also obvious. If the later synthesis was to be freer and produced more significant results, its greater fruit must be attributed first to the broader base of Greek culture which was hammered out in the Dark ages; Mycenaean civilization was too dependent upon a limited circle about its monarchs. Another factor was the solid digestion of the earlier stimuli which occurred in the slow-moving centuries after the fall of the Mycenaean world.

In the most general terms, the mainland of Greece was hampered by an insoluble problem during its Late Bronze phase. It could not resist the attractions of the Minoan tradition, the dominance of which was very marked at the beginning of the Mycenaean period. Yet it was also driven to draw on its Middle Helladic inheritance. Bold experiment was, for the most part, barred by the alluring temptations of the more advanced Cretan motifs and techniques; innovation could only be feeble, halfconscious. The potters, in particular, were generally more interested in technique and in mass production than in originality. One modern student terms their work "more orderly than imaginative," and the terms "commercialization" and "copying" almost inevitably turn up in any discussion of this ware. Local variations, which are slowly becoming discernible as the pottery is better studied, were still quite limited until its very last stages.[8] Historically, the solution to the basic problem of integrating alien

---

[8] The quotation is from F. H. Stubbings, "The Mycenaean Pottery of Attica," *BSA,* XLII (1947), 1–75, at p. 69; on local variations, see also Wace and Blegen, *Klio,* XXXII (1939), 131–47, and Stubbings, "Some Mycenaean Artists," *BSA,* XLVI (1951), 168–76. Furumark, *Opus. arch.,* VI (1950), 186–91, has much the same view of Mycenaean forces as that which I reached independently, but overstresses the degree to which Late Bronze craftsmen were able to resolve their problems.

and native inspirations was to be collapse and a new beginning on a far simpler level. Men at that time inherited much from the Mycenaean age but could move more freely.

DECLINE AND COLLAPSE OF THE MYCENAEAN WORLD

By the middle of Mycenaean III.B, in the mid-thirteenth century, the Aegean world was on a pinnacle of unprecedented prosperity. The palace at Pylos, which was begun at the opening of the period, was rebuilt; extensive remodeling took place at Mycenae. Interconnections both to the west and to the east, to judge from the pottery, were ever closer; the III.B style of vases is by far the most common of all Mycenaean wares. The volume of this pottery found in Syria shows that trade to the Orient was extensive, but in return the Aegean was drawing much from the East, both in physical objects and in intellectual and political concepts. The Mycenaean lands seemed on the way toward falling in place as satellites of the Oriental cultures, which were themselves drawing closer together in the bloom of the Late Bronze age.

This whole world was actually on the verge of collapse. The first step, internal decline, is especially obvious in Egypt, where the central political system was already weakening, overseas economic activity and local agricultural stability were waning, and artists were losing their sense of style and originality. In other parts of the Middle East much the same pattern can be demonstrated.

Then came the whirlwind as a fresh irruption of Indo-European peoples raced across an already weakened world.[9]

[9] Egypt: John A. Wilson, *The Burden of Egypt* (Chicago, 1951), 234 ff.; W. F. Edgerton and J. A. Wilson, *Historical Records of Ramses III* (Chicago, 1936), 35 ff.; W. F. Albright, *AJA*, LIV (1950), 170, lowers the dates to about 1175–1172; see also G. L. Huxley, *Bulletin of the Institute of Classical Studies*, University of London, No. 3 (1956), 19–20. Hittites: Ekrem Akurgal, *Phrygische Kunst* (Ankara, 1955), 112–13, 116–17; Mellaart, *Belleten*, XIX (1955), 126–29; E. Laroche, *Revue d'Assyriologie*, XLVII (1953), 70–78; Goetze, *Kleinasien*, 184–85.

Egypt, the farthest removed, barely beat off first an invasion by sea about 1230 and then a far greater wave which came about 1190–1185 by land, moving through Syria. Thereafter it lay in torpor, subject to internal conflicts and to Libyan and Ethiopian penetrations. On the coasts of Syria, Palestine, and Cyprus many great trading ports were sacked or deserted about 1200; inland towns on the mainland fell to the Semitic-speaking Habiru and Arameans, who pressed in from the desert. Assyria rode out the storm and remained an organized state, but its imperial ambitions, recently hatched, were quenched for centuries. The Hittite kingdom in Asia Minor vanished about 1180 or a little later. Virtually everywhere in the Fertile Crescent the civilized superstructure tottered, and society sank into the era of abject poverty and localism which archaeologists call the Early Iron age.

Both stages, decline and invasion, also afflicted the Aegean world. The preliminary phase of internal deterioration is most obvious in the artistic evidence, alike in Crete and on the mainland.[1] Very rapidly after the fall of Cnossus about 1400 Cretan pottery decoration became formalized and the earlier unity of Minoan styles dissolved. Within two centuries vase forms on the island had become stiff, the clay often was poorly prepared, and artists feebly imitated a limited repertory of inherited motifs. Earlier, the Cretan figurines had been lithe and vital—motion incarnate, as it were—but by 1200 they were commonly abstract, inorganic masses which breathe an air of decadence. Mainland artists, who were striving to move outside the Minoan patterns, found themselves in great distress. More and more their mass production was a mechanical copying of old motifs, which were no longer understood (see Plates 4d, 5a); the shapes of the vases became rigid; and both technical skill and artistic firmness underwent an absolute deterioration. While some of the late Mycenaean products are still fine products and the Warrior Vase,

[1] Cretan pottery: Furumark, *Mycenaean Pottery*, 175–76; Doro Levi, *Annuario*, X–XII (1927–29), 625 ff.; Pendlebury, *Archaeology of Crete*, 225–31, 271. Cretan figurines: Levi, *Annuario*, X–XII (1927–29), 612 ff.; Valentin Müller, *Frühe Plastik in Griechenland und Vorderasien: ihre* *Typenbildung von der Neolithischen bis in die griechisch-archaische Zeit* (*rund 3000 bis 600 v. Chr.*) (Augsburg, 1929), 41–42, 54. Mainland: Furumark, *Mycenaean Pottery*, passim; Mogens B. Mackeprang, "Late Mycenaean Vases," *AJA*, XLII (1938), 537–59.

in particular, shows a vigorous realism (Plate 3b), very many are poorly made and sloppily decorated.

In the long run these mainland changes might have resulted in a new style, for what art historians term "artistic decline" is often no less than the herald of fresh ideas. But the artists of the Mycenaean kings were not to have an opportunity to pursue their path indefinitely; political and economic disruption was already appearing, though hazily to our ken, by 1200. The fact that local pottery styles increasingly went their separate ways from the beginning of III.C onward in Cyprus, Rhodes, and elsewhere suggests an incipient breakdown in intercommunications; Crete, too, displays less contact now with the mainland.[2] The so-called Close Style, which emerged in the Argolid, was taken up by only a few other mainland sites, though it does show on Rhodes and Cyprus.

Through the countryside of Greece all was not well by this time. To prove the fact, some scholars make much use of the traditional tales of early internal feuds, such as the conflict of Atreus and Thyestes at Mycenae or the wars between Mycenae and Thebes. Far more reliable are the archaeological hints of serious trouble before the great wave of invasion.[3] Thebes, thus, was destroyed apparently during Mycenaean III.A, in the middle of the fourteenth century. The kings of Mycenae itself extended the fortified area in the late thirteenth century to safeguard access to a well, and constructed basement storerooms in the so-called Granary; the houses outside the wall were sacked and burned while III.B pottery was still in use, perhaps about 1250

---

[2] Pendlebury, *Archaeology of Crete*, 229; Furumark, *Opus. arch.*, III (1944), 200–02, 206–09, 263.
[3] Legends: Mylonas, *Mycenae*, 72–73; Whitman, *Homer and the Heroic Tradition*, 35–38; cf. P. J. Reimer, *Zeven tegen Thebe: Praehelleense elementen in de Helleense traditie* (Diss. Amsterdam, 1953). Thebes: *Arch. eph.* 1909, 57–122; Vermeule, *AJA*, LXI (1957), 198; but Blegen, *AJA*, LXIV (1960), 159, suggests the transition from III.B to III.C. Mycenae: Mylonas, *Mycenae*, 37–38, 72–

73; Wace, *BSA*, LI (1956), 120. Athens: Oscar Broneer, "What Happened at Athens," *AJA*, LII (1948), 111–14, and "A Mycenaean Fountain on the Athenian Acropolis," *Hesperia*, VIII (1939), 317–429 (esp. 423–25). Wace sees vigor rather than decline in this fortification, *Historia*, II (1953), 88 ff.; my view of the era differs radically from his. Miletus, too, was fortified in the fourteenth century, apparently for the first time: Weickert, *AnatSt*, VIII (1958), 31.

but surely before the fall of the mighty fortress itself. Nearby, the walls of Tiryns were much enlarged. Other settlements such as Zygouries, Aegina, and Prosymna were abandoned by or before the end of III.B; sites showing the next stage of Mycenaean pottery are far fewer and are widely separated. Off to the north, Aghios Kosmas in Attica was fortified. At Athens itself a stairway east of the later Erechtheum was blocked, and the main walls were reinforced; the lords of this place expended great energy in opening up a new well more than a hundred feet below the summit, which could safely be reached from the Acropolis itself. Soon the houses on the slopes below the Acropolis wall were hastily evacuated, at the end of the III.B style. Whether unrest at home or threats from abroad caused these precautions and preliminary disasters, we do not know, though the peasants may well have found heavy the yoke of their ambitious masters. Clearly the kings of the Mycenaean world felt uneasy before their system toppled.

In the Aegean basin, as elsewhere, the end of the Late Bronze age was not a matter of simple dissolution. The last tablets on the floor of the Pylos record room reflect a major effort to strengthen the coastal defenses under the local lords; apparently a force of rowers, 443 men at the very least, was assembled to move northward to Pleuron on the Aetolian coast.[4] At Pylos the rest is silence—tumbled tablets and marks of fire, after which the palace lay forever deserted. Elsewhere, too, the evidence is somber. From Iolkos in Thessaly to Malthi in Messenia, at Krisa and Kirrha near Delphi, at Aghios Kosmas in Attica, in the thickly settled countryside about Corinth, in the very heart of the Mycenaean world at Tiryns, Argos, and Mycenae itself—almost everywhere the Mycenaean settlements went up in smoke or were deserted, to lie roofless and decaying in wind and rain.

Once the palaces went, writing disappeared. That fact measures the degree of collapse in the Aegean. In Oriental lands civilization was long-seated, and most areas there rode out, though barely, the storm; the use of writing continued to have

[4] Ventris and Chadwick, *Documents,* 124–25, 138, 183–94, 191–95; but cf.   Vermeule, *AJA,* LXI (1957), 201.

political and economic advantages and advanced in most areas to true alphabetic scripts. In the Aegean, as in Asia Minor, the political and economic frame of civilization was so shallow-rooted that it fell catastrophically. By 1100, or soon thereafter, Greek lands had reverted to a simpler form of life than they had known for centuries.

It is not likely that this terrific collapse was purely the result of internal factors, especially in view of what was happening elsewhere in the eastern Mediterranean. The Aegean, too, must have experienced an invasion of new Indo-European peoples, and there is no valid reason to deny the basic truth of the later Greek tradition that the kernel of these invaders was the Dorians.[5] Folk memory, whether of epic or mythical form, is, as I have already commented and shall discuss again, a dangerous tool for the historian in its details; but so great an event as the present one is of a different order. The great invasion which ended the Age of Heroes lay immediately in the background of a continuous evolution which proceeded thereafter without further breaks into historic Greek times.

If we do accept the equation of invaders and Dorians, this assumption in itself does not require belief in all the legends which later Greek speculation attached to the return of the Heraclids and the Dorian sweep.[6] I do not propose to criticize in detail the reconstructions of the invasion and the manner in

[5] K. J. Beloch, Griechische Geschichte, I. 2 (2d ed.; Strassburg, 1913), 76 ff., and Gaetano de Sanctis, Storia dei Greci dalle origini alla fine del secolo V, I (Florence, 1939), 152–54, are prominent among those who deny any validity to the Dorian invasion. Others argue that the Dorians of legend infiltrated after unnamed invaders had delivered the main blows: Milojčić, AA 1948–49, 12–36; Fritz Schachermeyr, Poseidon und die Entstehung des griechischen Götterglaubens (Bern, 1950), 8; cf. Demargne, La Crète dédalique, 95. An entirely novel approach is that of M. Andronikos, "'Η 'δωρικὴ εἰσβολὴ' καὶ τὰ ἀρχαιολογικὰ εὑρήματα," Hellenika, XIII (1954), 221–40, who attributes the fall solely to internal discontent.

[6] N. G. L. Hammond, "Prehistoric Epirus and the Dorian Invasion," BSA, XXXII (1931–32), 131–79; Franz Miltner, "Die dorische Wanderung," Klio, XXVII (1934), 54–68, whose argument that they drove for Crete and then fanned out eastward as well as back to the Argolid is very tempting (see Eduard Meyer, Geschichte des Altertums, III [2d ed.; Stuttgart, 1937], 248; Demargne, La Crète dédalique, 93–94); Gerhard Vitalis, Die Entwicklung der Sage von der Rückkehr der Herakliden (Diss. Greifswald, 1930); a brief survey with bibliography in Hermann Bengtson, Griechische Geschichte (Munich, 1950), 46–51.

which modern studies utilize it to push other peoples about the Aegean. The myths, the tales of city foundations, and other materials are simply not adequate foundations for such lofty structures. That the Dorians spoke Greek seems a reasonable hypothesis, though the Dorian dialect of later times, as will be shown in Chapter 4, was largely evolved after the invaders had settled down in southern Greece, from the Peloponnesus through Crete to Asia Minor.

Presumably, as a new Greek-speaking people, the Dorians had lived earlier on the fringe of the Mycenaean world, and the most likely area for this home is that given them by tradition, the modern Epirus. Scrupulous investigations by archaeologists have not yet been able to prove this probability, but occasional hints in the shapes of the *fibulae* or metal safety-pins, metalware, and pottery motifs may suggest ties with the northern Balkans, particularly with Yugoslav sites. These signs, however, are more convincing along the northern fringes of the Greek world than in the old Mycenaean lands.[7] One of the three Dorian tribal names, Hylleis, may have an Illyrian root; another tribal name, Pamphyloi, suggests that they either were initially a mixed people or picked up others as they pushed through Greece.

To sum up, the Mycenaean world first underwent decline in the thirteenth century. Then, in the next hundred years, the internal deterioration was catastrophically complemented by invasions from the north, which wiped out the political and economic systems built around the kings and their palaces. A modern observer who today walks about the glittering showcases of the Mycenaean room in the National Museum, Athens, or stands

---

[7] Childe, *Proceedings of the Prehistoric Society*, n. s. XIV (1948), 177–95 (but cf. his restatement in *Acta congressus Madvigiani*, I, 296–97), and C. F. C. Hawkes, "From Bronze Age to Iron Age: Middle Europe, Italy, and the North and West," ibid. 196–218; Vladimir Milojčić, "Die dorische Wanderung im Lichte der vorgeschichtlichen Funde," *AA* 1948–49, 12–36; Theodore C. Skeat, *The Dorians in Archaeology* (London, n. d.), which much misreads the pottery evidence. European bronzes appear in tombs xxii and xxix of Deiras cemetery at Argos, along with III.C pottery (*BCH*, LXXX [1956], 361–65); the spectacle *fibulae*, too, are generally agreed to be a northern import (Lorimer, *Homer and the Monuments*, 363; Furumark, *Chronology of Mycenaean Pottery*, 91–93).

Hylleis: Kretschmer, *Glotta*, XV (1927), 194, after Ulrich von Wilamowitz-Moellendorf, *Hellenistische Dichtung*, II (Berlin, 1924), 177.

at the Lion Gate of Mycenae must have somber thoughts when he considers the fate of Greece in the twelfth century B.C. Not for half a millennium to come were men of these lands again to be organized so firmly in political units, to practice such varied and skillful arts, or to have the intangible and physical strengths which must underlie an advanced civilization—and by that point the Greek heart was to beat in a different rhythm.

THE FALL OF MYCENAE AND GREEK CHRONOLOGY

Two ASPECTS of this collapse deserve special note, though each must lead us somewhat far afield into certain major problems of early Greek history. The first, which is connected with the principles of Greek chronology, is the date of the final fall of the Mycenaean world.

With respect to absolute dates in early Greek history, we either may rely on lines of archaeological reasoning, as supported by contacts with Oriental chronology, or can appeal to the learned calculations of historic Greek chronographers. The former approach, which rests upon the truly contemporary materials, is more in keeping with sound historical principles insofar as it yields usable results. The storerooms of Pylos are loaded with amazing quantities of III.B pottery, which here and there was just shifting toward III.C; [8] many other sites came to an abrupt close about the same time or during the first phase of III.C; Mycenae itself lasted long enough to display considerable development of III.C. If the absolute dates suggested above for these styles are valid, then Pylos was sacked about 1200, but the citadel of Mycenae endured to about 1150. [9] Like Rome during

[8] Blegen's comments, *AJA*, LX (1956), 95–101, and LXI (1957), 129–35, on the presence of possibly III.C ware, he has been kind enough to inform me, must not be pressed too far; Furumark placed it all in III.B. See now Blegen's statement in *AJA*, LXIV (1960), 159.

[9] The fall of Mycenae is put *c.* 1150 by Furumark, *Chronology of Myce-*

naean Pottery, 115 n. 2, and *Opus. arch.,* III (1944), 263; *c.* 1200 by Bérard, *Studies to D. M. Robinson,* I, 142–44; *c.* 1100 by A. J. B. Wace, "The Last Days of Mycenae," *Aegean and Near East,* 126–35. Dates such as 1050–1000, given by A. R. Burn, *Minoans, Philistines, and Greeks* (London, 1930), 49–51, and H. T. Wade-Gery, *Cambridge Ancient History,* II

the Germanic invasions of the Roman Empire, Mycenae apparently fell toward the end rather than at the beginning of the Dorian assault.

The first threats from the north may well have come late in the thirteenth century, shortly after Macedonia seems to have been overwhelmed;[1] and the Aegean was probably rising in storm by 1200. The time when the fortified nuclei of the area collapsed, however, should apparently be put at 1200–1150. This conclusion accords reasonably well with the historical and archaeological evidence of the Middle East, which experienced its greatest unrest at and just after 1200. The Aegean and the Orient, it will be remembered, were in relatively close contact; and some of the peoples who beset the East, such as the Akhaiwasha, Peleset, and others, seem to have come out of the Aegean. Even off in Sicily and Italy, interestingly enough, many villages had fortified themselves in vain and collapsed toward the end of the thirteenth century.

While these dates will be accepted here, their hypothetical character should not be overlooked. Cross-checks between Aegean and Oriental archaeological levels are the ultimate basis of this chronology, for datable Oriental records which refer unmistakably to Aegean events are virtually absent down to 500 B.C. Even the general references to the Greeks in the inscriptions and literature of Assyria, Persia, Egypt, and Judaea are scanty and commonly of little chronological value. And, unfortunately, extensive synchronizations between the physical evidence of the Aegean and of the Orient exist only in eras when large-scale commerce throve—i.e., only at the height of the Mycenaean age and again *from 700 B.C. onward.* For the long stretches of time which intervened, our bases for absolute dates are inferences

---

(Cambridge, 1924), 525, now seem out of the proper range. Massimo Pallottino, "Μυκήνας καθεῖλον," *Archeologia classica*, III (1951), 186–91, suggests that the physical destruction of Mycenae took place early in the fifth century B.C. at the time of the Argive conquest. It is a great pity that solid stratification is really lacking at Mycenae.

[1] Milojčić, *AA* 1948–49, 14–15; W. A. Heurtley, "Early Iron Age Pottery from Macedonia," *Antiquaries Journal*, VII (1927), 44–59. Since the ceramics connected with the Macedonian conquest did not come down into Greece, it would be possible to argue that these invaders set in motion the Dorians.

from archaeological stratification, which is not easily come by in the poverty of Aegean sites, and estimates of the length of pottery styles. The evidence now at hand is sufficient to prevent making gross mistakes of a century or more, but accurate dating of events or of specific vases to a definite decade or even a quarter of a specific century cannot be achieved by this method —though, let me warn, a casual observer of much archaeological literature might be misled into thinking such dating was simple.

Scholars who cherish precision have accordingly tried to save the specific dates assigned to early events by Greek chronological traditions. Here, however, they run into even worse difficulties very swiftly. The canonical date for the fall of Troy, for instance, is 1184/3 in the scheme of Eratosthenes and others, though variant dates range from 1334 to 1135;[2] but anyone who holds to the Homeric picture of a joint attack by all Greece on Troy cannot then accept the general direction of the archaeological evidence which suggests that the mainland was already under attack by 1200. One common solution to this impasse is to depress the date of the Dorian invasion down well toward the end of the twelfth century so as to save the Eratosthenian date; others seek rather to adhere to the archaeological picture and pick one of the earlier, variant dates for the Trojan war.[3]

[2] Eratosthenes: Clement of Alexandria, *Stromateis* I. 21. 139 (as Eusebius, Velleius Paterculus I. 8, Dionysius of Halicarnassus II. 1–2, Diodorus I. 5). Other ancient views may be found in John Forsdyke, *Greece before Homer: Ancient Chronology and Mythology* (London, 1956), 62–63; F. Jacoby, *Die Fragmente der griechischen Historiker* (Berlin, 1923–), under the several authors.

[3] Jean Bérard, *Recherches sur la chronologie de l'époque mycénienne*, in *Mémoires presentés pars divers savants à l'Académie des Inscriptions et Belles-Lettres*, XV. 1 (Paris, 1950); and Oscar Broneer, "Athens in the Late Bronze Age," *Antiquity*, XXX (1956), 9–18, are examples of the effort to save archaeological appearances and the Homeric tradition together. But cf. R. M. Cook, *JHS*, LXVI (1946), 68; Furumark, *Opus. arch.*, VI (1950), 182–83; and among the many treatments of the development of myth, Ludwig Radermacher, *Mythos und Sage bei den Griechen* (Leipzig, 1938), Erster Teil.

The fall of Troy VI has been put about 1300, that of Troy VII.A about 1250 (or before the fall of Pylos), by Blegen, *X Congresso internazionale di scienze storiche*, VII (Rome, 1955), 128–29. Incidentally, if a Greek attack on Troy did take place, it was not necessarily like a modern interallied armada, and might have been launched by some parts of Greece even while others were already under Dorian assault. The emperor Majorian fitted out an expedition against the Vandals in A.D. 461 at a point when much of his European realm was in German hands. The fall of Troy VII.A

The proper answer, however, is neither alternative. Sober historical judgment must discard the ancient chronological schemes *in toto;* they are nothing more than elaborate harmonizations of the myths and legends which were known in later times and have no independent value whatever for historical purposes. Not until the fifth century B.C. did the historic Greek world come to date even contemporary events on a coherent scheme. Both Herodotus and Thucydides are careful on chronological matters, but do not concern themselves greatly over the yardstick of time. Their contemporary Hellanicus and other Greek antiquarians began to systematize earlier developments, and by Hellenistic times Eratosthenes, Apollodorus, and others had constructed a detailed picture which ran well back into the second millennium B.C. The yardsticks which were employed were to some extent a table of Olympiads beginning in 776 B.C., but more often the chronographers used genealogical lists, as of the kings of Sparta or Athens or of the priestesses of Hera at Argos. Generations were assumed to cover 40, 33⅓, and other spans of years.[4]

While the calculations were sometimes ingenious, they often were simply guesses; Duris of Samos assumed that Troy fell in 1334 in order to place the event a thousand years before Alexander crossed into Asia. The often striking differences in dates

---

may be due either to such an attack or to invaders from central Europe; although III.C pottery appears in a brief settlement (VII.B1) thereafter, this cannot disprove a conquest from the northwest.

[4] We do not know that the Olympian games actually began in 776, that they were given every four years in the eighth and seventh centuries (Th. Lenschau, *Philologus*, n. f. XLV [1936/37], 396–411, for instance, telescopes 776–584 B.C. down to a brief period, 632–584/3, by arguing for yearly games in early days), or that events placed in any Olympiad were correctly located. Probably Greek scholars affixed events, which they knew *independently*, to the 4-year Olympic scheme; see Ed. Will,

Korinthiaka (Paris, 1955), 351–52, on the battle of Hysiae; and Beloch, *Griechische Geschichte*, I. 2, 148–54, on the lists of Olympic victors.

Generations: Eratosthenes seems to have proceeded on a basis of 40 years per generation (from Hecataeus, according to Eduard Meyer, *Forschungen zur alten Geschichte,* I [Halle, 1892], 170). To assume that folk-memory was accurate in terms of generations and that Eratosthenian dates simply should be lowered by calculating generations at 30–35 years each is somewhat naïve; but see A. B. Burn, "Dates in Early Greek History," *JHS,* LV (1935), 130–46, and "Early Greek Chronology," *JHS,* LXIX (1949), 70–73.

assigned to early events are not incidental flaws in a generally solid tradition but reveal the fundamental weaknesses of the underlying principles. The Greeks believed their legends were historically true, and eventually, as they arranged their own times in sequences, they constructed elegant schemes for the past as well. We, however, need not follow them far. Since writing was used from at least the late eighth century B.C. onward, we can trust that major events and persons of the seventh and sixth centuries are approximately in the right *sequence*, though such figures as Pheidon of Argos float in a void; but so apparently reliable an absolute date as Solon's archonship of 594—perhaps the first solid point in Greek history—has been seriously questioned.[5]

Before the eighth century, on the other hand, no traditional date deserves credence in itself, and belief even in traditional events is largely a matter of faith. At the most, the historian can only hope that the main line of folk memory and genealogical tradition preserve the most outstanding developments in the right sequence; men in historic times thus knew that the Dorian invasion must be put well back before their own background and assigned to it dates which would so locate it. For the actual development of Greek civilization, fortunately, the archaeological evidence suggests the main stages, and the importance of this step in Western civilization is such that we may follow it with interest even though our story must lack the precision of absolute dating and the mass of attendant circumstances which are available in more historic epochs.

[5] T. J. Cadoux, "The Athenian Archons from Kreon to Hypsichides," *JHS*, LXVIII (1948), 70–123, examines the problem of Solon (pp. 93–99). The date assigned by modern students to the Cypselid domination of Corinth still wavers over a generation; Will, *Korinthiaka*, has recently argued forcefully for the era 620–550, as against the conventional date of 655–*c*. 580. The first useful tie between Greek and Oriental written chronology is the figure of Gyges of Lydia, who was active according to Assyrian records until about 652; as Herodotus reckoned back, he placed this king about 716–679. See Hermann Strasburger, "Herodots Zeitrechnung," *Historia*, V (1956), 129–61; Hans Kaletsch, "Zur lydischen Chronologie," *Historia*, VII (1958), 1–47.

THE SIGNIFICANCE OF THE DORIANS [6]

THE OTHER absorbing problem connected with the end of the Mycenaean world which must be considered here is the significance of the northern invaders. This issue links very directly to the substance of the next chapter, which will consider the Aegean world in the early Dark ages and the first appearance of a truly Greek outlook. More relevant at the present point, a consideration of the problem enables us to look back over the whole span of early Aegean evolution down to the fall of Mycenaean society and to assess its bearing on the rise of historic Greek civilization.

There is no need here to review in detail the factual aspects of Aegean progress through the Neolithic and Bronze ages, other than to reiterate that the stages thus far considered are not Greek in the sense in which that term is employed in this volume. They are the ancestors of that culture, but one must look closely to detect the family lineaments under the sharply defined physiognomy of archaic and classic Greek centuries.

If we pass from the specific to the general, the history of the early Aegean may perhaps assume different proportions. A very great part of modern scholarship thus tends to explain the Greek genius as the ultimate but essentially predictable flowering of a recognizable force which was introduced into the Aegean basin in the period before 1100. While this process of explanation is widely shared, its adherents differ fiercely among themselves in identifying the force in question. Three main contenders have been paraded: the original Mediterranean stock, Oriental civilization, and the northern Indo-European invaders.

[6] Judicious statements of the archaeological evidence may be found in the studies listed in n. 7 (p. 63). A few examples of the more sweeping interpretations are Hans Krahe, *Die Indogermanisierung Griechenlands und Italiens* (Heidelberg, 1949); Wilhelm Kraiker, "Nordische Einwanderungen in Griechenland," *Die Antike*, XV (1939), 195–230, who followed the same line in the official *Kerameikos* reports; Friedrich Matz, *Geschichte der griechischen Kunst*, I (Frankfurt, 1950), 38, 202, 344–45; Friedrich Wirth, "Der nordische Charakter des Griechentums," *Mannus*, XXX (1938), 222–46. Even that independent critic, Beloch, accepted the basic premises of the Nordic theory in *Griechische Geschichte*, I. 1, 92–95.

Of these three, the Oriental myth is the oldest and is once more strongly in the field today. Since it is often reinforced by arguments based on the Orientalizing wave in Greek times, we may postpone its consideration until the time when the Aegean and the Orient renewed their contacts (in Chapter 6). The other two, however, must be exorcised now lest they warp our view of the fundamental drives in Greek history.

The effort to prove that the basic qualities of Greek civilization bubbled up from the *Urbevölkerung*, the primeval Mediterranean stock, is often a reaction against the Nordic argument. It is to be found especially, but not exclusively, among scholars of Mediterranean origin; but it arises out of the same racialistic background as its more formidable contender.[7] I need not, accordingly, deal with its theoretical principles by themselves. On its purported factual proofs, drawn from such matters as round or oval architectural ground plans, the worship of a Great Mother, and so on, little comment is needed; their ascription to a basic Mediterranean outlook, static across the ages, commonly will not stand critical investigation. Worse yet, the political, religious, and spiritual attitudes of the earliest Mediterranean levels, as I have noted in Chapter 1, are not easily ascertained.

The Indo-European school has had a long and triumphant career. Its origins, as a conscious theory, lie in the early nineteenth century, very soon after linguistic students had discovered the wide spread of this group of languages and in the era when German scholars were liberating themselves from French cultural domination. The first major work which stressed the Nordic origin of Greek culture was K. O. Müller's study *Die Dorier*, published in 1824, which was actually in part a healthy reaction against the common interpretation of Greek culture at that time as a simple offshoot from Oriental sources. Since then the view

---

[7] Adolf Furtwängler put this view succinctly in 1900, "Das eigentlich künstlerisch Schöpferische ging wahrscheinlich von dem vorgriechischen Element der Urbevölkerung aus" (quoted by Franz Dirlmeier, *Gnomon*, XXVI [1954], 151, with other examples); see also Guido von Kaschnitz-Weinberg, *Die mittelmeerischen*

Grundlagen der antiken Kunst (Frankfurt, 1944). On the significance of ground plans, the remarks of C. A. Boëthius, "Mycenaean Megara and Nordic Houses," *BSA*, XXIV (1919–21), 161–84, still point in the right direction; see also Chap. 1, n. 1 (p. 20). Fertility cults: see below, Chap. 5, n. 6 (p. 177).

that Greek (and also Roman) civilization was the product of *indogermanisches Volkstum* has permeated not only nationalistic German scholarship but also an amazing range of other work all across the continent of Europe; its insidious influence can often be detected in studies the authors of which would be among the first to reject the basic theses of the school.

These theses have necessarily undergone amplification and change, though only on details, as our archaeological knowledge has progressed. Nowdays it is no longer possible to deny that the first impetus to Aegean development came from the Orient, but once the Nordic specialists have grudgingly admitted this influence into the Greek Neolithic era they do their utmost to redeem the situation. The basic pattern of life which resulted from the arrival of agriculture is termed a "closed peasant culture" which in itself could never have progressed.[8] To enliven this backward world, invaders from the north magically appear to contribute their dynamic, inventive spirit—first the Dimini people, then (though not commonly) a wave in Early Helladic days, and the Achaeans at the beginning of the Middle Helladic era. But these waves were drawn aside by the siren temptations of the "Mediterranean" culture of Crete. "The last, most fundamental, and decisive turning point" (in Kraiker's words), accordingly, was the Dorian invasion, which so strengthened the Nordic spirit of Greece that it became capable of the heights of the Hellenic achievement. To give the real flavor of this line of argument, early Aegean development must be described virtually in melodramatic terms of the struggle of good and evil.

My utter inability to accept any part of the Nordic theory will already be apparent. On the factual level, adherents of the school have had to yield every position which they have taken up, one after another. Neither the Dimini wave nor changes in Early Helladic times can be clearly attached to the north; and

[8] Kraiker, *Die Antike*, XV (1939), 196; cf. Kunze, *Orchomenos*, III, 91. The efforts to explain later variations in Greek religious outlooks on racial terms will be considered below in Chapters 5 and 8; an example of this approach is the study by C.

Theander, "'Ολολυγή und 'Ιά," *Eranos*, XV (1915), 99–160, and XX (1921–22), 1–50, which takes these Greek religious calls as survivals. The pre-Greek population thus is assumed to have been more inclined to emotional outbreaks.

the Middle Helladic invasion in itself brought nothing positive which can be seen in the archaeological evidence. If any era may be called rural and backward in early Greece, this epoch probable best deserves the term! As for the Dorians, scholars a generation ago were inclined to attribute to this wave an impressive range of physical gifts, such as iron, slashing swords, a new style of clothing pinned at the shoulders by *fibulae,* the house plan of rectangular shape known as the *megaron,* and burial by cremation; but increasing evidence and a greater precision in its chronological interpretation have shown conclusively that none of the major innovations at the end of the second millennium, which will be taken up in the next chapter, are to be connected with the Dorians.

These were a barbarian folk invading a far more civilized land. They gave a final push to what seems to have been already a tottering political and economic structure; they looted, killed some of the natives, and married native women; and at least on simple levels the new masters took over the previous patterns of culture. Proponents of the Nordic theory have been especially embarrassed by the fact that the greatest type of Protogeometric pottery, the first true mark of a Greek outlook as we shall see shortly, emerged in Attica—for this was not linguistically a Dorian land, though roundheads of Alpine type sifted into the area and were buried in its cemeteries in appreciable numbers.[9]

The strength of such a line of thought does not lie in factual evidence, which is mere window-dressing for more basic modern prejudices; the theoretical dictates of this outlook, however, have resulted in more misreading of the archaeological record of early Greece than any other single factor. With respect to the basic drives behind the Nordic theory, we may as well be brief, for the true believer in any cult will not yield his belief to logical argument. On the racialistic side, it may be noted that the terms "Dorian," "Ionian," etc., are simply linguistic in character, and

[9] Angel, *Hesperia,* XIV (1945), 322–23, 328; Emil Breitinger, *Kerameikos: Ergebnisse der Ausgrabungen,* I (Berlin, 1939), 223–55. This actually is our best evidence so far on the increase of dolichocrane skulls in the Greek graveyards of the late second millennium; see also Robert P. Charles, "Etude anthropologique des nécropoles d'Argos," *BCH,* LXXXII (1958), 268–313.

that the Dorian-speaking peoples of later Greece possessed no specific political or cultural attitudes merely by virtue of their dialect.[1] Nor does it follow that if a potter speaks in an Indo-European tongue, his fingers will be mystically impelled to give his pots a marvelous sense of structure. This proposition, I should perhaps observe, is actually very often asserted.

Not all of the wide acceptance either of the Nordic or of the Mediterranean theory, to be sure, is due to modern race tenets. In explaining any great development historical students tend to search for a pre-existent cause; the proposition that the Dorians are this force has often been innocently accepted because it seems a simple, all-illuminating explanation of the otherwise mystifying rise of the great Greek civilization of later days. History is not quite so chemical a process. To repeat an observation made at the close of the previous chapter, each people and each culture which contributed to the early evolution of the Aegean lands gave something which was of lasting value, but those contributions were not static, fixed entities to which clearly distinguishable parts of the later population clung. Far more they were living influences which entered subtly into ever changing patterns. By 1100 basic social and intellectual foundations had emerged from the interplay and interfusion of the many earlier forces which we have thus far examined; the rise of the Hellenic outlook itself is to be explained only when and as we consider its actual appearance.

The Dorians themselves are nonetheless of very great importance in Aegean history. The Nordic theorists are right—but for the wrong reasons—when they assert that the invasion at the end of the Mycenaean age was a vital condition for the emergence of Greek civilization. In many ways the invasion was a catastrophe, for it brought wide-scale destruction and broke down a relatively advanced political superstructure. Mycenaean pottery, which tells the tale well, progressed into a sub-Mycenaean phase which can only be termed degenerate. Yet in the

---

[1] The principles of modern racial study, which can be found in any respectable handbook, are applied to the issue at hand by Édouard Will, *Doriens et Ioniens: essai sur la valeur du critère ethnique appliqué à l'étude de l'histoire et de la civilisation grecques* (Paris, 1956).

fact that the Dorians did end the Mycenaean age lies their significance.

Greek civilization could never have arisen if that disruption had not occurred and had not shaken the old conventions. In the dull, repetitive cases of Mycenaean pottery which can be seen in modern museums, in the palace tablets which now show the centralizing drive of royal masters, we can sense that the Mycenaean world was far too attached to outside models ever to develop an independent outlook of its own. These links were broken by the barbarian invasions of Greece and of the Middle East at the end of the Late Bronze age; the declining palace economies of the Mycenaean lords were shattered; and so men were set free to create new political and intellectual views, once the worst of the chaos was over.

In that work the Aegean was to be essentially sundered from the Middle East for three centuries. This break was its decisive, critical opportunity. Potters and craftsmen moved on from the underlying tendencies in late Mycenaean art, yet already by the eleventh century they were expressing a new outlook on life. Although the Greek genius was not a gift from the wild forests of Indo-European Europe, we cannot do without the Dorians in essaying to explain the world in which the first clear marks of Greek civilization appeared.

PART II

THE DARK AGES

a) *Sub-Mycenaean vase (K. 436), showing the deterioration of Mycenaean shapes and motifs (Kerameikos Museum).*

b) *Ripe Protogeometric amphora (K. 1073), fully developed in the new style (Kerameikos Museum). Photographs courtesy Deutsches Archäologisches Institut in Athens.*

PLATE 5 · *The Revolution of the Eleventh Century*

(a)

(b)

(c)

(d)

(a) Sub-Mycenaean vase (K. 421) with degenerate floral motif on shoulder (Kerameikos
Museum).
(b) Amphora from Argos, on the verge of a
Protogeometric shape (Argos Museum). Photograph courtesy École française d'Athènes.
(c) Early Protogeometric amphora (K. 522)
at the beginning of the new style (Kerameikos Museum).
(d). Early Protogeometric amphora (K.
556) with more developed shape and separated circle motifs (Kerameikos Museum).
Photographs a, c, and d courtesy Deutsches
Archäologisches Institut in Athens.

PLATE 6 · *Emergence of the Protogeometric Style*

CHAPTER 3

AFTER

THE MYCENAEAN COLLAPSE

ᒪᒧᒪᒧᒪᒧᒪᒧᒪᒧᒪᒧᒪᒧᒪᒧᒪᒧᒪᒧᒪᒧᒪᒧᒪᒧᒪᒧ

As THE LAST EMBERS flickered out at the destroyed Mycenaean palaces, darkness settled over Greece. Men continued to
live in most parts of the Aegean, to beget families, and to die; but
their dull routine of daily life and final burial deposited only the
scantiest of physical remains. Not until the eighth century B.C.
does this obscurity slowly begin to lift. The material evidence
then grows more extensive and more varied, as sculpture and
architecture emerge alongside the ever present pottery; myth is
occasionally usable; and writing of a new type spreads over the
Aegean basin. Once more the Aegean and the Orient resume
contact on an extensive scale.

By 750 there can be no doubt that the type of civilization
which we call Greek had appeared. It had already produced one
of its greatest fruits, the *Iliad,* and was ready to enter upon a
great stage of revolution and crystallization, leading to the
archaic world of *kouroi* and *korai* statues, stone temples of Doric
order, Solon and Sappho, and the consolidated city-state. So dim
is the background to these magnificent achievements that many
scholars have assumed the Hellenic outlook arose only after
800 B.C. This point of view distorts the actual course of events
badly, as does the more recent argument which assigns the
decisive steps to the Mycenaean age.

Thirty years ago it was possible, perhaps inevitable, that
the ill-lit centuries between the fall of Mycenae and the emer-

gence of historic times should be summed up briefly as an un-differentiated, apparently static, and relatively unimportant era. Since then decisive archaeological discoveries have provided adequate signposts to the tempo, stages, and direction of change in the years from 1150 to 750. In this age, it is now clear, the inhabitants of the Aegean settled on the patterns of thought which continued directly into historic times as the main marks of Greek civilization. More specifically, the fundamental aspects emerged abruptly in the period immediately after the fall of the Mycenaean world. They then developed, very slowly but none-theless surely, across the following centuries down to the great outburst of the late eighth century.

This long period of four hundred years falls into three stages. Each, fortunately, has a clearly distinguishable pottery style. First comes the evolution of the most basic qualities of Greek civilization, a step which is aesthetically expressed in the rise of Protogeometric pottery. This development took place independ-ently in Attica, the Argolid, and other areas in the decades down to about 1000. The second phase is the consolidation of the new outlook across the tenth and ninth centuries, the era when the Protogeometric formulas yielded to the first stages of the Geo-metric style. At this time the linguistic and cultural unification of the Aegean basin was completed. In the third period, which runs directly on into the great age of revolution, the Greek world was secure enough to begin its intellectual and geographical ex-pansion. The greatest marks of this phase, the early eighth cen-tury, are the *Iliad* of Homer and the famous Ripe Geometric or Dipylon pottery of Athens.

Each of these three major eras deserves independent con-sideration. In the present chapter, which will consider the first, our attention must be focused upon the theses that unmistakable tokens of Greek civilization can be detected in the eleventh cen-tury B.C. and that these aspects emerged from native roots.

THE BACKGROUND OF CHAOS

DURING the invasions and unrest which ended the glowing Mycenaean age, Greek lands experienced a terrific shock. Everywhere men continued to make the most essential household tools and wares in the ways of their forefathers, but in a dreary, lifeless spirit which archaeologists term sub-Mycenaean. Commonly the only physical evidence is that provided by the scanty furnishings of simple graves—pottery of limited types and restrained decoration; occasional *fibulae,* pins, arms, and a few other metal objects, usually of bronze but now occasionally of iron. Gold and silver almost vanish; the little clay figurines which appear frequently in late Mycenaean graves are no longer to be found. Over the whole of the Greek mainland only a few remains of poorly constructed houses have thus far been turned up to demonstrate how abysmally building skills had sunk from the days when the architects of Mycenaean kings had the daring and resources to construct great palaces and *tholos* tombs.[1]

Quite probably the population of the Aegean basin dropped terrifically. This was the result not of the actual rapine and destruction or occasional emigration but of the collapse of order and settled life; human existence is even more deeply dependent upon a solid social and political framework than upon economic and technological skills. If we feel that major sites, at least in part, were still occupied, this is only an inference from their later history; our evidence is still too scanty to permit us to determine where inhabitation did continue. Archaeologists have not, thus far, succeeded in discovering a site at which men left a *continuous* stratified deposit all the way from the height of the Mycenaean age on down into the Dark ages. Even at Argos, Cnossus, and Athens, where settlements must have existed, new cemeteries were begun in the sub-Mycenaean phase.[2]

[1] N. Valmin, *Opuscula atheniensia,* I (1953), 31–40, on Malthi; Milojčić, AA 1955, 196, on the Gremnos mound in Thessaly; Gallet de Santerre, *Délos primitive,* 215, who accepts Vallois' argument for the very early date of the building under the later structure known as the Oikos of the Naxians.

[2] Decline: V. R. d'A. Desborough, *Protogeometric Pottery* (Oxford, 1952), 296–97, who may exaggerate its degree, especially for the islands; but the depopulation which often takes place here in times of crisis is

Many areas may well have sunk back into nomadic life, which always revives in Greek lands when civilization declines. The scantiness of remains from villages of the plains in the early Dark ages is perhaps not accidental; and the lowest point, when measured for Greece as a whole in physical terms, quite possibly came at and just after 1000, when the last sub-Mycenaean remnants flickered out in a number of areas. Settled sites become steadily more noticeable again after about 900. The development may reflect the slow restoration of order and growth of population as peoples which had previously wandered, each within its own tribal area, became fixed in location and turned to agricultural life.

The point at which the last waves of northern invasions died away cannot be precisely set. Throughout the eastern Mediterranean the major migrations had come to an end by 1000 B.C., though scattered movements and slow infiltrations continued thereafter. Within the Aegean, some archaeologists have essayed to demonstrate a new invasion just after 1000, and others feel that northerners sifted in for some time to come.[3] The possibility of movements in a fluid world cannot be gainsaid, but after the

illuminated for modern times by Hasluck, *BSA*, XVII (1910–11), 151–81. See, however, Gallet de Santerre, *Délos primitive*. The change in burial sites took a remarkable form at Fortetsa, near Cnossus; Late Minoan tombs seem to have continued in use but were swept virtually clear of earlier remains (J. K. Brock, *Fortetsa: Early Greek Tombs near Knossos* [Cambridge, 1957], 216).

Nomadism: Daniel Faucher, "Les Conditions naturelles de la vie agricole en Grèce continentale," *Mélanges de la société toulousaine d'études classiques*, I (1946), 5–22, who notes that Chateaubriand saw Albanian flocks on the ruins of Athens and Corinth. Cf. Johannes Hasebroek, *Griechische Wirtschafts- und Gesellschaftsgeschichte bis zur Perserzeit* (Tübingen, 1931), 1–6; H. Bolkestein, *Economic Life in Greece's Golden Age* (Leyden, 1958), 13; Thalia P. Howe, "Linear B and He-

siod's Breadwinners," *Transactions of the American Philological Association*, LXXXIX (1958), 44–65, who argues that grain-raising only slowly replaced livestock. Renewed settlement might be argued for Corinth with T. J. Dunbabin, "The Early History of Corinth," *JHS*, LXVIII (1948), 59–69, though we know too little of its early history to speak with confidence. A surer example of oscillation between nomadism and settled population is that of Jericho (Kenyon, *Digging Up Jericho*, 186–87, 192).

[3] Milojčić, AA 1948–49, 19–22, and "Einige 'mitteleuropäische' Fremdlinge auf Kreta," *Jahrbuch des römisch-germanischen Zentralmuseums in Mainz*, II (1955), 153–69; Lenk s. v. Thrake in PW, 415–16, who sums up ancient speculation; Desborough, *BSA*, XLIX (1954), 266, but see below, n. 4 (p. 89), on the nature of hand-made vases.

initial, decisive blows the further introduction of new tribes, whether Greek, Illyrian, or Thracian in speech, had little cultural effect except insofar as it may have served to delay the restoration of local order and the resumption of enduring settlement.

The degree of the collapse which befell the Aegean world in the late second millennium must not be underestimated. Nor, on the other hand, had this area become entirely a *tabula rasa,* a cipher incapable of internal development. Some places were surely occupied continuously; the older patterns of life generally persisted on at least their simplest level; new steps, which essentially mark the birth of Greek civilization, were taken in the very era of turmoil. To see these aspects, we must turn primarily to the mountain villages of Crete and to the cemeteries of Attica.

The Cretan mountain villages arose at the end of Late Minoan times; they were not inhabited before the collapse, and were deserted again as soon as the plains had once more become safe.[4] These mountain eyries were mean settlements. Karphi, the best explored, lay thirteen hundred feet above the fertile plain of Lasithi in eastern Crete and must have been almost unendurable in winter. Its population, perhaps as much as thirty-five hundred souls, supported life by farming in the plain below, by herding, and perhaps by brigandage against neighbors.

The houses of Karphi were simple structures of native stone and clay or mud. Often they were one room, which at times assumed a *megaron* form, a rectangular shape with hearth in the center and foreporch. Others, however, were of a rambling Minoan pattern; one abode of more extensive nature seems to have been the mansion of the chieftain. The streets within the settlement were roughly paved, and the inhabitants improved their spring by walls to catch the water and lead it down into a tank in which animals could be watered; about this tank figures of oxen, sheep, and a man were discovered. An open space was perhaps a public square, on which a tavern may have faced.

[4] "Excavations in the Plain of Lasithi III: Karphi: A City of Refuge of the Early Iron Age in Crete," *BSA,* XXXVIII (1937–38), 57–145; Henri van Effenterre, *Nécropoles de Mirabello* (Paris, 1948); E. H. Hall, *Excavations in Eastern Crete: Vrokastro* (Philadelphia, 1914); Pendlebury, *Archaeology of Crete,* 303–13; Nicolas Platon, "'Ανασκαφαί περιοχῆς Σητείας," *Praktika* 1952, 630–48.

Though the village was unwalled and displays no clear architectural planning, its equal has yet to be found on the contemporary mainland. The *tholos* tombs which were discovered below the houses were assigned by the excavators to the local nobles; the graves of the peasants apparently were too simple to leave lasting traces.

Culturally, the hallmark of Karphi, as of Vrokastro, Olous, Dreros, and other early Cretan settlements, was conservativism. The inhabitants of these villages had little interest in breaking away from their inherited tradition, but yet had sufficient resources to maintain its basic aspects. Karphi possessed a temple or, rather, religious enclosure in which worship was conducted in Minoan style.[5] The figures found in this enclosure, like those discovered at Gazi near Cnossus, are of a female deity with upraised hands (probably in pose of epiphany) and complicated crown. However rudimentary their modeling and crude their design, no sculpture of similar size is known from the Greek mainland throughout the Dark Age. The religious emphasis, too, on the female principle went back into Minoan times and continued on down into later centuries.

The pottery of these sites is almost entirely derived from Minoan and Mycenaean prototypes. While the vases were impoverished in motifs and were poorly decorated, human and animal figures never quite disappeared from Cretan pottery, as they virtually did on the mainland; and in comparison with the ruthless simplification of mainland pottery styles the work of Cretan potters remained varied as well as conservative.

Even thus far, nonetheless, the changes which were taking place on the mainland found distant reflection. The Cretan villagers used iron sporadically; *fibulae* of Protogeometric types

[5] An altar in shrine form was found at Karphi, *AJA*, XLIII (1939), 130 fig. 8; Stylianos Alexiou,"Πρωτογεω-μετρικός ναΐσκος τῆς Συλλογῆς Γαμαλ-άκη," *Kretika Chronika*, IV (1950), 441–62, published a round shrine model with female deity within and two other figures (Dioscuri?) and a dog on the thatched roof. Figures of female deities: *BSA*, XXXVIII (1937), pl. xxxi; Spyridon Marinatos, "'Αἱ Μινωϊκαὶ Θεαὶ τοῦ Γάζι," *Arch. eph.* 1937, 278–91; Matz, *Kreta, Mykene, Troja*, pl. 59; Müller, *Frühe Plastik*, pl. xii, nn. 228–230. While the Karphi examples are ruder than Late Minoan work, the presence of feet and the different structural sense in the torso are significant changes.

appear in their graves, and the style of burial tended to shift from inhumation in clay coffins to cremation in large storage vessels known as pithoi. Some aspects of the pottery can perhaps be hesitantly called Protogeometric. One clay box (pyxis) which was found at Karphi well reflects the varied strands of Cretan culture in the era: its horns of consecration and double axes attest Minoan inheritance; its general shape is of Mycenaean character, as is also its decoration of birds; but its lid has a Protogeometric air. Only at such an open site as Cnossus near the sea, however, is there any positive evidence that men of Crete directly knew what was happening elsewhere in the Aegean before the ninth century.

Crete, in sum, is not the best area from which to illuminate the major developments of the early Dark ages. The island of Minos remained perhaps richer and more settled than the Greek mainland, but its population clung more fully to their inheritance from the second millennium. When they turned abroad again, they looked eastward toward Cyprus and the Orient as well as northward; we shall see later that Cretan progress did not follow quite the same line as that in other important Aegean districts. The main course of Greek civilization was determined by forces emanating from the even more barbarous but also more venturesome mainland.

NEW WAYS IN THE ELEVENTH CENTURY

WHEN WE MOVE to Greece proper, we must resign ourselves to relying primarily upon the evidence which can be drawn from its simple cemeteries; but men's provision for the dead throws considerable light upon their views about life. Material is now coming in from several parts of the mainland; future excavations will surely enlarge and deepen our knowledge. Attica, which remains the best lit, was quite clearly not the only center of evolution, but it seems generally to have stood in the van.

Archaeological evidence for the Mycenaean period attests that Attica was then a thriving district with several local centers

besides the Acropolis, which had a royal palace.[6] We cannot be
as sure as was ancient tradition that Athens escaped the wave of
invasions, nor was it necessarily a refuge into which desperate
fugitives poured on their way to colonize Asia Minor—the myths
of this movement will be considered in Chapter 4. What we do
know is that here best we can follow continuous development
across the dim period after the fall of the Mycenaean world.
However destructive the whirlwind which swept across the rest
of Greece, and even perhaps Attica itself, men dwelt uninter-
ruptedly in the favored land of Athena; their culture evolved
from earlier roots but underwent epochal changes in the eleventh
century.

The principal proof of continuity and the main key to Attic
development is the cemetery of a simple village which was
placed in the open land by the Eridanus brook, northwest of the
Acropolis on the Eleusis road. The cemetery in this area, later
known as the Kerameikos or Potters' Quarter, was begun in sub-
Mycenaean times and was used on down into the classic period.
To the present point it is the only site in all Greece which furnishes an uninterrupted record across this era. The importance of
the cemetery, accordingly, cannot be overestimated; and fortunately its excavation was conducted with the utmost care by the
German Archaeological Society, in part in 1913–16 (after some
probings from 1863 on) but more completely in 1927–40.[7] With
the aid of the unbroken chain of pottery development which can
be established here, the relative place of various other early
burials in Athens—in the Agora, on the sides of the Acropolis, at
Eleusis, on Salamis, and so on—can be determined, and one can
assess their significance in the whole line of progress.

The Kerameikos graves proper begin with simple sub-Myce-

[6] Illustrative material may be found
from H. G. Lolling et al., *Das Kuppelgrab bei Menidi* (Athens, 1880),
on to the tombs discovered in the
Agora excavations, *Hesperia*, IX
(1940), 274–91; AJA, LI (1947),
270–71; LVII (1953), 24; LVIII
(1954), 231–32. Cf. C. W. Blegen,
"Athens and the Early Age of Greece,"
HSCP, Suppl. I (1940), 1–9.

[7] Preliminary reports in *AA*; final reports now being published as *Kerameikos: Ergebnisse der Ausgrabungen*
(Berlin), I (1939), IV (1943), V. 1
(1954), VI. 1 (1959); new excavation is in course. Georg Karo, *An Attic Cemetery* (Philadelphia, 1943),
gives a brief but delightful sketch,
which pays due respect to the finan-
cial aid and encouragement of Gustav
Oberlaender.

naean interments in rectangular pits. Almost half of these earliest graves have no burial gifts at all to supply the corpse with its needs; the remainder have a vase or two for food, a container for wine (oenochoe) or oil (lekythos), and a bowl (skyphos) or cup (kantharos), with at times a clay box on a stand or an ointment jar (pyxis). The men occasionally have their weapons; the women, pins, rings, spirals, and the like; the children, milk jugs and miniature vases. The metal is almost exclusively bronze, though one spiral of gold appears. The pottery displays the tired shapes and weak decoration inherited from the Mycenaean world. Simple black bands cover much of the surface of the vase; motifs include concentric half-circles roughly drawn by hand, wavy lines, and once a very conventionalized octopus.

About 1100 three of these sub-Mycenaean burials, which were laid in round pits, were cremations; an amphora contains the ashes of the corpse.[8] On the island of Salamis a contemporary graveyard which yielded more than a hundred simple tombs had two cremation burials. Soon thereafter cremation became the almost universal custom all over Attica and remained predominant until about 800 B.C., when interment again was resumed on an extensive scale.

The appearance of cremation is easier to note than to explain.[9] This method of burial had been practiced sporadically

[8] *Kerameikos,* I, graves 56, 67, 75; Desborough, *Protogeometric Pottery,* 2–4.

[9] H. L. Lorimer surveys the material in "Pulvis et umbra," *JHS,* LIII (1933), 161–80, and *Homer and the Monuments,* 103–10. See also Desborough, *Protogeometric Pottery,* 306–07; Levi, *Annuario,* X–XII (1927–29), 543–46; M. P. Nilsson, *Geschichte der griechischen Religion,* I (Munich, 1955), 174–77; Joseph Wiesner, *Grab und Jenseits: Untersuchungen im ägäischen Raum zur Bronzezeit und frühen Eisenzeit* (Berlin, 1938), 101–03, 108, 113, 119–26. Cremation in purely Mycenaean contexts: *JHS,* LXXIV Suppl. (1954), 147; LXXVI Suppl. (1956), 7, 16; *Ergon* 1957, 89 ff. It occurs with Mycenaean ware at Tell Atchana, Woolley, *Alalakh,* 204 ff.;

and an example has been found in Cyprus in the second half of the twelfth century, George H. McFadden, "A Late Cypriote Tomb from Kourion, Kaloriziki No. 40," *AJA,* LVIII (1954), 131–42.

Product of refugees: Kraiker, *Die Antike,* XV (1939), 223; Lorimer, *Homer and the Monuments,* 105–06, whose view that the custom was carried from Attica to Ionia probably reverses the true current; J. de Vries, *Altgermanische Religionsgeschichte,* II (Berlin 1937), 26–27, finds that cremation accompanied the era of Germanic migrations. Views of afterlife: Karo, *Attic Cemetery,* 8; Erwin Rohde, *Psyche* (8th ed.; London, 1925), 19–22; but cf. Dumézil, *Naissance de Rome,* 134–37. Liberation of graves: Mylonas, *AJA,* LII (1948), 69–70.

over the ancient world for centuries, but it had never been a custom in the Aegean proper save at Troy VI and on the coasts of Asia Minor, together with inland Hittite districts. In the last centuries of the second millennium and in the early first millennium it spread widely into central Europe (the *Urnenfelder*); in Greece we find it as a convention only at a few points, primarily Attica, Boeotia, some of the islands, and also Crete (and here perhaps before the Athenian villages had shifted over).

In their sober effort to explain everything, modern scholars have proffered many desperate solutions to this riddle. The old view that the Dorians brought the custom has been universally dropped, for this ascription fits neither our sure chronological framework of the relative sequence of events nor the absence of the practice in many Dorian areas. More common nowadays is the argument that refugees, who had to carry their dead in the more transportable and hygienic form of ashes, introduced cremation into Attica. Against this interpretation, in turn, stand weighty objections. Why should the one area, Attica, where we can be sure of continuous settlement take up the new fashion most completely? The direction from which cremation apparently came, moreover, was the east. Nor does our knowledge of later Greek religious views furnish any illumination as to why Athenians burned their dead and nearby Corinthians and Argives continued to inhume. The most reasonable explanation is that which suggests cremation set loose the spirit of the dead quickly so that it could go to Hades; the grave area thus was liberated for new use.

Changes in the style of burial throughout history are not necessarily significant in themselves, but the appearance of cremation at the Kerameikos is truly important and indicative in one respect. It demonstrates that parts of mainland Greece were free in the eleventh century to adopt a new pattern—i.e., that the dominance of older customs had been broken. Of incidental importance at this point is the area primarily affected; the virtually new custom of cremation penetrated from Asia Minor into Greece at Attica and secondarily Boeotia, regions closely connected with the Greek expansion eastward across the Aegean in the eleventh and following centuries. To this subject I shall return in the next chapter.

Another change which is evident in the Kerameikos cemetery as well as elsewhere in Greece was the use of iron.[1] Rings and other adornments of iron had appeared in Mycenaean times and also in sub-Mycenaean graves; but one of the first transitional tombs at the Kerameikos had an iron sword, and weapons of iron became ever more common in cremation burials.[2] In this development, too, the center of diffusion was Asia Minor, the smiths of which had learned the difficult, slow art of working iron into useful steel tools and weapons in the last centuries of the Hittite period. Thence the knowledge spread southward into Syria and other Oriental lands and brought an end to the Bronze age in the technical sense; wandering ironsmiths carried the new skills into Europe, where various finds of their workshops and supplies have illuminated their trade. Later Greek traditions of the Telchines, Dactyloi, and so on suggest the reverence felt for ironsmiths; it is interesting that these myths indicate Greece learned how to work iron either from Phrygia or from Crete, though we cannot be certain these were the actual routes.

Thenceforth Aegean society could base much of its technology upon a strong metal far more widely found than tin or even copper; but Greece entered its true Iron age only in the era of revolution after 750. Down to that point copper and stone still remained the most common materials for tools, partly because the Aegean was still too poor to support a large iron trade, partly because Greece itself was relatively weak in native ores of

[1] Iron in general: R. J. Forbes, *Metallurgy in Antiquity* (Leiden, 1950), 87–91, 456–58; Stefan Przeworski, *Die Metallindustrie Anatoliens in der Zeit von 1500–700 v. Chr.* (Leyden, 1939: *Internationales Archiv für Ethnographie*, XXXVI). In Greece: Desborough, *Protogeometric Pottery*, 308–12; Levi, *Annuario*, X–XII (1927–29), 544 (at Mouliana with cremation); Lorimer, *Homer and the Monuments*, 111–21; *BSA*, LIII–IV (1958–59), 234.

[2] On the new shape of sword which appears at Mouliana in Crete, e.g., and in Egypt under Seti II (c. 1214–1210), see Childe, *Proceedings of the Prehistoric Society*, n. s. XIV (1948), 183–84; Sir Arthur Evans, *The Palace of Minos*, IV (London, 1935), 847–53; Furumark, *Chronology of Mycenaean Pottery*, 93–96; Levi, *Annuario*, X–XII (1927–29), 464 and fig. 589; Sir William F. Petrie, *Tools and Weapons* (London, 1928), pl. 32–33.

iron. While deposits occurred in Samothrace, Euboea, Sparta, and Boeotia, the Aegean had to import much of its iron in semi-finished condition from Etruria, the Black Sea, and other regions in historic times. Gold and silver were also scanty; throughout the Dark ages no grave of the Aegean basin is even remotely as rich as some of the royal burials of the third and second millennia. Society no longer concentrated its wealth in the hands of a very few, and that wealth itself was very limited.

Aesthetically, the most interesting among the scanty metal objects in the Kerameikos graves are the straight pins and the *fibulae*, which had held together the folds of cloth at the shoulders of the dead person or had decorated his attire.[3] *Fibulae* had been so employed since late Mycenaean days and were popular over Greece, Italy, and central Europe in the early first millennium B.C. Their shapes underwent significant changes. The late Mycenaean examples developed a simple arch or "stilt" so as to hold more cloth in their grasp; thereafter the arch became much thicker in the middle and often had two strengthening bulbs on either side of the central swell. The product was a combination of clearly defined, articulated parts, an aesthetic principle which slowly manifested itself also in the bulbs and disk heads of the amazingly long straight pins. These outwardly insignificant objects are straws in the wind to suggest both the receptiveness to change in the eleventh century and the direction in which that change was moving. In the history of Greek *fibulae*, the most pronounced break which ever occurred was that at the end of the Mycenaean era, after which evolution followed a steady path on to classic times.

[3] *Fibulae:* Chr. Blinkenberg, *Fibules grecques et orientales* (Copenhagen, 1926); Desborough, *Protogeometric Pottery*, 308–09; Matz, *GGK*, I, 90–92. Pins: Desborough, *Protogeometric Pottery*, 309–10; Paul Jacobsthal, *Greek Pins and Their Connexions with Europe and Asia* (Oxford, 1956), 1–5. Although Taylour, *Mycenaean Pottery in Italy*, 78–79, and others suggest that heavier clothing was needed, a climatic shift at the end of the second millennium is not proven.

THE ORIGINS OF PROTOGEOMETRIC POTTERY

THE MOST abundant evidence of the Kerameikos graves is the pottery. Two quite different kinds appear, one turned on the wheel and decorated, the other hand-made and left in a native clay color. The latter, which was known in the Mycenaean era, was rather common through the Dark ages and on down into historic Greek centuries. This is a puzzling ware, which deserves full investigation by pottery experts. The shapes of hand-made vases were few, chiefly bowls and pitchers which were not of large size; at least at some places in later Greek times it was shop-produced. When we find examples in temple offerings or side by side with the most luxurious pottery, as in the eighth-century Isis grave of Attica, we must suspect that they had some sacred or magical attributes. Hand-made vases were not simply kitchen ware, and the occasional suggestion that this type was the pottery of an intrusive element has virtually no merit.[4]

The decorated pottery links firmly onto the sub-Mycenaean wares of the past and leads directly toward the later Geometric style, but it is so distinctive that it fully warrants a special name, Protogeometric.[5] On Plate 5 I have set side by side photographs of the vase K. 436, which is a sub-Mycenaean product of the

[4] Desborough, *BSA,* XLIX (1954), 266; Frödin and Persson, *Asine,* 435–36; Miločič, *AA* 1948–49, 33–34, who notes its Early Helladic and Middle Helladic affinities. In graves this pottery is said at times to be restricted to female burials (Kübler, *Kerameikos,* V. 1, 127; Charitonides, *AJA,* LXI [1957], 170–71); but see Kübler, *Kerameikos,* VI. 1, 85. It is not safe to conclude with Frankfort, *Studies in Early Pottery of the Near East,* II, 142 n. 1, that hand-made pottery was women's work. Examples have turned up at the temples of Aphaia, Perachora, etc., as well as in tombs on the mainland and on the islands.

[5] This name seems to have been coined by Sam Wide, "Gräberfunde aus Salamis," *AM,* XXXV (1910), 17–36, though the Salamis vases are

more sub-Mycenaean than Protogeometric. See V. R. d'A. Desborough's preliminary essay, "What Is Protogeometric?" *BSA,* XLIII (1948), 260–72, and his monograph, *Protogeometric Pottery,* which is an excellent study apart from its overemphasis on Attic origins and tendency to date non-Attic ware late; in *JHS,* LXXVII (1957), 215, he is no longer confident that Protogeometric ware appears in Greece only in a period corresponding to that of Late Attic Protogeometric vases. Not until the past two decades has our understanding of this style become solid. Skeat, *Dorians in Archaeology,* drew the style from Thessaly and Macedonia; T. Burton-Brown, *The Coming of Iron to Greece* (Wincle, Cheshire, [1954]), 211–26, still tries to connect it with Cyprus.

Kerameikos graves, and of the developed Protogeometric amphora K. 1073. When one inspects the actual vases in the Kerameikos Museum and goes on to compare the whole mass of
sub-Mycenaean ware with the marvelous cases of Protogeometric
work which follow thereafter, the impression to be derived is
unmistakable. One style descends from the other, but the change
is a virtual revolution. On the sides here illustrated of K. 436 and
K. 1073, the motifs are the same—bands and concentric semicircles—but the relative firmness and precision of the Protogeometric decoration are striking. Impressive, too, is the skill
with which the potter of K. 1073 applied his paint to mark off the
parts of the vase: the narrow but solid foot; the swelling, buff-
colored sides; the handles and shoulder; and finally the black
neck. The parts of this Protogeometric vase are clearly distinguished, yet they are superbly proportioned to each other to
create a unity which is utterly absent in the dumpy sub-Mycenaean pot.

Any aesthetic discussion of K. 1073 must employ such terms
as proportion, balance, and sober solidity; one senses here a
dynamic tension of opposing yet elegantly co-ordinated parts.
These qualities, I need hardly point out, are characteristic of
historic Greek civilization, but as combined in that culture their
first appearance in Aegean art is on Protogeometric pottery.

Before we can consider the implications of this pottery, its
origins in Attica and elsewhere on the Greek mainland must be
placed against the Mycenaean background. That the Protogeometric style evolved out of tendencies in the Late Bronze age—
but by a jump—is a highly important point in the rise of Greek
civilization, and only through the pottery can we hope to sense
the causes of the changes in the eleventh century.

In the Late Bronze age the potters of Greece had initially
yielded their hearts almost entirely to Minoan styles, but even
before the beginning of Mycenaean III.A (*c.* 1425 B.C.) a native
artistic spirit began to struggle up through the borrowed finery.
Across the range of III.A–C (*c.* 1425–1050, including the sub-
Mycenaean stage) very significant and quite obvious changes
took place in the shapes of vases, in their decorative motifs, and

in the application of these motifs. If one follows any specific vase form through these centuries, its evolution is continuous but extensive. The clash between borrowed and native instincts often resulted in a really ugly product in Mycenaean III.A, but by the next stage vases tended "toward simple, well-defined, and regular outlines, toward shapes approximating to simple geometrical bodies." [6] Ovoid outlines became more popular, and the differentiation of structural parts was more perceptible (see Plates 4a and d, 5a). In many vase forms, as the high-stemmed goblet (Plate 4c), late Mycenaean potters worked themselves into a dead end, marked by extreme stiffness; such shapes were to die out in either the sub-Mycenaean or Protogeometric styles.

The decoration of III.A–C vases began with recognizable, naturalistic motifs such as octopi, cuttlefish, murex shells, and papyrus heads. Sometimes these motifs continued to be mechanically copied; more often they were increasingly dissolved into formalized patterns of straight and curved lines. If we did not have the links in the chain, it would often be impossible to discern in the later, geometric shapes any natural origin. At times, indeed, late Mycenaean potters jumped back to Middle Helladic motifs of abstract character, which had been virtually absent in the Minoan wave of Mycenaean I–II.

Beyond these detailed changes in pottery motifs, the general principles of composition underwent intriguing alterations. At the beginning of Mycenaean III, potters usually treated the whole surface of a vase as a unit and decorated it accordingly with a flowing pattern. More and more, however, they came to divide the surface into horizontal zones, a principle which had been known in Middle Helladic times but which now reappeared primarily in reflection of a desire to emphasize the parts of the vase and their dynamic interrelations (compare Plates 1d, 2a, 4d).[7] These zones, in turn, were sometimes subdivided into

[6] Furumark, *Mycenaean Pottery*, 108. See in general ibid. 497–582; Mackeprang, *AJA*, XLII (1938), 537–59, covers the late Mycenaean ware more briefly, but clearly.
[7] Furumark, *Mycenaean Pottery*, 539–540, argues correctly, I think, that the principle of horizontal division reappeared to satisfy a real need. For the difference from unit decoration, see ibid. 112–16, based on Matz, *Die frühkretischen Siegel*. Metopes: Matz, *Kreta, Mykene, Troja*, 141–43; Wace, *BSA*, XLIX (1954), 247.

separate units in a system which is called from its architectural parallel the metope-triglyph technique, so as to secure a slower, more sharply emphasized rhythm (see Plate 7b and 8b for later, Geometric examples). More often each zone had a continuous "carefully drawn, detailed, close net-pattern." [8] The best examples of this type of Mycenaean III.C, which Wace termed the Close Style (see Plate 4d), are quite well done, but not all potters were willing to take the necessary pains. Beside the Close Style appears also a Granary Style, which at times has little more than wavy lines as adornment.

On the surface, as we saw in Chapter 2, the later stages of Mycenaean pottery are marked by a dull mass production and the dominance of standard types of vases decorated with a limited variety of uniform motifs. The hidden forces which were at work struggled against a strong inheritance of Minoan influences, but had not gained a clear victory when the Mycenaean political and economic system collapsed. Immediately, the results of this catastrophe were an abysmal decline of the potters' work. Sub-Mycenaean vases were commonly small in size and were made of poorly prepared clay. Their shapes tended toward heavy, globular, lifeless forms and were at times irregular. The painted decoration now was crudely applied in a sloppy fashion (compare Plate 4d with 5a and 6a) and was composed of weary, debased motifs inherited from the old stock; these often stand in simple rows.

Then, suddenly, the potters of Attica and elsewhere broke decisively with their jejune tradition and struck out on the fresh path of Protogeometric pottery. Thanks to the careful excavation and reasonably sure relative dating of the Kerameikos burials, we can watch the potters following this path, which is illustrated on Plates 6a, c, and d, and 5b. The transition into the new style is not a tidy, step-by-step affair of simple evolution. Various

---

[8] Mackeprang, *AJA*, XLII (1938), 544. The Granary Style: Wace, *BSA*, XXV (1921–23), 38 ff.; Furumark, *Opus. arch.*, III (1944), 203–06. On the terra-cotta figurines which suddenly became popular in Mycenaean graves after 1400 B.C. (Müller, *Frühe Plastik*, 55–58), a somewhat similar style of painting in which wavy lines emphasize the various parts of the structure appears alongside a decorative system of rings about the figure, which came probably from Crete.

pieces show each an aspect of change, but the whole pattern comes together with evident suddenness. The vases elongate, grow more oval, become better proportioned, and impress one as more stable. The foot changes until it becomes the simple ring of Protogeometric vases; the position of the handles is shifted to the belly or the neck; new shapes emerge and the old tend to disappear. Decorative principles also develop. Horizontal bands emphasize the shape and parts of the vase, which has otherwise only limited decoration. Concentric circles or semicircles, formerly drawn by hand, are now carefully applied by a multiple brush; [9] the lines are ruler-drawn. The last direct imitation of the naturalistic Mycenaean motifs vanishes.

In every basic respect the Protogeometric potters turned for their decoration and shapes to ancestral elements. These were mainly of late Mycenaean origin, but at points elements of Middle and Early Helladic flavor appear. The latter are mostly in the realm of motifs, yet Protogeometric amphoras resemble at times some taut, dynamic products of Early Helladic Orchomenos.[1] There is no trace of any significant indebtedness to the Balkans or to the Orient; the Protogeometric style was a purely Aegean development.

Though its roots were old, Protogeometric pottery was something distinctly novel as a coherent system. The new product was marked by a more serious attitude; vases improved rapidly in technique from the slovenly sub-Mycenaean level. To attain

---

[9] This important motif has been assigned by many to a northern source, but N. M. Verdelis,'Ο πρωτογεωμετρικὸς 'Ρυθμὸς τῆς Θεσσαλίας (Athens, 1958), 58–60, is surely correct in deriving it from Mycenaean origins.

[1] Kunze, *Orchomenos*, III, pl. 1; Schachermeyr, *Die ältesten Kulturen*, 199, fig. 64, outlines comparable vases. The stress on Middle Helladic influence is sometimes designed to demonstrate that an Indogermanic spirit welled up in Protogeometric vases (e.g., Matz, *GGK*, I, 48–51); but quite objective students have noted in Middle Helladic pottery the "rigidly tectonic syntax and a pronounced pre-

dilection for abstract geometrical designs" (Furumark, *Mycenaean Pottery*, 234). Though we do not know how earlier motifs were preserved for later use, the very common archaeological assumption that potters imitated other wares, especially textiles (Kraiker, *Die Antike*, XV [1939], 228–29; Matz, *GGK*, I, 50) or metal ware (Pfuhl, *AM*, XXVIII [1903], 134–36), rather underrates the potters and explains *obscurum per obscurius;* we do not have the textiles. Note too the warning by Dorothy Kent Hill, "The Technique of Greek Metal Vases and Its Bearing on Vase Forms in Metal and Pottery," *AJA,* LI (1947), 248–56.

the new style, potters found it necessary to simplify drastically
the frame of shapes and decorations within which they worked
—only some fourteen shapes of vases were popular in early Attic
Protogeometric graves.[2] Almost always artists left the greater
part of the vase undecorated. The scanty paint which was applied was intended primarily to accentuate the flow and balance
of the shape of the vase and was laid in simple, abstract motifs
—zigzags, dogs' teeth, cross-hatched triangles, bands, circles,
and semicircles, all these rhythmically balanced and opposed to
each other within the frame of the parts of the vase, especially
the handle zone. Occasionally on Protogeometric vases there are
freehand wavy lines. These were an inheritance from the Granary
Style, and stand out as an alien intrusion into the new world.

The ruthless, stark simplification and the rigidity of Protogeometric pottery at times resulted in stiff, dull work. This was
not a rich, serenely confident age, and one critic of its work,
Furumark, is partially right in contrasting "the lifeless, anxiously
restrained curves of Protogeometric and Geometric vases" with
the more flowing shapes of Mycenaean and Minoan masterpieces
(compare Plates 2 and 6).[3] Yet any visitor to the Kerameikos
Museum must marvel at the remarkably varied results which
could be achieved from a very limited repertoire of shapes and
patterns of decoration; nor is the basic impression to be derived
from their careful draftmanship a sense of sterile fear. The potters
reduced their concepts to fundamentals. Thereby they gained
what they needed, a base for new vigor and for an ever surer
grasp of the problems of synthesizing the individual parts into
clear, harmonious beauty.

THE DATE AND HOME OF THE NEW STYLE

To PLACE the early centuries of Greek civilization on a
proper footing, it would be extremely useful if we could assign
a date and a home to the Protogeometric style. Both can be

---

[2] Desborough, *Protogeometric Pottery*,
120. But did the living so limit their
variety of vases?

[3] Furumark, *Opus. arch.*, III (1944),
221.

found, but not as precisely as is suggested in some recent discussions.

With respect to the date, one must remember that the term "Protogeometric" refers to a style, not an era, and that such pottery was made at various times in different parts of the Aegean; the critical question is its first appearance. Here, unfortunately, we are reduced to very dubious calculations forward and backward from points which are themselves not soundly fixed. After the fall of Mycenae the space of a generation or two must be allowed for the sub-Mycenaean stage. If the fall be placed at 1150, then the sub-Mycenaean pottery comes down to the beginning or into the first quarter of the eleventh century; but the basic date, as already noted, is of a very tentative character.

Chronological argument backward across the stages of Attic Geometric and Protogeometric pottery must proceed all the way from the Late Geometric pottery of the eighth century B.C. On this basis, one can scarcely do better than assign the beginning of the new outlook in potters' workshops to an indefinite point before 1000. Two Protogeometric pieces of developed style which are certainly not of Attic origin have been found in Cyprus, with local ware which is perhaps of about 900 B.C.; but neither this evidence nor the broader arguments which have been drawn from the transition of sub-Mycenaean to Cypro-Geometric ware furnish solid pillars.[4] Until recently scholars have clutched

[4] Protogeometric ware in Cyprus: V. R. d'A. Desborough, "A Group of Vases from Amathus," *JHS*, LXXVII (1957), 212–19. Cypriote basis: Arne Furumark, "The Mycenaean III C Pottery and Its Relation to Cypriote Fabrics," *Opus. arch.*, III (1944), 194–265; but note that van Beek (and Albright) try to elevate Gjerstad's basic dates very appreciably.

Cups with pendant semicircles: The first examples, from Tell Abu Hawam (Stratum III), were published by R. W. Hamilton, *Quarterly of the Department of Antiquities in Palestine*, IV (1935), 23–24, nn. 95–96 (pl. xii–xiii), and their importance asserted by W. A. Heurtley, ibid. 181 (pl.

lxxxviii). The date of this stratum initially was put at about 926. B. Maisler, *Bulletin of the American Schools of Oriental Research*, 124 (1951), 21 ff., lowers it; Gus W. van Beek, ibid. 28, and "The Date of Tell Abu Hawam, Stratum III," 138 (1955), 34–38, raises it. Whether the cups were of Thessalian origin, as Heurtley asserted, has also been much debated. The matter is put in a proper light by P. J. Riis, *Hama: fouilles et recherches 1931–38, II.3: les cimetières á crémation* (Copenhagen, 1948), 113–14; John Boardman, *BSA*, LII (1957), 8; Desborough, *JHS*, LXXVII (1957), 216–219.

desperately at the tiny sherds of Aegean cups, decorated with pendant semicircles, which were found at Tell Abu Hawam, Hama, and elsewhere in the Orient. This style of cup, however, seems fairly clearly to have been a late, specialized offshoot of the Protogeometric style, probably manufactured widely over the Aegean islands. Its major export eastward came as late as the eighth century, when Oriental contact was being resumed, and its earliest representatives do not carry us back very far.

The definite dates, thus, which have been given for the appearance of Protogeometric pottery at Athens—1075, according to the excavators of the Kerameikos; 1025, according to the most recent careful survey of the whole style—have no strong support.[5] At the best we can only conclude that somewhere in the eleventh century, probably neither at its beginning nor at its end, the potters of the Greek mainland struck out on the new lines. Having begun, they pressed on, surely and with great rapidity, in not more than a generation or two to set their basic patterns— the Kerameikos evidence adequately attests this important point.

Protogeometric material is most abundant in Attica, and this ware exhibits a marked artistic and technical superiority to any similar vases thus far found in the rest of Greece. These facts have led many students to conclude that Attic craftsmen initiated the Protogeometric style.[6] Attica, after all, was traditionally spared the worst of the Dorian invasions; its inhabitants knew the Mycenaean tradition but were freer to experiment in new ways than were the men of Crete. Quite clearly, too, Attic aspects of the Protogeometric style influenced other regions of Greece in the tenth century just as the great Attic Geometric style was later to have a wide range of imitation.

Never, however, is it safe to write the history of Greece purely in terms of Athens, either culturally or politically. The

[5] 1075 B.C.: Kraiker and Kübler, *Kerameikos*, I, 162 ff.; Kübler, *Kerameikos*, V. 1, 70; Matz, *GGK*, I, 53. 1025 B.C.: Desborough, *Protogeometric Pottery*, 294; Furumark, *Opus. arch.*, III (1944), 194–265, though in *Chronology of Mycenaean Pottery*, 115, 128, he had restricted the sub-Mycenaean style to 1125–1100 B.C. The danger-

ous insecurity of these dates may be suggested by the amazing fact that Furumark, *Opus. arch.*, III (1944), 261, must depress the Dipylon ware down to 700 B.C.; to prove the hypothetical he asserts the clearly impossible (see below, Chap. 7).

[6] Desborough, *Protogeometric Pottery*, 125–26, 291.

evidence of some Tiryns graves, published forty years ago, suggested strongly that potters in the Argolid had moved independently from sub-Mycenaean to Protogeometric and then Geometric styles. The French excavations now under way at Argos itself confirm and enlarge this fact abundantly. Each stage appears here; Protogeometric graves lie beside the sub-Mycenaean; and burials of the later period are widespread over Argos.[7] On one example of the new finds (Plate 6b) the circles are still interlocked in Mycenaean style, the decoration is freehand, and the odd motifs are very degenerate sub-Mycenaean in flavor. Yet the shape of the amphora quite obviously accords with the Attic evolution shown in the other pieces on this plate.

Most of the Argive material has yet to be published, and in any case it is not my intention in this volume to engage in detailed analyses of pottery parallels. Two comments may still be made. First, the shapes of the Argos vases and their motifs show marked similarities to pots found at Mycenae, Tiryns, Asine, and elsewhere in the Argolid. Secondly, while Argive Protogeometric style is very closely akin to that of Attica, it has yet its own flavor. Although the Argive material cannot be precisely dated, there is no obvious reason to consider it later than the Attic sequence.

Protogeometric vases are turning up ever more widely throughout the Greek mainland and the islands. Nowhere, unfortunately, do we yet have another consecutive cemetery like that of the Kerameikos, and the chronological and stylistic interrelations of these scattered finds are not easily established. Sober students of the non-Attic evidence, however, have felt justified in arguing local origins from the new style as far north as Thessaly, westward to Ithaca, and eastward in the Cyclades.[8] Even

[7] Walter Müller and Franz Oelmann, *Tiryns*, I (Athens, 1912), 127–64; Frödin and Persson, *Asine*, 434–36; Desborough, *BSA*, LI (1956), 129–30. The Argos excavations are reported in *BCH*, LXXVII (1953), on, and will be published by Paul Courbin. I must express my gratitude to him and to Ephor N. M. Verdelis for making available the material in the Argos museum, as yet unopened, and for discussing the finds with me.

[8] Verdelis's study on Thessaly (above n. 9; p. 93); W. A. Heurtley, *BSA*, XXXIII (1932–33), 63–65; Emil Kunze, "Eine protogeometrische Amphora aus Melos," *Jahreshefte des österreichischen archäologischen Institutes*, XXXIX (1952), 53–57; N. M. Kondoleon's report on the excavations in Naxos, *Praktika* 1951, 214–23; Gallet de Santerre, *Délos primitive*, 210–18; Taylour, *Mycenaean Pottery in Italy*, 166–68.

in southern Italy, intriguingly enough, the inheritors of the Mycenaean style moved on into a new fashion which has a somewhat Protogeometric flavor. In Crete, too, the same forces were spottily at work but faced so strong an inheritance from the past that one wonders whether to emphasize in Cretan pottery the Minoan survivals or the Protogeometric flavor.[9]

The vases used by Cretan mountain villages fall into stiff, provincial patterns; Attic potters, on the other hand, restlessly sought to create a new style and then to deepen its expression. This difference underlines the really significant conclusion which emerges from a search for the home of Protogeometric pottery. The main source of development certainly lay on the Greek mainland, and more specifically in its southeastern districts. The focus of Aegean culture was now firmly anchored in the area which was to be its home thenceforth throughout the Dark ages and the subsequent era of revolution. Attica was not the only center within this district. Athenian potters were, most surely, of great importance, and their products often please the modern eye more than do others; yet we cannot single out these workshops alone as the creative source.[1] That the Greek mainland moved together essentially as a unit is shown by the very remarkable similarity of its Protogeometric products, which reflect a common Mycenaean background; but regional variation, while still limited in comparison to that of following centuries, is also distinguishable within the general uniformity.

---

[9] The peculiar flavor of Cretan pottery is discussed by Brock, *Fortetsa*, 142–44; M. Hartley, "Early Greek Vases from Crete," *BSA*, XXXI (1930–31), 56–114; Doro Levi, *Early Hellenic Pottery of Crete* (Princeton, 1945), 2–4, and *Annuario*, X–XII (1927–29), 551–76; Humfry Payne, "Early Greek Vases from Knossos," *BSA*, XXIX (1927–28), 224–298, a gifted study. Desborough, *Protogeometric Pottery*, 233–71, takes up its Protogeometric aspects; Sylvia Benton, *JHS*, LXXVI (1956), 124, dissents on Vrokastro ware and calls this Protogeometric too. Furumark, *Opus. arch.*, III (1944),

230, insists, in taking up the sub-Minoan ware, that "there are no tendencies towards the creation of a geometrical style in the true sense of the word." I am indebted to Stylianos Alexiou of the Iraklion Museum for making available closed material.

[1] If this is true, then the principal theoretical substructure collapses on which Whitman, *Homer and the Heroic Tradition*, 54–55, has based an argument for the survival of the epic tradition solely through Attica; so, too, Webster, *From Mycenae to Homer*, 160.

THE IMPLICATIONS OF PROTOGEOMETRIC POTTERY

IN THE preceding pages I have gone at some length into the sources, character, date, and home of Protogeometric pottery; for this is one of the most important shifts, historically considered, in Greek art. Its implication, briefly put, is that the pattern of civilization which we call Greek emerged in basic outline during the eleventh century B.C. Although the roots of the Hellenic outlook lay in the past and were of native origin, a veritable "jump" occurred in the turmoil following the end of the Mycenaean age.

To conclude so much from a few sparsely decorated vases may seem overbold, but justification can be offered for basing such major historical generalizations upon the rise of a new pottery style. In any age of ancient Greece the products of the potters' fingers were the fruit of minds which shared its common impulses. This mutual sympathy is evident in the Mycenaean period, for the grave steles and other sculptural remains as well as the architectural principles incarnated in the palaces reflected the general line of evolution which was sketched above for its pottery. After the Dark ages, when sculpture and architecture were resumed, the same forces operated in these fields as in that of Orientalizing pottery; literature, as we shall see, falls into place beside the arts in expressing a common spirit.[2] On this point I

[2] A good illustration of the sympathetic interdependence of art and literature is T. B. L. Webster, *Greek Art and Literature, 530–400 B.C.* (Oxford, 1939); see the perceptive, careful statement by Meyer Schapiro, "Style," *Anthropology Today*, ed. A. L. Kroeber (Chicago, 1953), 287–312. On artistic sensitivity, see my *Civilization and the Caesars* (Ithaca, 1954), 287 ff.; and the remark by Sir Kenneth Clark, *Landscape into Art* (Pelican, 1956), 44, on seventeenth-century Dutch landscape: "As so often happens, art anticipated intuitively what science was beginning to formulate."

On pottery itself, the assertion by Myres, *Cambridge Ancient History*, I (Cambridge, 1923), 70, is sweeping but not far from the mark: "As every fragment is an original work of art, the evidence of pottery justifies broader and surer generalizations than almost any other human document; every potsherd in any waste heap being the response of somebody's hand and brain to somebody's need, at the same time individual and communal, industrial and aesthetic." See also Frankfort, *Studies in Early Pottery of the Near East*, I, 1–17; Martin Robertson, "The Place of Vase-Painting in Greek Art," *BSA*, XLVI (1951), 151–59; William Willetts, *Chinese Art*, II (Penguin, 1958), 393–415, 421–28.

may observe that in studying the intellectual development of
the Roman Empire, which has fairly abundant quantities of both
artistic and literary products, one can conclude that artists then
sensed and expressed more swiftly the new forces of that age
than did philosophers and poets. In the era just after the Mycenaean collapse, to return to our present concern, the pottery
stands virtually by itself; but is it not, even so, significant testimony to the general intellectual evolution of the period? If we
give our heart's blood to the ghosts of the past, a great scholar
once observed, they come alive; [3] for the eleventh century B.C.
the pots in the graves contain the only ghosts we can invoke.

The historian who accepts the principle of a *Zeitgeist* must
hasten to utter certain warnings against its application without
proper qualification. No age has an absolute uniform culture
which will be expressed exactly alike in all areas and in all its
physical products. The techniques of any period, moreover, do
not progress at the same rate; some may even be obdurate to new
currents. And the craftsmen who use these techniques commonly
employ them in a rote way. Especially in primitive societies men
do not often consciously break fresh ground, and in earning their
daily bread in a trade they have little time or incentive to brood
deeply upon the world about them.

Worst of all, though we may stand at the shoulders of the
Kerameikos potters and inspect their wares, the craftsmen are
shadows who cannot talk to us. Pots are not magical lamps from
the Arabian Nights, nor do they themselves speak. While products of clay were used for many purposes, they were after all only
physical objects which could not express clearly the ideals, aspirations, and fears of their makers. The surface of a vase, moreover, is a small area, and an ever curving plane to boot: a difficult
frame, to which the artist must adapt and simplify his artistic
canons.[4] In the period of Protogeometric pottery the narrow
gamut of motifs did not even include human representation;
when later the range of expression widened, one must take into

[3] Ulrich von Wilamowitz-Moellen-
dorff, *Greek Historical Writing* (Oxford, 1908), 25.
[4] Fritz Schachermeyr, "Der Begriff
des Arteigenen im frühzeitlichen

Kunstgewerbe," *Klio*, XXXII (1939),
339–57 (esp. 347–48). On the manner in which funerary purposes could
affect the decoration of vases, see
Kübler, *Kerameikos*, VI. 1, 152–53.

account the fact that many vases were deliberately intended for use in graves or in religious dedications.

The historian, in consequence, will use this pottery with due circumspection. He may—indeed, must—go beyond the limited range of most modern studies of the material, for specialists restrict themselves to descriptive or morphological classification with the aim of setting the chronology of evolution and the inter-relationships between different fabrics. This is a highly useful and necessary foundation which reduces the masses of scattered finds to orderly terms; but it is not all the story. On the other hand, the careful student will not be able to follow in their details the overly subtle, at times virtually mystical interpretations of early Greek pottery which have occasionally been advanced. Ancient potters cannot be psychoanalyzed. When they came to depict figured scenes, we may hope to grasp at least partially their intentions; but the meanings which lay behind their earlier, abstract motifs—if, indeed, these always had symbolic sense—cannot today be rescued. As a warning which will apply more directly to later pages, I may also note that some modern efforts to create great webs of artistic interconnections all across the ancient Orient and the Aegean on the basis of scattered, individual parallels in motifs, taken out of context, are highly dangerous. Equally disturbing is the frequent tendency to explain the sudden reappearance of earlier motifs as the fruit of a primeval racial current in the Greek world.

When once these qualifications have been set down, the basic fact remains that the historian can approach the development of early Greek civilization only through its pottery. If he may now hope to establish the phases and tempo of progress in this era, the greatest light to that end comes from the discoveries and analyses of Protogeometric and Geometric pottery within the past fifty years. Much remains to be done, particularly in defining the varieties and the interrelations of Protogeometric and Geometric wares but also in publishing adequately some of the most useful series. As this is done, our views of early Greek history will undergo further great change, yet it seems unlikely that the present framework of pottery development will require fundamental alterations. On this foundation, which is relatively sure in terms of sequences though not yet anchored to absolute chronological dates, rests the whole structure of the present study.

From the vases, then, the student of the origins of Greek civilization must draw his principal conclusions. Between the Mycenaean and historic Greek worlds there is, on the one hand, clear evidence of continuity. Protogeometric pottery had demonstrable roots in Mycenaean and earlier ages. So, too, the epic tradition, which eventually produced the Homeric masterpieces, seems to have developed over long centuries; some of the basic social, religious, and economic conditions of Greek life were likewise inherited from much earlier days.

Yet on the other hand it is equally obvious that great differences in outlook sunder the lords of Mycenae and the citizens of Greek city-states. In political, religious, and economic aspects Greek civilization differed markedly from the palace economies which had stamped the Mycenaean age. The two eras cannot simply be termed alternate facets of the same basic spirit.[5]

If we seek to determine the great point of change, our physical evidence points unmistakably to the eleventh century B.C. In grave customs, in the furnishings which the living placed with their dead, in the very sites of the cemeteries themselves at Argos and at Athens, the Greek mainland saw an epoch of major alterations at this time. Where literary evidence is lacking, one must be chary of drawing overspecific conclusions; but in general terms the artistic development just studied assumes important proportions. When the potters of Athens, Argos, and elsewhere changed from the sub-Mycenaean to the Protogeometric style, the alteration was gradual in the sense that we can follow its stages and can often see its roots, but it was both rapid temporally and so great in magnitude as to be a veritable revolution.

---

[5] Alfred Heuss, "Die archaische Zeit Griechenlands als geschichtliche Epoche," *Antike und Abendland*, II (1946), 26–62, puts the matter correctly, though in somewhat mystical terms; for Stier's views, see Chap. 4, n. 7 (p. 142). To give only one example of the view which I strongly disagree, Whitman, *Homer and the Heroic Tradition*, 20, finds "the first genuinely Greek civilization" in the Late Bronze age; all such statements must deal with the physical facts which are put briefly and clearly by Spyridon Marinatos, "Mykenentum und Griechentum," *Acta congressus Madvigiani*, I (Copenhagen, 1958), 317–22.

It is not improper to emphasize the visible characteristics of the very best Protogeometric vases such as K. 1073—a synthesis of clearly defined parts, which has a dynamic quality; a deliberate simplification of form and decoration into a structure capable of infinite variation; an emphasis upon rational principles of harmony and proportion (as Western civilization has understood these principles ever since); a sense of order in which the imagination is harnessed by the powers of the mind—and to note that every one of these qualities was thenceforth a mark of Greek civilization. From Protogeometric pottery the course of artistic development flowed continuously, without abrupt interruption, through the centuries of Geometric, Orientalizing, and ripe archaic ware down to the heights of the Attic black-figure and red-figure masterpieces. So, too, developed the Hellenic outlook, as we come to see its expression in one field after another during this period.

Only the most basic aspects of the later patterns, true, are visible in the stark, simple products of Protogeometric workshops; much was still to be elaborated. For the next three centuries development was steady, but slow. Then came the great outburst of the late eighth century, when the truly consolidated structure of Hellenic culture crystallized swiftly.

If the eleventh century is the turning point, the inevitable question is: why at this time? The era was one of poverty, scanty population, almost chaos in the wake of the Dorian invasion and the collapse of the magnificent Mycenaean superstructure of organized life. In this very epoch, nonetheless, men formed an outlook which their descendants amplified and enriched into one of the greatest achievements of the human mind.

On the basic problems of history men's solutions must vary widely. Some students are satisfied with answers which rest upon purely mechanical factors of geography and climate. Others parade racial theories, though no such explanation today can attribute the forces of change simply and directly to the Dorian invaders. Some of the innovations, such as cremation and the use of iron, point eastward across the Aegean; but it would be even more hazardous to postulate a large-scale migration west from

Asia Minor to Greece in the late second millennium than at the
beginning of Early Helladic times.[6]

The most illuminating shift, that from sub-Mycenaean to
Protogeometric pottery, was a consecutive development. This
fact is enough to force us to look inside Greece itself if we are to
furnish any convincing explanation for the origin of Greek civilization. The answer which I would give is so based. Its main lines
are implicit in the earlier discussion of the Bronze ages and more
specifically in the analysis of the change from sub-Mycenaean to
Protogeometric pottery; but for sake of clarity I may state my
views more formally here.

The dimensions and the unique nature of the changes in the
eleventh century will perhaps be clearer if the student widens
his ken for a moment. It will, for instance, be useful to hark back
to the collapse of the Aegean world at the end of the Early Helladic age. This event, like its parallel at the close of the second
millennium, was followed by poverty-stricken centuries in which
a new pottery style was dominant; but few would consider the
Minyan pottery of Middle Helladic times as artistically advanced as Protogeometric work. Why, then, was the latter a more
fertile seedbed from which historic Greek art could directly
develop?

Or, again, it will be useful to look out from Greece of the
Dark ages to central and southern Europe at the same point of
time. Both areas were obviously disturbed by movements of peoples at the close of the second millennium, but both thereafter
entered on paths of steady development. Why, however, was the
course of central Europe, through the Urnfield cultures to the
Hallstatt stage, so much slower than the amazing soar of the
Aegean world?

If we are to answer these problems, we shall come close to
pinpointing the basic forces of Greek civilization itself. Any
answer must keep steadily in mind the felicitous position of the
Aegean area, on the fringes of Europe and Asia. Throughout the
millennia of earlier history Greece had commonly stood in the
forefront of Europe proper, though it lingered behind the Orient.

[6] Burton-Brown, *The Coming of Iron*   gument upon this postulate.
to Greece, nonetheless bases his ar-

But if one is to account for the very different outcomes of Minyan and Protogeometric pottery, one must look carefully at the remarkable Mycenaean age, which at once advanced Aegean culture to a far higher stage and also experienced such a flood of foreign influences that it could not drive beyond imitation to originality.

The men who lived in the eleventh century received a rich inheritance of many strands from the Mycenaean world; their artistic outlook, as was once observed, "is unthinkable without the schooling which the decorative sense of the Greek learned during this era." [7] The earlier Middle Helladic style, which was itself geometric in many respects, gained a sense of organization and symmetry from the Minoan wave which swept over the mainland in Mycenaean days; so, too, the primitive political and economic structure of life in earlier Greece developed greatly in the days of the palaces. But, alas, while the potters struggled to reach a new synthesis of these many strands, they strove in vain.

Then came the collapse of the Mycenaean world, a tremendous disruption almost without equal in any Mediterranean society of the era. Those who survived were hurled back close to barbarism; but they were also set free from the old trammels to fuse their inheritance into a new, more solid pattern of life. In very truth, men were *forced* to this step if they were to survive the era of chaos. The simplicity of Greek political, social, and economic life, when we begin to see it in the next centuries, is matched by the stark and bare character of Protogeometric pottery, which reduced shape and decoration to the most basic essentials. To the men who endured this rude age it would have been scant consolation to know that in imposing upon themselves a new rigidity they were liberating themselves from the confines of an old pattern; I have already quoted Furumark's perception of the anxious restraint visible in this work.

The vases of the age show, nonetheless, that the decisive step to a new environment had been taken. The crucial question now was whether latent potentialities could be realized, and this

[7] Müller and Oelmann, *Tiryns*, I, 162. This remains one of the most perceptive pages thus far written on the artistic change from the sub-Mycenaean style.

in turn depended on two factors: Would the Aegean world be spared new catastrophe? And would its new synthesis be too soon exposed to alien cultural forces stemming from the Orient? Fortunately for Western civilization the Greeks were to be free to work out their destinies essentially unaffected by external influences until they themselves were ready to look once more abroad.

CHAPTER 4

TWO CENTURIES OF

CONSOLIDATION

THOUGH THE CHANGES of the eleventh century were fundamental, the next generations were not prepared to rush swiftly
along the new path. To our view the period 1000–800 is devoid of
spectacular developments, a poor age illuminated mainly by the
scanty deposits of vases which mourners placed in graves. Attic
potters worked within the Protogeometric framework down to
about 900, developing it steadily; then they passed into the Early
and Strong Geometric styles. Some bronze and other metal work
occurs in Attica and elsewhere, particularly at the shrine of Zeus
in Olympia. Hints of architecture and sculpture appear before
the end of the period. The one settlement of any significance
which shows the houses of the living is that of Old Smyrna on the
coast of Asia Minor; we can only hope that future excavation will
turn up a parallel site in Greece proper.

Limited though it is, this evidence proves that the tendency
to treat the two darkest centuries of early Greek history as an
undifferentiated, static era can no longer be justified. From the
pottery alone, the observer can see that Greek artistic attitudes
were constantly moving along a consistent path of evolution. The
main lines of pottery style had been established in the eleventh
century, but a comparison of Early Protogeometric and Strong
Geometric ware (Plates 6c and 8b) will suggest how great an
alteration had resulted by 800 from the steady increments of
change, each of which in itself may have been small. Similar

progress can be made out, though less securely, for many other phases of human life by the survivals into historic times of earlier linguistic patterns, of primitive social, political, and religious customs, and of myth and tradition. Such material can be used only with caution and even then will yield a distressingly generalized picture; yet its testimony on fundamental aspects agrees with that of the physical remains in showing that the world of 800 was markedly different from that which can be seen in the latest Mycenaean stages.

Another major characteristic of the age was a significant reduction in the direct influence of Minoan and Mycenaean patterns; or, to put the matter more properly, these inherited influences were absorbed and integrated into a simplified Aegean outlook. This development is clearly visible in the pottery, reasonably certain in religious and political institutions and attitudes, and rather probable in the field of language. Equally intriguing is the creation of a fructifying tension within a common unity. Many of the basic aspects of the Hellenic outlook became a system shared alike by Greece proper, by the islands, and by the coast of Asia Minor. But, whereas the Mycenaean world had been monolithic, local differentiations now emerged clearly; they were to serve thenceforth as a source of wide variation and experiment, which could be drawn upon by the whole of the Aegean basin much as modern European civilization has been fertilized by its many regional manifestations since the Middle ages.

Six facets of cultural growth—territorial coalescence, Aegean isolation, Greek linguistic distributions, political organization, social structure, and the artistic spirit reflected in the pottery—will concern us at this point. The fields of religion, epic, and mythology will fall to the following chapter.

TERRITORIAL CONSOLIDATION OF GREEK CULTURE

DURING the Dark ages the Aegean turned into a Greek lake, focused within itself. This had not been true earlier. At the beginning of the second millennium B.C. men of the Aegean had

*a) Ripe Protogeometric amphora (K.
60) with the earliest animal figure of the
[ser]ra (Kerameikos Museum).*

*b) Late Protogeometric amphora (K.
[2]76) foreshadowing the Geometric style
[in] its dark glaze and decoration (Keramei-
[k]os Museum). Photographs courtesy
[D]eutsches Archäologisches Institut in
[A]thens.*

PLATE 7 · *Later Stages of the Protogeometric Style*

(a) *Early Geometric amphora (K. 254) decorated with meander patterns (Kerameikos Museum).*

(b) *Strong Geometric amphora (K. 2146) with "picture" spaces on the handle zone (Kerameikos Museum). Photographs courtesy Deutsches Archäologisches Institut in Athens.*

PLATE 8 · *Development of the Attic Geometric Style*

been attached to many local, diverse cultures, which had often looked outward, such as the Helladic of the Greek mainland; the Cycladic of the islands; the Minoan of Crete, which had strong ties to the Orient; the Trojan and other Middle Bronze cultures of the Asia Minor coast, which were linked in various respects to the Anatolian plateau. Thereafter Mycenaean civilization had spread over the Aegean widely, but rather thinly (see Map No. 1). Even in Greece proper it appeared as a culture of palaces, which did not entirely replace Middle Helladic ways among the peasantry; Crete experienced an uneasy, incomplete amalgamation of Minoan and Mycenaean; and on the coast of Asia Minor Mycenaean influence seems, on the basis of our limited knowledge, to have been only partial. At Troy VI–VII this force remained an alien, though important factor; thus far a Mycenaean foothold appears certain on the east shore of the Aegean solely at Miletus. And everywhere Mycenaean culture itself reflected strong Oriental borrowings.

Now, however, the western and eastern coasts of the Aegean, together with the islands between, became a cultural unit which could serve as a solid base for later Greek expansion. The unification is manifest in the spread first of Protogeometric and then of Geometric pottery styles throughout the area, both styles deriving their main impetus from the evolution in the potters' workshops of the mainland; by 800 the Aegean—apart from its northern shores—also shared those qualities which the Athenians were later to single out as Hellenic in the Persian wars: "our common language, the altars and sacrifices of which we all partake, the common character which we bear." The end product is clear; its importance is suggested in the quotation from Herodotus (VIII. 144); the causes of the phenomenon are not quite so obvious. We face here the rise of a Greek character, but at the moment I shall consider only its initial territorial spread.

The Greeks of historic times were dimly aware that not all parts of the Aegean had earlier been unified culturally, and tradition explained the consolidation as a product of migration eastward from Greece, which began immediately after the Trojan war. In their details the legends of these movements are worse than suspect. As I have already suggested in Chapter 2, the

historian cannot safely employ legend, myth, and epic to explore
the Mycenaean age; the same grounds for caution still apply
when we come to the period immediately on either side of
1000 B.C., three centuries before writing began to be extensively
used in Greece. In the form in which we have the tales of migration, moreover, they clearly reflect a great deal of rationalization,
by which myths had been neatly interlocked into chains where A
moves B, B impels C, and so on. Pride of family and homeland
also played a part in the final casting of the legends: Athenian
antiquaries funneled the migrations through Attica, and great
families of later Asia Minor spun ancestral connections with the
heroes of the Trojan period.[1] The many modern efforts to rescue
this material by manipulations, in which each student selects the
detailed pieces he thinks appropriate and dismisses the rest, are
unsound in method and historically valueless in their conclusions.

The general weight of Greek tradition, nonetheless, should
not be discarded, however justifiable may be our suspicion of the
details. Once the invasions at the end of the Mycenaean age were
over, Greek evolution proceeded on a consecutive line down into
the age of writing; and the closer one comes to this stage the
more probable is the relatively secure memory of major developments. Genealogical traditions, for instance, carry a number of
families back well before 700; some chains, such as that of Hecataeus' ancestors, extend close to 1000, though the earliest links
in these lines are often of mythical quality. In the lines which the
poet Mimnermus of Colophon composed in the seventh century
(fragment 12 Diehl):

> When from the lofty city of Neleian Pylos we came on ship-
> board to the pleasant land of Asia, and in overwhelming
> might destroying grievous pride sat down at lovely Colo-
> phon . . .

[1] M. P. Nilsson, *Cults, Myths, Oracles
and Politics in Ancient Greece* (Lund,
1951), 60–63, firmly assigns the re-
molding to the late sixth century onward; contra, Webster, *From Mycenae
to Homer*, 140–54. See also Munro,
JHS, LIV (1934), 116–21; Cassola,
La Ionia nel mondo miceneo, 20–33,
74–109, and Chap. 2, n. 3 (p. 66).
   Genealogies: Herodotus II. 143
(Hecataeus); H. T. Wade-Gery, *The
Poet of the Iliad* (Cambridge, 1952),
fig. I (Heropythos of Chios); Beloch,
Griechische Geschichte, I. 2, 17–18.

a clear reference to migration, worthy of our respect, can be found.

The tendency of tradition, based probably on genealogical reckoning, was to set the major movement from Greece in the twelfth and eleventh centuries. This too is reasonable, though the historian must place more weight on the fact that both the Aegean and the Near East were then in a fluid state. At any later date extensive colonization of Asia Minor is virtually inexplicable. In the Dark ages the mainland was primarily engaged in rebuilding its social and cultural structure after a great collapse and had neither any serious surplus of population nor a strong enough organization to launch out overseas.

That migrations of considerable scope had taken place is strongly suggested also by the religious patterns of the later Greek world, by the distribution of dialects, and by the similarity of tribal organization over wide areas on the mainland, in the islands, and on the coast of Asia Minor. The close resemblance of the Attic and Ionic dialects, the existence of the same four tribes in both areas (alongside others in Ionia), and the common festival of the Apaturia in honor of the ancestors are points which cannot be explained away as the product of later cultural convergences; on the other hand, they do not justify Solon's sweeping claim that Attica was the fountainhead of Ionia. Similar resemblances among the Doric-speaking areas of Greece proper and Asia Minor are likewise not easily accounted for unless elements originally centered in Greece proper had expanded overseas.

While early migration thus probably occurred, on a scale which we have no means of measuring, this factor was but an ultimate basis for the consolidation of Aegean culture. Modern scholars have created many problems in essaying to reconcile the evidence of legend with that of the physical remains; the root of their difficulty lies in the unfortunate tendency to explain cultural shifts solely in terms of movements of population. What actually took place in the Dark ages was far more a process of cultural adaptation, an expansion of the Greek civilization of the

mainland.[2] Even before 800 the new Hellenic outlook was beginning to exhibit those remarkable powers of attracting other peoples which were to be so marked throughout its history.

If we analyze the archaeological evidence now available, it
appears that the islands declined abruptly and greatly at the end
of the Mycenaean age but were not, in the main, entirely deserted. By the tenth century Protogeometric pottery appears here
and there in the central Aegean, partly of native origin, partly in
imitation of the great Attic Protogeometric style.[3] Farther eastward pottery of mainland Greek types was continuously present
at Samos from at least 900 B.C. onward (see Map No. 2). On the
coast of Asia Minor itself, the recent excavations at Old Smyrna

[2] If we keep this fact in mind, the effort to reduce the major Greek migration down toward 800 B.C., when
Greek civilization becomes clear along
the coast of Asia Minor, is unnecessary. Cassola, *La Ionia nel mondo
miceneo*, 10–11, gives a bibliography
of this view. See especially R. M.
Cook, "Ionia and Greece in the Eighth
and Seventh Centuries B.C.," *JHS*,
LXVI (1946), 67–98; G. M. A. Hanfmann, "Horsemen from Sardes," *AJA*,
XLIX (1945), 570–81; "Archaeology
in Homeric Asia Minor," *AJA*, LII
(1948), 135–55; "Ionia, Leader or
Follower?" *HSCP*, LXI (1953), 1–37;
J. H. Jongkees, "The Date of the
Ionian Migration," *Studia Vollgraff*
(Amsterdam, 1948), 71–77; Carl Roebuck, *Ionian Trade and Colonization*
(New York, 1959), chaps. 1–2.
[3] Islands: J. M. Cook, *JHS*, LXXI
(1951), 250, and LXXII (1952), 106;
Hazel D. Hansen, *Studies to D. M.
Robinson*, II, 54–63; N. M. Kontoleon,
"Γεωμετρικὸς ἀμφορεὺς ἐκ Νάξου,"*Arch.
eph*. 1945–47, 1–21, and *Praktika*
1951, 214–23; Scholes, *BSA*, LI
(1956), 35, who comes down to almost sub-Mycenaean pots at Amorgos,
Melos, and Naxos; Desborough, *Protogeometric Pottery*, 153–66, 177–78,
212–15, who finds pottery of the era
on Ceos, Paros, Naxos, Amorgos, Melos, Siphnos, Andros, Tenos (see also
BCH, LXXX [1956], 332), Rheneia,

Delos, Scyros.
    Samos: Richard Eilmann, "Frühe
griechische Keramik im samischen
Heraion," *AM*, LVIII (1933), 47–145;
Werner Technau, "Griechische Keramik im samischen Heraion," *AM*, LIV
(1929), 6–64. Old Smyrna: reports in
JHS, LXVII (1947), 41; LXXII
(1952), 104; LXXIII (1953), 124;
and now J. M. Cook, *BSA*, LIII–IV
(1958–59), 10–11; Ekrem Akurgal,
"Bayrakli kazisi Önrapor," *Ankara Üni-
versitesi Dil ve Tarih-Coğrafya Fakül-
tesi Dergisi*, VIII (1950), 1–97, concerns chiefly later levels. Miletus:
Chap. 2, n. 2 (p. 50); while Mellaart,
Belleten, XIX (1955), 129, is undoubtedly right that the collapse of
order in Anatolia aided early Greek
settlement, the evidence of Miletus
suggests they could settle there in
Late Bronze days.
    Other sites in eastern Aegean:
Desborough, *Protogeometric Pottery*,
215–18, 222–23; Hanfmann, *HSCP*,
LXI (1953), 12–14; Cook, *BSA*, LIII–
IV (1958–59), 11. At Rhodes a disturbance in settlement patterns
early in the eleventh century seems
clear (Desborough, *Protogeometric
Pottery*, 232–33); Furumark, *Opus.
arch.*, III (1944), 218–20, 264–65, attributes this to an Achaean influx. Cretan development: Chap. 3, n. 9 (p.
98).

give us a site where Protogeometric vases were used alongside native pots; the probings at Miletus, now renewed, reveal an uninterrupted succession from Minoan and Mycenaean days on into the era of Protogeometric pottery, which had evolved its own local pattern by the second half of the ninth century. Protogeometric ware has also been found at Lesbos, Chios (possibly), Cos, Rhodes, and Assarlik in Caria, usually in limited quantities beside native styles. All of this, and particularly the tentative manner in which Protogeometric vases enter local contexts, seems most easily explained as the fruit of growing cultural connections throughout the Aegean.[4]

By the ninth century the Greek mainland had progressed to the Geometric stage; abroad, this style was increasingly adopted in the late ninth and eighth centuries. At times the forms and decoration were clearly of native origin, for the Geometric style was far more subject to local variation than had been the Protogeometric type. Infused in these patterns, however, were motifs drawn from mainland styles, particularly from the outstanding Geometric expression of Attica, which in turn reflected Cycladic and other influences after 800. In Crete, for example, the survivals of Minoan-Mycenaean outlook which make it difficult for us to label any local pieces as truly Protogeometric yielded with great abruptness to a Geometric ware not directly derived from the earlier pottery but adapted from foreign models.

Much more extensive archaeological and artistic study will be required, particularly along the coast of Asia Minor, before the ceramic evolution of the Dark ages becomes clear, but it does seem certain at the present time, first, that pottery of Greek type appeared on the islands leading to Asia Minor and along the coast itself relatively early and, secondly, that by 800 Greek culture was dominant virtually throughout the Aegean, at least

[4] The process is well described for Old Smyrna by J. M. Cook, *JHS*, LXXII (1952), 104: "In the early stages the Protogeometric pottery looks like imported ware alongside the local monochrome pottery, but in the ninth century the painted ware becomes dominant; if the pottery can be used as a guide, it would seem that Smyrna had already passed completely in the hands of the Ionians before the end of the ninth century." See also his remarks in *BSA*, LIII–IV (1958–59), 13; the ethnic interpretation of cultural changes illustrates the conventional point of view with which I disagree.

in respect to pottery. That the same condition prevailed also linguistically will be shown shortly.

An explanation of this cultural fusion as the product of the expansion of ideas, rather than of peoples, is in accordance both with the earlier history of the Aegean, which we have already examined, and with the well-known course of cultural flow in historic times. Its vehicle was trade by sea, at least as far as the islands and Asia Minor were concerned. The inhabitants of the mainland and the islands had made use of the sea since at least the fourth millennium, if not before, and had been extremely active by sea in the Mycenaean age; this skill did not disappear entirely in the simplification of life which followed the Mycenaean collapse. The Protogeometric pottery of the mainland shows no real objects apart from a horse, and Early and Strong Geometric potters were almost as reluctant to move outside the realm of abstract motifs; yet a ship does appear on an Attic skyphos of about 875–850 (see Plate 9a) and on a Cretan crater of the tenth century.[5] While trade was not a major part of the economic life of the Dark ages, to judge from the scarcity of foreign objects in graves, the occasional appearance of alien vases shows that it cannot be dismissed as absolutely nonexistent. If the rather sudden interest abroad in Attic Protogeometric styles by 900 is a valid clue, seafaring may have begun to revive appreciably at that time; the increasing interconnections which appear in pottery during the next century suggest that it continued to grow.

As the civilization of mainland Greece expanded over the Aegean, it frequently met peoples who already spoke Greek dialects, small kernels scattered here and there in the Mycenaean age or immediately after its close in Crete, the islands, and the

[5] Kraiker, *Neue Beiträge*, 41; Brock, *Fortetsa*, n. 45 (cf. terra-cotta boat, n. 542).

The broadening out of pottery movements in the Dark ages is graphically illustrated in Wilhelm Kraiker, *Aigina: die Vasen des 10. bis 7. Jahrhunderts v. Chr.* (Berlin, 1951): Attic, perhaps also Argive, in the tenth century; Corinthian from 900 on; in

the ninth century Peloponnesian, Cycladic, Boeotian, Attic, Corinthian. Cf. Desborough, *Protogeometric Pottery*, 299–300. Against the later feeling that seafaring was absent in the Golden Age (e.g., Hesiod, *Works and Days* 236), place Aeschylus, *Prometheus Bound* 467 f., who lists seafaring as a contribution of Prometheus to man.

coast of Asia Minor. At other points alien elements were drawn in and were Hellenized by a process of imitation and absorption often repeated thereafter. The linguistic evidence, which shows the survival of non-Greek dialects spottily about the Aegean even in historic times, reflects the slow tempo of this cultural unification; so, too, does the maintenance of native social customs at some sites until late in the archaic period or even into the classic period. This factor, which Greek antiquarians were to explain as the product of intermarriage between Greek settlers and native women, may often have been a simple testimony to incomplete cultural absorption. It is not without significance in the present connection that in the *Iliad* the distinction between Hellenic and non-Hellenic was far from sharp and certainly was not contemptuous; [6] in the time of Homer, opines Thucydides (I. 3), "the Hellenes were not yet known by one name, and so marked off as something separate from the outside world."

The existence of a countercurrent, from east to west, has already been shown with respect to the appearance of cremation and iron on the Greek mainland; and the tendency of Attica, with its close cultural neighbor Boeotia, to take over most completely the custom of burning the dead is of weight in suggesting the main axis of cultural flow. Nonetheless, Asia Minor did not lead the Aegean culturally during the Dark ages. The essential developments in Greek pottery, sculpture, and architecture must be located in Greece proper, not Ionia; even economically the coastal settlements in the latter area lay on the fringe of the main sea routes until the seventh century at least.

AEGEAN LOCALISM

WITHIN THE AEGEAN, cultural patterns drew ever closer together on the simple level which prevailed in the Dark ages. Outside this enclave the wide net of foreign connections so noticeable in the Mycenaean age virtually disappeared. These two

[6] Santo Mazzarino, *Fra Oriente e Occidente: ricerche di storia greca arcaica* (Florence, 1947), 85–86, 90–92.

characteristics of the early Greek period are interconnected. If the outlook which had appeared on the mainland by about 1000 gained a strong hold throughout the Aegean, its success must be attributed at least in part to the lack of external competition and external diversion during a period of two centuries and more. To the west, Greek contact with Italy was almost entirely broken; only one or two Protogeometric sherds have been found in southern Italy.[7] The islands on the west coast of Greece manifested Protogeometric styles at points, and on Ithaca Corinthian Geometric ware was imported and imitated by the middle of the ninth century. For this latter development I should prefer to look to a process of cultural diffusion rather than to a hypothetical Corinthian colonization. To the north, the developing Hellenic patterns had an influence as far as Thessaly; Macedonia remained outside the orbit. On the east coast of the Aegean the forces of Greek civilization became firmly entrenched—and the interior was pacified—only toward 800 B.C. Thereafter Phrygia and Lydia began to swing slowly toward the Aegean.

Most important of all, connections between the Orient and the Aegean were almost, though not quite completely, broken. On neither side, to be sure, had seafaring disappeared during the chaos following the Late Bronze age. The Egyptian envoy Wen Amun traveled from Egypt to Syria about 1060 in search of wood and found in the Syrian ports a number of merchant vessels which were apparently organized in shipping guilds;[8] the story of Solomon's commercial ventures with Hiram, king of Tyre, in

[7] Italy: Taylour, *Mycenaean Pottery in Italy*, 159–68; only his Scoglio del Tonno nn. 165–66 seem Greek Protogeometric. Western islands: W. A. Heurtley and H. L. Lorimer, "Excavations in Ithaca I," *BSA*, XXXIII (1932–33), 22–65; Sylvia Benton, "Excavations in Ithaca III: The Cave at Polis, II," *BSA*, XXXIX (1938–39), 1–51; Sylvia Benton, "Further Excavations at Aetos," *BSA*, XLVIII (1953), 255–361; Desborough, *Protogeometric Pottery*, 272, 279–80; Will, *Korinthiaka*, 38–41, is justly doubtful of Corinthian settlement. Thessaly: N. M. Verdelis's study (Chap. 3, n. 9 [p. 93]); Milojčić,

AA 1955, 182–231; Desborough, *Protogeometric Pottery*, 130–37. The Marmariani ware published by W. A. Heurtley and T. C. Skeat, "The Tholos Tombs of Marmariane," *BSA*, XXXI (1930–31), 1–55, is mostly eighth-century (cf. Verdelis and Benton, *JHS*, LXX [1950], 18–20). Macedonia: Desborough, *Protogeometric Pottery*, 179–80; recent finds, *JHS*, LXXIV (1954), 159; LXXV Suppl. (1955), 15.

Phrygia and Lydia: see below, pp. 210–11.
[8] W. F. Albright, "The Eastern Mediterranean about 1060 B.C.," *Studies to D. M. Robinson*, I, 222–31.

the next century is famous. Yet contacts were reduced to an essentially insignificant level, partly because the markets offered by the Mycenaean palaces had disappeared, partly because men's energies and ambitions were rudely limited by the low plane of economic and social life.

It may be doubted if men in the Aegean could do without the ointments and spices produced in the Orient, but neither these items nor such return exports as slaves from the Aegean would make much mark in our physical record. A metal bowl of north Syrian origin was buried in a Kerameikos grave of about 850–825; the Pnyx has yielded a bronze tripod perhaps of about the same time; some Eastern motifs were being picked up by Geometric potters before 800, with Crete perhaps in the lead; and the ivories of Sparta, the earliest of which manifest Oriental indebtedness both in their material and in their techniques, may go back just before 800.[9] In the other direction, Protogeometric sherds of Aegean origin have turned up in Cyprus, perhaps about 900, and at Tell Abu Hawam and other Levantine sites from the ninth century on. Thus far, these isolated pieces are all that has been found to attest connections. More may well appear in the future in ninth-century or even tenth-century strata, but the negative impression which we must gain from the great bulk of the excavations, as well as from the purely local spirit of Greek Geometric styles, is very strong testimony that significant resumption of contacts via the eastern sea route took place in the Aegean only toward the beginning of the eighth century.

This cultural isolation of the Aegean may appear surprising when one reflects that men who spoke Greek dialects lived all along the eastern searoad during the Dark ages. The settlement of Greek-speaking peoples in Caria and Pamphylia probably occurred in the unrest at the end of the Bronze age, and may have been a product of their search for secluded, relatively safe

[9] Brock, *Fortetsa*, 22, on the Pnyx tripod (cf. Benton, *JHS*, LXX [1950], 17); Kübler, *Kerameikos*, IV, 17, 30–31, and V. 1, 159 n. 121 (bibliography), with "Eine Bronzeschale im Kerameikos," *Studies to D. M. Robinson*, II, 25–29. Greek ware in the East: Chap. 3, n. 4 (p. 95); Christoph Clairmont, "Greek Pottery from the Near East," *Berytus*, XI (1954–55), 85–139; Hanfmann, *Aegean and Near East*, 166–67, 174–75; Mazzarino, *Fra Oriente e Occidente*, 256 ff.

sites.[1] In Cilicia the appearance of late Mycenaean pottery at some sites has been taken to betoken earlier settlement; kings with Greek names, who traced their ancestry to Mopsus, a figure known in Greek myth, ruled over the Danauna or Danaians in this district late in the eighth century. The date at which Greek-speaking peoples took up their home in Cyprus is much debated; but, whether this wave came in late Mycenaean times or in the eleventh century, it was strong enough to endure throughout the Dark ages. None of these areas, however, participated in the initial evolution of Greek civilization; the only evidence of earlier Aegean connection which appears here is the survival of Greek dialects and, at points, of Mycenaean pottery motifs and shapes.

This fact throws perhaps our clearest light on the cultural consolidation of the Aegean itself. The substructure for the fusion was furnished by the migrations at the close of the Bronze age, but only the districts which lay thereafter in direct contact with the Greek mainland participated in the evolution of the Dark ages. The new spirit which had begun to unfold in the south-eastern districts of Greece proper had a full opportunity, unchallenged by outside models, to exert an attractive force on the rest of the Aegean for two full centuries; and the vehicle for that attraction was quite as much cultural proximity as similarity of racial background. Those Greek-speaking peoples who had driven beyond the effective range of mainland developments followed a different cultural path until Aegean civilization was ready to spread more widely after 800 and so to reclaim them. Within the Aegean itself the diffusion of mainland pottery patterns in the Dark ages and their interaction with local points of

[1] Caria-Pamphylia: Mellaart, *AnatSt*, IV (1954), 176–78; A. Heubeck, *Beiträge zur Namenforschung*, VII (1956), 8–13, on Pamphylian Greek. Cilicia: views on the Karatepe inscription, probably of the early seventh century, may be found in Cassola, *La Ionia nel mondo miceneo*, 110–18; Machteld J. Mellink, *Bibliotheca Orientalis*, VII (1950), 141–50. Mopsos, from Aeolian Cyme, was said to have founded Side and Colophon and to have been buried in Cilicia; note also

the stories of Amphilochos (Beloch, *Griechische Geschichte*, I. 2, 107–09). Schachermeyr, *Poseidon*, 175–78, and others connect the myth of Bellerophon with early Greek settlement in Lycia and Caria.

Cyprus: see Chap. 2, n. 4 (p. 52); on Mycenaean survivals into Cypriote Decorated (Debased Levanto-Helladic) and Proto White Painted ware, cf. Furumark, *Opus. arch.*, III (1944), 231–58, and Gjerstad, ibid. 75–77.

view had produced a rich variety in Greek Geometric pottery by 800 B.C.; the tendency to interpret common themes in local forms had an opportunity in the tenth and ninth centuries to become well set as an enduring force for later Greek history.

THE GREEK DIALECTS

GENERALIZATION from the evidence of the pottery to the course of early Greek civilization as a whole is strongly supported by the parallel linguistic developments in the Aegean. By 800 the Greek language had become the basic speech of the peoples living in Greece, on the islands, and along the western coast of Asia Minor. In this development and also in the existence of distinct dialects within the common tongue we have independent light of great value on the evolution of the Dark ages.

Most surely men in the Aegean had not been entirely Indo-European in the second millennium. The style of writing termed Linear A, which had been employed in Minoan Crete, cannot yet be read, but it does not seem to have been used for a Greek tongue. The place names of the Aegean world are largely drawn from an earlier speech which was probably not Indo-European. This stratum of Bronze-age tongues occasionally survived far enough into historic times to be employed in inscriptions, as on a famous but puzzling stone from Lemnos and on epigraphical material from eastern Crete, the home of the Eteocretans.[2] Whether the mysterious Pelasgians, Leleges, Carians, and other peoples whom Greek historians and antiquarians described as pre-Greek elements actually ever existed as such, or even neces-

[2] Eteocretan inscriptions: J. Friedrich, *Kleinasiatische Sprachdenkmäler* (Berlin, 1932), 147–48; Demargne, *La Crète dédalique*, 102–07; but the effort of Ernst Langlotz, "Eine eteokretische Sphinx," *Corolla Curtius* (Stuttgart, 1937), 60–62, to tie artistic monuments to this linguistic sphere is dangerous. Lemnos Stele: Margit Falkner, "Epigraphisches und archäologisches zur Stele von Lemnos,"

Frühgeschichte und Sprachwissenschaft (Vienna, 1948), 91–109, with bibliography there cited.

Pelasgians: Eduard Meyer, "Die Pelasger," *Forschungen zur alten Geschichte*, I, 1–124; Beloch, *Griechische Geschichte*, I. 2, 45–60, as Greek; J. A. R. Munro, "Pelasgians and Ionians," *JHS*, LIV (1934), 109–28, as the root of the Ionians.

sarily spoke non-Greek tongues, cannot now be firmly established; but the general tone of these references shows that Greek writers were aware of a process of linguistic consolidation in the Aegean. For there can be no doubt that the survivals of non-Greek languages were in the historic period no more than the fossils of distant ages. Men in the historic Aegean spoke Greek.

The background to this situation was in part the earlier external invasions and internal migrations of peoples who had learned Greek at their mothers' knees. One wave of Indo-European speech had probably entered the Aegean at the beginning of the Middle Helladic era; from this element came the lords of the Mycenaean palaces.[3] Their tongue, as reflected in the tablets of Linear B, has recently been well termed "south Greek," and seems to have been the same in Pylos, Mycenae, Boeotia, and Cnossus. At the close of the Mycenaean age a second wave of invasion introduced, apparently, what may be called a "north Greek" dialect.

Both the earlier and the later waves scattered bands of settlement across the Aegean in the Late Bronze age and in the unrest which marked its end. Neither in Greece nor abroad can we properly visualize these conquerors as wiping out the earlier peoples. Throughout history, except in parts of the modern European outpourings, invasions have been the work of relatively small groups who enter, conquer, and settle down on top of and beside a much larger native population. Already in the Mycenaean age, to judge from the non-Greek words appearing in the palace tablets, a process of linguistic unification was at work; by historic times over half the stock of words employed in Greek may have been of other than Indo-European origin.[4]

The increasing dominance of the Greek tongue as the basic structure of Aegean speech thenceforth was not due solely to

---

[3] There is no archaeological or epigraphic evidence for the view that two peoples, one speaking the ancestor of Ionian, the other of Aeolian or Achaean, came early in the second millennium, as suggested by Paul Kretschmer, "Zur Geschichte der griechischen Dialekte," *Glotta*, I (1909), 9–59; Nilsson, *Homer and Mycenae*, 92–97; C. D. Buck, "The Language Situation in and about Greece in the Second Millennium B.C.," *CP*, XXI (1926), 1–26; and many others.

[4] Hans Krahe, "Die Vorgeschichte des Griechentums nach dem Zeugnis der Sprache," *Die Antike*, XV (1939), 175–94.

racial reasons. Greek, thus, was widely scattered over the Aegean and so could serve as a medium of communication, particularly among the dominant political and economic elements; for the invaders did become masters of this world. Another factor was the relatively low plane of culture which had existed previously, except in Minoan Crete; and here, interestingly enough, the strongest survival of non-Greek speech seems to have occurred, among the Eteocretans. And finally, we must keep in mind the inherent attractiveness of Greek as a supple, logical tool of expression—the qualities of which were strikingly similar to those expressed in the logic of the also attractive Geometric pottery—together with the probability that Aegean mythology and epic tradition were encased within this framework.

If the inhabitants of the Aegean basin had come by inheritance and still more by absorption to speak a common tongue by historic times, they did so only in several distinct dialects, which differed more in pronunciation than in vocabulary. The Dark ages had a strongly local flavor, which worked toward divergence in speech as well as in pottery.

When Greece emerged into historic times, the west coast of Asia Minor was inhabited from north to south by men who spoke respectively Aeolic, Ionic, and Dorian dialects. These relatively well-defined varieties of Greek ran roughly westward across the islands of the Aegean to Greece proper: Dorian through Rhodes and Crete to the Peloponnesus, Ionic through the Cyclades to Attica, Aeolic through Lesbos to Thessaly and Boeotia. In Greece itself, however, the pattern was not so tidy. The hills in the center of the Peloponnesus were occupied by the Arcadians, whose tongue was most similar to that of Cyprus; Attic differed in certain respects very sharply from Ionic and in others approached Dorian; central Greece is divided by modern linguistic scholars among Boeotians, Thessalians, and Northwest Greeks.

The origin of these dialects cannot be fixed with precision, in the lack of sure epigraphic or literary evidence before the seventh century. Basically their geographical distribution has some connection with early movements about the Aegean, but only in the most general sense. Remarkably detailed but extraordinarily diverse pictures of these movements have been drawn

on the basis of dialectal evidence; the draftsmen of such reconstructions have quite ignored the archaeological evidence as a
rule and, worse yet, have commonly disregarded the fact that
spoken languages change with relative rapidity. To treat the
historic dialects as virtually fixed entities over long, analpha-
betic centuries is extremely unsafe.

Greek linguistic divergence seems rather to have experienced major steps after the end of the Mycenaean age. One recent suggestion, which is at least plausible, derives from Mycenaean or "south Greek" the Arcado-Cypriote dialect and also
Attic and Ionic.[5] From "north Greek" would come in the first
degree the Aeolic dialect, which in its Thessalian form may represent this earlier tongue most fully; and then also Dorian and
sundry other dialects of later Greece. The distinctions, indeed,
between Attic and Ionic may still have been crystallizing in the
eighth century.

The linguistic transformation of the Aegean from the Mycenaean era into the Dark ages shows once more the chain of
progress which we can see in the pottery. Historic Greek dialects,
like Protogeometric and Geometric pottery, were ultimately descended from roots in the second millennium; but the change
which had taken place was a very considerable one. The presence
of many dialects underlines the localism of the era; yet regional
and general ties also existed. The process of splintering did
not reduce the Aegean to a welter of mutually incomprehensible
tongues. By 800 the Aegean shared the same basic speech, and
at that time the Greek tongue in its highest form, the epic poetry

[5] W. Porzig, "Sprachgeographische
Untersuchungen zu den altgriechi-
schen Dialekten," Indogermanische
Forschungen, LXI (1954), 147–69;
Ernst Risch, "Die Gliederung der griechischen Dialekte in neuer Sicht,"
Museum Helveticum, XII (1955), 61–
76, and his surveys in Études mycé-
niennes (Paris, 1956), 167–72, 249–
63; John Chadwick, "The Greek Dialects and Greek Pre-History," Greece
and Rome, 2. ser. III (1956), 38–50,
and in Documents, 68–75. The new
light from the Mycenaean tablets is
leading to many studies on the subject; Vittore Pisani, for instance, takes
Ionian-Mycenaean as originating in
Asia Minor and overlaid by Aeolic
and Dorian in "Die Entzifferung der
ägaeischen Linear B Schrift und die
griechischen Dialekte," RM, XCVIII
(1955), 1–18. Cf. Cassola, La Ionia
nel mondo miceneo, 154–212.

Dialectal evidence: Carl D. Buck,
The Greek Dialects (Chicago, 1955);
Michel Lejeune, Traité de phonétique
grecque (Paris, 1947); Antoine Meillet, Aperçu d'une histoire de la langue
grecque (6th ed.; Paris, 1948).

of Homer, beautifully illuminates the most basic intellectual characteristics of Greek civilization. To this point I shall return in the next chapter, in considering the hexameter. In view of the racial theories which still plague our understanding of Greek history it might be well also to note once more that such terms as "Dorian" and "Ionic" are purely linguistic; their speakers did not necessarily have any fundamental, blood-carried differences in cultural outlook.

POLITICAL PATTERNS

FROM THE SPREAD of Protogeometric and Geometric styles over the Aegean as well as from its linguistic domination by one language, albeit divided into dialects, the historian can deduce the rise of a fundamental cultural unity. This process may be called a horizontal extension of Greek civilization. Another significant step was the consolidation in depth which resulted as the political, social, and cultural patterns in each area became more firmly established and integrated. This aspect of the Dark ages must concern us during the balance of the present chapter.

For the era 1000–800 the so-called "history" decked with specific names and dates, which was constructed in classic and Hellenistic times, had best be dismissed out of hand. It is a mere web of guesses to camouflage the obscurity of the age. Even the marvelous chapters at the beginning of Thucydides' history, which sketch the early evolution of Greece, have hypnotized too many modern scholars; Thucydides was usually a careful critic of events in his own time, but in turning to the past he could do no more than rationalize mythical lore. The legends which assert that the Dorians expanded from the Argolid northeast to Epidaurus, northward into the Corinthia and Megarid, or southwest to Sparta (see Map No. 2) may well have some validity, yet we cannot prove them purely on the basis of scattered archaeological hints.[6] Nor could such historical themes as

---

[6] Corinthia and Megarid: Dunbabin, *JHS*, LXVIII (1948), 63–64; N. G. L. Hammond, "The Heraeum at Perachora and Corinthian Encroachment," *BSA*, XLIX (1954), 93–102. Sparta: Skeat, *Dorians in Archaeology*, 31–35.

purposeful interstate relations and internal class struggles have
any real place in the simple society of those early centuries; true
wars, as distinguished from cattle-raiding and other border
skirmishing, could occur only in an age of well-organized states.

In political terms, all that we can hope to establish is the
character of the general framework by which men of the Dark
ages assured basic order to their life. If evolution occurred, it
probably should be sought in a consolidation of local units of
government after the chaotic movements at the end of the Mycenaean age and in an increasingly firm sense of political structure and spirit; but this suggestion is purely an inference from
the evolution of Geometric order. Our only useful evidence
comes from the very end of the age, in the epic poems. The
Homeric world, however, lies so decisively before the upheaval
which produced the city-state (*polis*) that one is probably
justified in taking its picture of tribally organized peoples and
"hereditary monarchy with established rights and limitations"
(Thucydides I. 13) as applicable in the earlier, slowly moving
centuries.

The abstract terms of political life which appear in the
Iliad are those familiar in historic times, but the system expressed in such terms as *polis, demos, boule, agora,* was still only
a rudimentary hint of later organization.[7] In the *Iliad, polis* and
asty are never sharply distinguished from each other in the
historic sense of "state" and "town"; both were inhabited, defensible localities. Their inhabitants seem to have considered themselves superior to the *agroikoi* or isolated inhabitants of field and
pasture; but, lest we judge too much from this feeling as to the

---

[7] Hermann Strasburger, *Gymnasium,*
LX (1953), 99, sums up the picture
briefly; full epic references may be
found in Adolf Fanta, *Der Staat in
der Ilias und Odyssee* (Innsbruck,
1882); see also Fritz Gschnitzer,
"Stammes- und Ortsgemeinden im
alten Griechenland," *Wiener Studien,* LXVIII (1955), 120–44. *Polis:*
Wilhelm Hoffmann, "Die Polis bei
Homer," *Festschrift Bruno Snell* (Munich, 1956), 153–65, overemphasizes
its place. *Demos: Iliad* XXIV. 481,

III. 50, VI. 158, IX. 634; *Odyssey*
XXI. 17, XIII. 233. *Boule:* Fanta, *Der
Staat,* 70–86. *Agora:* Fanta, *Der Staat,*
87–96; M. I. Finley, *The World of
Odysseus* (2d ed.; London, 1956),
84–90.

Basileus: De Sanctis, *Storia dei
Greci,* I, 237–38, 275; Fanta, *Der
Staat,* 46–69; Finley, *World of Odysseus,* 105–07, and *Historia,* VI (1956),
139; M. P. Nilsson, "Das homerische
Königtum," *Opus. sel.,* II (Lund,
1952), 871–97.

presence of city life, it must be remembered that the Greeks, even when they were purely farmers, tended to dwell together in groups. The term *polis* does at times have a vague connotation of "state," as in giving the name to an area. Chieftains and other heroes are occasionally identified as coming from a particular *polis;* a stranger may be asked what his *polis* is. But far more often the question is put: "What is your *demos?*"

The basic unit was not a firmly organized state in a territorial sense, nor was it simply a people; the *demos* was a people inhabiting a specific area. This *demos* was organized in subdivisions, tribes and phratries above all, for military purposes, for the preservation of law and order, and probably for most other purposes of communal life; even the gods are grouped in *phylai* or tribes in epic tradition. While the invading elements of a *demos* may have floated freely for a while at the end of the second millennium, they sooner or later settled down and amalgamated with the earlier population; and the area occupied by any one *demos,* which resulted from the fusion, came to be a generally definable tract which had commonly as kernel a *polis.* This seems usually to have been an inhabited site—i.e., a village; it also often served as the refuge and religious center of the people.

The political bonds, however, of the men who assembled here were not primarily territorial; they were far more those of tribal unity and of obedience to a particular *basileus.* The tribal ties, expressed in common cult and social customs, were of great, continuing importance, but were probably of an unconscious nature. Conscious political ties, to judge from the epic, must have been mainly on a personal basis; the *basileus,* as their focus, was an important element in the framework of society. To understand his nature we would do well to avoid the commonly employed equivalent, "king," for this inevitably suggests to a modern reader a position of great power and wide estate.

Greece had known such masters in the Mycenaean age, when each great palace fortress had served as center for a far-ruling *wanax,* supported by a bureaucracy of scribe-treasurers. Though every technical term in the Mycenaean tablets is still open to debate, it appears that a military retinue may have held its land for military service to the king. Below him there was a chain of local government, in which we can probably fit the officials called *pa₂-si-re-u* in the tablets and perhaps village spokesmen and councillors.[8] At the end of the Late Bronze era, however, this imitation of Oriental monarchy had fallen with a crash. The centralized political administration implied in the palace archives dissolved; the term *wanax* itself disappeared from the Greek vocabulary save as a term for gods and as an epithet in the Homeric poems. The *basileus* was a successor not of the *wanax* but of the local lords and the warleaders of the invaders who amalgamated with or superseded these *pa₂-si-re-u*.

In absolute terms this political change represented a great deterioration, which probably took place very swiftly. The modern argument that the *basileis* gradually lost their strength across the Dark ages, by granting out their domains to warriors, not only is sheer speculation but also is quite misleading; [9] whatever royal powers and domains the kings had held were dissipated, in the main, on the breakdown of political order at the end of the Mycenaean period. Nonetheless this development was one of the most important underlying steps in the rise of Greek civilization. Had it not occurred, Greek society could scarcely have become integrated as a basically unified structure, nor would the city-state of later days, the fruit of that structure, have emerged.

To understand both the political framework of the Dark ages themselves and the subsequent evolution out of this system, one must always keep in mind the limited strength of the *basileus*, who dominated only a small area. That the peoples of Greece may have felt cultural, religious, and linguistic ties over

---

[8] Ventris and Chadwick, *Documents*, 121–22 and passim. Little of this, however, has yet received complete assent. Giovanni Pugliese Carratelli, "Eqeta," *Minoica* (Berlin, 1958), 319–26, strongly attacks the military interpretation of that term; Page, *History and the Homeric Iliad*, 186, casts doubt on the significance of *pa₂-si-re-u*.

Anax: Bengt Hemberg, ΑΝΑΞ, ΑΝΑΣΣΑ *und* ΑΝΑΚΕΣ *als Götterna-*

men *unter besonderer Berüchsichtigung der attischen Kulte* (Uppsala, 1955); C. M. Bowra, *JHS*, LIV (1934), 54–55, 59–60, on Cyprus. In later times the Milesians remembered their first king as having been named Anax (Paus. I. 35. 6, VII. 2. 5); this surely had been his title.

[9] Beloch, *Griechische Geschichte*, I, 211–12; Nilsson, *Homer and Mycenae*, 243; and many others.

fairly wide districts is suggested above all by the religious leagues known in later times, which met for worship at especially sacred points.[1] Beyond the clues afforded by these and other traditional groupings, the main evidence for the political topography of the Dark ages should be the famous catalogue of the Greek army against Troy, in the Second Book of the *Iliad;* but this picture, though marvelously detailed, is not the guide we might wish. The epic geographic references are probably contaminated both by poetic fancy and by archaizing tendencies, though I much mistrust the recent ingenious manipulations of this material to prove its Mycenaean origin and topographic trustworthiness.[2] Worse yet, the artistic requirements of the epic limited the number of figures who could take part; both in the catalogue and in the list of leaders in *Iliad* IV. 250 ff. the major cultural and linguistic districts are assigned to only one or a few *basileis.*

In the practical terms of actual government, however, the area which looked to each individual warleader and so served as root for a later city-state had come to be very small before the end of the Dark ages. The resources of a *basileus* in so poor an era probably barely covered even the simple need of cult and rudimentary state. In some localities, indeed, the existence of several *basileis* side by side, which we find later in the *Odyssey,* at Elis, and elsewhere, may have been the case earlier.[3] Even in Homeric days the leaders were still intimately connected with the daily duties of farming and herding, as indeed they must be if they were to maintain any state for themselves and

[1] E. g., Panionian league of Poseidon: Wade-Gery, *Poet of the Iliad,* 4–5, 63–66; Carl Roebuck, "The Early Ionian League," *CP,* L (1955), 26–40, and *Ionian Trade and Colonization,* 25–31; Gallet de Santerre, *Délos primitive,* 206–07. Calaurian amphictiony: Will, *Korinthiaka,* 545 n. 1; J. P. Harland, "The Calaurian Amphictyony," *AJA,* XXIX (1925), 160–71.
[2] Mycenaean origins: V. Burr, "Νεῶν κατάλογος," *Klio,* Beih. XLIX (1944); Jula Kerschensteiner, "Pylostafeln und homerischer Schiffskatalog," *Münchener Studien zur Sprachwissenschaft,*

IX (1956), 34–58; G. R. Huxley, "Mycenaean Decline and the Homeric Catalogue of Ships," *Bulletin of the Institute of Classical Studies,* III (1956), 19–30; Page, *History and the Homeric Iliad,* 120–37. But cf. Wade-Gery, *Poet of the Iliad,* 49–57, and Gray, *Homer and His Critics,* 273–74 (whose remarks do not accord with Myres's own views of its early origin, p. 199). Epic magnification of kingship: Chap. 5, n. 6 (p. 164).
[3] L. H. Jeffery, *BSA,* LI (1956), 165; Gustave Glotz, *The Greek City and Its Institutions* (London, 1929), 63.

for their retainers (*therapontes*). Apart from gifts by foreigners
—to whom in turn countergifts had to be presented—the uncertain rewards of raiding, and not very well defined gifts by
their subjects, the Homeric *basileis* had to live by agriculture,
carried out both on their lands and on a *temenos* assigned
them by the tribal community; their reserves consisted mainly of
ancestral treasures, food, and stores of metals.[4]

That the chieftains continued to live in the old Mycenaean
palaces is often asserted, but there is no proof that any of these
were occupied across the Dark ages. Architectural and artistic
skills had certainly sunk too low for the construction of any new
palaces or great tombs; the "mansion" at Karphi, which was apparently the home of the village chieftain, may well have been
occupied by a man who called himself *basileus*.

The *basileis* did not stand far above their fellow tribesmen
either in economic or in political interests, nor apparently
did their plane of life and social customs differ radically from
those of the upper classes who fought beside them; among the
tombs of the early Dark ages at Athens there is no spectacular
divergence in the extent of burial gifts. Most significant of all, the
basileis did not absorb all the political powers of the community,
as the *wanax* had come close to doing in the Mycenaean age.
Even in that era the tablets seem to suggest that the villages had
local officials; when we again begin to see the Greek countryside, in the Homeric epics, it is quite clear that the chieftains
were not omnipotent, and did not "administer" through agents.
In the lawsuit depicted on the shield of Achilles, judgment
lay in the hands of village wise men.[5] Priests and seers con-
veyed the will of the gods, who could speak to any man if they
so desired. Assemblies of the folk and of the greater men occurred
sporadically for political, religious, and other functions. These,
too, did not proceed on regular rules and had no specific functions. The *agora* of the people voiced its opinion, if at all, only
by shouts and mob action; the nobles, when convened in meal
and council (*boule*), at times spoke their minds freely, yet their

[4] *Iliad* IX. 149–55; A. M. Andreades,
A History of Greek Public Finance, I
(Cambridge, Mass., 1933), 3–29; Fin-
ley, *World of Odysseus*, 104–06.

[5] *Iliad* XVIII. 497–508; on this much
vexed scene, see E. Wolf, *Griechisches
Rechtsdenken*, I (Frankfurt, 1950),
88 ff.

great days of power were still to come. Nonetheless *agora* and *boule* did have to take place as a medium by which chieftains and followers could sense each other's opinion; and the upper classes had an independent place.

In some recent studies it is suggested that the *basileus* reflects Indo-European principles of political organization.[6] The line of argument which reads back from the days of Germanic kingship often goes much too far in postulating clear political theories among the primitive peoples of north-central Eurasia, but we may grant that the invaders of Greece brought with them some views on the relations of chieftain and followers (though we do not really know what these were). More important forces, surely, arose from the facts of political life in the Dark ages. The simple economic and social plane of the era, which intensified the divisive forces of Greek geography, helped to turn the land away from a temporary imitation of Oriental monarchy on the grand scale and to tie men into small, practically self-sufficient political units.

Much of the governance of daily life was automatically executed in the operations of the social blocks into which the peoples were grouped; the areas of conscious choice for either *basileus* or subjects were very limited. In the eyes of his contemporaries the reputation of a *basileus* depended on his own prowess; only forceful men, who had "might," could hope to be chieftains in the neighborhood raids for cattle and female slaves. But their powers were always limited by the unwritten code of *themis,* "what is done." This fluid yet rigidly circumscribed situation changed little until the upsurge of Greek activity in the eighth century.

THE SOCIAL STRUCTURE OF EARLY GREECE

A MODERN CITIZEN of a firmly organized national state, reared in a metropolitan social and economic system, will have

[6] Specific applications of these ideas to Greek kingship may be found in Andrew Alföldi, *AJA*, LXIII (1959), 15–18; Jaan Puhvel, "Helladic Kingship and the Gods," *Minoica* (Berlin, 1958), 327–33.

as much difficulty in comprehending the social as the political
structure of early Greece. If we are to understand even the most
basic characteristics of its social life, we must place ourselves in
a very alien environment.

Economically its base was a primitive form of agriculture, in
which virtually everyone of working age had to labor to drag
food from the soil; but beside the villagers one must allow some
room, first, for nomadic herders, who were possibly more common then than in the eighth and following centuries, and, secondly, for at least a few artisans and adventurers by land and
sea. Socially the men and women who inhabited the Aegean
lands across the Dark ages were a primitive folk. From the findings of comparative anthropology on more recent, more easily
studied societies we can gain some insight into the probable
qualities of such a traditional, group-centered people, though
always the historian must proceed soberly and with care in
assessing the meaning of the fossilized customs which survived
down into historic Greece. It is better to speak only in general
terms on matters of classes, social groups, and social attitudes
than to create a misleadingly detailed picture on the basis of
current anthropological and psychological theories.[7]

Despite the strong efforts which have been made in recent
times to prove that Indo-European peoples had an underlying
caste organization of warriors, priests, and peasants, Greek history nowhere reveals any discernible signs of a true caste outlook.[8] Socially and economically distinct classes, however, did
exist from early times. Personal ownership of the land, in the
sense in which we know fee simple, seems to have been lacking,
and there are a few hints that communal exploitation of a people's territory had been known, particularly, perhaps, in connection with semi-nomadic ways;[9] but in virtually all areas the

---

[7] H. J. Rose, *Primitive Culture in
Greece* (London, 1925), 4–5, 36,
gives a judicious warning; cf. Leon
Robin, "Quelques survivances dans la
pensée philosophique des Grecs d'une
mentalité primitive," *REG*, XLIX
(1936), 255–92.
[8] Georges Dumézil, *Jupiter, Mars, Qui-
rinus* (Paris, 1941), 252–57; L. R.

Palmer, *Achaeans and Indo-Europeans* (Oxford, 1955), who tries to
find the three groups in the Mycenaean tablets; Nilsson, *Cults and Politics*, 143–49, who essays to prove
economic divisions in the Ionian tribes.
[9] The most recent surveys of this
thorny question are M. I. Finley,
"Homer and Mycenae: Property and

arable land, whether held by clans or other social groups, was not evenly divided among the possessors. To this condition of inequality the effects of the invasions at the end of the Mycenaean age must have contributed; tendencies to class division were already present at least from Early Helladic times.

On the one side, to judge from the evidence of the Homeric epics and later materials, were peasants, poor day laborers, and slaves. The slaves, who were chiefly women, worked in the households as maids, processors of wool, concubines, and the like. Shepherds and other masculine slaves appear in Homer, but large-scale agricultural slavery was never to be common in Greece.[1] Some slaves were house-born; others were captives of wars or raids. "Zeus takes away half his worth from a man," says Eumaeus, "when the day of slavery comes upon him"; but while slaves could know blows, they were also at times respected and even owned their own slaves. In the worst position of all, apparently, were the landless laborers, the *thetes*, for while slaves at least had firm attachment to some household, the *thetes* were adrift in a world where economic and social security was based on group ties. When Odysseus in the underworld praised Achilles' position as king of the dead, his erstwhile comrade-in-arms rejoined that it would be far better to serve as *thetes* some peasant of small acres on earth.

In later days the landholding peasants themselves were at times to be serfs, as in Crete, Thessaly, and elsewhere. The

Tenure," *Historia*, VI (1957), 133–59; Éd. Will, "Aux origines du régime foncièr grec: Homère, Hésiode et l'arrière-plan mycénien," *REA*, LIX (1957), 5–50. Finley seems more correct in rejecting any extensive continuity in patterns of landholding. The case for early communal ownership gains its best support from *Iliad* XII. 421, cf. XVIII. 541–59; one must also take into account the state contribution to the meals of the warriors, as on Crete (Aristotle, *Politics* II. 7. 3. 1272a; Athenaeus IV. 143a-b; R. F. Willetts, *Aristocratic Society in Ancient Crete* [London, 1955], 252). George Thomson, "On Greek Land-

Tenure," *Studies to D. M. Robinson*, II, 840–50, seeks to reinforce his argument in *Studies in Ancient Greek Society: The Prehistoric Aegean* (rev. ed.; London, 1954), 297 ff.; but see Chap. 11, n. 2 (p. 358).
[1] Slaves: my study, "An Overdose of Slavery," *Journal of Economic History*, XVIII (1958), 17–32; Bolkestein, *Economic Life*, 74–76; Denys Page, *The Homeric Odyssey* (Oxford, 1955), 105, on the limited terms in Homer. Their treatment: *Odyssey* XVII. 320–23; cf. IV. 244–45, XI. 190–91, and XIV. 59–61 against XV. 403 ff., XV. 376–79, XIV. 449–52. Thetes: *Odyssey* XI. 489–91.

legal refinement which drove them down to this position may
well have been the product of aristocratic consolidation in historic times and will be considered as such in Chapter 9; even
then the peasants were generally free and enjoyed a relatively
secure, if humble, place in society. We can, I think, postulate
no less for the Dark ages.

To what extent the peasants represented the older population, and the upper classes the invading elements, one can only
guess. Our knowledge of conquest aristocracies at other times in
history suggests that due allowance must be made for possibilities of some initial amalgamation between old and new upper
levels as well as for the likelihood of intermarriage; certainly a
general social integration took place in the centuries of the Dark
ages. At least by the end of the era the upper and lower classes
of Greece formed a consolidated society with a common pattern
of civilization and speech, subject only to the inevitable cultural
variations which result when some men possess wealth and
wider contacts—and the very minor nature of these variations is
suggested by the general uniformity of the tombs.

This integration was, from the social point of view, one of
the greatest bequests of the period to later Greek history.
Nowhere in historic times is there any valid evidence that the
upper classes of one area differed in culture from those of another because of *racial* background, nor within any one people
did the upper and lower classes have basically different cultural
inheritances. Modern assertions that the masters preserved a
Nordic outlook and so were more capable of culture are pure
nonsense, bred of modern racial prejudice, not of the ancient
evidence.

In the primitive Aegean world of the early first millennium
B.C. the upper classes, moreover, were far simpler than the
nobility of medieval western Europe, who inherited much from
the developed pattern of the Roman Empire. On this important
point we must be clear. The leading elements in Homer did
stand sharply apart from the poorer peasants or landless *thetes;*
their social position as the warriors of the community tended to
give them a special standard of life, dominated by the need

to show bravery; and they expressed their distinctive position in some physical possessions. The ownership of horses, animals of limited economic utility in the day-to-day labors of Greek farming, seems to have been one of the most prized of these attributes. The early tripods of Olympia and elsewhere were probably dedicated by horse-owners who had won chariot races; when real objects began to appear more commonly on vases in the Strong Geometric style, these were often horses, either drawn or simply modeled plastic decorations (individually or in teams) on the lids of pyxides.[2] None of these qualities, however, connotes the presence of a truly aristocratic spirit, a great force in later Greek history but one which we can trace back only to the end of the eighth century. By that date, however, the earlier essential uniformity of all free men in the *demos* was beginning to jell into concepts of the rights and duties of the free citizen.

Throughout the Dark ages men lived not by and for themselves but within a strong web of groups. Topographically, the countryside of Greece almost forces its population into clusters; socially, this turbulent era was not one for men to dwell apart or to maintain life on an individual level. The main social units which survived into historic times were those of family, clan, warrior band, and tribe.

Basic, but only in a practical sense, was the family (*oikos*), vital for the purposes of procreation and child-raising but too small for independent action. The clan (*genos*) was at least theoretically a group of related families; while it was probably an early unit, its era of greatest importance perhaps came

---

[2] K. 560 (Plate 5a); K. 290 about 825–800 B.C., *Kerameikos*, V. 1, 127–28, 135–36, 179 n. 176; K. 257 about 800 (Plate 8b). Cf. Sylvia Benton, "The Dating of Horses on Stands and Spectacle Fibulae in Greece," *JHS*, LXX (1950), 16–22; Sidney D. Markman, *The Horse in Greek Art* (Baltimore, 1943), whose dates are badly in error.

Tripods: Sylvia Benton, "The Evolution of the Tripod-Lebes," *BSA*, XXXV (1934–35), 74–130; Emil Kunze, *Olympia-Bericht*, IV (1944), 110; Karl Schwendemann, "Der Dreifuss," *JdI*, XXXVI (1921), 98–185; Franz Willemsen, *Dreifusskessel von Olympia: Alte und Neue Funde* (Berlin, 1957), 50–51, 167–68, 148–54 (horses on caldrons).

Emergence of aristocracy: Chap. 9.

when aristocrats began to play a larger part in Greek political and social life.[3]

The main groupings of a people, at least in Homer, were the warrior bands and tribes. The former was an institution which often appears in modern primitive societies; its Greek form was the *hetairia*, which was commonly the same as the phratry.[4] Male citizens of Sparta and still more of Crete still ate together in historic times at the "men's house" (*andron*) in common meals, at which the young boys participated as attendants. These youths were trained in bands and then were formally initiated into manhood and adult responsibilities as husbands and warriors. Survivals of such patterns can be found at Athens and elsewhere; the importance of this early principle of military organization is visible in Nestor's advice to Agamemnon to separate the warriors by tribes and phratries "that phratry may bear aid to phratry and tribe to tribe." [5] Only within the phratry structure could a man be certain of mutual defense and protection; an outcast, who was unable to get along with his fellows or his father or had murdered a member of his own social group, had to seek out some alien *basileus* as protector.

Over all stood the tribe (*phyle*) as the basic building

---

[3] Family and clan: D. P. Costello, "Notes on the Athenian ΓΕΝΗ," *JHS*, LVIII (1938), 171–79; W. Erdmann, *Die Ehe im alten Griechenland* (*Münchener Beiträge zur Papyrusforschung und antiken Rechtsgeschichte* XX, 1934), 112–32; Gustave Glotz, *La Solidarité de la famille dans le droit criminel en Grèce* (Paris, 1904); C. Hignett, *A History of the Athenian Constitution to the End of the Fifth Century B.C.* (Oxford, 1952), 61–67, who shows the problems connected with the clans in Athenian history and notes they had no place in Attic law; Thomson, *Prehistoric Aegean*, 332–34, who tries to prove that clans had an occupational character.

On the group character of early Greek society, cf. Glotz, *Greek City*, 36–37; *Iliad* II. 362 ff.; Finley, *World of Odysseus*, 56–63. Its results in ethics will be considered in connection with

Homer in Chap. 5.

[4] M. Guarducci, "L'istituzione della fratria nella Grecia antica e nelle colonie greche d'Italia," *Memorie della Accademia nazionale dei Lincei*, 6. ser. VI. 1 (1937), VIII. 2 (1938); H. Jeanmaire, *Couroi et courètes* (Lille, 1939), with the critique by Louis Gernet, "Structures sociales et rites d'adolescence dans la Grèce antique," *REG*, LVII (1944), 242–48, and the skepticism of Nilsson, *Gnomon*, XXV (1953), 8; Nilsson, *Cults and Politics*, 150–70; Ch. Picard, "Prépélaos et les courètes éphésiens," *RA*, 6. ser. XXXVII (1951), 151–60, on an example overlooked by Jeanmaire; Willetts, *Ancient Crete*, 18–23, on the basis primarily of Strabo X. 4. 16–21, C. 480–84.

[5] *Iliad* II. 362–63; cf. II. 668; *Odyssey* XV. 273.

block of the various Greek peoples.[6] In areas where men spoke Dorian the population was commonly grouped in three tribes, the Hylleis, Dymanes, and Pamphyloi; in Attica there were four, the Geleontes, Hopletes, Argadeis, and Aigikoreis, which reappear in Ionic-speaking areas with others, especially the Boreis and Oinopes. This organization, which served purposes of military organization and probably local government—at Athens each *phyle* had a *phylobasileus*—evidently went far back into the period of migration; but we cannot discern its origin or fully account for the local variations in the numbers and names of the tribes. If the tribes were institutions of the invaders, the natives must somehow have been absorbed; in historic times no one seems to have stood outside these units. During the early centuries with which we are here concerned, all the events of daily life took place within this tissue which was at once social, economic, religious, and political.

The social code of the Dark ages cannot be established save by a very limited interpolation backward from historic conditions. Such matters as the relations of the sexes, the mutual attitudes of parents and children, and behavior among one's peers are among the most vital forces in human existence; but even in historic times these areas were taken so much for granted that they appear only sketchily in our sources. For individual caprice in basic social patterns there certainly was little room. Marriage bonds continued in later centuries to have a strong air of property transactions, and were appropriately arranged by parents within the confines of clan and class requirements; children were bound firmly in family and clan units; and even as adults individuals had to move within traditional requirements in sexual and other relations.[7]

[6] H. E. Seebohm, *The Structure of Greek Tribal Society* (London, 1895); Emil Szanto, "Die griechischen Phylen," *Ausgewählte Abhandlungen* (Tübingen, 1906), 216–88; we do not know if the Aeolian area was tribally organized. In terming the *phylai* building-blocks, I do not infer they existed before the state chronologically;

cf. Eduard Meyer, "Über die Anfänge des Staats und sein Verhältnis zu den Geschlechtsverbänden und zum Volksthum," *SB Berlin Akademie* 1907, 508–38.
[7] Erdmann, *Die Ehe im alten Griechenland*, 204–12, 342–63, sums up our later knowledge. The traditional, superstitious side of Greek social life

To what extent the rules which governed this life were drawn from earlier eras we cannot hope to determine. Proto-geometric pottery evolved out of Mycenaean and sub-Mycenaean roots; the later dialects owed their origin to second-millennium speech; so, too, probably many ways of life carried on, particularly inasmuch as the economic mode of life remained much the same. This logical argument, however, must not be carried too far; the really great changes which took place in the eleventh century forbid us simply to assume uninterrupted continuity in basic social outlook. If Bachofen's theory were correct that the pre-Greek inhabitants of the Aegean preferred mother-right and the Indo-European invaders introduced a patriarchal structure, we should have to postulate a general reorganization of social standards in the Dark ages.[8] This argument rests, as far as factual evidence is concerned, upon the prevalence of female figurines in early Aegean contexts as against their absence in the Iron age, and upon the presumed importance of mother goddesses. Essentially, however, the adherents of the mother-right theory have compounded dubious anthropological principles, which distinguish agricultural, female-based villagers from herding, male-based nomads, together with those racial prejudices which contrast virile Nordic peoples and the placid, backward, Mediterranean *Urvolk*. As applied to early Greece the theory of mother-right seems more than doubtful.

The only certain fact is that men and women throughout the Dark ages continued to contract unions from which sprang successive generations, and that they imparted to their children a basic set of social principles and beliefs on which life could

---

is marked in the concern over intercourse, pregnancy, childbirth, menstruation, etc., in Buck, *Greek Dialects*, no. 115 [*SEG* ix. 1, no. 72 (from Cyrene)]; cf. Rose, *Primitive Culture*, 109–33.

[8] J. J. Bachofen, *Das Mutterrecht* (Basel, 1861; reprinted in *Gesammelte Werke*, ii–iii, 1948). Pro: Thomson, *Prehistoric Aegean*, 149; Willetts, *Ancient Crete*, 87–88; and many others who are often of Marxist outlook.

Contra: Erdmann, *Die Ehe im alten Griechenland*, 117–24; Lewis R. Farnell, "Sociological Hypotheses concerning the Position of Women in Ancient Religion," *Archiv für Religionswissenschaft*, VII (1904), 70–94; Nilsson, *GGR*, I, 457–61; H. J. Rose, "Prehistoric Greece and Mother-Right," *Folk-Lore*, XXXVII (1926), 213–44; J. H. Thiel, "De Feminarum apud Dores Condicione," *Mnemosyne*, n. s. LVII (1929), 193–205.

continue. This morality was strongly group-oriented rather than resting consciously upon individual choice and responsibility; when first one begins to see its outlines in the Homeric epic, its terms of praise and expressions of virtue are overwhelmingly in communal terms.

Probably the greatest contribution of the Dark ages to Greek social conventions was their stabilization and consolidation after the unrest at the end of the Mycenaean age. To infer that such an era knew security may seem to go too far, particularly in view of the rigidly restrained patterns of Protogeometric and Geometric pottery. Superstition and primitive fears of the unknown were undoubtedly rife; famine and disease can never have been far absent; and most men could expect to be dead by the time they were thirty-odd, if indeed they survived the terrible gantlet of early childhood.[9] Yet mankind exists always under the shadow of death; the critical issue at any time is whether the social and intellectual framework gives humanity the strength to endure its dangers. The majestic development of Greek pottery across the Dark ages is enough to prove that society did regain its solidity after the upheavals at the end of the Mycenaean epoch, and the relentlessly swiftening tempo of Greek expansion from the early eighth century onward can be understood only against a background of earlier social reorganization.

The danger here was that early Greek society would overemphasize static principles in an effort to maintain itself in a difficult era. The task of sheer physical survival was critical; the primitive level of life made alteration and experiment dangerous. That change, however, could slowly take place is indicated by the territorial and linguistic unification of Aegean culture and by the development of Geometric pottery. When we come to the world of the epic itself, we shall find that communal loyalty and the conventions of the group had not entirely stifled the instincts of individual human beings to express themselves,

[9] J. L. Angel, "The Length of Life in Ancient Greece," *Journal of Gerontology*, II (1947), 18–24, who argues on very limited evidence that life expectancy rose down into classic times. Even about A.D. 1900 only one in three Greek infants lived to its first birthday (Myres, *Geographical History*, 20).

albeit within the limits imposed by these factors. The course
of historic Greek civilization was long marked by a happy blend
of individual experiment and social conservatism.

THE RISE OF GEOMETRIC POTTERY [1]

THE POLITICAL and social institutions of the Dark ages can
be described only in the most general terms, and even tentative
conclusions must be based on the evidence of epic and later survivals, which is of greatest value for the end of the era. To go
further in a search for precision on these topics must lead the
student either into speculation based on anthropological analo-
gies and the like or into hazardous combinations of legendary
materials; historically it is unsound to tread either path.

By only one means can we follow cultural threads across
the entire period—viz., the physical material. Within the range
of metal objects, which are a minor but useful source, bronze
continued to be most common; it turns up in *fibulae*, straight
pins, the earliest tripods of Olympia, and other forms which can
best be dated and appreciated against the ceramic background.
Iron was used primarily for weapons, which were less common
in the graves of this era than in the age of invasions. The most
sure and continuous testimony, however, is the pottery, and for
even this type of material we have only one site, the
Kerameikos cemetery, where a continuous chain can be arranged
across both the tenth and ninth centuries. With its aid the occasional partial stratification which appears elsewhere can be
properly interpreted, as well as the many isolated finds; for
pottery styles moved generally in sympathy throughout the
Aegean.

[1] No single survey of all manifestations of this subject has yet been published. The Attic chain is the best
treated; as by Peter Kahane, "Die
Entwicklungsphasen der attisch-geo-
metrischen Keramik," *AJA*, XLIV
(1940), 464–82; Kübler, *Kerameikos*,
V. 1, 3 n. 17 (bibliography), 44–48,
58–68, 160–62; B. Schweitzer, "Untersuchungen zur Chronologie und Geschichte der geometrischen Stile in
Griechenland II," *AM*, XLIII (1918),
1–152, and his thoughtful review-arti-
cle, *Gnomon*, X (1934), 337–53. The
later stages of Geometric will be considered in the next chapter.

The existence and bearing of this fact upon the territorial consolidation of the early Greek world have already been noted. So too the increased stability and economic advance by 800 B.C. can be sensed in the growth of the volume of surviving pottery and in its more extensive decoration. Most important of all at the present point is the illumination which the vases throw on the internal consolidation and cultural progress of the Dark ages.

The framework of pottery classification is now reasonably well established for the period. The Protogeometric style, which was dominant across the first half, has been divided in its Attic manifestation into Early (K. 522, 526; Plate 6c and d), Ripe (K. 1073, Plate 5b; K. 560, Plate 7a), and Late (K. 576, Plate 7b). Of these three stages the Late Protogeometric seems to have endured longest; Desborough, who assigns the beginning of Protogeometric pottery at Athens to 1025, places the Early phase 1025–980, Ripe Protogeometric 980–960, and Late Protogeometric 960–900.[2] While these dates can scarcely be lowered, in view of the great mass of Geometric pottery which follows in several stages, they can and perhaps should be raised by a quarter of a century or so, as I suggested in Chapter 3. Where the other Protogeometric styles of Greece fit in is not yet clear; but some styles certainly evolved independently of the Attic experiments.

In its simple, restrained forms and decoration the Protogeometric pottery of Athens reflects the stark simplicity of contemporary life; but no observer can call it "primitive" in the sense in which Early and Middle Helladic vases were primitive. The achievements of the Mycenaean age were not entirely lost, and ceramic memories of that era are still fairly discernible in Early Protogeometric work. Neither at Athens nor elsewhere in the Aegean, moreover, were the potters blindly following paths of rote memory. At least by the Late phase Attic experiments became known abroad, and a great body of changes appeared at home.

This intellectual activity is well illustrated in the differences between K. 560 (Ripe) and K. 576 (Late) on Plate 7. The two

[2] Desborough, *Protogeometric Pottery*, 294.

amphoras are generally alike in their basic shape, which reflects
—though at remote distance—Mycenaean proportions; but the
makers were evidently seeking different effects in their decoration. The wavy lines of the earlier vase, which allowed room
for a freehand horse (the only motif from nature thus far found
in Protogeometric pottery at Athens), are a survival from Mycenaean days; below and above this zone are bands of different
thickness, and on the shoulders appear concentric semicircles.
The vase K. 576, on the other hand, is entirely covered by a
painted ground except in the handle zone, which is given over
to a carefully composed, fine pattern based on a central triglyph
and two metopes, each occupied by concentric circles.[3] The impression which its potter created is clearly more unified.

Other Late Protogeometric vases exhibit motives which had
been almost suppressed in immediately preceding decades, as
well as motives which were virtually pre-Mycenaean. Thus, the
meander pattern (the source of our Greek key), which had been
little used in the Aegean since Middle Helladic times but was
popular in central Europe, began to gain that great vogue which
marked Geometric workshops; rectangles consisting of alternate
brown and white squares (the chessfields) occurred; and the
very shapes of the vases elongated subtly and stiffened. In
much of their product Late Protogeometric potters seem to a
modern student to have worked themselves into dead ends
while exploring the opportunities of the style.

The basic drive within these changes was toward a new outlook, unified in shapes and decoration, which is called Geometric; and the Geometric pottery of Greece was to have a
remarkably fruitful, long history down almost to 700 B.C. In its
Attic phase Geometric pottery was marked by a great reduction
in the use of concentric circles and several other favored motifs
of Protogeometric days; in their place came the meander, Greek
key, triangles, dots, and so on (see K. 254, 2146 on Plate 8).
The placing of the decoration likewise changed. While most of

[3] Metopes: Chap. 3, n. 7 (p. 91);
Kahane, *AJA*, XLIV (1940), 473, re-
buts the concept of Oriental origin.
Meander: Kraiker, *Kerameikos*, I, 176;
Kübler, *Kerameikos*, IV, 18–19 (with
bibliography), and V. 1, 46; Milojčić,
AA 1948–49, 34 (but cf. Kraiker,
Gnomon, XXIV [1952], 455). Stiff-
ness: Kübler, *Kerameikos*, I, 209–10;
IV, 8–9; V. 1, 186.

(a) Strong Geometric skyphos with one of
the earliest pictures in Greek pottery. Photograph from AJA, XLIV (1940), pl. XXI. 6.

(b) Pyxis (K. 257) of about 800 B.C. (Kerameikos Museum). Photograph courtesy
Deutsches Archäologisches Institut in Athens.

PLATE 9 · *Enrichment of the Attic Geometric Style*

(a) Fragments from Athens and Louvre A531 (now Brussels, Musée du Cinquantenaire) of a sea battle and warriors. Photograph courtesy Deutsches Archäologisches Institut in Athens.

(b) Warriors with crested helmet, shield, two spears and dagger, and probably greaves (National Museum 726, Copenhagen). Photograph courtesy National Museum, Copenhagen.

PLATE 10 · *The Dipylon Style*

the vase was at first simply painted with a uniform tone, the widest part was emphasized by a zone of motifs. Here at times the decoration ran around the vase, but at other times it was broken up by vertical accents between which a virtual picture space was left.[4] Generally this space was occupied by an abstract motif, as the concentric circles of K. 2146. Geometric artists viewed life in a generalized sense; and we may even infer that specific events which demanded commemoration did not yet take place in their world. On one Attic skyphos (Plate 9a), nonetheless, a real object, a ship, is depicted; from this humble start were to come in the eighth century the magnificent pictures of the Dipylon vases. In their shapes, too, the vases underwent significant alterations. While some Protogeometric forms continued to be popular, others vanished or were transmuted into new types, which commonly were more elongated and articulated, as in the example K. 254 (Plate 8a).

Within Geometric pottery itself, which covers two centuries of Greek history, further extensive developments occurred which are summed up in its modern divisions into Early (a little before 900–850), Strong (850–800), Ripe (800–750 or a little earlier), and Late (750–700).[5] These dates rest in their upper reaches on the framework of Protogeometric dating and in the lower phases depend on the Greek colonization of Sicily and Italy; they are only approximate guides, which are more useful in handling great masses of pottery than in placing individual vases or small grave groups found by themselves. The detailed stylistic criteria which lie behind these divisions seem generally valid, but I shall not here embark upon this complicated field. From the historical point of view the important problems are, first, the significance of the emergence of a new pottery style and, secondly, its illumination of the intellectual outlook of the ninth century.

If one compares typical Attic products of the developed Protogeometric and Geometric styles, the change which has taken place assumes very considerable proportions. Yet we can

---

[4] Matz, *GGK*, I, 56; Carl Weickert, "Geburt des Bildes," *Neue Beiträge*, 27–35; R. S. Young, *Hesperia*, XVIII (1949), 287.

[5] These are the dates of Kahane, *AJA*, XLIV (1940), 478–81, which have been widely accepted (so Dunbabin, *JHS*, LXVIII [1948], 68); Kübler, *Kerameikos*, V. 1, 70, 182–83, puts Early Geometric at 950 onward.

follow the stages of transition clearly enough to be sure this was a locally inspired development. The old argument that the Dorians introduced Geometric pottery had to be given up once pottery specialists disentangled its general chronological phases, and in more recent years it has become clear that even the meander motif, which was long assigned to central European sources, was known in the second-millennium Aegean. Nor can any significant contact be proven between the pottery of the Aegean and of Asia Minor and Syria.[6] Though the latter areas developed pottery styles with a limited number of abstract motifs which were combined in much the same spirit as in Greek ware, this "geometric" outlook was an independent product, rising out of parallel political and social simplification and based upon a similar inheritance from the second millennium. If we are to explain the change from Protogeometric to Geometric styles in Greece, we must search within Aegean evolution itself.

Basically, what had occurred was a consolidation of the main lines of the Hellenic outlook, as that spirit had been expressed in pottery from the eleventh century onward. The rise of the Geometric style, that is to say, does not mark the first appearance of that outlook; if one compares the change from sub-Mycenaean to Protogeometric pottery with that which is now under consideration, the earlier shift is much more crucial, particularly in its mainland phases.[7] In the Kerameikos Museum one can perhaps best sense that the first change, to Protogeometric,

---

[6] Danubian source: Emil Solle, *Počátky hellénské civilisace* (Prague, 1949), which I know only from *Fasti Archaeologici*, 1949, no. 674. Oriental origin: Anna Roes, *De Oorsprong der geometrische Kunst* (Haarlem, 1931), and *Greek Geometric Art: Its Symbolism and Its Origin* (Haarlem, 1933), who seeks to establish Elamitic origins. The contemporary "geometric" art of Anatolia and the Near East is considered below in Chap. 6.

[7] Against this generalization, contrary examples may naturally be found, as in Crete (Chap. 3, n. 9 [p. 98]) and in other areas where men dully

clung to old ways. At Delphi, for instance, L. Lerat, "Tombes submycéniennes et géométriques à Delphes," *BCH*, LXI (1937), 44–52, could not sharply distinguish sub-Mycenaean from Protogeometric; the clear break was to Geometric. H. E. Stier, "Probleme der frühgriechischen Geschichte und Kultur," *Historia*, I (1950), 195–230, accordingly divides Greek history into the eras 1200/1150— c. 900, c. 900—750/650, c. 750/650 —classic. The basic break, however, seems to me to be that put in the text; see also Chap. 3, n. 5 (p. 102).

was a real jump, while the second, to Geometric, was more evolutionary; but this significant point can be made clear by comparing the sub-Mycenaean vase K. 436 (Plate 5), the Ripe Protogeometric K. 560 (Plate 7a), and the Strong Geometric K. 2146 (Plate 8b). The first stands quite apart from the two later amphoras. Though these are themselves quite different in artistic spirit, they share a common tautness and sharpness of thought, a dynamic spirit which is harnessed within a balanced composition, and an essential harmony—the fundamental hallmarks of Greek art.

Geometric ware, nonetheless, manifests the outlook far more clearly. While Protogeometric potters still breathed an inheritance directly from the Mycenaean world, this influence had been eliminated or integrated by 800 B.C. through a long process of recombination and reinterpretation. Protogeometric pottery, again, displayed synthesizing qualities, which we might call Greek, in a somewhat muffled manner; but Geometric potters held a firm mastery over clearly understood principles of logical analysis. In their Early Geometric phase they concentrated upon the vase as a unit and severely limited their decoration, but a Strong Geometric vase such as K. 2146 exhibits an over-all unity composed of many different elements, each in itself simple but assembled, one beside and below the other, to form a coherent whole. Protogeometric vases were constructed on an additive principle, while Geometric potters both co-ordinated and subordinated their motifs.[8]

The reasons which now led potters to draw meanders, chessboards, lozenges, and the like we cannot hope to understand; but, to speak in general terms, the spirit which animated the artists of the ninth century was not a naïve pleasure in manipulating straight lines and, more rarely, circles. On the one hand, as was already observed, we may feel that their environment was not yet a sharply conceived pattern of specific events, and so genuine pictures did not appear; yet, on the other, as these men emphasized the structure of their vases by applying decoration, they were expressing a view, no doubt unconsciously, of the form and structure of the world about them. The

[8] Matz, *GGK*, I, 55.

commonly accepted term "Geometric" is thus somewhat misleading in its suggestions of purely mathematical calculation;
these vases, as a German critic has justly said, were "bildlos aber
nicht inhaltlos." [9] Whenever artists, indeed, turned to actual
representations or molded three-dimensional figures, which
were rare down to 800 B.C., they tended to reflect reality (see
Plate 6a, 9b); a schematic, abstract treatment of men and
animals, *by intent,* rose only in the late eighth century.

To speak of this underlying view of the world is to embark upon matters of subjective judgment. At the least, however,
one may conclude that Geometric potters sensed a logical order;
their principles of composition stand very close to those which
appear in the Homeric epics and the hexameter line. Their
world, again, was a still simple, traditional age which was only
slowly beginning to appreciate the complexity of life. And perhaps an observer of the vases will not go too far in deducing that
the outlook of their makers and users was basically stable and
secure. The storms of the past had died away, and the great upheaval which was to mark the following century had not yet
begun to disturb men's minds.

Throughout the work of the later ninth century a calm,
severe serenity displays itself. In the vases this spirit may perhaps at times bore or repel one in its internal self-satisfaction,
but the best of the Geometric pins have rightly been considered
among the most beautiful ever made in the Greek world. The
ninth century was in its artistic work "the spiritually freest and
most self-sufficient between past and future," [1] and the loving
skill spent by its artists upon their products is a testimonial to
their sense that what they were doing was important and was
appreciated.

[9] Wilhelm Kraiker, "Ornament und
Bild in der frühgriechischen Malerei,"
Neue Beiträge, 36–47 (at p. 40); and
Gnomon, XXIV (1952), 451. Attempts
to fathom this spiritual change have
been made by Kübler, *Kerameikos,* V.
1, 43–44; Schweitzer, *AM,* XLIII
(1918), 78–79, 138.

[1] Kübler, *Kerameikos,* V. 1, 182. Pins:
Jacobsthal, *Greek Pins,* 5; cf. the tripod leg, Olympia B 1250, which Willemsen, *Dreifusskessel,* 169, places in
the Strong Geometric style.

THE AEGEAN IN 800 B.C.

GEOMETRIC POTTERY has not yet received the thorough, detailed study which it deserves, partly because the task is a mammoth one and partly because some of its local manifestations, as at Argos, are only now coming to light. From even a cursory inspection of its many aspects, however, the historian can deduce several fundamental conclusions about the progress of the Aegean world down to 800 B.C.

The general intellectual outlook which had appeared in the eleventh century was now consolidated to a significant degree. Much which was in embryo in 1000 had become reasonably well developed by 800. In this process the Minoan-Mycenaean inheritance had been transmuted or finally rejected; the Aegean world which had existed before 1000 differed from that which rises more clearly in our vision after 800. Those modern scholars who urge that we must keep in mind the fundamental continuity of Aegean development from earliest times—granted occasional irruptions of peoples and ideas from outside—are correct; but all too many observers have been misled by this fact into minimizing the degree of change which took place in the early first millennium.

The focus of novelty in this world now lay in the southeastern districts of the Greek mainland, and by 800 virtually the entire Aegean, always excepting its northern shores, had accepted the Geometric style of pottery. While Protogeometric vases usually turn up, especially outside Greece proper, together with as many or more examples of local stamp, these "non-Greek" patterns had mostly vanished by the later ninth century. In their place came local variations *within* the common style—tentative, as it were, in Protogeometric products but truly distinct and sharply defined as the Geometric spirit developed. Attica, though important, was not the only teacher of this age. One can take a vase of about 800 B.C. and, without any knowledge of its place of origin, venture to assign it to a specific area; imitation and borrowing of motifs now become ascertainable. The potters of the Aegean islands thus stood apart from those of the mainland, and in Greece itself Argive, Corinthian, Attic, Boeotian, and other Geometric sequences have each their own hallmarks. These local variations were to become ever sharper in the next century and a half.

The same conclusions can be drawn from the other physical evidence of the Dark ages, from linguistic distribution, and from the survivals of early social, political, and religious patterns into later ages. By 800 B.C. the Aegean was an area of common tongue and of common culture. On these pillars rested that solid basis for life and thought which was soon to be manifested in the remarkably unlimited ken of the *Iliad*. Everywhere within the common pattern, however, one finds local diversity; Greek history and culture were enduringly fertilized, and plagued, by the interplay of these conjoined yet opposed factors.

Further we cannot go, for the Dark ages deserve their name. Many aspects of civilization were not yet sufficiently crystallized to find expression, nor could the simple economic and social foundations of this world support a lofty structure. The epic poems, the consolidation of the Greek pantheon, the rise of firm political units, the self-awareness which could permit painted and sculptured representations of men—all these had to await the progress of following decades. What we have seen in this chapter, we have seen only dimly, and yet the results, however general, are worth the search. These are the centuries in which the inhabitants of the Aegean world settled firmly into their minds and into their institutions the foundations of the Hellenic outlook, independent of outside forces.

To interpret, indeed, the era from 1000 to 800 as a period mainly of consolidation may be a necessary but unfortunate defect born of our lack of detailed information; if we could see more deeply, we probably would find many side issues and wrong turnings which came to an end within the period. The historian can only point out those lines which were major enough to find reflection in our limited evidence, and must hope that future excavations will enrich our understanding. Throughout the Dark ages, it is clear, the Greek world had been developing, slowly but consistently. The pace could now be accelerated, for the inhabitants of the Aegean stood on firm ground.

CHAPTER 5

THE EARLY EIGHTH CENTURY

⊓⊓⊓⊓⊓⊓⊓⊓⊓⊓⊓⊓⊓⊓⊓⊓⊓⊓⊓⊓⊓⊓⊓⊓⊓⊓

THE LANDSCAPE of Greek history broadens widely, and rather abruptly, in the eighth century B.C., the age of Homer's "rosy-fingered Dawn." The first slanting rays of the new day cannot yet dispel all the dark shadows which lie across the Aegean world; but our evidence grows considerably in variety and shows more unmistakably some of the lines of change. For this period, as for earlier centuries, pottery remains the most secure source; the ceramic material of the age is more abundant, more diversified, and more indicative of the hopes and fears of its makers, who begin to show scenes of human life and death. Figurines and simple chapels presage the emergence of sculpture and architecture in Greece; objects in gold, ivory, and bronze grow more numerous. Since writing was practiced in the Aegean before the end of the century, we may hope that the details of tradition will now be occasionally useful. Though it is not easy to apply the evidence of the *Iliad* to any specific era, this marvelous product of the epic tradition had certainly taken definitive shape by 750.

The Dipylon Geometric pottery of Athens and the *Iliad* are amazing manifestations of the inherent potentialities of Greek civilization; but both were among the last products of a phase which was ending. Greek civilization was swirling toward its great revolution, in which the developed qualities of the Hellenic outlook were suddenly to break forth. The revolution was well under way before 700 B.C., and premonitory signs go back virtually across the century. The era, however, is Janus-faced. While many tokens point forward, the main achievements stand

as a culmination of the simple patterns of the Dark ages. The
dominant pottery of the century was Geometric; political organization revolved about the *basileis;* trade was just beginning
to expand; the gods who protected the Greek countryside were
only now putting on their sharply anthropomorphic dress.

The modern student, who knows what was to come next, is
likely to place first the factors of change which are visible in the
eighth century. Not all men of the period would have accepted
this emphasis. Many potters clung to the past the more de-
terminedly as they were confronted with radically new ideas;
the poet of the *Iliad* deliberately archaized. Although it is not
possible to sunder old and new in this era, I shall consider in
the present chapter primarily the first decades of the eighth century and shall interpret them as an apogee of the first stage of
Greek civilization.

On this principle of division I must postpone the evolution
of sculpture, architecture, society, and politics; for the developments in these areas make sense only if they are connected to
the age of revolution itself. The growing contacts between Aegean and Orient are also a phase which should be linked primarily to the remarkable broadening of Hellenic culture after
750. We shall not be able entirely to pass over these connections
to the East as we consider Ripe Geometric pottery, the epic and
the myth, and the religious evolution of early Greece; the important point, however, is that these magnificent achievements,
unlike those of later decades, were only incidentally influenced
by Oriental models. The antecedents of Dipylon vases and of
the *Iliad* lie in the Aegean past.

DIPYLON POTTERY

THE POTTERY of the first half of the eighth century is commonly called Ripe Geometric. The severe yet harmonious vases
of the previous fifty years, the Strong Geometric style of the late
ninth century, display as firm a mastery of the principles underlying Geometric pottery; but artists now were ready to refine and

elaborate their inheritance. The vases which resulted had different shapes, far more complex decoration, and a larger sense of style.

Beyond the aesthetic and technical aspects of this expansion we must consider the change in pottery style on broader lines. In earlier centuries men had had enough to do in rebuilding a fundamental sense of order after chaos. They had had to work on very simple foundations and had not dared to give rein to impulses. The potters, in particular, had virtually eschewed freehand drawing, elaborate motifs, and the curving lines of nature, while yet expressing a belief that there was order in the universe. In their vases were embodied the basic aesthetic and logical characteristics of Greek civilization, at first hesitantly in Protogeometric work, and then more confidently in the initial stages of the Geometric style. By 800 social and cultural security had been achieved, at least on a simple plane; it was time to take bigger steps, to venture on experiments.

Ripe Geometric potters continued to employ the old syntax of ornaments and shapes and made use of the well-defined though limited range of motifs which they had inherited. In these respects the vases of the early eighth century represent a culmination of earlier lines of progress. To the ancestral lore, however, new materials were added. Painters left less and less of a vase in a plain dark color; instead they divided the surface into many bands or covered it by all-over patterns into which freehand drawing began to creep. Wavy lines, feather-like patterns, rosettes of indefinitely floral nature, birds either singly or in stylized rows, animals in solemn frieze bands (see Plates 11–12)—all these turned up in the more developed fabrics as preliminary signs that the potters were broadening their gaze.[1]

---

[1] Motifs: Kahane, *AJA*, XLIV (1940), 470–77; Kübler, *Kerameikos*, V. 1, passim; Schweitzer, *AM*, XLIII (1918), 81–93. Oriental animal rows: Dieter Ohly, *Griechische Goldbleche des 8. Jahrhunderts v. Chr.* (Berlin, 1953), 133–35; Frederik Poulsen, *Der Orient und die frühgriechische Kunst* (Leipzig-Berlin, 1912), 16–17; Emil Kunze, *Kretische Bronzereliefs* (Stuttgart, 1931), 153–65, who points out that rows of grazing animals as such appear entirely Greek in origin. The earliest row on a Greek vase, according to Ohly, is Munich 1250. Other external influences: Kübler, *Kerameikos*, V. 1, 167–70, 174 n. 160, 177 n. 171. Plants: Kunze, *Kretische Bronzereliefs*, 133, 144–45.

The rows of animals and birds, in particular, suggest awareness of Oriental animal friezes, transmitted perhaps via Syrian silver bowls and textiles, but the specific forms of these rows on local vases and metal products are nonetheless Greek. Though the spread of this type of decoration in the Aegean has not yet been precisely determined, it seems to appear first in the Cyclades, which were among the leading exporters of pottery throughout the century.[2]

As the material at the command of the potters grew and the volume of their production increased, the local variations within a common style became more evident. Plate 12 illustrates four examples, which are Ripe or Late Geometric work of common spirit but of different schools. These local manifestations I shall not consider at length lest our understanding of the main forces be confused. By all odds the greatest type was the Attic, and here we can penetrate most deeply into the new currents.

The potters of Athens had earlier stood in the van of Proto-geometric and Geometric development. Shortly after 800 their eminence became greater than at any time before the evolution of the black-figured style in the sixth century. The ancestral strength of Attic workshops gave the eighth-century craftsmen a sure foundation; but to explain their force and daring one must also keep in mind the evidences of prosperity and foreign contacts visible in Attic tombs of the period. The artists themselves were evidently in touch with all that was happening throughout the Aegean; in this *relatively* cosmopolitan center they felt confident enough both of their abilities and of social support to launch out on a truly great step, the drawing of human and animal figures not merely as decorative elements but as real pictures.[3]

[2] N. M. Kontoleon, *Arch. eph.* 1945–47, 1–21, presents powerful reasons for broadening the range of Cycladic exports in the eighth century, as against Rodney S. Young, *Late Geometric Graves and a Seventh Century Well in the Agora* (*Hesperia*, Suppl. II: Athens, 1939), 222, on Attic Geometric exports. He may have over-emphasized the Cycladic sources, though Brock, *Fortetsa*, 189–91, ac-cepts his principles. In any event Cycladic pottery was much indebted to Attic impulses, which extended across the Aegean to Miletus (*Istanbuler Mitteilungen*, VII [1957], 122–23).

[3] Pictures: Walter Hahland, "Zu den Anfängen der attischen Malerei," *Corolla Curtius* (Stuttgart, 1937), 121–31; Kraiker, *Neue Beiträge*, 36–47, and *Gnomon*, XXIV (1952), 451–53; Kübler, *Keramaikos*, V. 1, 135–36,

This development was a relatively sudden one. Virtual picture spaces had been created on Strong Geometric vases, but commonly potters had been inclined only to put abstract motifs within their windows. Now, on the smaller Attic vases, appear simple scenes, such as two horses facing a tripod of victory, a man holding the reins of two horses, lions devouring domestic animals, and the like. Such pictures are as starkly bare, as concentrated in their action, and as generalized in meaning as the similes of the *Iliad*.[4] To adorn the noble grave mounds by the Dipylon gate of later Athens, potters also fashioned great amphoras and craters, which stand five to six feet high. These works not only manifest the technical skill and bravado of their makers but also, in their rich combination of ornament and more extensive pictures, are the first easily recognizable testimony to the aesthetic genius of Greek civilization.

The earliest of the famous Dipylon vases, the amphora of Athens (CC 200), is also the greatest; in its harmonious majesty it quietly dominates all other eighth-century vases. This must be placed well before 750. Contemporary with it are several of the fragments in the Louvre and elsewhere; shortly thereafter come the Hirschfeld crater (CC 214) of Athens and the crater of the Metropolitan Museum.

In shape and in over-all composition of the decoration, the

175–80 (bibliography, 175 n. 163), who overemphasizes metalwork origins; Matz, *GGK*, I, 58–67; Schweitzer, *AM*, XLIII (1918), 127–52, who overstresses Eastern origins; Weickert, *Neue Beiträge*, 27–35. The earliest Attic Geometric pictures are the ship (Plate 9a), a land and sea battle (Kraiker, *Neue Beiträge*, pl. 2); a horse between two warriors (*Kerameikos*, V. 1, pl. 111 and 141), a chariot race (Athens NM 806; *AJA*, XLIV [1940], pl. 25).

Dipylon vases: François Chamoux, "L'école de la grande amphore du Dipylon: étude sur la céramique géométrique à l'époque de l'"Iliade,'" *RA*, 6. ser. XXIII (1945), 55–97; Kübler, *Kerameikos*, V. 1, 172–73, who tries to lower their date; Emil

Kunze, "Bruchstücke attischer Grabkratere," *Neue Beiträge*, 48–58; Gerda Nottbohm, "Der Meister der grossen Dipylon-Amphora in Athen," *JdI*, LVIII (1943), 1–31, who goes so far as to acclaim the potter of CC 200 as the first great comprehensible personality in European art, more influential than any other except Giotto; Frederik Poulsen, *Die Dipylongräber und die Dipylonvasen* (Leipzig, 1905). The Louvre fragments are now well reproduced by François Villard, *CVA France* XVIII (= *Louvre* XI, 1954); see his essay, "Une amphore géométrique au musée du Louvre," *Monuments Piot*, XLIX (1957), 17–40.
[4] Roland Hampe, *Die Gleichnisse Homers und die Bildkunst seiner Zeit* (Tübingen, 1952), esp. 23–26.

Dipylon amphora (see Plate 11) stands directly in the main stream of Greek artistic principles of Geometric days; from such Protogeometric masterpieces as K. 1073 (Plate 5b) a clear, unbroken line leads directly to this work. Yet how much more developed and more supple was its artist's imagination! The impression which one first derives from the amphora is one of simple, dignified formality; on closer study the surface becomes a mass of many interrelated bands, which are separated by the three lines customary at this time. Though the patterns are simple and are repeated, the subtle variations in width of the bands and the balancing of motifs produce a varied rhythm. The potter has avoided monotony as successfully as did Homer in manipulating the flow of his simple hexameters.

The new spirit which distinguishes Dipylon work appears in the rows of deer and goats on the neck and especially in the picture to which these draw one's eyes. Inserted in a field on the shoulder is a scene of death. The corpse lies on its funeral couch (*prothesis*) with coverlet displayed above; wife and child stand at the head, friends and relatives raise their hands in grief while musicians accompany their wails, and the warriors are at the far left, poised to take away the bier (*ekphora*). The artistic quality of the event is well suggested by a great modern student of Attic art:

> Viewed as a rendering of life it is a solemn scene reduced to its barest terms, terms telling from their very bareness. Here is an artist who has not attempted more than he could exactly perform; an art not childish, but planned and austere.[5]

Within the next generation the interest of Attic painters in figured scenes grew tremendously. On the New York crater the *prothesis* scene has expanded greatly in breadth and claims almost all the viewer's attention; below it a procession of chariots

[5] J. D. Beazley, *The Development of Attic Black-figure* (Berkeley, 1951), 3; cf. Hampe, *Die Gleichnisse Homers*, 24–26; Kahane, *AJA*, XLIV (1940), 476. Funeral ceremonies: John Boardman, "Painted Funerary Plaques and Some Remarks on Prothesis," *BSA*, L (1955), 51–66; Eugen Reiner, *Die rituellen Totenklage der Griechen* (Stuttgart, 1938); Willy Zschietzschmann, "Die Darstellungen der Prothesis in der griechischen Kunst," *AM*, LIII (1928), 17–47.

and warriors, armed with great shields and spears, marches in solemn memory of the funeral cortège and the accompanying games. On other vases, known only through fragments, scenes of battle by land and sea hark back to events of life.

In this work the potters were still so reluctant to distinguish their pictures sharply from the decorative elements that they filled the vacant spaces within their scenes with simple ornaments.[6] The drawing, too, is schematic to modern eyes. Chariots, horses, even human bodies are visualized not as a whole but as a combination of parts. The torso is a triangle descending to a narrow waist, below which are pronounced, triangular hips; the legs and arms are elongated; the painters provided for the heads a very scanty equipment of rudimentary noses, eyes, and other features (see Plate 10). Yet, however primitive the detailing drawing may be in comparison to Oriental work, there is no evidence of any Oriental prototypes or influences; the Dipylon pictures are a vehicle of native meditation.

The unifying factor in these scenes—for they are unified— is the underlying sense of action. On Dipylon vases, as in the *Iliad,* man is because he acts, and the deed is shown, not the human being as such.[7] Within the framework of Geometric decoration, born purely of the mind, occur now scenes born ultimately of nature, the first conscious artistic reflections of life in Greek civilization. The battle scenes are as violent in their action as are Homeric duels, and dying men are seized in the very moment of their death; note, for instance, the figure in the lower right corner of the fragment Louvre A 531 (Plate 10a). The scenes of *prothesis,* though outwardly static, convey with dramatic impact the emotions of the living at the point when the funeral procession of the dead must begin toward the eternal grave. If one reflects upon the few simple pictures of ninth-

---

[6] Kahane, *AJA,* XLIV (1940), 472. Kraiker, *Neue Beiträge,* 41, however, properly notes that the figures are not woven into the ornament as in Celtic and other styles but stand beside the ornament.

[7] Chamoux, *RA,* XXIII (1945), 80–82, 87–94, who gives detailed parallels of Homeric and Dipylon battle scenes;

Kraiker, *Neue Beiträge,* 42–44; Émile Cahen, "Sur la représentation de la figure humaine dans la céramique dipylienne et dans l'art égéen," *REG,* XXXVIII (1925), 1–15; Bruno Snell, *The Discovery of the Mind: The Greek Origins of European Thought* (Oxford, 1953), 6–20; Webster, *From Mycenae to Homer,* 202–07.

century Attic vases, such as the skyphos with ship (Plate 9a),
the skill and clarity with which potters now grouped simple
elements into complicated scenes is as impressive in its sudden appearance as is the contemporary consolidation of the
Iliad.

The extent to which these scenes are efforts at literal representations of actual events has been much debated. One must,
I think, conclude that on the Dipylon vases, as in the *Iliad*,
events are "indefinite as to time and space, and general in
their narrative content."[8] Nor did the painters look at their
world in specifically mythical terms. The epic and mythical
traditions, which had already long been in existence, were
seized and used to give a heroic cast to the pictures, but representations of definite mythological scenes are not certain in
any art medium until about the close of the eighth century. The
present development, however, gave to artists the ability to
depict specific events when they came to desire to do so. That
desire was to be one of the great gifts of the age of revolution to
Greek civilization; the Dipylon pictures could scarcely be other
than typical portrayals of life and death.

To consider these vases primarily from the artists' point of
view is not quite enough to explain the bold, virtually deliberate
experiment in figured scenes. The potters themselves must have
been technically ready for this step; and this readiness may be
proved from the developments in Strong Geometric ware. Yet we
must also look outside the realm of artistic impulses. The society
of the age evidently was prepared to condone, even to foster
novelty. If potters were to move so swiftly beyond old traditions,
they needed great spiritual support; the artists who spent so
long on the minute decoration of individual masterpieces required considerable material aid. The upper classes of the early
eighth century were only now moving toward a truly aristocratic
outlook—a great development for the future, which will be
treated in Chapter 9—but both the Dipylon vases and the
Iliad make manifest their pride in valor by land and sea

[8] George M. A. Hanfmann, "Narra-
tion in Greek Art," *AJA*, LXI (1957),
71–78 (bibliography, p. 72 n. 5);
Kraiker, *Neue Beiträge*, 45; Webster,
From Mycenae to Homer, 168–77. On
representations of myth in art, see
Chap. 8, n. 1 (p. 261).

and that family dignity which must be duly expressed upon a noble's death.[9] The contemporary tombs of the well-to-do are often richly equipped with vases, objects of bronze, and even at times with gold, ivory, and faïence; the pomp of funeral is well described in the burial of Patroclus and is illustrated with care by these very vases.

That delight in horses, too, which had already marked Strong Geometric pottery became far more evident in the early eighth century over much of Greece, as in the clay figures of horses atop Attic pyxides, the increasing abundance of horses on Argive pottery, and the bronze figurines of horses set on tripod-caldrons at Olympia. The intensely competitive, or agonal, spirit which was later to be a pronounced aspect of the Greek aristocratic outlook is already visible in these representations, in the dedications of actual tripods of bronze at Olympia and elsewhere, and in the epic poetry. While the chronological tradition which sets the first Olympic games at 776 has no value in itself, it has placed the event in the right period.[1]

Having gone so far through outside encouragement and internal artistic spirit, the Attic potters had shot their bolt; or rather, perhaps, their aristocratic patrons became less inclined to commission great funeral vases in the closing decades of the eighth century. But it is also true that the artists of Athens had developed their form of Geometric style to a point beyond which it was difficult to go but which was equally difficult to abandon. By yielding to an urge for representation they had introduced a force which was to produce mighty results when linked to conscious efforts to depict the specific events of myth.

[9] Kraiker, *Neue Beiträge*, 44, 47; Young, *Late Geometric Graves*, 56–57, 229–30, whose remarks extend too widely to Geometric work as a whole. The important problem of the emergence of the Greek aristocratic outlook is considered below in Chap. 9.
[1] Horse and tripod: *BSA*, XXXV (1934–35), pl. 25. 2, Empedocles collection. Four-horse chariots were new at this time: *Iliad* XI. 699 ff., VIII. 185; *Odyssey* XIII. 81; Athens NM 810; Agora P 4990 (three-horse). Agonal spirit: Victor Ehrenberg, *Ost*

und West (Brünn, 1935), 63–96. Games: Julius Jüthner, "Herkunft und Grundlagen der griechischen Nationalspiele," *Die Antike*, XV (1939), 231–64; above, Chap. 2, n. 4 (p. 67). Benton, *BSA*, XXXV (1934–35), 114–15, connects the decline in use of tripods with Phlegon's statement, *Fragmenta historicorum Graecorum*, ed. C. Müller, III (Paris, 1849), 602–04, that crowns were first given at Olympia in 748 B.C., but Willemsen's arrangement, *Dreifusskessel*, will not altogether support this argument.

Immediately, however, this new element clashed severely
with the abstract, decorative tradition of the pure Geometric
style. At the mid-century mark Attic pottery began to display
signs of stress. It had taken up the new, liberalizing forces of
Oriental and local origin perhaps more freely than had any other
Aegean fabric; but now there appeared increasing rigidity, stiffness, even archaism in decoration. Vase forms, often tending
to elongation, became harsh; the human figures stretched out
likewise and lost their sense of import.[2] That this was a general
aesthetic problem in Athens by 750 is attested by the same loss
of volume and life, the same tendency to reproduce stiff formulas, in the gold bands made by Attic smiths at this time.

Artists outside Athens had not developed their Geometric
inheritance so far, and in this very backwardness were perhaps
more easily able to modify their styles. By 750 potters in the Cyclades, on Crete, and especially at Corinth were also experi-
menting with freer forms of decoration, still largely Geometric
in spirit but also at times including figured scenes.[3] Soon, in the
later decades of the century, came from these roots the great
revolution of Orientalizing pottery, which was to overpass the
bonds of the Geometric inheritance. Though Attica lingered
behind in this development, the artists who had created the
Dipylon vases had shown what heights the old tradition could
reach ere it came to an end.

EPIC AND MYTH

A NOTHER great source for the early eighth century is the
circle of epic, which was now being cast in its lasting mold; with

[2] Kübler, *Kerameikos*, V. 1, 135–36,
163–67, 178; Matz, *GGK*, I, 48; Ohly,
Griechische Goldbleche, 96–118, who
dates some of the gold work too early.
[3] Corinthian scenes: Delphi inv.
6401–2, a large crater with human
beings in chariots (P. Amandry, *BCH*,
LXII [1938], 317–20); the famous
ship vase from Thebes is rather late.

Samian: prothesis scene (Technau,
AM, LIV [1929], pl. II). Argive:
horses (*BCH*, LXXVII [1953], fig.
50). Cretan: prothesis scene (Brock,
Fortetsa, 36 n. 339); siren from Prai-
sos (Levi, *AJA*, XLIX [1945], 280–
93; cf. *Annuario*, X–XII [1927–29],
597–604).

this I shall place for my purposes its country cousin, myth. When the historian approaches the *Iliad*, the first great monument of Greek literature, he may at first sigh in relief. Aegean civilization was growing vocal; thenceforth an increasing body of literature will liberate us from entire reliance on the mute testimony of physical objects. Very soon, however, the historical student must realize that the epic is surrounded by a range of violent controversies almost without equal. The epic war which eddied to and fro on the plains of Scamander lasted only ten years; the modern battles of Homeric scholarship were not new in the days of F. A. Wolf's *Prolegomena ad Homerum* (1795) and rage on, far from decision. Whatever any expert says today about epic or myth has been said before, and has been scornfully rejected by scholars who think otherwise.[4]

My concern with these materials is primarily to see if we can place them within a specific environment and so use them as historical sources. In the Homeric field the historian must pay proper attention to the findings of epic specialists, but his own discussion cannot hope to review their many answers in detail. Each man will read the epic for himself and, having framed his views, needs to suggest principally the main grounds for his solutions. The main articles of my own belief are that the Homeric epic and myth cannot safely be used to restore a specific picture of events for any epoch, Mycenaean or otherwise; that they, nevertheless, do throw general light on the main characteristics of the Greek outlook, and for this end are among our most precious sources; that the evidence of the epic, in particular, bears best on the early eighth century. Like Ripe Geometric pottery, the *Iliad* represents a culmination of native evolution through the Dark ages.

Many grounds will force the historian to be careful in his assessment of epic and myth. This material is, in the first place,

[4] Introductions to earlier Homeric scholarship may be found in Paul Cauer, *Grundfragen der Homerkritik* (3d ed.; Leipzig, 1923); A. Delatte and A. Severyns, *L'Antiquité classique*, II (1933), 379–412; Nilsson, *Homer and Mycenae*, 1–51. On recent developments, see E. R. Dodds, "Homer," in Maurice Platnauer, *Fifty Years of Classical Scholarship* (Oxford, 1954); Dorothea Gray, in Myres, *Homer and His Critics*, 252–93; Albin Lesky, *Die Homerforschung in der Gegenwart* (Vienna, 1952); Wolfgang Schadewaldt, *Von Homers Welt und Werk* (2d ed.; Stuttgart, 1951).

not precisely datable. Neither solid external tradition nor clear internal references suggest a date for the *Iliad;* its author, Homer, is as impersonal as the creator of a Dipylon vase. For the vases, at least, we can usually determine a place of manufacture, and ceramic materials can be arranged in chronological sequence. The *Iliad* stands alone, save for its mighty sibling, the *Odyssey;* scholars have placed it by persuasive arguments anywhere from the twelfth to the sixth century B.C. Both bounds are generally, and properly, judged to be much too extreme; but, historically speaking, we can feel reasonably sure only that the *Iliad* had assumed its enduring form before 700 B.C. While some small bits were added thereafter, the poem was written down soon enough to prevent serious distortions; the epic tradition, moreover, ceased to be really productive by the middle of the seventh century.[5]

The situation with respect to myth is even worse. One may rightly feel, I think, that the main core of Greek mythology had also been well set by the eighth century.[6] References to some of its tales in the *Iliad* take them as well known, and Late Geometric vases and metal work began to draw from the mythological repertoire by the end of the century. Yet no canonical form of expression existed to safeguard the myth from later adaptation. Myth-making was a simpler, more widely spread art than the complex epic technique, which was entrusted largely to specialized bards; and so the creation of myths continued far

---

[5] Recent arguments, which do not seem sound, have been made that the epic was written from the outset; see Sir Maurice Bowra, *Homer and His Forerunners* (Edinburgh, 1955); Albin Lesky, "Mündlichkeit und Schriftlichkeit im homerischen Epos," *Festschrift für Dietrich Kralik* (Horn, 1954), 1–9; Wade-Gery, *The Poet of the Iliad;* Webster, *From Mycenae to Homer,* 272–73. Miss Lorimer's statement, *Homer and the Monuments,* 526, seems sensible.

The effort, on the other hand, to delay written exemplars to the era of Pisistratus is equally extreme; see most

recently Reinhold Merkelbach, "Die pisistratische Redaktion der homerischen Gedichte," *RM,* XCV (1952), 23–47; and the survey by Whitman, *Homer and the Heroic Tradition,* 65–83.

[6] See generally Radermacher, *Mythos und Sage bei den Griechen;* Carl Robert, *Die griechische Heldensage,* 3 vols. (Berlin, 1920–26); more briefly, Nilsson, *GGR,* I, 17–35. Hans Herter, "Theseus der Athener," *RM,* LXXXVIII (1939), 244–86, 289–326, gives a well-documented study of changes in the myth of Theseus; see also Chap. 4, n. 1 (p. 110).

longer. Virtually all extensive bodies of Greek myth underwent rationalization and systematization throughout the seventh and sixth centuries; and much which is to be found in modern manuals of mythology goes back in its details only to classic, Hellenistic, or even Roman times.

Mythology was, after all, a way of reflecting life. In spinning their tales the Greeks amused themselves, and this aspect must not be forgotten when we set about wresting deep meanings from mythological stories. Myths served, too, as a release for the tensions and problems of human fallibility, as an explanation of natural (and unnatural) phenomena, as a commemoration of great events, as a crystallization of religious views. Greek mythology was always in process of creation until more abstract types of thought became dominant—or pushed myth-making down below the surface of our ken. While we can detect some parts of the later adaptations, we can rarely be sure how much of the store already present in 700 was at that time relatively new, a reflection of the broadening of view and intensification of intellectual activity in the eighth century, and how much comes from earlier days.

Epic and myth, thus, are not easily dated. Nor, in the second place, were they designed to be history, even though later Greeks took them as factually truthful. Efforts to draw historical events out of such myths as those of Bellerophon, Heracles, Theseus, or the Seven against Thebes, to name only a few which have been so analyzed, are hopeless practically and unsound logically, as I have noted in preceding chapters. The tellers of myth were not endowed with the critical qualities of a modern scholar; they were not interested in history; and in any case there was no history, in the modern sense, in the Dark ages. If we treat the deeds of Theseus as deliberately symbolic versions of specific historical conflicts between Athens and Megara and so on, we are taking fairyland as real. Any interpretation of the *Iliad* must also keep in mind the artistic requirements of the plot and the literary conventions of epic technique, for these factors seriously affected the treatment of social relationships and political institutions, let alone the course of the Trojan war itself. The historian cannot expect to disentangle specific events from epic passages; nor may he safely press too great meaning out of single phrases.

Epic and myth alike, nevertheless, were framed by human beings, and the product reflects contemporary views on the basic relationships among men and their attitudes toward the physical world and divine forces. The underlying outlook in this material has an interesting uniformity. On the details men's beliefs did change, and the older explanations are occasionally embodied like fossils in the myths; on major points no evidence appears for sharp breaks in early Greek thinking. From a modern point of view the mythical and epic interpretation of the world and of man often seems primitive; but any comparison of the myth and epics of Mesopotamia with those of Greece will show how remarkable was the civilization, basically rational, human, and confident, which had developed in the Aegean world by the eighth century.

Since the Dark ages were an epoch of slow alteration, we may postulate that the evidence of epic and myth is generally applicable to the whole period. As we have already seen, Ripe Geometric pottery was the highest expression of a spirit which was common to earlier phases as well. Yet in important respects, I believe, the epic bears most specifically on the early eighth century. Implicit in this opinion is my judgment that the *Iliad* assumed the form in which we have it just before the mid-mark of this century. The tale of the wrath of Achilles was composed as a unit by one great poet, who poured into his lines their dramatic drive and impact.[7] This author most probably lived on the coast of Asia Minor and must be placed almost two generations before the poet of the *Odyssey*, which will accordingly appear only incidentally in this chapter. The marked differences in tone and outlook of the two epics, which support this distinction, will be considered in Chapter 8.

In general, Homer was no freer to invent absolutely afresh than were the Geometric potters of Athens, and the story he cast

---

[7] Therein lay his chief originality, as is noted by Frederick M. Combellack, "Contemporary Unitarians and Homeric Originality," *AJP*, LXXI (1950), 337–64; and Whitman, *Homer and the Heroic Tradition*.

in its final shape was undoubtedly long in creation.[8] But for neither the *Iliad* nor the *Odyssey* can we hope to dissect levels of development of the story and of characterizations solely on the basis of internal evidence, even if logically we may assume that such development did underlie their present form. Those flaws of composition and the inconsistencies which modern students use toward the end of determining layers of accretion are highly subjective discoveries, if not at times the fruit of modern over-subtlety. Comparative studies of the Greek and other, more modern epic techniques throw some light on the probable mode of evolution of the Homeric oral style; but I think that one may gain as much illumination on the epic use of stock phrases and on its verse forms from examining the stiff principles of composition in Geometric vases. That a man could take inherited motifs and group them suddenly in a masterpiece has already been shown in the great Attic amphora CC 200.

Detailed arguments to support the date which I have just given can be drawn from archaeological parallels, topographic references, and the level of epic social and political development, though on the latter point we must be careful not to argue in a circle (inasmuch as our principal evidence here comes from the epic itself).[9] The most conclusive grounds,

---

[8] Limits to epic freedom: Hermann Fränkel, *Dichtung und Philosophie des frühen Griechentums* (New York, 1951), 64–75; A. W. Gomme, *The Greek Attitude to Poetry and History* (Berkeley, 1954), 1–48; Page, *History and the Homeric Iliad*, 223, 230, who suggests that between four fifths and nine tenths of the *Iliad* is made up of "ready-made phrases, remembered from the past, not created for the present." Nilsson, *Homer and Mycenae*, 272 ff., suggests somewhat greater liberty. The efforts to analyze the *Iliad* into layers have been resumed since World War II, as in Peter von der Mühll, *Kritisches Hypomnema zur Ilias* (Basel, 1952), which follows many earlier dissections—e.g., Paul Mazon, *Introduction à l'Iliade* (Paris,

1942). Contra, J. A. Scott, *The Unity of Homer* (Berkeley, 1921).
[9] Eighth-century date: Gomme, *Greek Attitude*, 41–42; Lesky, *Anzeiger für die Altertumswissenschaft*, V (1952), 7; Lorimer, *Homer and the Monuments*, 464–67; Wade-Gery, *Poet of the Iliad*. References to arguments for other dates may be found therein, and in the works listed in n. 4 (p. 157).

Artistic parallels: Chamoux, *RA*, XXIII (1945), 87–97; Karo, *Greek Personality*, 35–36; Matz, *GGK*, I, 98–101; J. L. Myres, "Homeric Art," *BSA*, XLV (1950), 229–60; Webster, *From Mycenae to Homer*, 206–07, 259–67, and "Homer and Attic Geometric Vases," *BSA*, L (1955), 38–50; Whitman, *Homer and the Heroic Tradition*, 87–101, 249–84.

however, are the close relations in style and outlook between Ripe Geometric pottery and the *Iliad*. As literature, the latter is far more explicit than is the pottery of the era, which must appear at first sight primitive and backward to the reader of Homer; and yet the principles of composition of this "ordered structure of manifold verse" accord best with the techniques of Ripe Geometric potters, both in the manipulation of the hexameter, in the construction of scenes, and in the basic structure of the whole poem.[1] So, too, as has often been pointed out, the flavor of the similes of the *Iliad* and at many points their very subjects, such as the frequent illumination of the wildness of nature by the lion theme, have their best parallel in Ripe Geometric art.

Underneath both art and literature lies the same spirit: an ability to create mighty works, a drive to do so, and an ultimate confidence in life.[2] This spirit, one may feel, is a reflection of the early eighth century, when the old framework of Greek civilization was being enlivened but still stood firm as a secure support for creative activity; when the leading classes of Greece were willing, even eager, to support artists and poets in their mighty summations of ancestral inheritances.

If one thus sets the date of the *Iliad*, and by extension reckons that myth then had begun to come into focus, this conclusion warrants our employment of the evidence only to illuminate the general outlook of the period in question. The poet of the *Iliad* could not escape reflecting the temper of his milieu, yet any single part of his materials may have been of much earlier origin. In establishing the tempo of change across the Dark ages, the historian must advance from the physical evidence, far more surely to be dated, and can use the hints of epic and myth solely insofar as they fit into the solid framework already at hand. To proceed primarily from Homer, or to label the early Greek centuries the "Homeric Age," is to narrow our vision far too much.

---

[1] Democritus, fragment 21. Homeric hexameter: Hermann Fränkel, *Wege und Formen frühgriechischen Denkens* (Munich, 1955), 100–56, and more briefly, *Dichtung und Philosophie*, 39–43; Lorimer, *Homer and the Monuments*, 455–61.

[2] The frequent assertion that Homer takes the present world as decadent must be treated with reserve; cf. Max Treu, *Von Homer zur Lyrik* (Munich, 1955), 30.

The *Iliad,* moreover, was created in a relatively timeless
era, in which past, present, and future were not rigidly separated.[3] Cultural distinctions between Greek and non-Greek
were still in process of creation, as I noted in considering the territorial consolidation of the Aegean in Chapter 4; internally,
political divisions were still amorphous. Homer does not reflect
sharply the attitudes of any specific area or of any local variant
of Greek culture. If his product can be compared best to
Attic pottery, this does not mean he was an Athenian or that
his epic tradition stemmed primarily from Attica. While the
potters of Athens were the greatest of their age in exploring the
common artistic inheritance of the Geometric Aegean, another
area might nurture the greatest poet.[4] Homer, again, knew well
that change had occurred, but in his aim of creating a generalized story cast his work in an archaic vein.

Any assertion that the epic and myth reflect first the spirit
of the early eighth century and then, more generally, the pattern
of life in the Dark ages must cope with the very frequent efforts
to assign this material either to Mycenaean origins or to Oriental
roots. On the former point, we simply do not know to what extent Greek myth was derived from Mycenaean sources. Enthu-
siastic efforts have been made to discover representations of
Europa on the bull and of other mythical figures on Mycenaean
seals, jewels, and vases, but more sober analysts have had little
trouble in disproving any equations which have been offered.[5]

[3] F. M. Cornford, *From Religion to
Philosophy: A Study in the Origins of
Western Speculation* (London, 1912),
140: "The first notion of causality is,
thus, not temporal but static, simul-
taneous, and spatial." The generalized
character of the Dipylon vases stems
from the same sense. See also Fränkel,
Wege und Formen, 1–22; Treu, *Von
Homer zur Lyrik,* 123, 224; Thad-
daeus Zielinski, "Die Behandlung
gleichzeitiger Ereignisse im antiken
Epos," *Philologus,* Suppl. VIII (1901),
407–49. The sense of time, however,
is not entirely absent: *Iliad* V. 303–04;
VII. 87–91.
[4] Rohde, *Psyche,* 94–95, saw this; but
Whitman, *Homer and the Heroic Tra-*

dition, builds much of his picture of
Homer on the contrary view.
[5] Mycenaean myth: Nilsson, *Minoan-
Mycenaean Religion,* 34–40, and *The
Mycenaean Origin of Greek Mythol-
ogy* (Berkeley, 1932); Persson, *New
Tombs at Dendra;* Webster, *From
Mycenae to Homer,* 43–63, 114–27.
Skepticism: Luisa Banti, "Myth in Pre-
classical Art," *AJA,* LVIII (1954),
307–10; Doro Levi, "La Dea micenea
a cavallo," *Studies to D. M. Robinson,*
I, 108–25, on the so-called Europa;
Emily Townsend Vermeule, "Mythol-
ogy in Mycenaean Art," *Classical Journal,* LIV (1954), 97–108. Mycenaean
chariot craters (see Plate 4a):
Sara A. Immerwahr and V. Kara-

Though men in the Mycenaean era may well have had myths, they cannot now be identified.

In recent years, as interest in Mycenaean development has risen greatly, Homeric scholars have asserted an extensive Mycenaean survival in the epic tradition. While one may sympathize with their efforts to gallop down a fresh path, the results are not very convincing. With respect to physical objects mentioned in the epic poems, a few can be shown to have been Mycenaean, though these are far fewer than is often suggested —and the possibility of transmission of heirlooms must not be forgotten.[6] The more one learns from the Mycenaean tablets of the political, social, and economic organization of that earlier era the less comparable becomes the evidence of the Homeric epics on these subjects. The Homeric *basileus*, for instance, was not a Mycenaean *wanax*. If Agamemnon were leader of the allied force against Troy, his position in the epic derived not so much from a possible wide domination by the ruler of Mycenae before 1200 B.C. as from the requirements of the plot that the Greek army have a commander. In general the position of the epic *basileus* wavers between feebleness and a considerable authority. The former characteristic reflects that evolution of the Dark age which we examined in Chapter 4, as a result of which the chieftain was, apart from his necessary control in battle itself, a *primus inter pares;* the hints of greater power and self-assertion by "Zeus-nurtured" monarchs may well be not a vague memory of days when kings were great in Greece but a contemporary reflection of a temporary growth in royal power during the eighth century itself.

All in all, I should be much disinclined to postulate for the

---

georghis, *AJA*, LX (1956), 137–49; C. F. A. Schaeffer, "Sur un cratère mycénien de Ras Shamra," *BSA*, XXXVII (1936–37), 212–35; S. S. Weinberg, *Hesperia*, XVIII (1949), 156–57; Vassos Karageorghis, "Myth and Epic in Mycenaean Vase Painting," *AJA*, LXII (1958), 383–87.

[6] Physical objects: Chap. 2, n. 6 (p. 47). Kingship: Gunther Jachmann, "Das homerische Königtum," *Maia*,

n. s. VI (1953), 241–56, based on E. Bethe, "Troia, Mykene, Agamemnon und sein Grosskönigtum," *RM*, LXXX (1931), 218–36. The Olympian state of the gods does not reflect any early political domination by Mycenae. For the conventional picture of Agamemnon, cf. Nilsson, *Homer and Mycenae*, 238–39. The political developments of the eighth century are considered below, in Chap. 10.

Iliad any marked inheritance from as far back as the Mycenaean era either in substance of plot (save for the basic memory of an attack launched across the Aegean to Troy) or in epic spirit. What did survive perhaps from Mycenaean days was far more the aspect of techniques—i.e., the creation of the epic dialect, of the hexameter, or of stock formulas. Even here the age of invasions and the Dark ages probably caused changes the dimensions of which we cannot measure.

ORIENTAL LITERARY INFLUENCES

ANOTHER possible source for Greek epic and myth, which has gained a vogue in recent work, is the Orient. Our growing knowledge of Hittite, Hurrian, and Canaanite tales in the past few decades has led some students to construct an imposing picture of a common eastern Mediterranean stratum of poetic composition and mythical lore which produced eventually on the one side Homer and on the other the Old Testament.[7] This view strikes me as even more unlikely than the arguments of Mycenaean origins. Worse yet, its basic assumption must lead one into serious misunderstandings which can only obscure the tempo and sources of early Greek culture and the close relations between the achievements of the eighth century and of the Dark ages.

The possibility of literary or intellectual contacts between East and West from the late ninth century on does exist, for resumption of trade between the two areas had then begun. We must, indeed, go even further: in some few cases it can now

---

[7] Various aspects of this line of thought may be found in Charles Autran, *Homère et les origines sacerdotales de l'épopée grecque*, 3 vols. (Paris, 1938–44), and *L'Epopée indoue* (Paris, 1946); Franz Dirlmeier, "Homerisches Epos und Orient," *RM*, XCVIII (1955), 18–37; Cyrus H. Gordon, *Homer and Bible: The Origin and Character of East Mediterranean Lit-* erature (Ventnor, N. J., 1955), and *The World of the Old Testament* (Garden City, New York, 1958), 101–12; T. B. L. Webster, "Homer and Eastern Poetry," *Minos*, IV (1956), 104–16, and more fully in *From Mycenae to Homer*, 64–90; on its application to the *Odyssey*, see Chap. 8, n. 7 (p. 265).

be demonstrated that Greek myth, like Hebrew literature, did draw directly from the Oriental stock. The tale of the castration of Uranus by Kronos comes from a Hittite-Hurrian story in which Kumarbi treated Anu in similarly unpleasant fashion. The Song of Ullikummi, again, was the prototype of the battle between Typhon and Zeus, which the Hellenistic scholar Apollodorus still localized on Mount Casius, the scene of a much earlier Phoenician version.[8] In other instances Oriental monsters came into the Greek ken and were explained by the creation of myths.

Wherever the route of transmittal from the East can be tentatively identified, it runs via northern Syria—Phoenicia, not Asia Minor; the time of borrowing is thus far a difficult problem. The Aegean had had extensive contacts with the East in Mycenaean times, but at this time we do not know what kind of myth was prevalent in the Greek world. The facts, first, that many of the details in the myths just mentioned are common to East and West and, secondly, that these myths are not of a truly folk character are very difficult to explain if they were remembered orally for centuries on the Greek side but survived in writing in the Orient. Most, if not all, of this influence, one must feel, was a product of the renewed connections from the late ninth century onward. Some tales were taken over well before 700, but others thereafter; Greek mythology was not a static, closed body.

These occasional evidences of borrowing, in any case, do not justify a sweeping inference that all Greek mythology was drawn from the Orient. Even before the connection of the

[8] H. G. Güterbock, *Kumarbi: Mythen vom churritischen Kronos aus den hethitischen Fragmenten zusammengestellt, übersetzt und erklärt* (Zürich, 1946); "The Song of Ullikummi," *Journal of Cuneiform Studies,* V (1951), 135–69, and VI (1952), 8–42; "The Hittite Version of the Hurrian Kumarbi Myths: Oriental Forerunners of Hesiod," *AJA,* LII (1948), 123–34. See also R. D. Barnett, "The Epic of Kumarbi and the Theogony of Hesiod," *JHS,* LXV (1945), 100–01; Alfred Heubeck, "Mythologische Vorstellungen des alten Orients im archaischen Griechentum," *Gymnasium,* LXII (1955), 508–25; Albin Lesky, "Zum hethitischen und griechischen Mythos," *Eranos,* LII (1954), 8–17, and "Hethitische Texte und griechischer Mythos," *Anzeiger der Oesterreichischen Akademie,* LXXXVII (1950), 137–59. Oriental monsters: see Chap. 8.

Kronos and Kumarbi stories was known, students had been struck by the un-Hellenic savagery of this particular myth, which, we can now see, was somehow introduced virtually intact from a quite different system. In other examples the Oriental tales were largely stripped of the grotesque and magical and were cast in more human terms by the Greeks.

As far as the epic is concerned, it is possible that some parallel turns of phrase in Homer and Oriental literature were adapted by the Greek epic tradition, either in the Mycenaean age or in the last stages of the Dark ages; yet many of the parallels which have been so triumphantly paraded are no more than the incidental products of similar social and economic backgrounds or of roughly comparable levels of thought in the two areas. To be blunt about this matter, it is fantastic to jump from the level of trivial similarities to assert that the Greek epic was based either in technique or in content upon an Oriental background. The general spirit of the Homeric poems is one of our earliest, clearest demonstrations of the rise of the Greek view of life, an independent creation of a virtually self-contained Aegean enclave.

This important point is evident if one compares the epic of Gilgamesh, king of Uruk, with the epic of Achilles. The two are superficially similar in outlook, for they were born of man's musing on his nature; fundamentally, they are products of entirely different civilizations. The story of Gilgamesh was Sumerian in root but was more fully formulated about 2000 B.C. into a truly mighty reflection upon the nature of man, who strives but in the end must die:

> Who, my friend [says Gilgamesh] is superior to death?
> Only the gods live forever under the sun.
> As for mankind, numbered are their days;
> Whatever they achieve is but the wind! [9]

[9] Trans. E. A. Speiser, *Ancient Near Eastern Texts Relating to the Old Testament,* ed. James B. Pritchard (Princeton, 1950), 79. I cannot follow Webster, *Minos,* IV (1956), 114, when he observes: "It is difficult to believe that the mourning for Patroclos is not influenced by the mourning for Enkidu," or argues (*From Mycenae to Homer,* 82, 120) that the figure of Achilles was recast to bring him into agreement with that of Gilgamesh.

The epic is, as well, a paean to friendship, exemplified by the hero Gilgamesh and his friend Enkidu, and an explanation of the meaning of civilization. Gilgamesh, though harsh, protects his city against the violent forces of nature, which are symbolized in the monsters he kills. Like the *Iliad*, the Babylonian epic moves on two planes, the divine and the human, and of the two levels the divine is the one which decides what is to happen.

But in many respects the tale of Homer is vastly different from that of the Babylonian poets. The earlier story is balder and has less artistic unity; it is more naïve, far earthier; monsters are prominent in its plot; its appeal is rather to emotion and to passion than to reason, as is that of the *Iliad* in the end. Above all, the epic of Gilgamesh throws light on humanity, but not on individual human beings; and its tone is a far blacker one. The heroes of the *Iliad* know as well as does Gilgamesh that the gods made the world and that men must die, but while alive they throb with delight in the world about them. In reflection of the growing pride and individualism of the upper classes who were slowly becoming self-conscious in the eighth century, Homer fashioned a dream of emancipated heroes, competing for honor in the eyes of men, which was thenceforth to be a polar companion to the equally strong Greek feeling for cooperation of the group. From Gilgamesh and Enkidu there stems no fructifying development of man's understanding of his own nature; from the men of the *Iliad* comes a steadily onrushing exploration of the qualities of mankind, the fruits of which we shall consider in the age of revolution.

Only a great poet could have infused the *Iliad* with its majestic interpretation of life which leads inevitably to death and yet is the stage of man's glory. Achilles knows beforehand that if he goes to Troy he will die there, but his honor drives him to go, once his mother's effort to hide him fails. He knows full well that the gods determine all, but he is free to act as he wills. When the goddess Athena descends to calm him, she must begin carefully: "I came to check your passions, if you will listen"; and Achilles reluctantly but freely decides: "I must observe your bidding, goddess, angry though I am indeed. It is better so. What the gods command you, do, then the gods will listen to *you."* [1] Here the ultimate dominance of reason, though forced to strive with elemental passion, stands sharply defined. In the *Iliad* as a whole the basic differences between Greek (and Western) civilization and the Babylonian view of life cannot be mistaken.

The greatest debt of Greece to the East in literary matters was its borrowing of the alphabet. This, like much else which the Aegean was to take from the Orient, was a technical device, but its literary importance was great. The fixing and amplification of the major myths was much assisted by the appearance of a Greek script, and by the seventh century efforts to systematize aspects of the material were well under way in the Hesiodic *Theogony* and *Eoiae*. So, too, the preservation of the epics in a relatively unaltered state must be due to the fact that they could be written down very soon after their consolidation.

While the Phoenician origin of the Greek alphabet is clear both from the shape of its earliest letters and from the names given to them in Greek, the date, place, and reasons for the borrowing lie too far back to be entirely visible. The oldest remains of Greek writing are words incised or painted on Late Geometric vases and plaques from Attica (Mount Hymettos, the Agora, Dipylon, and Eleusis), Aegina, Ithaca, and Ischia, none of which can be dated before the two final decades of the eighth century.[2] Shortly thereafter appeared the first inscrip-

[1] *Iliad*. I. 206 ff.; cf. the analysis of Achilles in Whitman, *Homer and the Heroic Tradition*, 182–220.

[2] Attica: *Inscriptiones Graecae*,[2] I, 919 (Dipylon prize jug); C. W. Blegen, "Inscriptions on Geometric Pottery from Hymettos," *AJA*, XXXVIII (1934), 10–28; Young, *Late Geometric Graves*, 225–29, and "Excavation on Mount Hymettos, 1939," *AJA*, XLIV (1940), 1–9. Aegina: Boardman, *BSA*, XLIX (1954), 184–86. Ithaca: Robertson, *BSA*, XLIII (1948), 81–82. Ischia: G. Buchner and C. F. Russo, *Rendiconti della Accademia nazionale dei Lincei*, 8. ser. X (1955), pl. III. The Corinthian material published by Agnes N. Stillwell, "Eighth Century B.C. Inscriptions from Corinth," *AJA*, XXXVII (1933), 605–10, is on Late Geometric vases and could accordingly be put after 700, especially since the letters are well formed; see M. Lejeune, *REA*, XLVII (1945), 106–10. Wade-Gery, *Poet of the Iliad*, 66–67, gives a list of inscriptions on bronze and stone. For names on gravestones, which do not seem to go back of the sixth century, cf. Wiesner, *Grab und Jenseits*, 98; Pfuhl, *AM*, XXVIII (1903), 86–87, on Thera grave 111; Kübler, *Kerameikos*, VI. 1, 102 n. 49. See generally H. L. Lorimer, "Homer and the Art of Writing: A Sketch of Opinion between 1713 and 1939," *AJA*, LII (1948), 11–23.

tions on bronze (the Mantiklos statuette, Plate 20b) and on stone (probably the Perachora bases), but extensive use of writing to label mythical characters on pottery, to identify artists and dedicants, or to set in public view state acts came only slowly in the seventh century.

Unless one wishes to argue that writing in the Aegean prior to these testimonials was exclusively on papyrus and other perishable materials, the conclusion appears inevitable that the Greek alphabet was developed no earlier than some point in the eighth century. Such a date accords with our other evidence of firm Oriental contacts only at and after 800 B.C. On the other hand, the early appearance of Phrygian and Etruscan alphabets, derived from the Greek, makes it impossible to lower the Aegean development proper into the last decades of the century.[3]

From the internal history of the Greek alphabet, which underwent both expansion and contraction in its letters, and from the varying forms of the letters in different regions, modern opinion has inclined to agree that the most archaic Greek alphabet is that of Melos, Thera, and Crete; here or at Rhodes—areas which lay on the main route eastward—the origin of the alphabet is placed.[4] It is, however, surprising that no really early

[3] The earliest Etruscan alphabets must be placed just after 700 at the latest (Giulio Buonamici, *Epigrafia Etrusca* [Florence, 1932], 101–15); the Phrygian alphabet has been found on material before 700 (Rodney S. Young, *ILN*, May 17, 1958, 828). See also for the alphabets of Asia Minor, Akurgal, *Phrygische Kunst*, 106–07; Mazzarino, *Fra Oriente e Occidente*, 261–68.

Efforts to fix the date of the Greek alphabet by comparing Greek and Semitic letter forms must face the lack of established canons either in Phoenician or in early Greek scripts; such attempts have resulted in very divergent dates: B. L. Ullmann, "How Old Is the Greek Alphabet," *AJA*, XXXVIII (1934), 359–81, eleventh or twelfth century (as Wilamowitz and others); G. R. Driver, *Semitic Writ-*

ing: From Pictograph to Alphabet (rev. ed.; Oxford, 1954), 171 ff., midninth century; W. F. Albright, *Aegean and Near East*, 162, late ninth to mideighth centuries; Rhys Carpenter, *Folk Tale, Fiction and Saga in the Homeric Epics* (Berkeley, 1946), 10 ff., and elsewhere, about 700. Cf. David Diringer, *The Alphabet* (2d ed.; London, 1954), 451 ff.
[4] This is the "green" alphabet of Kirchhoff. Cyprus: Lorimer, *Homer and the Monuments*, 128–29. Al Mina or Tarsus: T. J. Dunbabin, *The Greeks and their Eastern Neighbours* (London, 1957), 61. Rhodes: Carpenter, *AJA*, XXXVII (1933), 27–29; L. B. Holland, *AJA*, XLV (1941), 356; Margit Falkner, "Zur Frühgeschichte des griechischen Alphabetes," *Frühgeschichte und Sprachwissenschaft* (Vienna, 1948), 110–33. Rhodes or

writing has thus far turned up in these regions, in contrast to Attica. The common combination of over-all Greek cultural uniformity and local variation is evident once more in Greek writing, for a cluster of local alphabets became well set during the eighth and seventh centuries in the Aegean world, from which they were transmitted to the colonies, to the Etruscans, and to Asia Minor.

The most important problem in connection with the alphabet is that which is least often considered: the reasons for its appearance. Students of the subject almost universally have assumed that the Greeks began to write because of commercial motives, although Greek traders, like simple merchants throughout history, got along very well without writing even in historic times.[5] The fact, again, that the Greeks felt compelled to write their vowels as well as their consonants rarely receives its proper emphasis. The inventors of the Greek alphabet remodeled drastically the symbols which they borrowed in order to create a supple tool for human expression. Though the alphabet was probably not created primarily to set down literature in permanent form, its wide use depended on its general utility, intellectual as well as economic, and on the rise of a relatively large aristocratic class. The very appearance of the Greek alphabet may be taken as a token of the increasing consciousness of Greek civilization in the eighth century; the rapid spread of writing is another testimonial to the quickening life of the era. Neither characteristic was Oriental in origin.

EARLY GREEK RELIGION

ONCE WRITING comes to be used to set down the thoughts of man, the historian has another lens with which to peer into the past. The testimony of physical remains and of written words

---

Crete: Demargne, *La Crète dédalique*, 148–49. Thera: Mazzarino, *Fra Oriente e Occidente*, 261–67. Crete: Margherita Guarducci, "La Culla dell'alfabeto greco," *Geras A. Keramo-*

poullou, 342–54.
[5] Johannes Hasebroek, *Trade and Politics in Ancient Greece* (London, 1933), 10–11, 89; cf. Wade-Gery, *Poet of the Iliad*, 13–14.

does not always accord perfectly, partly because one source is essentially objective and the other is more liable to subjective distortion by the writers, partly because actual objects cannot well express all the non-material sides of man's life. In any epoch, nonetheless, the same framework of basic concepts will dominate all its sources; from the point when the *Iliad* became essentially set, soon to be written down, we begin to be able to interrelate one type of evidence with the other.

It becomes possible, accordingly, to see some major aspects of early Greek religion. At all times humanity's views of its gods are an important subject for the historian. Religion reflects the innermost thoughts of men on their own nature, and its beliefs are the basic bond which holds together a society and enables its members to endure the travails of life. Yet discernment of these thoughts is a delicate task, for they are not always directly expressed; they will, moreover, vary widely from class to class, from area to area, and even among individuals who stand side by side. To discuss Greek religion purely on the basis of the very scanty physical testimony of the Dark ages is not only dangerous but also limited in rewards. Men must often feel, and feel deeply, religious beliefs which they do not know how to represent in physical form, or care to express thus. I have, therefore, postponed consideration of this significant side of early Greek civilization until we can draw on epic evidence.[6]

Both the physical and the written testimony shows, first, that historic Greek religion took its source from Mycenaean days, if not before. This information also suggests that at the end of the Mycenaean era and in the Dark ages changes occurred in religion which were as great as those already noted in aesthetic views and political organization. While the alterations within the Dark ages proper cannot be spelled out in detail, it is possible to detect that by the eighth century religious evolution had proceeded a great distance; by this date development begins to be more visible and more speedy. The

---

[6] In considering Greek religion, too, one must remember that it was not "revealed" at any one time in a sacred book and was not the preserve of a dedicated priesthood: Nilsson, *GGR*, I, 1–2. This work, together with his *Minoan-Mycenaean Religion*, gives basic references to the sources and to the great volume of modern literature.

*Dipylon amphora with
mourning scene and
deer inserted into Geo-
metric motifs (National
Museum 200, Athens).
Photograph courtesy
Friedrich Hewicker.*

PLATE 11 · *Height of the Geometric Spirit*

(a)

(b)

(c)

(d)

(*a*) *Corinthian amphora from Corinth (Corinth Museum). Photograph courtesy YDAP, Athens.*

(*b*) *Cycladic amphora from the Artemisium on Delos, in the last stages of Geometric style (Delos Museum). Photograph from Délos XV (Paris, 1939), pl. XVIII.*

(*c*) *Rhodian oenochoe from Delos (Delos Museum). Photograph from Délos XV, pl. XLVI.*

(*d*) *Argive vase from Mycenae (Nauplia Museum 53–337). Photograph from BSA, XLIX (1954), pl. XLV.*

PLATE 12 · *Non-Attic Geometric Styles*

major areas of discernible change are in the actual conduct of worship, the relations of the gods to the kings, burial beliefs, and the very nature of the gods.

Throughout the Dark ages and into the eighth century the major religious remains are scanty deposits of votive pottery and other objects and the residues of burnt sacrifices which were offered to the gods at open altars in sacred areas. Often these altars stood on sites which had apparently been of religious significance in the Mycenaean age; Delphi, Delos, Eleusis, and other great shrines of historic times have Mycenaean levels.[7] There is, however, no physical testimony to prove that exactly the same kind of cult persisted at these points. The earliest Cretan temples, which go back to the ninth century or beyond, reproduced in part Minoan architectural ideas, but these principles were not to have any great influence on the canonical patterns of Greek temples. When the first simple shrines appeared on the Greek mainland, generally not before the early eighth century, they borrowed their style of single room and foreporch from the *megaron*. The development of this structure will be considered in Chapter 7, for the great steps in architecture must be assigned to the age of revolution; so, too, the evolution of the major international centers of Hellenic religion can be shown fairly clearly to have begun only after 750.

In Minoan and Mycenaean times the royal palaces had private, domestic chapels, where the kings worshipped goddesses, presumably on behalf of their subjects—though we do not actually know to what extent common folk could approach the divine protectors independently. In many respects the *wanax* seems to have had the qualities of a priest-king. This situation did not continue to obtain in the Dark ages; as the

[7] Delphi: Desborough, *Protogeometric Pottery*, 199–201; Nilsson, *GGR*, I, 339–40. Eleusis: Nilsson, *GGR*, I, 475; George E. Mylonas, *The Hymn to Demeter and Her Sanctuary at Eleusis* (St. Louis, 1942), and "'Η προέλευσις τῆς ἐλευσινιακῆς λατρείας," *Geras A. Keramopoullou*, 42–53. Epidaurus: J. M. Cook, *JHS*, LXXI (1951), 240–41, and LXXII (1952), 98. Amyclae: Ernst Buschor, "Vom Amyklaion," *AM*, LII (1927), 1–23. Delos: H. Gallet de Santerre, "Délos, la Crète et le continent mycénien au 2ᵉ millénaire," *RA*, XXIX–XXX (1948), 387–400, and with J. Tréheux, "Rapport sur le dépôt égéen et géométrique de l'Artemision à Délos," *BCH*, LXXI–LXXII (1947–48), 148–254, and *Délos primitive*, 89–100 (note his references to continuity at other sites, 96–99).

wanax disappeared and local *basileis* took his place, they were either unable or unwilling to exercise complete control over religious machinery. The occasional argument that the old palace shrines continued to be centers of cult and so became the focuses for civic worship is very ill-founded. Such a continuity cannot be proven, and if temples were eventually erected atop some Mycenaean palaces the commanding position of these points, as well perhaps as the availability of already worked stone, was primarily responsible.[8] As warleaders, the *basileis* offered up sacrifices in Homer and in myth; in their pride of lineage they considered themselves Zeus-sprung and Zeus-nurtured; but beside the chieftains stood priests and seers who came from upper-class clans. In the Dark ages Greek religion became basically a common tribal matter, conducted throughout all levels by group organizations.

Even clearer testimony to the changes and consolidation of Greek religious attitudes in the early first millennium B.C. is afforded by the graves, for here new customs, such as cremation, merged with other customs which ran back to Early and Middle Helladic times.[9] Generally corpses were now buried with a relatively simple provision of food, drink, and intimate possessions—arms occasionally for the men; pins, *fibulae,* and spinning whorls for the women—in pits which were at times, but not always, deliberately oriented in an east-west direction. At Athens and several other sites adults were usually cremated down through 700, while small children were buried in large pithoi; elsewhere inhumation remained standard throughout

---

[8] J. A. Bundgaard, "A propos de la date de la péristasis du mégaron B à Thermos," *BCH*, LXX (1946), 51–57; Leicester B. Holland, "The Hall of the Athenian Kings," *AJA*, XLIII (1939), 289–98, argues that the prytaneion, not a temple, succeeded the *megaron* on the Acropolis. At Tiryns, Blegen, *Korakou*, 130–34, denies that a temple replaced the *megaron* (vs. Nilsson, *Minoan-Mycenaean Religion,* 475–78); Wace, in his introduction to Ventris and Chadwick, *Documents,* xxxi, agrees with Blegen.

[9] H. Groppengiesser, *Die Gräber von*

Attika (Diss. Heidelberg, 1907); Kübler, *Kerameikos,* IV, 2–4 and passim; Axel W. Persson, "Earliest Traces of the Belief in a Life after Death in Our Civilization," *Eranos,* XLIV (1946), 1–13; Pfuhl, *AM,* XXVIII (1903), 281–82; Wiesner, *Grab und Jenseits;* comparative material in T. Özgüc, *Die Bestattungsgebraeuche im vorgeschichtlichen Anatolien* (Ankara, 1948). Direction of graves: Kübler, *Kerameikos,* IV, 3–4, and VI. 1, 85, 103–04; Persson, *Asine,* 423; Pfuhl, *AM,* XXVIII (1903), 264, who found graves grouped by clans or the like.

the era. In the eighth century the graves of Attica attest an increase in the elaborateness of burials. A wide assortment of vases (often specially made for the graves) appears in the richer tombs; ivory figurines, Egyptian faïence, and other unusual objects were occasionally placed beside the corpse; and over the graves of dead nobles was built a mound topped by a great Dipylon vase. The social distinction thus evident in death must have been marked in life.

A cult of the dead also becomes evident. For the Mycenaean age such a cult is very dubious, but in the first millennium Greek burials manifest not only a funeral feast at the time of interment but also continued attention to the grave.[1] A feeding tube thus was provided, by which drink could be poured down to the grave proper—often the bottoms of the great Dipylon vases were knocked out so that libations and food could go down through them into the earth. Men in the second millennium had treated the bones of earlier burials in very cavalier fashion once the flesh had dissolved; now, when Greeks accidentally broke into old tombs, they tended to be respectful of the remains and began by the eighth century to create cults of heroes at these sites.[2] From Homer we should scarcely be able to guess the prominence of these beliefs about the dead, for the epic celebrates heroes only while living and views the dead as no longer of importance, once the corpses were properly buried.

Besides the rise of the cult of heroes and the more common construction of temples—and connected with these phenomena —the increasing personification of the divine forces governing

[1] Pro: C. W. Blegen and A. J. B. Wace, "Middle Helladic Tombs," *Symbolae Osloenses*, IX (1930), 28–37; Nilsson, *Minoan-Mycenaean Religion*, 587–615; Persson, *Asine*, 342; Wiesner, *Grab und Jenseits*, 179–80, 183–93. But see George E. Mylonas, "The Cult of the Dead in Helladic Times," *Studies to D. M. Robinson*, I, 64–105; and note the lack of Protogeometric remains in C. W. Blegen, "Post-Mycenaean Deposits in Chamber-Tombs," *Arch. eph.* 1937, 377–90. On the historic cult of the dead, see recently Bengt Hemberg, "ΤΡΙΠΑΤΩΡ und ΤΡΙΣΗΦΩΣ: Griechischer Ahnenkult im klassischer und mykenischer Zeit," *Eranos*, LII (1954), 172–90; and Mylonas, "Homeric and Mycenaean Burial Customs," *AJA*, LII (1948), 56–81.

[2] Respect for dead: Eleusis, *BCH*, LXXX (1956), 245; Asine, Frödin and Persson, *Asine*, 179. On hero cults, see Chap. 9, n. 8 (p. 319). Homer: Rohde, *Psyche*, 12–19. The common explanation that Homer here reflected upper-class attitudes is not entirely convincing.

the Greek world is a mark of religious change in the eighth century. This was an important step in creating the unique outlook of historic Greek religion, but it is not easily to be treated. We must look back across the entire course of Aegean development and must assess very carefully the somewhat divergent evidence of physical and literary remains if we are to understand the still ambivalent situation in 750.

Already in the second millennium, to judge from the evidence of carved gems, figurines, and other materials, men had visualized their divine protectors—at least in part—in anthropomorphic terms. From the Mycenaean tablets it would appear that at that time such gods and goddesses as Hera, Athena, and Dionysus stood over the Greek countryside,[3] though we cannot be sure whether their powers and character were conceived as in later ages. On the whole, however, the evidence of the myths, epic, and arts concurs in suggesting that the clear definition of the Greek gods of historic times was a magnificent achievement not easily attained and that it was far from complete by the early eighth century.

If the mainland Greeks had physical religious symbols in the Dark ages, they must have been the aniconic stones, trees, and the like which have a significant place in some myths and religious customs. In the eighth century figurines and plaques begin to appear in the rapidly swelling masses of sacred deposits, scantily at first but ever more abundantly as one goes down into the next century. Animals are more common than human figures, which are usually female.[4] The goddess thus

---

[3] Ventris and Chadwick, *Documents*, 125–27.

[4] On the religious aspects of the human figurines, see Demargne, *La Crète dédalique*, 265–68, 272–78, 286–303, and *BCH*, LIV (1930), 195–204; Emil Kunze, "Zeusbilder in Olympia," *Antike und Abendland*, II (1946), 95–113; Levi, *Early Hellenic Pottery*, 29; Walter A. Müller, *Nacktheit und Entblössung in der altorientalischen und älteren griechischen Kunst* (Leipzig, 1906), which is somewhat superficial. *Potnia theron:* Hansjörg Bloesch, *Antike Kunst in der*

Schweiz (Erlenbach-Zürich, 1943), 28–31; Karl Hoenn, *Artemis: Gestaltwandel einer Göttin* (Zürich, 1946); Nilsson, *GGR*, I, 295–96, 308–11, who traces her back to a Minoan-Mycenaean goddess of nature; she may as well have come, as an artistic type, from the Orient. *Polos:* Valentin Müller, *Der Polos* (Diss. Berlin, 1915), 24 ff. The artistic quality of this work will be considered in Chapter 7, but note that their human nature is sometimes almost lost, as in the Boeotian bell figurines (Frederick R. Grace, *Archaic Sculpture in*

depicted is often unclothed, but not always; frequently she bears a cylindrical crown (*polos*). Her hands are extended upward—an attitude probably not of human adoration but of divine power [5]—or hold her breasts, or later are often stiffly by her side. Occasionally she is flanked by wild beasts on either hand; these guard her or are held by their necks. In this pose of the *potnia theron* (Mistress of Wild Beasts) she is commonly winged, especially in the eighth century. Twin goddesses also appear, and more rarely male and female deities side by side. Male deities alone are rather unusual, but apart from a Master of Animals there are interesting examples presumably of gods fighting wild beasts or bearing a thunderbolt. Artistically this material is important as the true beginning of Greek sculpture, as aspect which will be assessed in Chapter 7. The first examples seem to be of purely Aegean origin, but the sudden, swift evolution of eighth-century plastic art owed much to Oriental models, alike in techniques, in motifs, and even in material (in the case of ivory). The creation of divine types in Greek art was heavily indebted to alien influences and only gradually swung into its own majestic path.

While the technical indebtedness is obvious, the conclusion does not necessarily follow that the goddess or goddesses who could now be depicted were also Oriental in origin, in powers, or in character. From Homer we can learn but little pertinent to these matters; the primary evidence is physical, and must be interpreted in the light of comparative anthropology. Female figurines, that is to say, had been made from Neolithic times in the Aegean, as in the Near East generally. Sometimes men worked in naturalistic styles, and at other times emphasized the female organs in schematic treatments.[6] Such figurines turn

Boeotia [Cambridge, Mass., 1939]).

Aniconic sacred objects: Lorimer, *Homer and the Monuments*, 437, who argues in "Δίπαλτος," *BSA*, XXXVII (1936–37), 172–86, for a possible example of the shift from impersonal to personalized representation.
[5] Arnold von Salis, "Neue Darstellungen griechischen Sagen. 1. Kreta," *SB Heidelberg*, XXVI (1935–36), 43

n. 1; approved by Kunze, *Antike und Abendland*, II (1946), 99.
[6] Early figurines: Müller, *Frühe Plastik*, 30–37; Wiesner, *Grab und Jenseits*, 131–33, 138, 150–51; Leonhard Franz, *Die Müttergöttin im vorderen Orient und in Europe* (*Der alte Orient*, XXXV 3, 1937). Cult of Earth Mother: Jean Przyluski, *La grande déesse* (Paris, 1950); Gallet de San-

up in Neolithic Sesklo, Lerna (see Plate 1a), and elsewhere; in
the Early Cycladic cultures; on Minoan Crete; and—after a
break in Middle Helladic times—in Mycenaean graves from
about 1300 to the end of the Mycenaean age. Then a break again
occurs in Greece proper, but cult figures of female deities have
been found at Karphi and elsewhere in Crete; these had, however, no direct influence on the development of Greek plastic
art.

Modern scholars generally interpret these female figurines
as reflecting the worship of a Great Mother by an agricultural
population. Primitive men, it is argued, represented symbolically
the force of Mother Earth, which brings to humanity the fruits
by which it may live, in the figure of child-bearing woman, on
whom the endurance of the race depends. Such fertility cults
are known in historic times in the Near East in the instances of
Cybele, Astarte, and the like, and also in Greece, in the worship
of Demeter and other goddesses. Twin female deities can be
explained in this framework as representing the maternal and
virginal aspects of woman, a concept which led into the later
cults of Demeter-Persephone at Eleusis, Demeter-Despoina in
Arcadia, and so on. Male and female deities side by side, at
times in a pose where the male touches the breasts of his
consort, may be taken as representing a sacred union, the
hieros gamos, celebrated in historic cults of Samos and Cnossus
and in the annual ritual marriage of Dionysus and the wife of
the *basileus* at Athens.[7] The *potnia theron,* finally, suggests the
general sway of this divine figure over the wild forces of nature.

In general this line of explanation must be correct. Early
farmers had few reserves and little likelihood of gaining food

---

terre, *Délos primitive,* 128–34; Wiesner, *Grab und Jenseits,* 172–73 (bibliography, p. 172 n. 2); Nilsson, *GGR,*
I, 457–63. As the latter points out
(pp. 593–94), one notable aspect of
fertility ideas in later Greece, the
phallic symbol, seems unknown until
the Dark ages; he also (pp. 287–
88) prefers to interpret the figurines
as servants, concubines, or adorants
(cf. Mylonas, *Mycenae,* 78–83).

[7] This motive goes back to Early Helladic times (Wiesner, *Grab und Jenseits,* 176); interesting examples of
archaic style are to be found in *Catalogue raisonée des figurines et reliefs
en terre-cuite grecs, étrusques et romains,* I, ed. Simone Mollard-Besques
(Paris, 1954), B 168 (p. 30); and
AM, LXVIII (1953), Beil. 13, from
Samos (one of the very few wooden
objects from early Greece).

from other areas if their own fields failed; the success of the annual crops was one of the most basic concerns in life. In all eras until very recently, when agricultural chemistry and botany have made great strides, mankind has surrounded its farming activity with a great mass of magic and religious rites. So, too, did the ancient Greeks; a strong fertility cult, revolving largely about a female deity, was a major strand of early Greek religion. Classical philologists have often been shocked by the primitive manner in which the Greeks frequently satisfied this deep religious need; but the evidence of myth and religious customs shows abundantly that what we would call obscenity and ritual murder, together with other irrational beliefs, long survived down into historic times.

Recent reactions against an overidealization of Greek religion have, however, often gone much too far. That the inhabitants of the Aegean in the third, second, or even early first millennium conceived a Mother Goddess as sharply as we find her portrayed in historic cults cannot be proven on the basis of the figures. Nor need every one of these have been conceived and made in deeply solemn purpose; fancy and artistic impulse must never be ruled out of court. And, finally, fertility cults clustered about female figures were far from being the sum total of early Greek religious views.

Even in the physical testimony there stand beside the goddesses a large number of representations of animals. At times these are domestic beasts, which may be partly connected with fertility concepts or with sacrifice; but in part they seem to have symbolic value as representing men or forces of nature. An example of the former is the bird which is placed by the corpse of a dead man on Dipylon vases, to show apparently the spirit of the deceased.[8] The latter aspect is illustrated in the figure of the horse, which reflects aristocratic pride and also the sense of

[8] Compare the bird perched on the terra-cotta funeral cart of Vari: *AJA*, LXI (1957), 281; cf. Ohly, *Griechische Goldbleche*, 135. Kübler, *Kerameikos*, V. 1, 177, suggests religious significance for the bull, horse, snake (on which see also Nilsson, *GGR*, I, 198–99); the use of animal figurines in sacrifice is clear at the Samian Heraeum (Ohly, *AM*, LXV [1940], 81, 91, 99). The horse can even speak in early Greek literature (*Iliad* XIX. 404 ff.) The signs of stress visible in the frequency of monsters and beasts of prey are considered in Chap. 8.

divine speed and power in this mighty animal, and especially in the beasts of prey and monsters which appear frequently on vases, gold bands, bronze armor, *fibulae*, tripods, and the like by the later eighth century. These fierce figures are not simply artistic motifs, but rather are superb testimony to the awe which men felt toward the uncontrollable, indefinite forces of nature encompassing their frail endeavors. We are here at a point where we must remember that the distinction between human, animal, and divine worlds was not sharp throughout most ancient society: while men might come to venture to make their gods in human form, they could also feel that human beings in turn reacted to and even incorporated generalized forces of nature.

Besides the physical evidence there is, moreover, the religious material of the epic and the myths. If Homer passed over fertility cults virtually in silence, he did so partly because his subject was war, not the daily life of a farming community in peacetime. Partly, too, it may be argued that he molded his tale to fit the tastes of the nascent aristocracy of the eighth century —though one must not go too far in postulating that the upper classes had a fundamentally different religious outlook from that of the peasants. But, above all, the divine machinery of the epic throws our most valuable light upon the tendency of the Greeks to see their entire world as directed by divine forces incarnated in human shape.

The drive to personify the gods had proceeded so far by the time the *Iliad* was formed that we must take it as a continuous evolution across the Dark ages. Alternatively, the process might be considered an inheritance from the Mycenaean world, but this I much doubt; in the epic and myth there still lingers a strong unpersonalized sense of divine forces, as in the tales of centaurs and the like. The term *daimon* is used particularly in the *Odyssey* to indicate a general religious power which surrounded the gods who *had* crystallized.[9] Nonetheless, the divine

---

[9] P. Chantraine in *La notion du divin depuis Homère jusqu'à Platon* (Bern, 1954); Ove Jörgensen, "Das Auftreten der Götter in den Büchern ι-μ der Odyssee," *Hermes*, XXXIX (1904), 357–82, who points out that clearly conceived gods appear in Homer's narrative and myth but that undefined divine forces are dominant in the speeches; Wolfgang Kullmann,

world of the epic was essentially a panorama of gods in human form, who lived in pagan revel on Mount Olympus but came down to earth to consort with human beings.

Quarrelsome, adulterous, and skillful in trickery, these gods were strikingly differentiated and had become general forces for all the Aegean; the processes by which local deities were being eliminated or equated with the great gods is reflected particularly in mythology. Though the advanced religious thinker Xenophanes was later to criticize Homeric religion as crudely polytheistic, the epic shows that the Greeks had by the eighth century directed the higher aspects of their religious beliefs toward the plane of the rational, the beautiful, and the human. Their gods had gained a superhuman nobility and represent, like Ripe Geometric masterpieces, a meaningful, orderly world within which men felt they might work, even though the essential decisions lay on the divine plane.

The religious achievement is more strikingly manifest in epic than in art, for it is not yet possible in the eighth century to identify the goddesses of the figurines securely with classical figures.[1] So too the aesthetic principles of the early Hellenic outlook are more easily visible in the *Iliad* than on a Dipylon vase; but the epic religious evidence will thus warn us against taking the still fumbling efforts of the first sculptors as necessarily indicating that all divine figures were generalized.

Throughout the Dark ages the men of the Aegean must have been evolving their views about their gods, and had drawn from many sources, which the modern students of comparative religion have essayed to disentangle.[2] The great god Apollo, who

---

Das Wirken der Götter in der Ilias (Berlin, 1956), which is rather unsatisfactory; Nilsson, *GGR*, I, 217 ff., Fernand Robert, *Homère* (Paris, 1950).

[1] Observe the difficulty in identifying the figurines on the earliest Sumerian seals (Henri Frankfort, *The Art and Architecture of the Ancient Orient* [Pelican, 1954], 12, 37–38); Dumézil, *Naissance de Rome*, 12–22, offers a useful warning against efforts to equate such figures with gods known in classic literature.

[2] See generally Nilsson, *GGR*, I. Apollo: Nilsson, *GGR*, I, 529–64; also Machteld J. Mellink, *Hyakinthos* (Utrecht, 1943), who emphasizes a Cretan aspect, and Chap. 8, nn. 9, 1 (p. 288). Other aspects of Greek religion which may be derived from Asia Minor are itemized by Barnett, *Aegean and Near East*, 218–26.

Athena: Nilsson, *GGR*, I, 433–44. Levi, *AJA*, XLIX (1945), 297–98, is right in emphasizing Athena's primary role as goddess of energy, skill, and craftsmanship; her place as pro-in later days was best to exemplify the highest plane of Greek rational religion, seems to have entered the Aegean from Asia Minor, and the myths which depict his triumph over other deities at Delphi, Sparta, and elsewhere may reflect dimly his increasing popularity during the Dark ages. Athena, the majestic patron of the arts, is generally agreed to have descended from the palace deity of the Mycenaean age—the palace, it will be remembered, was an economic center in that era. From the Minoan world came apparently the tales of the birth and death of Zeus and perhaps some aspects of later Greek mysticism; temples, cult statues (largely of goddesses), and religious paraphernalia in Crete show an uninterrupted continuity of very old ideas.[3] Zeus himself, however, as the Father of the Gods was an Indo-European god of the sky, the only one whose name proves that he accompanied the northern invaders. Other members of the Greek pantheon, again, probably came from the Orient.

Yet, as in Greek history generally, the basic issue is not the source of the elements in Hellenic religion. What must be explained is their reworking and amalgamation from the Dark ages onward. Here particularly the tendency of many religious students to distinguish between an emotional, chthonian, mystical attitude of a pre-Indo-European stratum and a rational, ethical outlook of the Indo-Europeans themselves puts the development in entirely the wrong light. Tensions in later Greek religion, as we shall see, are to be explained only on social, economic, and psychological grounds, and its earlier developments cannot properly be attributed to any one area or to any one class.[4] By the early eighth century a long, unseen process of

---

tectress in war was a product of the development of the city-state. The problems involved in searching for the origins of such gods are well illustrated by the fact that Poseidon to Schachermeyr (*Poseidon*) is an ancient Aegean deity; to Lesky (*Thalatta*, 92–98), an Indo-European import.
[3] Brock, *Fortetsa*, nn. 546–50, 1047, 1414, 1440, 1568, give a good conspectus of the peculiar Cretan flavor;

on its Minoan background, cf. Groenewegen-Frankfort, *Arrest and Movement*, 214–16, and Nilsson, *Minoan-Mycenaean Religion*, 447–56, 576–82.
[4] Contra, Schachermeyr *s.v.* Prähistorische Kulturen Griechenlands in PW, 1481–86, and *Poseidon*, 109–13, 122–29; Nilsson, *GGR*, I, 324, 610–11; see Chap. 2, n. 8 (p. 71), and Chap. 8, n. 9 (p. 288).

analysis had reached the level which we can detect in the physical and literary evidence of this era. The sculptors had come to the point where they felt able, and compelled, to represent some divine forces in human form; in doing so they were soon to gain inspiration from the more polished arts of the Orient. Beside them, however, stood the poet who fashioned the *Iliad* and placed within it a divine picture which was in its turn to stimulate further artistic and literary advances based on these native roots. To what extent Homer deliberately shaped the picture of the divine world which overlooked the struggling Greeks and Trojans we cannot securely determine; but I should be inclined to suspect that rather rapid advance occurred in this matter, as in Dipylon pottery and in the formulation of the epic itself. Always in considering Greek religion, however, one must remember that below its developed level lay more primitive strata of magic, superstition, and generalized views of divine power, which were to endure throughout classic civilization.

THE MEN OF THE EARLY EIGHTH CENTURY

As MEN CAME to visualize the gods more sharply in forms like themselves, so they became more aware of their own nature. Probing, conscious reflection upon the essential marks of mankind and upon its place in the world, which was to be one of the most magnificent marks of Greek culture, was principally a conquest of the age of revolution; but its first stages had taken place by the early eighth century. There are, in testimony, the Dipylon vases; there are also the marvelous portraits by Homer, whose "acquaintance with the passions of mankind"[5] was to make his work an enduring manual of human life in later centuries. Wily Odysseus, garrulous but sage Nestor, bluff Agamemnon, wrathful Achilles—from such skillfully characterized types and their interplay arises the human plot of the *Iliad*.

The psychological advances of the past half-century have

[5] Dio Chrysostom, *Orations* LXI. 1.

led us to see more clearly that the Homeric portrait of mankind was still limited in major respects. In part this limitation was the result of the stylization of an epic, oral technique, which forced poets as well as Dipylon potters to work within a framework of accepted motifs and simple composition. Only thus could order be brought into the chaos of life. Homer, again, made no effort to be a Dante and to embrace all the knowledge and thought of his era. Quite obviously, whole phases of human activity could not enter into the epic story of war; aspects of life which were to be expressed in the seventh-century work of Hesiod, Archilochus, and black-figure potters may already have existed, as yet unvoiced, in the age of Homer.

A more basic limitation, which characterized eighth-century thought as a whole, was the epic inability to visualize men physically as an integrated whole, moved internally. Detailed analysis of Homer's vocabulary and turns of expression has demonstrated that to the poet the human frame was a collection of parts, as it is represented on the Dipylon pictures. In the *Iliad*, to repeat an earlier observation, man exists only to act; in the *Odyssey* an inner force and a deliberately thoughtful consideration of one's course of action are about to make their appearance.[6] Between the two epics lies the beginning phase of the revolution in Greek civilization which defined its course for all subsequent centuries; the *Iliad* is our greatest landmark of the development in the Dark ages which prefaced that revolution.

Yet, though the heroes of the *Iliad* still drew their strength and their folly from divine impulse, they were characters endowed with freedom of will. Though encompassed by a wild nature and themselves committed to the task of killing, they were basically rational, reflective, and purposeful. Though generalized and subject to the iron dictates of communal standards, they displayed individual passions just as did the men who listened to the tale of their exploits. They exhibited, in fine,

[6] Joachim Böhme, *Die Seele und das Ich im homerischen Epos* (Leipzig, 1929); Fränkel, *Dichtung und Philosophie*, 111–13, 120–32; Treu, *Von Homer zur Lyrik*, 10–17, and passim; and the works cited by Lesky, *Gnomon*, XXVII (1955), 483, against the views of Homeric psychology here accepted.

the major characteristics which we call Greek. If any proof is needed that Greek civilization had emerged before the upheaval which produced archaic society, it may most obviously be found here; but let me suggest that adequate corroboration of this view can be found also in such small details as the logical qualities of the hexameter line or the meander pattern on a Geometric vase.

The men of the early eighth century were not consciously proud of their achievements—such egotism came in the next period. When they turned back to look at the past, they saw first a grim era, the age of iron in Hesiod's famous description. Beyond that lay a great period, the age of heroes, when men, said Homer, could hurl stones which two men of his age could not lift. The Dark ages had not been tranquil, superficially secure centuries of rapid progress; and yet, as we have seen in the preceding three chapters, they had witnessed basic developments.

Particularly by studying the stages of Protogeometric and Geometric pottery, but also by using other hints, the historian today can establish the tempo of change. First had come the emergence of new patterns in the eleventh century. Then followed two centuries of slow consolidation as the population of Greece again settled down into villages and replenished its numbers; this progress produced a basic cultural unification of the Aegean basin and also a host of local variations of the common structure.

Finally, in the early eighth century the pace quickened appreciably. The increasing richness of the graves of nobles, the appearance of figurines and shrines in far greater numbers, the sudden emergence of the Dipylon figured scenes, the Greek adoption of the alphabet, the cult of heroes—all these are unmistakable, essentially *datable* testimony that Greek culture was moving toward a new phase. On the solid basis of these indicators we may hope to date the *Iliad*, the fixing of myth, and the crystallization of the Olympic pantheon to approximately the same era.

One great problem of historical study, the determination of stages of amplification and alteration, can thus be answered for early Greek civilization. The other issue, the cause of these changes, is not simple. "All change," wrote Thoreau, "is a miracle to contemplate; but it is a miracle which is taking place every instant." The historian of early Greece may yet hope to determine, in the broadest terms, the motive forces of its development. These forces I would find first in a happy blend of tensions which at once produced a stable system and yet left seeds for dynamic movement: the combination of a common Aegean culture and strong local variations; the presence both of group unity and of individual self-assertion; the fusion of the Minoan-Mycenaean inheritance with patterns deriving from earlier Greek ways and those of the invaders. But Greek civilization was not simply a meeting of opposites. One must keep in mind as well the shock of collapse, which had forced men to think afresh at the end of the second millennium, and the subsequent temporary isolation of the Aegean basin from new outside forces.

Is even this enough? When the historian looks back across his story thus far, he may still feel amazement; the dimensions and outward sureness of development in this period are an unusual miracle of human ability. The heroes of Homer feel that their achievements are extremely difficult, and repeatedly call upon divine aid if they are to act; the poet himself implores the aid of the Muses to tell his story. And so it was in reality. Every step taken by the Greeks of the Dark ages which even in the slightest degree changed ancestral patterns must have been extraordinarily difficult; yet the steps were taken, slowly, often unconsciously, but along an essentially consistent path in the long run.

Inheriting a mass of earlier elements, the generations which lived in the Aegean from 1100 to 750 fused them into a coherent outlook and social structure which, by the time of the *Iliad*, must be labeled Greek. As we look onward, it is with the knowledge that this world was ready to expand both culturally and politically, without losing its own identity.

PART III

THE AGE OF REVOLUTION

CHAPTER 6

THE ORIENT AND GREECE

╓╥╥╥╥╥╥╥╥╥╥╥╥╥╥╥╥╥╥╥╥╥╥╥╥╥╥╥╥╥╓

FOR CENTURIES Greek civilization had crawled laboriously. Then suddenly, in the late eighth and early seventh centuries, the Aegean world blazed out in revolutionary change. The remarkable progress of this era is sharply apparent in our physical evidence; one fine example is afforded by the contrast in two shrines of Hera at Perachora opposite Corinth.

The earlier of the two, which was dedicated to Hera Akraia (of the Height), lasted down to about 750. The men who worshipped here brought the gifts of a still simple world: a limited amount of local pottery, with a few Argive pieces; simple pins and *fibulae;* gold disks and rings of primitive character; three scarabs of faience; four glass beads or pendants; one amber pendant; three terra-cotta figurines. Nearby a new shrine of Hera Limenia (of the Harbor) was constructed about 750. The change itself is significant; the finds, moreover, from the new site are far more abundant and varied. There is pottery not only of Corinth but also of Argos, Athens, the Cyclades, and Boeotia; developed pins and *fibulae* of many types in bronze, ivory, and amber; dozens of glass and amber beads; over a hundred ivory objects; bronze and clay figurines; scarabs of faience in numbers. As its brilliant excavator observed, these shrines reveal in their juxtaposition both the limited horizon of the era of Geometric pottery and then "how suddenly the geometric world was opened, by the expansion of trade, to new influences; how in the second half of the eighth century the first great expansion in the west coincides with the new wealth, both of materials and of ideas, which Corinth at this time derived from the East." [1]

The age of revolution, 750–650, was the most dramatic development in all Greek history. Change was many-sided and was intricately connected in all fields; and the connections both with basic earlier patterns of the Aegean world and with outside cultures deserve careful study. Upheaval, too, means different things from different points of view. Men of the age, I suspect, felt the difficulties of change more than its blessings; there are very evident tokens of mental and physical stress as well as of conservative efforts to cling to old ways. These we must keep in mind if we are to appreciate fully the marvelous achievements of the period.

Swiftly, with simple but sharp strokes, the Greeks erected a coherent, interlocked system politically, economically, and culturally, which endured throughout the rest of their independent life. In field after field the modern student can trace back to the early seventh century, but no further, the developed lineaments of the Hellenic outlook; beyond lie only primitive, almost inchoate foundations. The century from 750 to 650 thus witnessed a great expansion of trade, the wide outrush of Greek colonization, and the consolidation of the city-state under aristocratic domination. Beside this vehicle of Greek localism, however, the concept of Hellenic civilization became a consciously felt, generally unifying force in the Aegean. In the field of art, pottery shed its rigid geometric dress; Protocorinthian, Protoattic, and other potters created the forms and elaborated the motifs of succeeding centuries. The great mold of Greek architectural thought, the stone temple, made its appearance. Sculptors gained the confidence to work on a large scale in stone and metal; from the first simple modeling of human forms in figurines they advanced swiftly to such noble types as the *kouros,* the idealized nude athletic male. While the epic tradition continued long enough to produce the *Odyssey* and Hesiod's work, new forms of literature appeared, and the Greek view of human personality gained new depth in the lyric.

[1] Humfry Payne, *Perachora: The Sanctuaries of Hera Akraia and Limenia,*   I (Oxford, 1940), 33–34.

Fortunately for the historian, the body of available literature and physical remains now increases greatly in quantity and in variety. General histories of Greece have commonly floundered, in a cursory chapter or two, through the "Homeric age," but begin their real treatment with the later seventh century. In doing so, their authors have relied primarily upon the ancient literature; today the historian must also consider an ever increasing number of monographs which are reducing to order specialized areas of the physical evidence, such as Protocorinthian and Protoattic pottery, Attic gold bands, Cretan bronzes, the early passage of vases and artistic motifs between Greece and the Orient, and so on. Much remains to be done, as in the fields of Greek ivories and East Greek pottery; and the strong likelihood of major new discoveries renders tentative any detailed conclusions. The main lines of evolution, however, seem clear, and upon these we must concentrate at the cost of passing over many intriguing side paths. Yet no student of Hellenic culture can entirely ignore its wide range of local variations, which now became increasingly well defined and enduringly significant.

Thenceforth, too, we can no longer treat the Aegean entirely by itself. The great wave of invasions from the north had ended; whatever lasting imprint the barbarians had placed on Greek culture in its initial stage was now an indivisible part of that outlook, a continuing inheritance from the Dark ages. By the eighth century, on the other hand, direct contact with the Orient was resumed and increased steadily until the days of Alexander's conquest. Greece became again linked to the eastern Mediterranean, first culturally, then politically, to a far greater degree than had been true in the Mycenaean age. This new element in Aegean history deserves careful inspection before we turn to the age of revolution itself. In particular we must assess the mode, date, and significance of the ties between East and West in the era leading up to the great changes in Greece.

THE SIGNIFICANCE OF THE ORIENT

THE SIGNIFICANCE of the Orient in Greek civilization is a subject on which the views of scholars have swung between opposite poles. Down to the eighteenth century students still largely accepted the early Christian (and Jewish) efforts to prove that Mosaic civilization had preceded that of Greece and Rome. Though the arguments for Hebrew priority steadily lost ground, the inherited presupposition of heavy Greek indebtedness to the East gained support for a time from the translation of the Phoenician language (1750–8) and from a growing acquaintance with the antiquities of Mesopotamia and Egypt.[2]

In the nineteenth century this point of view came under heavy attack. Philologists created the concept of a common body of Indo-European languages and, by extension, of an early Indo-European culture; German scholars especially seized upon the new evidence as the basis for a shibboleth that Nordic blood was the primary force in Greek civilization. Beside this product of nineteenth-century nationalism stood the liberal strain of thought, confident in the powers of human reason, which dreamed a mighty picture of the rational, human-centered culture of Periclean Athens. In many majestic panoramas of the classic glory of Greece which were written toward the end of the century one will search in vain for any suggestion that Oriental influence had a serious role in the origins of Western culture.

More recently the pendulum has swung back. While some scholars continue to flog the Nordic myth zealously, the excesses of their assertions have now become obvious. Humanists still fashion a timeless heaven of wit and reason out of classic Greece; but the realities of historical fact can no longer be entirely ignored in an age which now has a deeper sense of the irrational factor in human activities. Although one may sharply separate

---

[2] The opening chapter of Mazzarino, *Fra Oriente e Occidente,* furnishes a good survey of early opinions on the place of the Orient; see also W. F. Albright, *Studies in the History of* *Culture* (Menasha, Wisconsin, 1942), 37–40. For more recent argument by Barnett, Gordon, Roes, Webster, et al., see above, Chap. 5, nn. 7–8 (pp. 165–66).

the rational glow of Greece from the "superstition-ridden" Orient, the accumulating weight of evidence stands against the possibility that Greek civilization sprang full-blown from the head of Zeus. In 1912 Poulsen's *Der Orient und die frühgrie-chische Kunst* put the demonstration of the artistic interrelations of East and West in the eighth and seventh centuries on a new level; and a host of detailed studies, which will be considered later, have further illustrated the Greek artistic borrowings from the rich Oriental culture of the time. For many decades the art and sculpture of Greece during the age of revolution have been termed "Orientalizing."

As our knowledge of the links between East and West, especially through the arts and letters of Syria and Phoenicia, has increased, there has even come a revival of the old thesis that Greek civilization was essentially an extension of the Orient; that the eastern Mediterranean as a whole formed a cultural unit out of which Hebrew thought and the Greek achievement rose as twin mountain peaks. Adherents of this point of view link Homer directly to the Oriental epic tradition, stress the indebtedness of Greek mythology to the body of Near Eastern myth, and make Greek religion and thought generally a direct continuation of an Oriental inheritance. In the fields of the arts, students of this persuasion incline to find so many Oriental prototypes for Greek artistic motifs and forms of the age of revolution that Greek art might well be called "Oriental" rather than "Orientalizing." [3]

Only a small minority holds views so radical. There is a twofold error at the root of this argument: first, civilization is rather simply conceived as an indivisible continuum; and, secondly, external borrowings are not distinguished from internal spirit, which alone gives meaning to historical inheritances. The arguments of the Orientalists are rushing and far-flung in scope, but on analysis will often be found to be based upon single artistic or literary motifs wrenched out of a wide context

[3] E.g., R. D. Barnett, "Ancient Oriental Influences on Archaic Greece," *Aegean and Near East,* 212–38, observes (p. 233): "It was the fall of Susa and the change in the Oriental prototypes that caused the change from the early to the later, coarser Wild Goat style in Greece, and perhaps also the change from Protocorinthian to Corinthian."

and treated in a mechanical form. Worse yet, the efforts to link closely Greece and the Orient must draw upon materials of very differing value, which range over many centuries.

Sober scholars have generally rejected the more extreme claims of this type, as applied to *specific* bodies of evidence, but the realization that links did bind the Orient and Greece by the eighth century has all too often led men to unwarranted general assumptions. The connections between Greece and the East were indeed important all across the sweep of Aegean history. Throughout the earlier millennia which we have already examined, Greece was a mediator between Europe and Asia, and Aegean civilization had developed as a local response to the Oriental spur. In the age of revolution the Greeks once more knew the world of the Orient. The tempo of Aegean progress and even its forms in part were much affected by that knowledge.

Yet these are not the points which one must keep primarily in mind. First of all, Greek civilization had already appeared by this date and was, in its origins, an Aegean product. In the centuries of the first, great, and decisive steps toward this formulation the Greek world had, largely by its own choice, little contact eastward.

Then again, the great revolution of the eighth century did not start from the Orient. If Greece was now to resume close contact with the Orient, this connection rose largely because men of the eighth-century Aegean were ready to widen their ken and to build more loftily; partly, too, because the Orient itself had developed during its own Dark ages a more cosmopolitan, attractive culture than it had known in the Bronze age.

From this Eastern culture, finally, the Greeks in and after the eighth century borrowed extensively in motifs, in forms, and, above all, in inspiration that certain things *could* be done. Without this aid, the Greeks entirely on their own might not have achieved so much; for what made Hellenic civilization truly outstanding was the once-for-all juxtaposition of fresh Greek energy and the inherited lore of the Orient. But always in human history the question is not so much whence inspiration comes as this: what do men do with external stimuli in their own minds?

The proof of this point of view will be the burden of subsequent chapters. Here we must draw Greece and the Orient together. That the early eighth-century Aegean was in a stage of increasing ferment has already been shown; it is time now to sketch the political and cultural development of the Near East down to the same point. The significant renewal of contacts between the two areas, which then ensued, also offers several serious problems as to its mode and date.

THE UNIFICATION OF THE ORIENT

THE FIRST CENTERS of civilization in the Near East had been the river valleys of Mesopotamia and Egypt. Here firmly organized states, grouped about kings and temples, had appeared before the end of the fourth millennium B.C. in a process which seems to have been one of swift crystallization. Within a space of only two or three centuries both Egyptian and Mesopotamian cultures had set the main outlines on which they developed for thousands of years. The achievements of this period must stagger the modern observer, yet the men who lived in the river valleys paid a heavy price for their victories. Only by erecting the symbols of god-king, as in Egypt, or of a divine state of omnipotent gods, as in Babylonia, were men able to group themselves in the closely knit collective units on earth which could attain so much. The epics and myths of Mesopotamia reveal the hidden anxiety that humanity had been overbold in creating civilization, and the patterns of life, once created, settled into firm conventions which discouraged free experimentation.[4]

From Mesopotamia, in particular, vital impulses radiated out, eastward as far as India and apparently even to China,

[4] Origins of civilization: Chap. 1, n. 7 (p. 24); also Wilson, *The Burden of Egypt*, 145 ff., 308. Anxiety: the Atrahasis epic, in which the gods punish by flood the clamors of busy mankind, *Ancient Near Eastern Texts*, 104–06; Frankfort, *Birth of Civilization in the Near East*, 51–52; Georges Contenau, *Everyday Life in Babylon and Assyria* (London, 1954), 301–02, who attributes part of this feeling to the oppressive climate.

westward along the course of the upper Euphrates to Syria-Palestine in the third millennium. By the end of this period Assyrian merchants were trading into southeastern Asia Minor, and soon thereafter the Hittites of central Anatolia began to fashion civilized states. The development of the Aegean, and especially of Crete, also owed much to Oriental example, though the flavor of civilization there always remained distinct. In the second millennium, once the initial wave of invasions and movements had subsided, the Near East rose to a peak of culture. The international politics of Egypt, Syrian princedoms, Assyria, and the Hittites assumed almost a modern flavor; international trade drew in even the bold inhabitants of Mycenaean Greece; and artistic influences radiated widely. Yet the gleam of this superstructure cannot obscure the fact that culture remained essentially local throughout the Near East; there was in the Bronze age no one Oriental civilization.

Internal decay paved the way for a great series of invasions at the end of the second millennium. The invaders from the north, as we have seen, destroyed the fragile structure of civilization in the Aegean and Asia Minor and shook much of the rest of the Near East; Semitic-speaking peoples such as the Arameans and Habiru pressed into Palestine, Syria, and Mesopotamia from the Arabian desert. The product everywhere was a marked reduction in the level of culture. The empires vanished; many cities were abandoned; in some areas peasants had to struggle bitterly to maintain settled life even on a village plane. The early first millennium was a dismal, poverty-stricken age.

Throughout the Near East, however, civilization was not quite as catastrophically overturned as in the Aegean. Egypt and Assyria survived as kingdoms, albeit weakened. The Arameans, Hebrews, and others who came into Syria and Palestine took over the structure they found and erected small principalities, the most famous of which were the Phoenician city-kingdoms and the territorial kingdom of David and Solomon. Neither the literary nor the artistic inheritance of the past was entirely lost. Much of the Orient has an artistic gap in major products, which in our present knowledge seems to have extended over two centuries and more (*c.* 1150–950),[5] and even in Egypt, which was less markedly affected than any other area, monuments of this dull era were on a minor scale. Yet the Hebrews picked up a wealth of ancient myth from their neighbors; Phoenician craftsmen built and adorned palace and temple for Solomon; Ahab erected a house of ivory. In smaller objects the working of ivory, bronze, and stone continued; and an ancestral treasury of motifs, some purely decorative, others of human, animal, and monster forms, endured. Along the Syrian coast, an area which must particularly interest the student of Greek evolution, artistic styles of the first centuries after 1000 B.C. were an amalgam of old influences from Egypt, Mesopotamia, and the Minoan-Mycenaean world, encased in a stiff, even "geometric" form. Though no one can mistake these products for Greek, much the same simplification and resort to rigidity occurred in Syria as in the Aegean (and also in Asia Minor).

While old political, economic, and cultural patterns thus survived, their earlier dominance was seriously shaken; the resurgence which followed the collapse was not simply a revival of earlier ways. Among the many aspects of this resurgence, which has not yet received its full attention, those of greatest interest here are, first, the increasing unification of the Orient and, secondly, the fact that revival in the Orient preceded the Aegean age of revolution by a century or more.

In the eastern Mediterranean trade by sea had never quite disappeared. It now fell largely into Phoenician hands and began to expand rapidly by at least the ninth century. The first clear evidence is the establishment of Phoenician trading posts in Cyprus, which should probably be dated to the period just before 800 B.C.; Phoenician exploration and trade in the western Mediterranean probably came largely after this date,

[5] Frankfort, *Art and Architecture of the Ancient Orient*, 164–66, stretches out the gap virtually to 1200–850; W. F. Albright, "Northeast Mediterranean Dark Ages and the Early Iron Age Art of Syria," *Aegean and Near East*, 144–64, essays to close it as far as possible. Geometric flavor: Müller, *Frühe Plastik*, 103–36; Adolf Furtwängler, *Antike Gemmen*, III (Leipzig-Berlin, 1900), 65; Edith Porada, "A Lyre Player from Tarsus and His Relations," *Aegean and Near East*, 185–211.

though the problem is a thorny one.[6] On land the Arameans of North Syria held commercial primacy. By the ninth century their princes were wealthy enough to decorate cities such as Tell Halaf with imposing monuments which could not be equaled, at least for size, anywhere in contemporary Greece.[7]

A concomitant of this economic advance was the Assyrian effort to gain political dominance over the Near East and so to translate an increasingly unified economic world into empire. The chain of Assyrian conquests commenced in the ninth century but achieved fruition only in the days of Tiglath-Pileser III (744–727), when Assyrian rule extended from the Persian Gulf to the Mediterranean. Under his successors, especially Sargon II (721–705), the Assyrians even gained the submission of the seven kings of Ia, the Greeks, i.e., of Cyprus.[8] They also conquered Cilicia, where other Greek-speaking people were domiciled.

To call the Assyrian domination of the Near East "Empire," as is commonly done, overregularizes a situation which was never firmly consolidated. The Assyrian warlords were not able to exercise enduring control over the mountains to their north, where the state of Urartu had risen in the modern Armenia by the eighth century, and Assyrian rule even in the lower lands of

[6] Einar Gjerstad, *Swedish Cyprus Expedition*, IV. 2, *The Cypro-Geometric, Cypro-Archaic and Cypro-Classical Periods* (Stockholm, 1948), 436–40, offers the most solid analysis of the Cypriote evidence; for the western Mediterranean, see below, Chap. 11.

[7] Ekrem Akurgal, *Späthethitische Bildkunst* (Ankara, 1949); illustrations in *Tell Halaf*, III, ed. Dietrich Opitz and Anton Moortgat (Berlin, 1955). See also Carchemish, D. G. Hogarth and C. L. Woolley, *Carchemish*, I–III (London, 1914–52), which remained "Hittite" to a greater extent down to its fall to Assyria in 718 (Goetze, *Hethiter, Churriter und Assyrer*, 165); Frankfort, *Art and Architecture of the Ancient Orient*, 182–83, notes this but limits the Hittite character (cf. p. 165).

[8] *Ancient Near Eastern Texts*, 284, 286–87, 290–91 (Esarhaddon); Berossus, *FHG*, II, 504, fragment 12 on Cilicia. The problem of the origin and precise meaning of the terms Iaman, Iatnam, and Iavan (Genesis 10:2, 4) is much vexed; see the material in Mazzarino, *Fra Oriente e Occidente*, 89, 113–26; W. Brandenstein, "Bemerkungen zur Völkertafel in der Genesis," *Festschrift Debrunner* (Bern, 1954), 57–83; Dunbabin, *Greeks and Their Eastern Neighbours*, 30–31; C. F. Lehmann-Haupt, "Zur Erwähnung der Ionier in altorientalischen Quellen," *Klio*, XXVII (1934), 74–83, 286–94. However derived (and the origin of the Greek word for Ionians, 'Ιάφονες, is unclear) the term in Assyrian records surely means no more than the Greek-speaking inhabitants of Cyprus (and at times of Cilicia).

Mesopotamia and Syria was imperiled by repeated revolt. The brutality and militarism which stamp Assyrian records are perhaps a testimony to this insecure position. In the end, Nineveh fell in 612, and the Hebrew prophets far off in Palestine rejoiced greatly.

The Assyrians nonetheless went far toward breaking the political localism of the Near East and toward accustoming its traders and local magnates to accept over-all political unity; of this development the milder Persians were to reap the profit. Another product of the political and economic revival, as well perhaps as of the quieting down of northern Eurasia, was the increasing ability of the Near Eastern military and political system to bar outside invaders. After the Cimmerian onslaught, which swept as far as Egypt early in the seventh century, the Orient was not again seriously affected by attacks of northern invaders until long after the time of Christ.

For Greek history the political unification of the Orient was eventually to have tremendous influence, but the slow tempo of its initial stage was an incalculable blessing. Tucked off in an obscure corner behind the seas and the forbidding mass of Asia Minor, the Greeks of the eighth and seventh centuries were able to develop their own political institutions almost without foreign influence. The end product, the *polis* or city-state, was to be vitally different from the political pattern of the Orient. From Sumerian days Eastern kingship had been divinely appointed, "lowered from Heaven" in the conventional phrase, and kings had gained their glory largely by war. Of the earliest known conqueror, Sargon I, later chroniclers reported that "he marched against the country of Kazalla and turned Kazalla into ruin-hills and heaps of rubble. He even destroyed there every possible perching place for a bird." [9] The Assyrian monarchs boasted unendingly, both in word and in the grimly fascinating reliefs of their palaces, which display mounds of human heads and the fierce storming of cities; and by this date the gods who supported earthly rule had shrunk far into the background.

[9] *Ancient Near Eastern Texts*, 266; the rise of kingship over communal as-   semblies need not be considered here.

Leading their nobles and peasants in looting expeditions was not the only task of the kings, who piously supported justice and also directed vast palace economies of traders and artisans; but as a whole the institution of Oriental imperialistic monarchy, boasting its wealth from "the incoming taxes of all inhabited regions," [1] was far removed from the tiny city-states of archaic Greece, both in size and in spirit. Beside the kings in their palaces stood the great temples, the scenes of highly developed cult attended by a vast array of specialized priests who manipulated a complex, inherited lore. In Greece, on the other hand, simple mud-brick chapels and ash altars still served as the focus for communal worship of the basic forces guarding human existence.

So, too, the intellectual framework of the Assyrian world, which drew heavily from all earlier tradition, differed greatly from that of the contemporary Aegean. Much more advanced on the factual level, Oriental knowledge was encased in bonds which were to prevent it from developing as amazingly as did the Greek world thenceforth. Mesopotamian thought did not have that analytical and synthesizing quality already visible in Greek Geometric pottery and in the *Iliad*. The basic process was one of analogical reasoning, and the end product was often simple classification; the same difficulty in co-ordination appears in the poetic tendency to heap up parallel expressions one after another. In the Orient, nonetheless, the practical sciences had been the subject of experiment, however unconscious, for millennia of enduring civilization. Knowledge of the stars and of mathematics had already made great strides; the body of Mesopotamian myth contained a great deal of speculation about the nature of man's life. [2] The Greeks were to draw upon this material to a marked extent but so transmuted their borrowings that we are not always aware of the source; as far as myth is

---

[1] Ibid. 311 (Nabonidus). Contenau, *Everyday Life*, 113–41, sketches the nature of Eastern monarchy; its developed flavor appears sharply in the Assyrian royal inscriptions.

[2] See generally Contenau, 158–59; Henri Frankfort et al., *Before Philoso-* phy (Penguin, 1949); Otto J. Neugebauer, *The Exact Sciences in Antiquity* (2d ed.; Providence, R. I., 1957); Charles Singer, E. J. Holmyard, and A. R. Hall, ed., *A History of Technology*, I (Oxford, 1954).

concerned, men of the Western world have gained much more direct knowledge of Babylonian tale-telling from its adaptation by the Hebrews. In many ways, incidentally, this small people in the hills of Palestine fitted as poorly into the main Oriental tradition as did the Greeks. But Israel lay directly adjacent to the centers of the Orient. Its political catastrophes, while promoting the search of the Hebrew prophets for the deeper meaning of religion, may suggest how much the more distant Greeks were spared.

The artistic development of the Assyrian period reflects the political and economic unity of the time. In the great palaces of Sargon and Ashurbanipal architecture made great strides toward solemn monumental complexes; the reliefs which paneled the walls of the palaces reached an unprecedented height in the depiction of action, of realistic agony of dying animals, even of the suggestion of space.[3] But these were far-off masterpieces which the first Greek traders probably never saw, or, if they did, could have no hope of emulating. The smaller arts—textiles, ivory and gold, bronze statuettes and bowls—were far more important as vehicles by which the Aegean world could learn of Oriental techniques, motifs, and concepts, first as they were practiced along the littoral of Syria and Phoenicia and then, in the seventh century, in their Assyrian forms.

As an outside observer considers the minor arts, he feels strongly inclined to deduce that the craftsmen of the Orient were developing in the ninth and eighth centuries a fairly uniform, generalized style well suited for far-flung sale. Ivory plaques depicting a comely courtesan at her window, pierced reliefs of opposed animals or grazing cattle, faïence scarabs, carved tridacna shells, bronze dishes intricately worked with rows of animals or scenes of siege and war, great caldrons

---

[3] Groenewegen-Frankfort, *Arrest and Movement*, 169–81; Frankfort, *Art and Architecture of the Ancient Orient*, 84–101; Contenau, *Everyday Life*, 101–13; Goetze, *Hethiter, Churriter und Assyrer*, 182–84, who emphasizes the root in Hurrian art. We cannot determine how Greek *fibulae* made their way to the palace of Sargon (G. Loud, *The Palace of Sargon*, II [Chicago, 1938], pl. 59) or Greek vases (one sub-Mycenaean, one Protogeometric, one Rhodian) to Nineveh (R. W. Hutchinson, *JHS*, LII [1932], 130). Assyrian relief had a limited influence even in northern Syria, according to Frankfort, *Art and Architecture of the Ancient Orient*, 179.

whereon were riveted winged figures (Assurattaschen) to hold the handles, delicate gold earrings—all these and a thousand other items were sold over the Near East and soon made their way far afield in the Mediterranean.[4] The craftsmanship is generally tidy, the composition neat, the drawing realistic within its conventions; the aim is clearly decoration rather than deep artistic probing of the universe. The consumer, whether priest, king, or foreign trader, obviously dominated the artist.

Yet one must be cautious in thus reducing the arts of the Near East to a common formula, for wide variations can be sensed in these products. While the work of Phoenician shops reflected an Egyptian inheritance and often was soft and sickly sweet, that of North Syria drew little from this source. Far firmer and more vigorous, it turned instead to so-called "Hittite" prototypes. The distinctive flavor of Urartian bronze work, again, is only recently coming into focus as distinct from Assyrian styles.[5] Greek art which drew on this material varied in minor details according to its source; lions on seventh-century Corinthian vases thus were designed in two perceptibly different styles, the "Hittite" first and then the Assyrian.[6] Within a

[4] This art awaits its major study; see pro tempore, Helmut Th. Bossert, *Altsyrien* (Tübingen, 1951); Frankfort, *Art and Architecture of the Ancient Orient*, 164–201; Müller, *Frühe Plastik*, 103–36; Poulsen, *Der Orient*. Ivories: R. D. Barnett, "The Nimrud Ivories and the Art of the Phoenicians," *Iraq*, II (1935), 179–210; "Phoenician and Syrian Ivory Carving," *Palestine Exploration Quarterly*, 1939, 4–19; "Early Greek and Oriental Ivories," *JHS*, LXVIII (1948), 1–25; *A Catalogue of the Nimrud Ivories* (London, 1957); also Demargne, *La Crète dédalique*, 203–14; C. Decamps de Mertzenfeld, *Inventaire commenté des ivoires phéniciens et apparentés découverts dans le Proche-Orient* (Paris, 1954).
[5] Pierre Amandry, "Chaudrons à protomes de taureau en Orient et en Grèce," *Aegean and Near East*, 239–61; George M. A. Hanfmann, "Four Urartian Bulls' Heads," *AnatSt*, VI

(1956), 205–13; Massimo Pallottino, "Gli Scavi di Karmir-Blur in Armenia e il problema delle conessioni tra l'Urartu, la Grecia e l'Etruria," *Archeologia classica*, VII (1955), 109–23; K. R. Maxwell-Hyslop, "Urartian Bronzes in Etruscan Tombs," *Iraq*, XVIII (1956), 150–67 (Urartian bronzes at Olympia, p. 167); R. D. Barnett, *Iraq*, XII (1950), 37–39; Bittel, *Grundzüge der Vor- und Frühgeschichte Kleinasiens*, 78–81; Goetze, *Kleinasien*, 187–200; Frankfort, *Art and Architecture of the Ancient Orient*, 186, 189, 244 n. 55, 258 n. 105, who denies any original character to Urartian bronze work but admits the possibility that its smiths influenced the West (though not by land).
[6] Hanfmann, *HSCP*, LXI (1953), 18, 34–35; Humfry Payne, *Necrocorinthia* (Oxford, 1931), 19, 53, 67–69, 146–147; Dunbabin, *Greeks and Their Eastern Neighbours*, 41–42, 47–49; Akurgal, *Späthethitische Bildkunst*,

general uniformity of outlook the artistic styles of the Near East yet differed notably in Assyrian times. Unfortunately for the Greek student who wishes to disentangle the skeins of Oriental influence in the eighth- and seventh-century Aegean, these variations have not yet received definitive treatment.

The main points nonetheless are clear. Taken en masse, the arts of the Near East were by the eighth century as far in advance of the work of Aegean craftsmen as were the armies and political concentration of the Assyrian realm. These products were, moreover, of a cosmopolitan, graceful flavor which could well be attractive to the less advanced inhabitants of the farther Mediterranean shores. Human and animal representation was a commonplace; lines were supply curved; ornament was rich and harmonious. Equally important from our point of view, this was a style of superficial grace. Neither in Egypt nor in Syria was true artistic vigor, the expression of the human spirit, pulsating when the Greeks came to the shores of the Orient.[7] If this spirit appears in Greece during the great age of revolution, it was not a foreign gift.

THE RE-ESTABLISHMENT OF CONTACTS

THE ORIENTALIZING movement which bulks so large in Greek history did not affect solely the Aegean basin; if we broaden our gaze, we can see that it was a very general force. The Orient now was able to offer attractive wares and ideas; and any district elsewhere in the Mediterranean which was ready politically, economically, and intellectually reached out for the new materials. Most instructive to the student of Greek history is the course of change in the Etruscan domains of Italy, where political and cultural developments speeded up

---

76–79. Amandry, *Syria*, XXIV (1944–45), 161, also defines a Syrian type of lion (of the second millennium).

[7] Wilson, *Burden of Egypt*, 308–17, discusses the dull, lifeless spirit of Egypt in the first millennium; "there could be no worse teacher for a young and eager culture." Poulsen, *Der Orient*, 73–74, suggests that it was fortunate the Greeks met the adaptive arts of Syria and Phoenicia rather than the greater art which lay behind them.

amazingly in the late eighth century. In the sculpture and other arts of Etruria the stimulus of Eastern contacts is evident from about 750–725.[8] The sources for the Orientalizing wave were the same for the Aegean and for Etruria; even such detailed repercussions as the stylistic shift from "Hittite" to Assyrian renderings which was just noted on Corinthian vases appears in Etruscan work. Yet each area tapped the riches of Syrian-Phoenician art independently, at least at the outset.

The major results, too, varied significantly between Greece and Italy. Both districts had geometric backgrounds and tended to geometricize their borrowings at the outset; but in Etruria the native reaction was less lively, less continuous, less independent. Only in Greece, of all non-Oriental lands, did local artists succeed in absorbing the alien influences and then proceed to new heights of original stamp. It was Greece, not Etruria, which evolved a more supple alphabet out of the Phoenician model and passed its discovery on to other Mediterranean lands. The Greek success was due in part to its native Geometric synthesis, which had already reached a high level; in part to its inheritances from the earlier rapprochement between Mycenaean and Oriental lands in the Late Bronze age; and also in part to the probability that contact between the Aegean and the Syrian coast had never been broken, even at the lowest ebb of civilization. The physical evidence for tenuous links, while scanty, does exist, as we saw in Chapter 4.

Yet only as that artistic development occurred in the East which has just been sketched, and only as the Aegean itself began to burgeon were the necessary conditions at hand for significant borrowing. *A priori,* Oriental imports could be expected to appear in the most developed areas of Greece, and local arts could begin to reflect the stimulus of Oriental ideas, by the late ninth century at best. Truly significant influence,

---

[8] The most useful studies on the present aspect are P. J. Riis, *Tyrrhenika: An Archaeological Study of the Etruscan Sculpture in the Archaic and Classical Periods* (Copenhagen, 1941); Georg Hanfmann, *Altetruskische Plastik I: Die menschliche Gestalt in der Rundplastik bis zum Aus-* gang der orientalisierenden Kunst (Würzburg, 1936). The effect was still limited in the eighth century; E. H. Dohan, *Italic Tomb-Groups in the University Museum* (Philadelphia, 1942), 108, places the main influx of Oriental and Greek products at 680–650.

(a) Linear Geometric crater found in North Cemetery, Corinth (Corinth Museum). Photograph from AJA, XXXIV (1930), 413, no. 7.

(b) Linear Geometric kotyle from Aegina, in an important new shape (Aigina, no. 154).

(a)

(b)

(c)

(d)

(c) Early Protocorinthian cup from Aegina, which combines rays and freehand elements with decadent meanders and other Geometric motifs (Aigina, no. 180).

(d) The Rider Kotyle, of Early Protocorinthian style, from Aegina (Aigina, no. 191). Photographs b, c, and d courtesy Deutsches Archäologisches Institut in Berlin.

PLATE 13 · Rise of Protocorinthian Pottery

(a) Fragments of large vase with four rows of animals from Aegina (Aigina, no. 273). Photograph courtesy Deutsches Archäologisches Institut in Berlin.

(b) Aryballos combining floral, mythical, and animal elements in the perfected Protocorinthian style (Museum of Fine Arts, Boston). Photograph courtesy Museum of Fine Arts, Boston.

PLATE 14 · *Triumph of the Protocorinthian Style*

however, would not come until the eighth century. Similar reaction in the less advanced regions would be a matter for the seventh century and even later. This is the actual pattern of what did occur.

Against this background the otherwise puzzling brief appearance of a curvilinear pottery style at Cnossus (Protogeometric B) in the era 850–820 is a significant phenomenon, if it has been correctly dated.[9] When the most advanced potters of Crete, at this time probably still the richest part of the Aegean, began to turn from the debased sub-Minoan styles which had lingered in the island, they apparently were willing to make some experiments with materials of Oriental origin. But the brief duration of the style, a flash of light in a wintry Geometric sky, is equally interesting—even the Greek land closest to the Orient was not yet prepared to broaden its horizons so far. Very soon Geometric impulses from the mainland gained the upper hand at Fortetsa and remained dominant in its pottery well down into the eighth century.

Potters were often among the most conservative craftsmen, and enduring contact between Crete and the East showed itself in other fields very soon after the eighth century began.[1] Worshippers at the sanctuary of Zeus on Mount Ida dedicated there a mass of ivories in which Eastern styles were clearly reflected—indeed, some of the work may have been Phoenician. Even more impressive are the famous Idaean bronze shields, thin sheets of bronze shaped like shields or percussion instruments and decorated elaborately with repoussé reliefs. The

[9] Brock, *Fortetsa*, 143: running spiral, arc, cable. One could wish that the stratigraphic evidence to assign this ware firmly to the ninth century were much more certain.
[1] Ivory: Emil Kunze, "Orientalische Schnitzereien aus Kreta," *AM*, LX–LXI (1935–36), 218–33; both Nimrud and Loftus types appear, according to Barnett, *JHS*, LXVIII (1948), 3–4. Gold: R. W. Hutchinson and J. Boardman, *BSA*, XLIX (1954), 215–30, on the Khaniale Tekke tombs. Bronze: Kunze, *Kretische Bronzereliefs*, who discusses well the Oriental parallels.

Fragments of similar, apparently Cretan work have been found at Miletus and Delphi (*BCH*, LXVIII–LXIX [1944–45], pl. 3. 1); cf. Demargne, *La Crète dédalique*, 217–43; Levi, *Early Hellenic Pottery*, 8, who points out the Greek aspects of this work. Kunze's dates are supported by Hencken, *AJA*, LIV (1950), 297–302; but are lowered by Sylvia Benton, "The Date of the Cretan Shields," *BSA*, XXXIX (1938–39), 52–64, and XL (1939–40), 52–54; Pendlebury, *Archaeology of Crete*, 336.

earliest of these works smack clearly of Phoenician influences, and the indebtedness to several Eastern artistic styles in subjects and in the plumpish outlines of the human figures remained profound throughout the course of their manufacture, which was dated by Kunze from 800 at the latest on down into the seventh century. Other students have not agreed in placing their inception so early, but even if one lowers the first shields toward 750 this body of material remains one of the earliest and most direct testimonials to continuous Greek interest in things Oriental. Crete, however, did not stand alone, nor was it an intermediate point through which all Oriental influence flowed into Greece; enduring, if yet limited, contact with the East had generally been established by the more developed areas of the Aegean by the mid-eighth century.

The evidence for this resumption of links lies partly in the areas of the alphabet, borrowed myth, and other phenomena which were considered in the previous chapter; more surely datable is the appearance of Oriental objects and motifs on the mainland of Greece. Accurate studies in this fascinating field have been well carried out in recent decades. Some of their results, which rest upon careful analysis of large masses of material, can be summarized here; others will be noted in subsequent chapters, when we shall also have to consider the degree to which Greek economic, political, and intellectual progress was indebted to Oriental stimulus.

To the north of Attica there is almost no firm evidence of Oriental contacts in the eighth century proper. Boeotia, Phocis (including Delphi), Thessaly, and other northern districts lay off the main path. On the western side of the Peloponnesus, again, Olympia and other sites were at this time virtually as bare of Oriental materials as was northern Greece.[2] The main testimony derives from Sparta, the Argolid, Corinthia, and Attica. The southeastern districts, in sum, were the initial beachhead, from which alien influences penetrated the rest of the mainland only after 700.

Attic vases began to show Oriental influence to a limited degree rather early in the eighth century, perhaps earlier than

[2] Kunze, *Kretische Bronzereliefs*, 252–53.

any other mainland fabric.[3] Objects and materials of Oriental origin are, in absolute terms, few in Attica down to 700, but relatively are more numerous than anywhere else in Greece; in evaluating this fact, however, one must always keep in mind the more careful archaeological exploration of Attic soil. An ivory tusk was imported, and was worked locally into five nude female figurines, which were buried in a Dipylon grave of the mid-eighth century (see Plate 19a). The material and the form are Eastern, and in the modeling of these exquisite ladies great Syrian influence has been argued by some scholars; indebtedness at least is certain, though the whole spirit is Greek. In a grave of Eleusis, called the Isis grave, a noble woman was buried in the second half of the eighth century with a rich equipment of vases, some of which must have been family heirlooms from much earlier times. Besides native treasures the grave contained a chain of pearls of Egyptian porcelain, her earrings with three amber pieces in gold, a chain of small ivory beads and long Egyptian porcelain beads, an ivory brooch, and scarabs as well as the Egyptian idol from which the burial gains its name. A probably Phoenician amulet of blue glass, which should perhaps be placed before 750, was found in another grave in the Agora. By the eighth century gold became more plentiful in Attica and was worked into thin plates for jewel chests and diadems. These plates were stamped with designs in rectangular blocks, which could be repeated or rearranged *ad libidinem;* their minor elements are purely Geometric, but the major figures are imaginary monsters of Oriental type, lions slaying other animals or human beings, and so on—we shall have occasion later to consider the macabre spirit of death which was manifested here.

Elsewhere in southern Greece the principal evidence of

---

[3] Oriental pottery motifs: Chap. 5, n. 1 (p. 149). Dipylon ivories: Chap. 7, n. 5 (p. 255). Isis grave: A. N. Skias, *Arch. eph.* 1898, 106–10; on the much disputed date, see T. J. Dunbabin, *The Western Greeks* (Oxford, 1948), 462; *Kerameikos*, V. 1, 70 n. 101; Roland Hampe, *Frühe Griechische Sagenbilder in Böotien* (Athens, 1936), 3–4. Note that obsidian also appeared, and beside the developed Geometric vases two hand-made pots.

Agora amulet: R. S. Young, "An Early Amulet Found in Athens," *Hesperia*, Supp. VIII (1949), 427–33. Gold plates: Ohly, *Griechische Goldbleche.*

Oriental contact consists of new pottery motifs, especially at Corinth, of ivory, and of faïence. Ivory has been found at Corinth (Perachora), at Sparta (Artemis Orthia), at Argos (Heraeum), and elsewhere. Most of the pieces come after 700, but some plaques, brooches, and other items may be placed earlier. While the style is commonly Greek, the subjects are often Oriental-type monsters.[4] The scarabs and other faïence objects of Egyptian spirit which appear spottily at Perachora and elsewhere in the Aegean are a great problem, both in date and in origin. Some may be Phoenician, others Rhodian;[5] true Egyptian ware turns up in Greece well after 700, when the Greeks opened trade directly with the Nile delta.

In addition to ivory, faïence, and gold, the southeastern districts of the Greek mainland were probably importing textiles, papyrus, incense, and spices by the eighth century; presumably finished products in bronze, iron, silver, and gold also came, though virtually no certainly Oriental metal products of this century have yet been found west or north of Crete.[6] Students of Orientalizing styles in Greece and Etruria alike face a serious crux in the fact that demonstrably Oriental objects are far too uncommon to explain fully the evidences of Eastern imitation by local potters, sculptors, and smiths; no surely Oriental

---

[4] The Spartan ivories, which Barnett, *JHS*, LXVIII (1948), 14–15, calls "the most important though the dullest in Greece," he assigns to the eighth-sixth centuries. Dawkins, *Artemis Orthia*, 203–04, placed them from the first half of the eighth century on; Albright, *Aegean and Near East*, 162, would date them back into the late ninth century at least.

The source of ivory, according to Barnett, ibid. 1–2, was Syria (to the eighth century), but the Sudan, etc., must not be overlooked. Since ivory passed through Oriental middlemen, its true origin was unknown down to the days of Aristotle.

[5] Scarabs: Pendlebury, *Perachora*, I, 76–77, who notes the problem of their appearance in the deposits of Hera Akraia before 750; Lorimer, *Homer and the Monuments*, 88; Freiherr von

Bissing, *Zeit und Herkunft der in Cerveteri gefundenen Gefässe aus ägyptischer Faience* (Munich, 1941), on Rhodian origins. Tridacna shells: Blinkenberg, *Lindiaka* II-IV (Copenhagen, 1926), 5–31; Poulsen, *Der Orient*, 59–74. See also generally Pierre Amandry, "Objets orientaux en Grèce et en Italie aux VIII° et VII° siècles avant J.-C." *Syria*, XXXV (1958), 73–109.

[6] Luristan (or similar) bronzes: Crete, mid-ninth or mid-eighth century, Brock, *Fortetsa*, no. 1570, p. 199; Samos, 750–650, Buschor, *Forschungen und Fortschritte*, VIII (1932), 161; Corinth, perhaps seventh-century, *Perachora*, I, 138–39. The Phoenician bowl of Delphi (*Fouilles de Delphes*, V, pl. 18–20) and similar pieces are of the seventh century and later.

ivories, for instance, have yet been found in eighth-century Greek levels. The bearing of this situation will reappear when we consider the mode of contact between East and West.

ROUTES OF CONTACT

BY THE seventh century the Aegean was in contact with the Orient by several avenues.[7] One route was a great loop via the west, for the Greeks of the western colonies were early in touch with both Phoenicians and Etruscans. Another sea lane ran southward to Egypt from the late seventh century onward. A third extended up the Aegean into the Black Sea to the new colonies of Trapezus, Sinope, and others, and thence on to the northeastern corner of Asia Minor, where bronzes, iron, and textiles from Urartu and farther inland made their difficult way by caravan down to the shore. The fourth, and major, artery ran from Syria to the southeastern corner of the Aegean and thence primarily to the states bordering the Saronic Gulf, with spurs to Ionia on the one side and to Crete on the other (see Map No. 1).

This age-old route along the south coast of Asia Minor must have been virtually the only link during the first contacts between the Aegean and the East. Trade by land across Asia Minor, in particular, was certainly of no great importance in the early centuries of the first millennium B.C. Geographically, the mountains, deserts, and the very extent of the terrain hampered any extensive use of the land route by human or animal porters; political conditions in the peninsula were long as primitive as those which existed in Greece after the invasions of the late second millennium. In Asia Minor the earlier civilized structure of the Hittite realm was ended by barbarian tribes,

[7] Western route: Will, *Korinthiaka,* 74–75. Egyptian: Poulsen, *Der Orient,* 92, 100, 170. Black Sea: Barnett, *Aegean and Near East,* 228–32, who places Trapezus much too early. Asia Minor: Barnett, *JHS,* LXVIII (1948), 24. Mazzarino, *Fra Oriente e Occi-* dente, 285, postulates (erroneously, I think) that by land came military skills, religious ideas, mystical forces, money, astronomy; by sea, luxuries, the alphabet, artistic influences, commerce.

which apparently poured across the Hellespont. The chief of these tribes, to judge from later records, was the Phrygian, which is only now beginning to manifest itself in excavations at Gordium, Boghazköy, and elsewhere; its most recent student, Ekrem Akurgal, even suggests that the Phrygian people remained nomadic down virtually to 800 B.C. This is perhaps too desperate a conclusion in view of the still limited archaeological exploration of Anatolia, but the sites so far uncovered are marked by a very low plane of life.

Only after 800 did ordered states appear in Asia Minor.[8] Far to the east, Urartu became consolidated under Assyrian pressure; just inland from the west coast, kings in Phrygia and Lydia grew powerful enough to establish capitals with palaces and tombs. Of early Lydia one cannot yet speak, but the excavations at Gordium have shown that by the end of the eighth century Phrygia was gaining contact with the outside world. A native alphabet, derived from the Greek, was in use, and the well-known type of Cycladic bowl with pendant semicircles had found its way to Larisa shortly after 750;[9] a vase of Cypriote manufacture or influence and faïence work probably

---

[8] Urartu: Goetze, *Hethither, Churriter und Assyrer*, 172–76. Lydia: Dunbabin, *Greeks and Their Eastern Neighbours*, 69–70; G. M. A. Hanfmann, "Prehistoric Sardis," *Studies to D. M. Robinson*, I, 160–83. Phrygia: Akurgal, *Phrygische Kunst*, whose effort to link Phrygian and Greek is not convincing; G. and A. Körte, *Gordion: Ergebnisse der Ausgrabung im Jahre 1900* (*Jahrbuch des deutschen archäologischen Instituts*, Erganzungsheft V, 1904, 1–27); Seton Lloyd, *Early Anatolia*, 191–203; Dunbabin, *Greeks and Their Eastern Neighbours*, 63–68; Bittel, *Kleinasien*, 75–76, 81–86; Rodney S. Young's reports on his continuing Gordium excavations in *AJA*, LXI (1957), and following. Frankfort, *Art and Architecture in the Ancient Orient*, 186, denies the existence of a specifically Phrygian art; on Phrygian pottery, which has an interesting geometric character in some types, see

Dunbabin, *Greeks and Their Eastern Neighbours*, 65–66. Roebuck, *Ionian Trade and Colonization*, 42–60, considers relations with the interior.

[9] Johannes Boehlau and Karl Schefold, *Larisa am Hermos III: Die Kleinfunde* (Berlin, 1942), 170. Cypriote work: Young, *AJA*, LXI (1957), 328; the earliest Greek vase at Gordion thus far found is an East Greek bird-bowl of about the mid-seventh century, *University of Pennsylvania Museum Bulletin*, XVII. 4 (1953), 33. Samos finds: Akurgal, *Phrygische Kunst*, 33 (Buschor, though, called them "sicher samisch"); I agree with Miss Mellink, *AJA*, LXI (1957), 393, that Akurgal reverses the current in calling these a Greek export to Phrygia. Midas: Aristotle, fragment 611, 37 (Rose); Pollux IX. 83; Herodotus I. 14. 2; *Ancient Near Eastern Texts*, 284–85; Eusebius dated Midas 738–696/5.

came to Gordium from the coast. In the other direction a few Phrygian pots were discovered at Samos in strata before 700, and King Midas both married a Greek wife from Cyme and dedicated offerings at Delphi. To the east as well Phrygia now had relations, which were rather closer: huge caldrons of Urartian origin were placed in the tomb of a Phrygian king, and the Sargon Annals of Assyria refer under 712 and 709 to Mita (Midas) of Phrygia.

Virtually all of this evidence, however, is from very near the end of the eighth century. Then came the terrific wave of Cimmerian invaders. These peoples, the first horse-mounted nomads who touched civilized lands, broke across the Caucasus and wreaked wide havoc in the Near East early in the seventh century.[1] While Assyria eventually repelled the threat, Phrygia fell, in either 696/5 (Eusebius) or 676 (Julius Africanus); even along the coast of Asia Minor the Greeks shivered and had to beat off bands of the barbarians. In the place of Phrygia, which seems to have remained a land of small states, the more southerly inland kingdom of Lydia rose in the later seventh century and pushed its rule both eastward and especially west down to the Greek coast. The picture which Herodotus suggests of active Lydian commerce refers to this later period.

For the era with which we are here concerned, then, there is thus far no evidence of any important trade route across Asia Minor. The products of Urartu may at this time have made their way west mainly via North Syria, which the kings of Urartu controlled for a time early in the eighth century; and the "Hittite" influence which occurs in Orientalizing Greece almost surely came by this road from its home in the upper Euphrates–North Syrian district.[2]

---

[1] L. A. Jel'nizkij, "Kimmerijzy i Kimmerijsskaya Kul'tura," *Vestnik Drevnej Istorii*, 1949. 3, 14–26, summarized in *Historia*, I (1950), 344; Mazzarino, *Fra Oriente e Occidente*, 135–39; Herodotus I. 6. 3, Jeremiah 6: 22–23; Ezekiel 38–39. Dunbabin, *Greeks and Their Eastern Neighbours*, 68–69, suggests that the Cimmerian settlement in Cappadocia forced the rest of Asia Minor to turn westward and so opened it to Greek influence.

[2] Akurgal, *Späthethitische Bildkunst*, 145, and *Phrygische Kunst*, 108–10; Dunbabin, *Greeks and Their Eastern Neighbours*, 62; Smith, *Antiquaries Journal*, XXII (1942), 92–94, 102–04; on Urartu, Amandry, *Syria*, XXIV (1944–45), 164–65, remains uncertain.

GREEKS OR PHOENICIANS?

WHILE MODERN VIEWS on the date and route of the renewed contacts between East and West have not always been in agreement, the most vocal controversy has long swirled about the identity of the traders themselves. Were they Greeks or Phoenician-Syrians? And insofar as they may have been Greek, just which Greeks? On both points the answers which one returns are significant for a just appreciation of the vigor of Aegean society and of the relative significance of its various areas in the eighth century.

As between Greeks and Phoenicians, the initiative in resuming Eastern contacts lay, I think, firmly in Greek hands. That this is the correct view is now often accepted, though many still cling to the earlier opinion which accorded to the Orient the place of honor. The various Greek localities entitled *Phoinikous* or the like have been considered evidence for Phoenician trading factories; at Corinth the cult of Melikertes is equated with that of Phoenician Melkarth; and the appearance there of temple prostitutes of Aphrodite seems to smack of Oriental background. The worship of the Kabiri at Samothrace and elsewhere also has been assigned to an Eastern origin, especially when connected with Herodotus' tale of Phoenician settlement at Thasos.[3] The most influential testimony which has promoted general acceptance of Oriental primacy is that of myth and epic. Such Greek tales as the story of Cadmus credit Eastern adventurers with settlements and innovations at many places; in Homer there are several references to Phoenician merchants.

[3] Herodotus II. 44, VI. 47. 1, IV. 147 (Thera), I. 105. 3 (Cythera), II. 49. 3 and V. 57–58 (Thebes). Pro-Phoenician arguments may be found in V. Bérard, *Les Phéniciens et l'Odyssée*, 2 vols. (Paris, 1902–03); E. Maas, *Griechen und Semiten auf den Isthmus von Korinth* (Berlin, 1903). See more recently Demargne, *La Crète dédalique*, 119–28; Dunbabin, *JHS* LXVIII (1948), 66, and *Greeks and Their Eastern Neighbours*, 52, 54–55; Lorimer, *Homer and the Monuments*, 67–76; Bengt Hemberg, *Die Kabiren* (Uppsala, 1950); Will, *Korinthiaka*, 67–72, 169, 229–31; and in general Beloch, *Griechische Geschichte*, I. 2, 65–76. Albright, who certainly does not underestimate Phoenician activity, concludes (*Studies in the History of Culture*, 44) that the Phoenicians did not colonize the Aegean, but set up temporary "factories."

Virtually none of this material will bear any weight on the issue at hand. The term "Phoinix," for instance, is a Greek word for "date palm," and appears only in the southernmost reaches of Greece where this tree can grow. Melikertes is surely of Greek origin; though both the goddess Aphrodite and phases of her worship may reflect the East, she is not necessarily a late arrival; the Great Gods of Samothrace are equally Greek. In considering the myths generally, one must remember that to a very great extent they were consolidated or even formed after 700, in an era when the Greeks *were* acquainted with the Orient and realized its cultural precedence over the Aegean. The Homeric evidence, of which so much has been made, must be assessed with particular care. In the *Iliad* there is only one reference (XXIII. 741–745) to Phoenician trade, and Phoenicia seems a far-off land (VI. 289 ff.). The more extensive passages in the *Odyssey* (XIII. 272 ff., XIV. 288 ff., XV. 415 ff.) show us Phoenicians as trading westward along the coast of Crete and the south and west shores of Greece, but they do not depict Phoenicians in the Aegean proper. And, finally, the physical evidence for interchanges points both in Greece and in the East primarily to Syria, not to Phoenicia.[4]

The wide-scale appearance of Phoenician traders in the Aegean is thus a fiction, but in its place some students are now erecting a hypothesis that Oriental craftsmen—ivory workers, bronze smiths, and so on—migrated westward in the eighth century to teach the backward Greeks new skills.[5] The view has attractive elements; above all, it would serve to explain the presence of Oriental borrowings on a scale which cannot be satisfactorily accounted for by direct Oriental imports in Greece. Yet I cannot feel that in the end this view puts the mode of Ori-

[4] Dunbabin, *Greeks and Their Eastern Neighbours*, 35, who points out also that the first imports into Greece were Syrian, not Phoenician; Smith, *Antiquaries Journal*, XXII (1942), 94–96; Clairmont, *Berytus*, XI (1954–55), 85–139; on the recent finds of Greek pottery of before 700 at Tell Sukas, see *Archaeology*, XII (1959), 283.

[5] Barnett, *JHS*, LXVIII (1948), 6;

Dunbabin, *Greeks and Their Eastern Neighbours*, 41, 49; Cyrus H. Gordon, "Ugaritic Guilds and Homeric ΔΗΜΙΟΕΡΓΟΙ," *Aegean and Near East*, 136–43. Kunze, *Kretische Bronzereliefs*, 263–64, underlines the hypothetical nature of this migration; Frankfort, *Art and Architecture of the Ancient Orient*, 259 n. 123, is very skeptical.

ental contacts in the proper light. The Aegean was sadly lacking in kings and great lords who could attract such craftsmen. Would they have been inclined to leave the surer markets of their far richer world, where Assyrian might was beginning to bring order and to provide royal markets? Is there, again, any reason to deny the equally logical assumption that Greek craftsmen would have found profit in picking up the still simple skills of the East? Greek artisans, as we know, did make their way later as far afield as Etruria.[6] While Eastern traders or skilled workers may well have entered the eighth-century Aegean on occasion, there are weighty grounds, both logical and factual, for discounting the significance of this element.

We tend, after all, to misread most early commerce in terms of the modern expansion of Europe overseas. Throughout history the less civilized areas have quite commonly tended to take the initiative in seeking the riches of the developed areas, either by trade or by invasion (as one meditates on the relative cultural levels of western Europe in the Renaissance and of contemporary India and China, it is possible to argue that such a pattern was true even in early modern times). We have seen that the Mycenaean Greeks sought out Syria and Egypt, rather than the reverse; the same pattern was true in later, classic times down to the days of Alexander; there are no logical grounds for postulating an inverse flow during the eighth century alone.

Moreover, anyone who wishes to draw a portrait of venturesome Phoenician merchants and artisans must, on the basis of our evidence, accord the same audacity to the contemporary Greeks. The distribution of Protogeometric and Early Geometric pottery within the Aegean shows that internal trade had already revived by 800. During the next century the social and political framework of the Aegean was obviously infused with a remarkable vigor, for the Greeks spilled out in all directions, to the uncivilized West as well as toward the cultured East. Attic, Corinthian, and other vases of the age depict ships, and the Attic scenes of coastal raiding suggest that not all of the Greek seafaring was of peaceful nature.[7] On the manner in which this

[6] See below, Chap. 11, n. 9 (p. 370).
[7] G. S. Kirk, "Ships on Geometric Vases," *BSA*, XLIV (1949), 93–153, who argues that the appearance of

"trade" was conducted in the eighth century I shall essay to be more specific in Chapter 11; here the most important matter is the degree to which objects and ideas moved between East and West, and in whose ships.

The most useful factual evidence on the direction of flow between East and West has recently been uncovered on the North Syrian coast in the excavations at Al Mina, by the mouth of the Orontes River. At this seacoast end of a main route to Mesopotamia a trading colony, surely of Greek origin, which has left a mass of Greek pottery, was established at least by the middle of the eighth century, and perhaps a little earlier—the lowest levels of the site have been swept away by the Orontes.[8] No similar deposit of Oriental ware has yet been found in Greece, and in my opinion the likelihood of such a discovery is not great.

The Greek traders at Al Mina, to judge from their pottery, came chiefly from the Cyclades, secondarily from Rhodes and the "East Greek" area. This distribution suggests the identity of some of the major trading areas to the East; we have only recently come to appreciate the wide-scale activity of the Cyclades in particular, both eastward and to the western Mediterranean.[9]

ships on eighth-century ware may reflect the greater skill of the potter in depicting complicated objects; R. J. Williams, "Ships in Greek Vase-painting," *Greece and Rome*, XVIII (1949), 126–37, 143–44.

[8] Leonard Woolley, "Excavations at Al Mina, Sueidia I: The Archaeological Report," *JHS*, LVIII (1938), 1–30, 133–70; Martin Robertson, "The Early Greek Vases," *JHS*, LX (1940), 1–21, and LXVI (1946), 125; Sidney Smith, "The Greek Trade at Al Mina," *Antiquaries Journal*, XXII (1942), 87–112. Hanfmann, *Aegean and Near East*, 175, puts the earliest material back to 800 on the basis of unpublished sherds; Dunbabin, *Greeks and Their Eastern Neighbours*, 25–30, supports this conclusion when he observes that the Cycladic cups with pendant

semicircles do not appear in western colonies. R. M. Cook, *JHS*, LXVI (1946), 78–83, tends to pull down the date of Al Mina.

On the usual identification of this site with the Poseideion of Herodotus (not of Strabo), cf. Smith, 96–98; Will, *Korinthiaka*, 343 n. 3, 53 n. 6. Even if it were so called, Dunbabin's suggestion, *Greeks and Their Eastern Neighbours*, 28, that it was named from the Panionian shrine of Poseidon Helikonios or other Ionian influence seems doubtful.

[9] See above, Chap. 5, n. 2 (p. 150). Note, however, that such a transit point as Thera remained conservative in its own pottery: Buschor, *AM*, LIV (1929), 162; Charles Dugas, *La Céramique des Cyclades* (Paris, 1925), 175; Will, *Korinthiaka*, 62–63.

While the islanders may often have served as intermediaries on the long, dangerous haul from the mainland of Greece to Syria, it would be a serious mistake to assume that Eastern influence poured into Greece through this single funnel. The daring of Greek seafarers as a whole must not be underestimated; by the eighth century traders from many parts of the Aegean—Ionians, islanders, Cretans, and men of the mainland as well—were surely beginning to tread the eastern path. One Corinthian vase, thus, has turned up at Al Mina before 700, and the varied evidence of Oriental materials and ideas in Athens, Corinth, and elsewhere in Greece proper seems scarcely explicable as the fruit of indirect contact.

This is an important point. Since the mainland states of southern Greece were the principal leaders along the main line of Hellenic development, it is a significant matter whether they drew directly from the East or, as too often argued, through such an intermediary as the islands, Ionia, Crete, or Cyprus. As far as the old claim of Ionia is concerned, we may now be brief. Undoubtedly a spur of the main trade route curved north along the west coast of Asia Minor. Wares which must thus far be described rather vaguely as East Greek appear at Tarsus as well as Al Mina;[1] Samos was importing Cypriote figurines in numbers by the eighth century and knew Oriental ivory traditions; and other evidence that the cities of Asia Minor were in contact with the East by sea—but not this early by land—will probably appear as archaeological investigation proceeds. Yet nothing so far suggests that Ionia gained Eastern contact before the mainland of Greece; East Greek pottery, too, is very rare in Crete, in Aegina, and on the coasts of Greece proper even in the seventh century.[2] As we shall see later, trade must have moved across

---

[1] East Greek exports: G. M. A. Hanfmann, "On Some Eastern Greek Wares Found at Tarsus," *Aegean and Near East*, 165–84, speculates on Rhodes and Samos as sources. He here revises his argument (*AJA*, LII [1948], 142) that Greek trade in Cilicia began only with the seventh century. Scattered evidence of Greek Geometric sherds in surface finds at Cilician sites (including Mopsuhestia) is summed up by M. V. Seton-Williams, *AnatSt*, IV (1954), 136–37. Samos: Ohly, *AM*, LXV (1940), LXVI (1941); Nimrud-type ivory, Barnett, *JHS*, LXVIII (1948), 3.

[2] Kraiker, *Aigina*, 33–34; Brock, *Fortetsa*, 190; Roebuck, *Ionian Trade and Colonization*, 83–86. Note on the other hand the abundance of Corinthian ware at Old Smyrna, J. K. Anderson, *BSA*, LIII–IV (1958–59), 138–51.

the Aegean, but the dominant current therein seems rather to have set from west to east.

The place as tutor of Greece that Ionia was once granted is now often assigned to Crete.[3] This island was the ancestral home of Minoan culture, which had earlier played a similar role; it seems to have remained richer and more settled even in the Dark ages; and alike in religious practices and in that development of the arts which the later Greeks associated with the figure of Daedalus, Crete held a large role in Greek tradition.

And yet the early interest of Cretan smiths and potters in Oriental styles really proves no more than that the native traditions of the island made them receptive to patterns which were ultimately based to some extent upon that Minoan-Mycenaean background as transmitted eastward in the second millennium. Nor did Cretan Orientalizing developments have a powerful influence on the Greek mainland. If one looks attentively at the emergence of Orientalizing pottery in Greece, Cretan mediation cannot be shown to have any major role; even in Corinthian work its effect has been overstressed.[4]

The place of Crete, in sum, in stimulating mainland Greece is not entirely to be dismissed, but on the other hand it must not be magnified. If Crete was perhaps the first truly Greek land—for Cyprus does not count in this respect—to open its mind to Eastern whispers, it lay nonetheless to one side of the really vital line of communication. Its artistic styles were not the seedbed

[3] Demargne, *La Crète dédalique*, passim; Levi, *Early Hellenic Pottery*, 7–8, with references to Loewy et al., and "Gli scavi del 1954 sull'acropoli di Gortina," *Annuario*, XVII–XVIII (1955–56), 207–88; Kunze, *Kretische Bronzereliefs*, 261, puts the matter best in observing that, however significant Crete might have been, this does not eliminate direct contact between the Orient and other Greek areas.
[4] Cretan influence on Corinth: Demargne, *La Crète dédalique*, 341–46; K. Friis Johansen, *Les Vases sicyoniens* (Paris, 1923), 62–66; Levi, *Early Hellenic Pottery*, 16–18, and

"Κρήτη καὶ Κόρινθος ἢ 'Αρχαιολογία καὶ ἀκριβεῖς ἐπιστῆμαι," *Kretika Chronika*, IV (1950), 129–92; Payne, *Necrocorinthia*, 4–6, 53, and *Protokorinthische Vasenmalerei* (Berlin, 1933), 11. Contra: Brock, *Fortetsa*, 191, 218–19, 160; Dunbabin, *JHS*, LXVIII (1948), 66; R. M. Cook, *JHS*, LXVI (1946), 93; Kübler, *Kerameikos*, V. 1, 153–54; Matz, *GGK*, I, 255–61; Weinberg, *Corinth*, VII. 1, 22–23; Will, *Korinthiaka*, 59–67; Jörg Schäfer, *Studien zu den griechischen Reliefpithoi des 8.–6. Jahrhunderts v. Chr. aus Kreta, Rhodos, Tenos und Boiotien* (Diss. Tübingen, 1955–56), 42–43, 108–09.

from which the great development of Greece 750–650 was to spring, and even the interesting achievements reached at the most lively center in Crete, Cnossus, had come to a sad end by 650.

A fourth candidate for the role of intermediary between the East and the Greek mainland has occasionally been advanced: the island of Cyprus. The light which has been thrown on Cypriote development in recent decades by the excavations of the Swedish Cypriote Expedition and others has better defined its native development, and has shown that the island lay in a backwater until the seventh century. On the eastern side the Phoenicians were active by 800; on the north and west coasts a somewhat different pottery tradition of black-on-red ware had ties with Cilicia. These coasts also had contact with the Aegean, and in the eighth century their wares began to appear in some quantity in Crete and on the Greek mainland.[5] So, too, some bronze work of the Aegean perhaps stems from Cyprus, while on the other hand Attic and Cycladic Late Geometric vases have been found on the island. This evidence shows no more than that a spur of the main trade route linked Cyprus with the west. No direct evidence attests that the Greeks made their acquaintance with Oriental products in the harbors of Cyprus—the history of the alphabet, for instance, reveals that the Cypriote syllabary played no part in the creation of the Greek alphabet from a Phoenician prototype.

If we are to visualize properly the renewed links between East and West, we must virtually eliminate Asia Minor proper from consideration and fix our attention upon the sea route from the Aegean to North Syrian ports. Along this path tiny ships had

[5] Brock, *Fortetsa*, 190–91, 217–18; Roebuck, *Ionian Trade and Colonization*, 65–67; Dunbabin, *Gnomon*, XXIV (1952), 193–94, and *Greeks and Their Eastern Neighbours*, 49–51; Gjerstad, *Swedish Cyprus Expedition*, IV. 2, 262–69; Lorimer, *Homer and the Monuments*, 78. Cypriote models may have influenced such Greek vases as K. 1327 (*Kerameikos*, V. 1, 4, 170); *Asine*, 325 fig. 221, nn. 7–8; and an unpublished contemporary vase of Argos. Cypriote bronze work: Brock, *Fortetsa*, 22. Dunbabin, *Greeks and Their Eastern Neighbours*, 72–73, lists twelve early Attic vases in Cyprus beside two Corinthian and five or six Cycladic; cf. Young, *Late Geometric Graves*, 222, on Curion. But see above, Chap. 5, n. 2 (p. 150).

occasionally ventured throughout the Dark ages, but from the very last days of the ninth century—and still more in the eighth—sailors from the Aegean dared the dangerous trips in growing numbers. The increasing stability and riches of the Aegean states and a native energy which was already springing the confines of the Geometric pottery made these areas now ready to receive what they found in the East. To a degree which cannot be specified, but must have been minor, traders and artists from the East may have made their way westward, seeking their fortunes. Yet the weight of the drive lay in the Aegean, and cannot be localized in any one district.

Once resumed in a continuous fashion, contacts with the Orient were to multiply rapidly as the Aegean passed into the seventh and then the sixth century. Greek mercenaries served Egypt and Babylon, traders settled down at Egyptian Naucratis by the end of the seventh century, and such men of inquiring bent as Hecataeus followed. Herodotus affords clear evidence that by the sixth century political connections were growing; the upshot was the wave of Persian attack and at long last the conquest of Alexander. Throughout subsequent chapters the Orient must frequently appear in our story, for from the eighth century Greece no longer lay remote and virtually insulated from the eastern Mediterranean.

In the first steps, which have alone been considered in this chapter, much remains dark. "The time is not yet come," observes R. D. Barnett on the connection of East and West, "when we can sufficiently explain more than half those early influences. There are still too many unknown factors. The threads of different origin cross and recross one another and cannot be unravelled." [6] Apart from the alphabet and some evidence of myth, the only signposts are those of physical objects which passed to and fro, and not even all of these—textiles, for instance—have survived. The effects upon Greek social, religious, and political developments from these initial contacts are ticklish problems on which little more than hypothesis will be possible.

The basic issue, however, is this: did Oriental influence have an overpowering weight in setting the course of Greek civ-

[6] *JHS*, LXVIII (1948), 7.

ilization? My answer, which has already been given and will be substantiated later, is a firm negative, on the basis of the evidence so far in hand and of the main course of Greek history. Set off behind the buffers of Cyprus, Rhodes, and Crete, the Aegean had still by 700 only limited contact with the Orient. The material which has been adduced in the preceding pages is in truth very scattered and limited; beside it must be placed an infinitely greater amount of evidence for purely local progress.

In the revolution which was under way in the more advanced areas of Greece by 700 and to which we must now turn, the vigor came from strong native roots. Only in its surface modes of expression did indebtedness to the Orient appear; those artistic motifs and principles of composition which can be traced to Oriental roots underwent a significant sea change as they passed over the tossing waters of the eastern Mediterranean. Parenthetically, it may also be observed that as the Greek artists began to liberate themselves from earlier conventions there was one other source from which they could draw inspiration: the heirlooms and survivals of the freer Minoan-Mycenaean styles. These, too, occasionally served as points of departure.[7] In its basic form, nonetheless, the age of revolution was a new step in human history.

---

[7] This remains a very debated point in art as in religion and other fields. Kunze, *Kretische Bronzereliefs*, 131, almost eliminates any survivals, as do many others; apparent Minoan-Mycenaean motifs would have come back from the Orient. See also Demargne, *La Crète dédalique;* Valentin Müller, "Minoisches Nachleben oder orientalischer Einfluss in der frühkretischen Kunst?" *AM*, L (1925), 51–70; Poulsen, *Der Orient*, 76–77.

Yet the logical and historical possibility of minor survivals cannot be ruled out of court; see Schäfer, *Reliefpithoi*, 57–58, 66; Levi, *Annuario*, X–XII (1927–29), and *AJA*, XLIX (1945), 292; and below, Chap. 7, n. 8 (p. 244).

CHAPTER 7

THE INTELLECTUAL UPHEAVAL: I

ௗௗௗௗௗௗௗௗௗௗௗௗௗௗௗௗௗௗ

DURING THE AGE of revolution the Greek outlook on life was definitively consolidated. The origins of this outlook lay much earlier, and its magnificent potentialities had already been partly demonstrated. Just before the intellectual upheaval commenced, a mighty surge of human life and passion had welled forth in the *Iliad;* the potters of the great Dipylon vases had created stiff but poignant pageants of war and death. These twin products were the summation of what had gone before and the herald of the onrush which was immediately to follow.

The century of most evident change covered the decades 750–650. In this era potter, smith, and poet developed amazingly their skill and clarity. The media of architecture and large-scale sculpture, new to Greek civilization proper, made their appearance. No longer must we be content to handle a Geometric vase and to sense instinctively in it the qualities of logic and symmetry which mark Hellenic civilization; for by the end of the age of revolution many of the basic values of this outlook had attained clear expression in physical and intellectual form. Taken in sum, the achievements of the epoch represent an enlarged dimension for Greek civilization and, by extension, for Western culture.

The intellectual development was attended by, and rested on, great political, social, and economic changes; yet these facets in turn depended on the new views in men's minds. If first things are to be put first, any study of the age must begin with the major forces driving Greek civilization as a whole. This chapter will consider the evidence of the arts; the next, the evidence of literature. Then we shall be ready to analyze the parallel social, political, and economic progress. In this fascinating epoch, unfortunately, the observer cannot treat every aspect in detail; but we must at least be careful to note the signs of stress and conservatism as well as the marks of triumphant advance.

THE TEMPO OF CHANGE

IF THE SPECIAL QUALITY of the age of revolution is to be appreciated fully, its amazing rapidity must be recognized. This recognition, in turn, is possible only if one discards or seriously modifies the conventional concepts of historical change as a purely evolutionary process.

It is not my purpose here to treat the problem of historical tempo at length in philosophical terms. The step from historian to philosopher is deceptively easy, and often is fatal to the practicing historian. The saving grace of the historical discipline is its base upon specific fact in specific time. Yet, in marshaling the facts, one inevitably employs broad concepts which are nonetheless philosophical for being applied, usually, in an unconscious manner; and we need to be clear as to the nature and bearing of these concepts.

Current views of historical change have not been easily attained. While a rudimentary sense of the passing of time is a common trait of most peoples, anthropologists have shown that primitive societies often have no true concept of chronological development. In historic Greece Thucydides penned a marvelous picture of gradual but true change in the opening chapters of his history, but only rarely was ancient historiography able to come up to this intellectual level. Far more common in both Greek and Roman thought were tales of sudden creation and then essentially unchanging endurance of religious and political institutions, on which time washed to and fro in insignificant froth. The advent of Christianity, which emphasized human progress toward a divine destination, marked only a partial break in this pattern; true belief in substantial development as a historical principle has been a slow development in Western civilization. The rise of the division of historical time as "ancient," "medieval," and "modern" from the Renaissance on marks one stage; further progress came in the nineteenth century as Western civilization entered upon a rapid period of external alteration. The consequence was the interest in history which has been obvious in recent generations and the general fascination of archaeology as an intensive search for man's remote past.

The historical canon of evolution has commonly been couched in terms which are markedly similar to the concept of change accepted by the biological and physical sciences since the days of Darwin and Lyell—not, to be sure, through direct borrowing by the historian from the scientist but rather as an expression of a common intellectual outlook. History, that is, has been written as a slow process of continuous development. Beside and implicit in this view is the doctrine which the biologists call the preformation of characteristics: "The characters of all organisms were present from the start of evolution and the progress of evolution is wholly due to their becoming expressed in the bodies of organisms." Or, as V. Gordon Childe put the doctrine succinctly in historical terms, "In the first innovations the germs of all subsequent improvement were latent." [1]

This conceptual scheme has been of immense value to the historian. It has enhanced his standing in society, for he may claim the right to explain the present as a product of the past; it has also given him a simple scheme for ordering investigations of historical fact. That it also imposes blinkers upon one's view has not been so apparent. Students of human development, moreover, have failed to appreciate the warning implicit in the recent drift of scientific thought on the problem of change. In their detailed investigations of the physical and biological worlds, scientists have not been able fully to substantiate the general doctrines of continuous development, useful though these theories have been in many respects for practical research. The discoveries of the quantum theory in physics and of mutations in

[1] William Bateson, Presidential Address to the British Association in Australia, 1914, as summarized by George Stuart Carter, *A Hundred Years of Evolution* (New York, 1957), 122–23; Childe, *Dawn of European Civilization*, xv.

biology have shown the possibility of sudden changes not implicit in the pre-existing structure.

It is high time, too, that historians gave over compressing their materials into a Procrustean bed of slow evolution. Students of revolutionary eras have stumbled over difficulties which they do not always fully comprehend; the apparent suddenness and magnitude of these flood tides do not seem entirely explicable by an analysis of pre-existing stresses and forces. More recently investigators of early human history have found themselves confronted by what appear to be discontinuities, the appearance of *new* characteristics, and rapid spurts in development. The truth is that man's rise has been a shifting process of slow evolution and of sudden alteration. In epochs of the latter type new patterns of life are rapidly set on foundations which, no doubt, were slowly constructed in previous centuries; yet the resulting structure is stamped with a solidity and breadth which could not be predicted from these foundations. Such a period, for instance, was the late fourth millennium B.C., when civilization emerged in Mesopotamia and Egypt.[2]

The development of Greek civilization can only be understood if its tempo is conceived as one of varying rapidity. The eleventh century B.C. was an era when men swiftly established the basic patterns of Hellenic culture, but our evidence is much too limited to permit entire determination of the speed and dimensions of so fundamental a step. Movement in the next centuries was treacle-slow; modern students, in keeping with their evolutionary bias, have probably exaggerated the inevitability of continuous development in the Dark ages. Then, with amazing speed, a violent period of upheaval broke out shortly after 750.

This revolution is too notable to have been entirely overlooked by students of early Greece, but its true nature has not often been appreciated. Archaeological or philological specialists, in pursuing their particular interests, have seen only limited aspects, and have failed to comprehend the tremendous width of interlinked change which then occurred in virtually every field

[2] Frankfort frequently stressed this aspect, as in *The Birth of Civilization in the Near East;* see also Sir Mortimer Wheeler, *Archaeology from the Earth* (Penguin, 1956), 23–25.

of life. Scholars of more general interests have, on the other hand, often begun with the age of revolution proper and have not measured either its connections to earlier stages or the precise dimensions of its alterations.

Above all, the fact that the main wave of change took place in only a few decades is rarely comprehended. Establishment of this point requires more precise chronological calculations than have been necessary in the earlier centuries which we have already traversed. While the relative chronology of progress is reasonably certain, the historian who tries to convert archaeological sequences into absolute dates B.C. quickly feels that he has fallen into a bottomless morass; any chronological system now advanced will have to remain provisional and approximate, barring some unbelievably lucky finds of datable Oriental items in Greek lands. Still, the morass is not absolutely bottomless. A student who proceeds with care can win through to sufficient clarity on the basic objective—viz., the determination of the bounds on either side of the age of revolution.

The chronological schemes of later Greek historians and antiquaries reach back with some certainty as far as about 600 and furnish less secure materials running on to the middle of the eighth century. If one investigates these indications in detail, they display a noticeable concentration of activity in the last decades of the eighth century and the first half of the next century: a great outburst of colonization; much more extensive political activity at home in the form of wars and internal reorganization of political structures; the international popularity of certain religious and athletic festivals and the introduction of new religious rites; and even the appearance of named artists and artistic inventions. This material, of course, is open to doubt. Popular memory of events long past is notably untrustworthy; writing, again, came into common use only about the end of the eighth century; and there are serious chronological inconsistencies. Safe employment of the body of tradition is possible solely if we can link it to physical evidence, which remains our surest guide on *relative* chronology down to the sixth century.

Within the physical evidence, the most useful material is that afforded by the pottery, which was ever changing in motifs and shapes. The decorative patterns in themselves are not always safe criteria for dating vases, inasmuch as motifs could be copied from earlier work (as in some Late Geometric vases of Athens); but pottery specialists seem agreed that changes in types of vases and the development of shapes within each type are reliable guides to pottery evolution. On these bases, successions of styles and substyles in Attic and Corinthian pottery have been firmly established across early Greek history, and soon should be possible for Argive work. Down to Late Geometric or even Orientalizing ware, however, similar chains are not yet fully certain for the islands or along the eastern coast of the Aegean. In the major traditions it is also possible to go some distance in distinguishing schools or masters, especially in Attic and Corinthian work from about 700 B.C., for pottery of artistic quality was made at only a few workshops in any early Greek state.

While this material is extremely useful for establishing relative development, the historian must always remember that any absolute dates assigned to early Greek pottery are, at best, skillful guesses. Stylistic evolution did not necessarily proceed evenly over the entire Aegean basin or even at the same pace in all shops in any one area. Backward-looking potters, who clung to sub-Geometric styles, existed side by side with progressive craftsmen well down into the seventh century. Heirlooms, too, are always turning up in any extensive set of graves along with much later material. To make proper use of the pottery evidence, one must be careful never to build too much on a single vase, and must also attempt to peg the sequences to absolute dates drawn from other sources.

Efforts to this end have already been advanced in Chapters 2 and 3 for the beginning phases of Greek history. For the period now in question, the two main avenues are Oriental connections and the establishment of the Greek colonies in the West. On the Oriental side, unfortunately, no method yet exists to link Greek physical remains continuously with the absolute chronology of these lands until after 700, when political contacts began. The later stages of the Greek trading post at Al Mina can be tied down sufficiently for us to be sure that the earlier Greek material at this site is of the eighth century, though how far back it goes in the century cannot be entirely established. The Assyrian conquest of Cilicia is physically marked in the strata of Tarsus, which Sennacherib took in 696, and the Cimmerian devastation of Asia Minor, well dated to the early seventh century from Assyrian records, enables us to place the Phrygian tombs recently uncovered at Gordium before 700. Scattered finds of Greek vases in Syrian and Palestinian sites, which have already been noted, give further suggestions of absolute dates; but on the whole the material thus far at hand is too limited and fragmentary for safe conclusions on a wide scale. The surest ties between Eastern chronology and Greek pottery remain the Greek settlement at Naucratis *c.* 610 and the Lydian destruction of Old Smyrna a little after 600.

The main path toward establishment of absolute chronology for Greece lies in the second alternative, a roundabout detour through the Greek colonies of Sicily and Italy. For some of these colonies Thucydides gives specific dates in his brief sketch of early Sicilian history; for the others generally consistent colonization dates are preserved in the Greek chronological tradition. Cumae, on this material, is placed about 750; Syracuse, 733; Megara Hyblaea, 728; Gela, 688; Selinus, 628; and so on.[3] At most of these points modern archaeological exploration has turned up pottery of Corinthian origin—the first Orientalizing experiments (kotylai and aryballoi) in the earliest tombs of Cumae, somewhat more developed Protocorinthian vases in the first burials at Syracuse, and successively thereafter more advanced stages of Protocorinthian styles down to the foundation of Selinus, where these styles scarcely appear and Corinthian work proper begins to hold the field. On this correlation of specific colonization dates and vase styles depends the chronology of Corinthian vases; on this in turn rest most of

[3] Thucydides VI. 3–4; other authors give quite variant dates (Eusebius, e.g., assigned Cumae as far back as 1051). Dunbabin, *Western Greeks,* 435–71, especially 460–70, discusses the literary evidence in detail. See also R. M. Cook, *JHS,* LXVI (1946), 74–77; Robertson, *BSA,* XLIII (1948), 54; A. R. Burn, "Dates in Early Greek History," *JHS,* LV (1935), 130–46, and LXIX (1949), 70–73, who lowers Thucydides' dates by artificial juggling. The fall of Old Smyrna is now discussed by J. M. Cook, *BSA,* LIII–IV (1958–59), 24–27.

the absolute dates assigned to Greek artistic development in the late eighth and seventh centuries. A subsidiary support for the scheme exists in early Etruscan tombs; at the Bocchoris tomb of Tarquinia, for instance, a Phoenician faïence vase with the name of Bocchoris, pharaoh of the Egyptian Delta about 718–712, was laid beside Italian imitations of Protocorinthian ware which should not be more than a generation younger, say 690.[4]

This scheme is ingenious, useful—and slightly shaky. Though the progress of Protocorinthian and then Corinthian pottery agrees reasonably well with the succession of Thucydides' dates, it cannot be entirely reconciled; modern opinion is thus forced to prefer Diodorus' date of 650 for Selinus. Nor is this the only breach. Even more problematical are the beginnings of the chain, the dates for the foundations of Cumae and Syracuse. Most scholars put the Greek colonization of Cumae about 750, but others have strong grounds for feeling that this extends Protocorinthian (and also Protoattic) pottery over much too long a period; accordingly they lower the date of Cumae to about 730–725. If this step is taken, then Syracuse must be depressed below 733, for the first Corinthian pottery at the Sicilian site is later than that of Cumae.[5]

[4] Dohan, *Italic Tomb-Groups*, 106–08, lowers the burial to 670; A. W. Byvanck, *Mnemosyne*, 3. ser. XIII (1947), 245, dates the deposit to 715–690; other dates are noted in *Kerameikos*, V. 1, 142, n. 110. Cf. Riis, *Tyrrhenika*, 152–59.

[5] Selinus: René van Campernolle, "La date de la fondation de Sélinunte (circa 650 avant notre ère)," *Bulletin de l'Institut historique belge de Rome*, XXVII (1952), 317–56; Georges Vallet and François Villard, "La date de fondation de Sélinunte: les données archéologiques," *BCH*, LXXXII (1958), 16–26, which reports their discovery of late Protocorinthian and also Transitional ware.

Megara: Vallet and Villard, "Les dates de fondation de Mégara Hyblaea et de Syracuse," *BCH*, LXXVI (1952), 289–346, who place Megara earlier; see also their article, "A propos

des dates de fondation de Mégara Hyblaea, de Syracuse et de Sélinunte," *Bulletin de l'Institut historique belge de Rome*, XXIX (1955), 199–214 (criticized by van Campernolle, ibid. 215–40); and their excavation reports in *Mélanges d'archéologie et d'histoire* 1951–55.

The foundation of Cumae is placed about 750 by Dunbabin, *Western Greeks*, 5–6; Kraiker, *Neue Beiträge*, 43; Schweitzer, *AM*, XLIII (1918), 43. About the 730's by Kübler, *Altattische Malerei* (Tübingen, 1950), 5; *Kerameikos*, V. 1, 141, with full bibliography in n. 109; VI. 1, 112. About 725 by Kahane, *AJA*, XLIV (1940), 479–81. To go back as far as 800 (Johansen) and 775–750 (Blakeway and Matz) seems unjustifiable; on the earlier settlement of Ischia, see below, Chap. 11. Pottery of Cumae: *Monumenti antichi*, XXII (1913), 93,

Such manipulations shake the basic underpinning of all absolute chronology for the age of revolution, for if Thucydides' dates are not completely reliable, neither is the placing of pottery styles which is based thereon. In the end we must remember that, however careful Thucydides was on events of his own day, he had to rely, in dealing with the early West, upon traditions— to put the matter baldly, his dates are *not* absolutely sure.

The whole pattern of calculation from the western colonies, on the other hand, does not become utterly useless merely because it must be adjudged provisional. The succession of Protocorinthian styles, now reasonably firm, cannot be arbitrarily stretched out or shrunk by half a century in either direction, and finds of this ware in the West do accord in general with the historical tradition. With all due reserve, then, I shall place the beginning of Protocorinthian ware at about 720, and the beginning of true Protoattic—after experiments which went back two decades—at about 710. From this point on, absolute dates might be assigned somewhat as follows:

CORINTH [6]		ATHENS	
720–690	Early Protocorinthian	710–680	Early Protoattic
690–650	Middle Protocorinthian	680–630	Middle Protoattic
650–640	Late Protocorinthian	630–610	Late Protoattic
640–620	Transitional		(with which Black-
620–590	Early Corinthian		figure overlaps)
590–575	Middle Corinthian		
575 on	Late Corinthian		

111; on grave 103bis, XIII (1903), 273–75; cf. Byvanck, *Mnemosyne*, XIII (1947), 246–47; Blakeway, *BSA*, XXXIII (1932–33), 200 ff.; Hencken, *AJA*, LXII (1958), 270.

[6] Except at the beginning, where I agree with Kraiker, *Aigina*, 16, the Corinthian dates are generally those of English students; see Dunbabin, *JHS*, LXVIII (1948), 68, after Payne, *Protokorinthische Vasenmalerei*, 20, and *Necrocorinthia*, 21–27, which is much lowered from Johansen, *Les Vases sicyoniens*, 179–85. Kübler, *Kerameikos*, VI. 1, 105–20, sets Proto-

corinthian 740/35—640/35 and gives full references. Villard, "La Chronologie de la céramique protocorinthienne," *Mélanges d'archéologie et d'histoire*, LX (1948), 7–34, reduces the series throughout by ten to twenty years, as does A. W. Byvanck, "The Chronology of Greek and Italian Art in the 8th and 7th Centuries," *Mnemosyne*, 3. ser. XIII (1947), 241–53, and Jack L. Benson, *Die Geschichte der korinthischen Vasen* (Basel, 1953). The effort of Åke Åkeström, *Der geometrische Stil in Italien* (Lund, 1943), to lower the scale by

Many of these divisions are subject to movement up or down by a decade or so in the varying schemes of modern analysts, but the general tempo of artistic development seems reasonably secure. With the pottery goes the evolution of sculpture, which had reached its Protodedalic stage by at least 680;[7] and the emergence of stone temples is also best defined by accompanying pottery deposits.

The vital point to be attained is the conclusion that our chronological tradition pointing to a great outburst just before and after 700 accords essentially with the archaeological evidence and also, though less securely, with the Oriental materials. To encompass all aspects of the age of revolution we must consider the whole century from 750 to 650. Yet in many points the crucial era was far briefer; from the beginning of Early Protocorinthian to the end of Early Protoattic is only four decades (*c.* 720–680). The men of one generation, it is not too much to say, dared to release Greek civilization from its earlier bonds. Not only did they break, very abruptly, with old trammels; Aegean life rose swiftly in these years to a new plane of cultural, political, and economic organization which enduringly stimulated men, first in its archaic and then in its classical stages.

ORIENTALIZING POTTERY: PROTOCORINTHIAN

THE SHARPEST visual impact of the age of revolution will come to the modern student when he looks at its pottery. This can be studied in a number of chains, Corinthian, Argive, insular, Cretan, Attic, and others.[8] Whatever series one picks, the

half a century has met virtually no acceptance.

The Attic dates are those of Dunbabin, *JHS*, LXVIII (1948), 68; for variations, see below, n. 4 (p. 243).

[7] R. J. H. Jenkins, *Dedalica: A Study of Dorian Plastic Art in the Seventh Century B.C.* (Cambridge, 1936), 61, 64–65, gives 680 as the latest possible date and suggests that even 700 might be possible.

[8] Discussions of this phase may be found in every history of Greek vases —e.g., Andreas Rumpf, *Malerei und Zeichung,* in *Handbuch der Archäologie,* VI (Munich, 1953), 23–30— but a comprehensive study of Orientalizing pottery as a whole remains a desideratum. On some details see Wolfgang Schiering, "Zur Ornamentbildung in der griechischen Vasenmalerei des siebenten Jahrhunderts," *Neue Beiträge,* 59–70.

change which it reveals for the late eighth and early seventh centuries is phenomenal. In the outwardly dull wooden cases of modern museums, the serried ranks of Greek vases tell a marvelous tale.

First come the serene, beautifully ordered products of the Geometric stage. Here shape and decoration are integrated, in the better specimens, to form a taut, vibrant, yet disciplined unity; the motifs, almost entirely rectilinear, are severely limited; much of the vase is evenly covered with a dark coat. Then suddenly a riot of curvilinear decoration, floral, animal, even human, bursts into vision and swirls over the entire surface of the vases; on some pieces all sense of Greek logic and restraint seems to have dissolved into the wildest of experiments. The pots themselves change shape: many of the new types are smaller, more carefully studied, even dainty in effect; others are poorly proportioned and ephemeral essays in breaking away from old restraints. And finally the very technique of drawing is elaborated as outline gives way in many workshops to solid black-figure painting, picked out and enriched by the use of supplementary color (white and purple especially) and of incision to render more specific detail than Geometric potters had ever deemed necessary.

In these developments lie hidden very significant changes in men's views of themselves and the world about, but these changes will best be considered after we have examined precisely the nature, date, and major workshops of the new "Orientalizing" ware. The term, unfortunately, is irretrievably incorporated into modern use, for though it has some validity in suggesting the indebtedness of Greek potters to Oriental motifs the connotations of the word "Orientalizing" are otherwise seriously misleading. Not only did Oriental pottery fail to resemble in any significant respect Greek ware; but also, and above all, the Greek world was at this very time becoming more sharply distinguished from the Orient. In the age of revolution a distinctive artistic outlook was evolving which led the Greeks straight on to classic expressions. But conventional classifications must often be employed, with due care to their limitations.

Among the many types of Orientalizing pottery the one to

be considered first is the most popular and also the most easily
analyzed fabric, the Protocorinthian.[9] The Geometric products
of Corinth were well summed up by Payne as "a colourless,
unambitious, but exceptionally competent series." The Early
Geometric vases are much like those of Attica in shape and
decoration, though far more limited in motifs and artistic skill.
By the eighth century, however, the two series were moving on
quite different lines. Corinthian potters, as far as we now know,
did not essay the marvelous experiments which led to the great
Dipylon vases, and their gamut of motifs widened only slowly
(see Plate 12a). On the other hand, and perhaps as a result of
their greater caution, the stiffening, rigidity, and overelabora-
tion which seriously affected Attic pottery by 750 are virtually
absent from Corinthian work. Vase shapes here became rounder
and more supple, rather than harder; new forms such as the cup
with flaring sides called the kotyle (Plate 13b) and the round
incense or perfume container called aryballos emerged; and the
steadily changing patterns of Corinthian decoration demonstrate that at least by the mid-century mark the potters found
their inherited framework no longer adequate.[1]

This is the basic point of importance in Late Geometric
Corinthian work. Craftsmen of Corinth evidently felt new
breezes and were groping within their simple inheritance to express a spirit not contained in ancestral patterns. The first results
are suggested by the upper two vases on Plate 13. The crater on
the upper left is an old form, as are many of its motifs, particu-

[9] This term was invented by Furtwängler. Johansen, *Les Vases sicyoniens*,
tried to pin the product to Sicyon, but Payne firmly located it at
Corinth in *Protokorinthische Vasenmalerei* and *Necrocorinthia*, with ad-
denda by R. J. Hopper, *BSA*, XLIV
(1949), 162–257. Excavation at Corinth confirmed the ascription; see
Weinberg, *Corinth*, VII. 1. The Potter's Quarter and the North Cemetery
still await publication, but the material visible in the Corinth Museum
well illustrates the change. See also
Benson, *Geschichte der korinthischen
Vasen;* T. J. Dunbabin and M. Rob-

ertson, "Some Protocorinthian Vase-
Painters," *BSA*, XLVIII (1953), 172–
81; Kübler, *Kerameikos*, VI. 1, 105–
57. My quotation of Payne is from
Necrocorinthia, 1.

[1] Changes in the mid-eighth century
are well studied in the Ithacan material by S. Benton, *BSA*, XLVIII
(1953), 260–64, who suggests the
kotyle emerged about 775–750; Weinberg, *Corinth*, VII. 1, 52, gives the
date 750–700. See also Weinberg,
"What Is Protocorinthian Geometric
Ware?" *AJA*, XLV (1941), 30–44;
Kraiker, *Aigina*, 13.

larly the main design set in a window on the shoulder—three horizontal zigzag lines connected above and below to the frame. Just below this design, however, is a band of short vertical freehand wavy lines, often found in Corinthian vases of the mid-eighth century, which may be construed as a timid effort to launch out on freer paths. Even more typical, and significant, is the manner in which the bulk of the vase below the shoulder zone has been treated. Previously this would have been a solid dark; now it is broken up into many thin lines, except at the base. This treatment, which gives the name of Linear Geometric to a large part of Late Geometric Corinthian work, is not a purely mechanical device, for the lines (as Payne observed) impart a sense of dynamic movement to the surface.

The kotyle on the upper right of Plate 13, which is very much like the earliest kotylai found at Cumae, represents further steps on the same path.[2] The horizontal lines about the vase are marked off more sharply; on the handle zone the meander of ancestral type is breaking down, and a motif new to Corinthian work, the butterfly (already known at Athens),[3] gains the emphasis. The shape of this vase is a new, Corinthian invention which obviously much pleased the Greek world, for examples of generally similar nature turn up not only in Cumae and Aegina but also at Delphi, Athens, and a number of other places.

Not all of the new motifs in Corinthian work at this time are purely geometrical, abstract devices. Beside the chevrons, vertical wavy lines, hourglasses, and butterflies appear rudimentary stars, leaflike patterns, birds at first singly and then in conventionalized rows, and even some scenes of human life. Especially remarkable is a rather late crater from Thebes, now in Toronto, which depicts a ship with hieratically stiff oarsmen seated in a long row.[4] This, like most of the larger Corinthian vases of the eighth and seventh centuries, was found elsewhere than at Corinth, for the best work was exported—a common fate of artistic products always. Corinthian trade was now growing to the west, where it began to oust Cycladic products; eastward through the

[2] Cf. *Corinth*, VII. 1, n. 123; Cumae, grave 103bis.
[3] Weinberg, *Corinth*, VII. 1, 89.
[4] Payne, *Protokorinthische Vasenmale-* rei, 9–10; cf. the Corinthian figured vase, *JdI*, XLVI (1931), cols. 241–42, fig. 18.

Aegean late eighth-century vases of Corinth turn up as far afield as Al Mina.[5] In return increasing quantities of foreign products, both Greek and Oriental, made their way to Corinth, as the deposits of the new temple of Hera Limenia at Perachora amply testify.

Insofar as we can explain the amazing development which next occurred, the basic factors were now present. Corinthian craftsmen were seeking new modes of expression; they were encouraged to boldness by their growing success in international trade; and a wealth of new ideas was pouring in to stimulate their minds. The product was the appearance of the Protocorinthian style in a matter of three decades (720–690).

To call this marvelous creation a "product" utterly disguises what had occurred. Protocorinthian pottery is not an evolution but a revolution, a spectacular testimony to the speed and sureness with which Greek civilization moved in these decades to a new, unpredictable plane. There are no neat transitional steps of evolutionary type between Linear Geometric and Protocorinthian; at best, remnants of the old framework linger on in the new style, to tell whence it came. The two lower vases on Plate 13, for instance, have still geometric bands with butterfly or meander; but these elements have shrunk far into the background, soon to disappear in favor of palmettes and other floral patterns. Beside the old elements on the cup appear bold, freehand S's, and the solid dark base has given way to rays. On the other, the Rider Kotyle from Aegina, the rays have become even more dynamic, and the body of the vase is occupied by a majestic procession of horses and riders. So impressive is this frieze that at first sight the viewer may not note the painter's failure to depict the right leg of the riders, except in one case, and his still rudimentary drawing of the men, who are akin to the rowers on the Theban ship crater. His main interest clearly has been to communicate a fresh sense of the power and life contained in the horses. Here one finds not only the use of black-figure technique, which was to be ever more skillfully developed, but also the first employment of incision in Corinthian work to mark out in

---

[5] Corinthian export began with Late Geometric ware (Weinberg, *Corinth* VII. 1, 32); see below, pp. 369–71.

specific, concrete clarity the internal modeling of the figures. In other vases white was already being used to this end, and purple was soon added to the potters' repertoire.[6]

On Protocorinthian vases, as in other Greek styles, clearly recognizable scenes of myth and epic events began shortly after 700 B.C. to replace the generalized, undefinable pictures of eighth-century art. Nowhere can we better sense than in these scenes the driving force of a new outlook on life; its effect in forcing the painter to ever more precise, clear, and detailed work is obvious. As between the demands of society as consumer and the active interest of the potter as artist to strike out on new paths we cannot determine the initiative, but certainly the potters made heavy weather at first of their experiments. The men and gods in Early Protocorinthian work are often awkward, ill-balanced and poorly proportioned, and not well composed.[7] Most craftsmen did not dare so much, but stuck to the easier materials of stylized floral-type patterns and animals, both real beasts and imaginary creatures such as sphinxes (see Plate 14b) of Oriental inspiration.

Despite these evidences that experiment was not always successful, the new Protocorinthian style displays from the first pieces a basically firm concept of what its makers wished to achieve. Virtually all at once they threw up a disciplined, co-ordinated system of shapes and decorations. Supple, complicated, yet sensitive, their work strikes the observer as consciously designed, a product of deliberate thought toward a fairly clearly conceived end. While the potter of the Late Geometric crater of Plate 13a still moved largely by instinct, the brain and hand of the man who made the Rider Kotyle were directly and purposefully linked.

By about 680 the most advanced potters of Corinth had sloughed off the external marks of the Geometric style. The

---

[6] Rays: Weinberg, *AJA*, XLV (1941), 37, who finds them first on the shoulders of round aryballoi, then on the base. Incision and technique: Kraiker, *Aigina*, 16–17; Payne, *Necrocorinthia*, 7; Robertson, *BSA*, XLIII (1948), 56–57. Color: Brock, *Fortetsa*, 188 n.

2, who gives Dunbabin's date 750–725 for the introduction of white; in Attica Kübler, *Kerameikos*, V. 1, 174, dates it to the 740's. Cf. Young, *Late Geometric Graves*, 197–98.

[7] Payne, *Protokorinthische Vasenmalerei*, 12.

ovoid aryballos of Plate 14b, with its spiral decoration on the rim, palmettes, confronted sphinxes, hares and dogs, and rays, is a fine example of early Middle Protocorinthian work. Corinthian aryballoi and other small vases decorated in a miniature style were tremendously popular over all the Greek world as containers for the incense and perfumes which Corinthian shops made from Oriental materials. A grander vase, from Aegina, is shown on Plate 14a; Payne well described it as "perhaps the finest existing example of Protocorinthian animal drawing," in its exhibition of "an astounding power of persuading natural shapes into calligraphic formulae." [8]

In the words "calligraphic formulae" is perhaps the hidden mark of the firm Greek inheritance from Geometric days which may explain—as far as anything can explain—why the Corinthian potters had moved so swiftly and surely. This pottery of Corinth, called Orientalizing, is nonetheless unmistakably Greek. To a student who knows primarily classic Greece, the vases on Plate 14 must appear more Greek than much of the Geometric product (e.g., Plate 8); yet the Protocorinthian style was born ultimately out of the main Greek tradition.

Students who cling to evolutionary concepts have naturally tried to find a basis for the explosion at Corinth in the pottery of Crete or Cyprus, and have asserted that Protocorinthian designs must be indebted to Oriental prototypes in textiles and metal work. Such arguments are not worth the effort expended on them. There can be no doubt that the potters of Corinth, searching as they were for new modes by the middle of the eighth century, were set free partly by observing the experiments of Cycladic and other artists with birds and freehand lines, partly by contact with Oriental motifs in non-ceramic media; but far more weight must be placed on the generally liberating spirit of the age of revolution. Once these craftsmen had dared to break away from the old patterns, they swiftly created a new scheme. As Payne observed, "the early Protocorinthian potters are, indeed, more purely Hellenic than those of

[8] Ibid. 12, 17–19. The famous Chigi vase (ibid. 14–16) I pass over here both because it is not in the main black-figure tradition and also because it falls after 650.

(a) Argive fragment from Argos, depicting the blinding of Polyphemus (cf. Plate 23b) (Argos Museum). Photograph courtesy Ecole française d'Athènes.

(b) Boeotian vase of a stiff, provincial flavor (National Museum 15300, Athens). Photograph courtesy Deutsches Archäologisches Institut in Athens.

PLATE 15 · *Other Orientalizing Styles (I)*

(a) Parian amphora made in the era of Archilochus (National Museum 1, Stockholm). Photograph courtesy National Museum, Stockholm.

(b) Cretan vase from Arkades, perhaps representing Theseus and Ariadne (Heraklion Museum). Photograph from Doro Levi, Early Hellenic Pottery of Crete (Princeton, 1945), pl. XVI.

PLATE 16 · Other Orientalizing Styles (II)

any contemporary school." Any *direct,* provable transfers of motifs from the Orient to Corinth commonly occurred after the seventh century was well under way—i.e., after the new artistic outlook was sufficiently set to permit its artists to feel secure in taking over such material.[9]

In their innovations the Protocorinthian potters followed a typical Greek procedure, which we shall find throughout the age of revolution. They chose a few types of shapes and decorations; and having thus limited their freedom of range, they concentrated their energies upon perfecting these types. The overwhelming bulk of the tremendous Corinthian vase output was in the form of small pots, such as aryballoi and kotylai, in extremely similar patterns of floral and animal decoration. Eventually, to be sure, this restricted range was to exhaust Corinthian inventiveness by Middle Corinthian times; the potters of Attica, who had followed a more bizarre path, were to gain the upper hand.

In concentrating upon the main line of Protocorinthian ware, I must note in conclusion, we run a serious risk of oversimplification. The products which Corinth sold on the international market were of the new model and reflected changes in fashion rather quickly. Thus they helped to speed the rapid adoption of the Orientalizing style all over the Greek world. At home not all men were ready to abandon their ancestral inheritance. One of the most interesting revelations of the Potters' Quarter at Corinth has been the volume of sub-Geometric ware which it contained; pots with straight Geometric designs or Linear Geometric patterns continued to be made beside the more developed vases all through the first half of the seventh century. Then the use of rays and other newer elements came into even the conservative workshops, but on down to 600 a strong tint of reluctance to yield ancient ways is perceptible.[1] Repeatedly in the age of revolution there are similar marks that not all elements and all areas were willing to move swiftly forward.

---

[9] Payne, *Necrocorinthia,* 10, 53, 67, 71; so also at Crete (Brock, *Fortetsa,* 144) and on the Idaean shields according to Kunze and Benton.

[1] Weinberg, *Corinth,* VII. 1, 72–73; *AJA,* XLV (1941), 39–40.

ORIENTALIZING POTTERY: PROTOATTIC AND OTHER

INTO THE MAKING of Protocorinthian ware inspiration had poured from several late eighth-century sources—the Cyclades, Attica, probably the Argolid, Crete, and the Orient proper. From Corinth, in return, the influence of the new style spread far and wide in the early seventh century, mainly through the export of the best, most developed Protocorinthian products and their local imitation, partly perhaps through the migration of craftsmen. Some of the inscriptions on Protocorinthian vases are in foreign alphabets and may betoken the residence of alien potters at Corinth; more certain evidence for the mobility of artists is the fact that Greek potters worked in the new styles in Etruscan clays.[2]

Throughout the new western colonies and in the fringe districts under native rule potters were able to do little more than imitate Greek models. No outstanding local types of pottery, except that which is known as Etruscan bucchero, arose in the West during the seventh and sixth centuries.[3] In Greece, on the other hand, some regions which previously had not produced Geometric pottery of any merit were now able to consolidate virtually independent fashions. Chief among these was Sparta, still devoted in the seventh century to the common path of aristocratic luxury; under the influence of Corinth and also of Argos,

[2] The four inscribed Protocorinthian vases show three alphabets (Robertson, *BSA*, XLIII [1948], 123); the Chigi vase, thus, has an Aeginetan flavor (Rumpf, *Malerei und Zeichnung*, 33). Cf. Michel Lejeune, "Vases 'Protocorinthiens' Inscrits," *REA*, XLVII (1945), 101–10; Matz, *GGK*, I, 247, who notes that the Corinthian alphabet appears mainly in Transitional and Corinthian styles. But the problem of alphabets on Greek vases is a perplexing one. The Protoattic Menelaus stand of Aegina is not inscribed in Attic (*JHS*, LXIX [1949], 26); the Euphorbos plate of East Greek style has an Argive-type alphabet (Rumpf, *Malerei und Zeichnung*, 36). Robert Eisler, "Eine semitische Inschrift auf einer 'protokorinthischen' Vase von Megara Hyblaea," *Klio*, XX (1925–26), 354–62, argued for a possibly Aramaic inscription in Corinthian alphabet; Lejeune (102) considers it meaningless. The effort to explain such alphabets in terms of alien purchasers, T. B. L. Webster, *Greek Art and Literature, 700–530 B.C.* (Dunedin, 1959), 20, is not convincing.

[3] F. Villard and G. Vallet, "Géométrique grec, géométrique sicéliote, géométrique sicule," *Mélanges d'archéologie et d'histoire*, LXVIII (1956), 7–27, have useful remarks on one local western adaptation.

the Laconian style emerged. In the Laconian III and IV stages (sixth century) this was exported to North Africa (Cyrene) and to East Greece (Samos especially).[4]

While Spartan Orientalizing ware seems almost entirely derivative in its original impulse, many other areas could build upon stronger Geometric roots and gained new inspiration only partly through Corinthian influence. The seventh century was the golden age of distinctive pottery styles in the Aegean; that process of local differentiation which had been ever more marked throughout Protogeometric and Geometric styles now reached its peak in pottery as well as in political history. By the early sixth century these individualized outlooks were to fade slowly away before the unanswerable competition of Attic black-figured ware.

This, however, is a later story. In the seventh century the Orientalizing pottery of Greece bears a common stamp both in its new repertoire of shapes, in its wider use of solid figures picked out by incision and color, and in its range of motifs, which vary from simple floral patterns to elaborate compositions of aristocratic warriors (and gods) in battles, chariot races, and scenes of myth and epic. Within this relatively uniform reaction to unifying forces, cross-currents of influence become sharply perceptible, and each local style has its own flavor.

The pottery of the Argolid, known from earlier finds at Tiryns and the Argive Heraeum and recently from Argos itself, was more powerful than has been recognized; in "horse-raising Argos" great, majestic horses had been depicted since Late Geometric days, and Homeric scenes, especially the blinding of Polyphemus by Odysseus, occur from the early seventh century (see Plate 15a).[5] Beside these relatively skillful Argive com-

[4] J. P. Droop, *Artemis Orthia*, 52–116; E. A. Lane, "Lakonian Vase Painting," *BSA*, XXXIV (1933–34), 99–189; Paola Pelagatti, "La ceramica laconica del Museo di Taranto," *Annuario*, n.s. XVII–XVIII (1955–56), 7–44. Protocorinthian ware at Sparta is noted by Droop, 113–14, and Lane, 100–01, where Argive influence is also found.

[5] Argos: Müller and Oelmann, *Tiryns*, I, 135–64; Anne Roes, "Fragments de poterie géométrique trouvés sur les citadelles d'Argos," *BCH*, LXXVII (1953), 90–104; J. M. Cook, *BSA*, XLVIII (1953), 34–50, who gives a list (p. 38 n. 10) of Late Geometric of the Argolid; Paul Courbin, "Un fragment de cratère protoargien," *BCH*, LXXIX (1955), 1–49, who illustrates also the Aristonothos vase.

positions the pottery of Boeotia (see Plate 15b) seems stiff and conservatively Geometric in pattern, and almost never occurs outside its homeland.[6] Cycladic workshops, on the other hand, while unable to meet Corinthian competition in the West, moved into a galaxy of Orientalizing patterns.[7] To a modern eye the large vases of Parian origin (see Plate 16a) are perhaps the most fascinating in their clean build, firm decorative sense, and marvelously depicted animals; but the grandly conceived scenes of myth on some Naxian work are equally unique. Farther east, the wares called East Greek now become more identifiable as to origin, particularly the Rhodian Wild Goat styles; these latter appeared suddenly about 650 and seem like tapestry in their richly decorated rows of animals.[8] To the south the potters of Crete produced from about 735 on down to the middle of the seventh century vases more loosely drawn in yet another Orientalizing pattern (see Plate 16b).[9] Cretan pottery showed Corinthian influence in the seventh century, but tended to

This is commonly taken as Etruscan; see Rumpf, *Malerei und Zeichnung*, pl. 6.

[6] Boeotia: Boardman, *BSA*, XLVII (1952), 17–18, 47, who discusses the pottery from Eretria.

[7] Cyclades: Charles Dugas, *Délos XVII: Les Vases Orientalisants de style non Mélien* (Paris, 1935); Ernst Buschor, "Kykladisches," *AM*, LIV (1929), 142–63; H. G. G. Payne, "Cycladic Vase-Painting of the Seventh Century," *JHS*, XLVI (1926), 203–12; J. K. Brock, *BSA*, XLIV (1949), 74–80, on the dates of the ware. The relief pithoi of Tenos show the same development very interestingly; cf. Athens NM 2475, Munich 7697, and others listed in Schäfer, *Reliefpithoi*, 67–73. Paros: Buschor, *AM*, LIV (1929), 142–52. Naxos: Christos Karusos, "Eine naxische Amphora des früheren siebenten Jahrhunderts," *JdI*, LII (1937), 166–97; Buschor, *AM*, LIV (1929), 152–58; Ernst Homann-Wedeking, *Die Anfänge der griechischen Grossplastik*

(Berlin, 1950), 137–39.

[8] East Greeks: Andreas Rumpf, "Zu den klazomenischen Denkmälern," *JdI*, XLVIII (1933), 55–83; Karl Schefold, "Knidische Vasen und Verwandtes," *JdI*, LVII (1942), 124–42; M. Robertson, *JHS*, LX (1940), 8 ff.; R. M. Cook, *JHS*, LXVI (1946), 93–94; W. Lamb, "Excavations at Kato Phana in Chios," *BSA*, XXXV (1934–35), 138–64, on the ties of Chiot Geometric and "Naucratite"; Technau, *AM*, LIV (1929), 20–40, on Samos; Wolfgang Schiering, *Werkstätten orientalisierender Keramik auf Rhodos* (Berlin, 1957).

[9] Crete: Brock, *Fortetsa*, 213–18, who puts Early Orientalizing at 735–680, Late Orientalizing at 680–630 on the basis of Protocorinthian parallels and three Egyptian scarabs (nos. 1076–1078), one of which is surely XXVI Dynasty. See also above, Chap. 3, n. 9 (p. 98); and on the relations of Crete and Corinth, Chap. 6, n. 4 (p. 217).

eschew figure composition; large polychrome amphoras are among its most outstanding products.

A detailed discussion of these styles would carry us much too far afield, and we need note only their manifold variety within a common spirit; but the developments in Attica cannot be dismissed so briefly. Here, best of all, is illuminated the struggle to move onto a new artistic plane and the quality of stress which marked the early seventh century. The Attic experiments, too, though immediately without any major effect on the rest of Greece, were eventually to be more decisive in shaping the course of Greek pottery than even the Corinthian styles.

Throughout most of the eighth century Attic pottery had been the most progressive in Greece. Freehand drawing had appeared in Athens by 750, but the rows of birds and other motifs which resulted were for a time integrated into the prevailing Geometric spirit. Shortly after the mid-century point signals of distress began to fly in Attic products. On the one side, the growing uncertainty of the potters led them to cling more desperately to the old patterns, and many vases are stiff both in shape and in overelaborate Geometric decoration. On the other hand, the more experimental artists found themselves dissolving the old crisp sureness of Dipylon scenes.[1]

A fine example of this very point in time is afforded by a vase from the site in the Kerameikos cemetery labeled by its excavators the first Opferrinne. The painter of K. 1356 (Plate 17a) evidently was essaying to depict noble action and life in more realistic terms than had his Dipylon grandfather. The parts of the bodies are better integrated, and even the parts of the vase itself flow more into one another than previously; but the looseness of drawing, in figures and in general patterns as well, suggests the difficulty of the experiment. An Oxford amphora (Plate 17b) has proceeded a step further. The chariot frieze

[1] Athens: Kübler, *Kerameikos*, V. 1 passim (esp. 135–36, 83–84, 171–81), and *Altattische Malerei*; Young, *Late Geometric Graves*, and "Graves from the Phaleron Cemetery," *AJA*, XLVI (1942), 23–57; J. M. Cook, "Athenian Workshops around 700," *BSA*, XLII (1947), 139–55, and "Protoattic Pottery," *BSA*, XXXV (1934–35), 165–219; Ohly, *Griechische Goldbleche*, 110–16, who draws parallels to the gold bands.

harks back to the earlier eighth century, but the runners on the neck exhibit a real flow of energy in their freer stride and more supple bodies.[2] Finally, the maker of a third vase, in the Louvre (Plate 18a), probably the painter of the famous Analatos hydria, has achieved the transition to Protoattic, both in the bands of naturalistic decoration and in the chariot frieze, the horses of which are internally defined by incision.

These three successive chariot scenes are extremely suggestive, particularly if we place them beside contemporary Corinthian work in the crucial decades about 700. The inheritance of the Dipylon figured scenes led the Attic potters to attempt far more than did their Corinthian confreres, but their vaulting ambition was for the moment much less successful. If one compares even the last of the three with the roughly contemporary Rider Kotyle of Corinth (Plate 13a) or with a Corinthian aryballos (Plate 14b), the difference is marked. The Attic vase is overly elaborate, even fussy in its pierced handles and applied wavy lines; the shape is stiffer and more Geometric; a *horror vacui* leads to too abundant filling ornament; and the Geometric inheritance, though still present in the meander of the Rider Kotyle, has evidently been much more successfully overpassed at Corinth than at Athens. Such a comparison of the two schools does not seriously introduce modern aesthetic prejudice, for the seventh century itself made much the same judgment: Corinthian ware captured the market, and Protoattic vases were scarcely exported at all, save to nearby Aegina.[3] As far as we can determine on the basis of admittedly hazardous stylistic criteria, no more than three major workshops were active in Late Geometric–Early Protoattic days in Attica, while the greater demand for Corinthian vases supported perhaps as many as eleven at Corinth.

The absolute dating of the development to the Protoattic

[2] Cook, BSA, XLII (1947), 150, derives the Mesogeia painter, of the first Protoattic days, from this workshop of the last Late Geometric years. Analatos shop: Cook, BSA, XXXV (1934–35), 166–69, 172–76.

[3] Cook, BSA, XXXV (1934–35), 204; Young, *Late Geometric Graves*, 222.

Note that even in Attica Corinthian ware appears in quantity, especially from the Middle Protocorinthian on; its popularity at Old Smyrna is apparent in BSA, LIII–IV (1958–59), 138–51. Number of workshops: Cook, BSA, XLII (1947), 143; Benson, *Geschichte der korinthischen Vasen*, 13–16.

style is much debated at present.[4] The publishers of the Kerameikos material place Opferrinne 1 in the early 730's and so ascribe the commencement of significant Orientalizing tendencies to 735–725; the Analatos hydria, on this basis, must be placed in the 720's. Others, however, have dated this vase to 710, to 700, and even to 690. On the whole the Orientalizing wave seems to have got under way about as soon at Athens as at Corinth, but was slower to reach a true basis for a new style, partly because Attic potters were much more ambitious, partly because their great inheritance stood in their path. As a result, Early Protoattic vases have been found in the same context with more developed Protocorinthian kotylai.[5] I incline accordingly to set the early phase of Protoattic proper at 710–680.

In many ways the first Protoattic pottery may be termed poor.[6] The vases often were not well made, their forms were bizarre experiments which did not endure, perfunctory Geometric ornament stood beside some of the most flamboyant work ever produced in historic Greek times. Modern surveys sometimes stress too much the lack of discipline in Protoattic decoration, for its creators were still, after all, Greek and were more heavily burdened by their inheritance than were most Orientalizing craftsmen. Yet it must be said that Attic potters occasionally displayed singular indifference to the limitations and requirements of vase forms, as when they sprawled huge animals over virtually the whole surface.

Modern students, however, are rightly at one in paying careful attention to the Attic experiments. In these vases the

---

[4] Earlier dating: Kübler, *Kerameikos*, V. 1, 141–56, and *Altattische Malerei*, 6–8; J. M. Cook, *JHS*, LXXVI (1956), 124–25, accepts this date for the Opferrinne, while Kraiker, *Neue Beiträge*, 43, suggests 725. Later dating: J. M. Cook, *BSA*, XXXV (1934–35), 202–05, puts Early Protoattic 710–680; R. M. Cook, *JHS*, LXVI (1946), 93, about 700; Young, *Late Geometric Graves*, 2–3, 221–22, 229, and *AJA*, XLVI (1942), 55–57, lowers it into the early seventh century (as does Buschor).

[5] The Lion Painter of the last Attic

Late Geometric occurs beside two Protocorinthian kotylai; see Kahane, *AJA*, XLIV (1940), 479–80 (Cook, *BSA*, XLII [1947], 143). The Phaleron graves display minor Protoattic work with a strong sub-Geometric flavor beside considerable Protocorinthian imports; see S. Pelekidis, *Deltion*, II (1916), 13 ff.; Young, *AJA*, XLVI (1942), 23–57; See also Cook, *BSA*, XXXV (1934–35), 201–02; *Kerameikos*, V. 1, grave 67 (K. 661).

[6] Young, *Late Geometric Graves*, 195–201, 212–16 (especially in sub-Geometric ware).

human beings and animals were growing plumper as draftsmen stated an observation of life more directly than Geometric conventions had permitted.[7] Motion had entered the artists' ken, and they were attempting to express action not by external attributes but within their figures. The individual elements, again, now interacted on each other, for the painters' skill in composition grew. In sum, through their technical experiments in color, incision, and black-figure with reserved spaces, Attic potters were manifesting as keen an interest in the world and man as one can find in any seventh-century style, more so indeed than most of the competent but increasingly conventional shops of Corinth. By the middle of the seventh century the great rage for experiment was waning in Attica, and its artists were beginning to settle down to a consolidation of their gains. The Kerameikos vase of Middle Protoattic style depicted in Plate 18b shows still the ambition of its maker in the huge figure of the sphinx but also reflects the surer sense of shape and decoration which led toward the creation of the famous Attic black-figure style before the end of the century.

The story of Protoattic development demonstrates even more clearly than does the Corinthian series how difficult were the problems of change in the early seventh century. The most advanced workshops tried much, but had great trouble in equating ambition and result. Beside their product a very strong strain of sub-Geometric pottery went on, as at Corinth, down to the middle of the seventh century.[8] Particularly puzzling and intriguing is the apparent revival of some Mycenaean motifs, which can be paralleled at Delos; in reaching forward, potters seem also to have reached back to earlier artistic levels. From these scattered suggestions of Mycenaean motifs one can per-

---

[7] Young, ibid. 218–20; Matz, *GGK*, I, 313–15, 343–44; Beazley, *Development of Attic Black-figure*, 4–5; Kübler, *Altattische Malerei*, 8, 15.

[8] Young, *Late Geometric Graves*, 2. Mycenaean motifs: Young, 177; *Délos* XV, 51 (Ae 71). Note too the appearance of the octopus on seventh-century ware: Crete, *BSA*, XLIX (1954), 222–23, fig. 6 no. 52; Samos,

Technau, *AM*, LIV (1929), 25 pl. III; Athens, Young, *Late Geometric Graves*, 126 fig. 88 (B. 58); *Hesperia*, II (1933), 575–76; B. Graef and E. Langlotz, *Die antiken Vasen in der Akropolis zu Athen*, I (Berlin, 1909), 37 no. 365; Corinth, *Necrocorinthia*, nos. 540, 629; Myconos museum, unpublished example.

haps read a general lesson that the strands of Greek civilization were many, and that the pattern of Aegean culture at any one time was not as uniform a plane as it is sometimes depicted. To suggest this, nonetheless, does not warrant the interpretation still occasionally advanced that the Orientalizing developments of the seventh century were a contest between primeval Mediterranean and new Nordic attitudes.[9]

EARLY ARCHITECTURE

IN CONSIDERING the major aesthetic changes of the age of revolution, the modern student must commence with the area which has just been surveyed, that of the pottery. Only here can we hope to understand against a continuous background the true nature and meaning of the great alterations which took place and to date the innovations with some precision; only in the ceramic field can we compare continuous chains of materials for a number of Aegean districts. By and large the Orientalizing potters were independent craftsmen. At times they drew inspiration from non-ceramic sources—textiles, bronze, and other objects of Oriental and local origin—for their treatment of decorative elements and of human and animal forms; but the degree of this dependence is, I think, often greatly exaggerated. Insofar as the fingers and minds of the potters responded to influences from outside their shop doors, the major debt was to the poets and to the tellers of myth and fable.

Whether the makers of vases reacted consciously to the developments in the sister arts is difficult to determine. In respect to the decoration of vases, the more complicated scenes may at times have reflected larger paintings on flat surfaces, though the existence of such work remains a hotly debated argument in an almost complete vacuum of evidence. For the seventh century there survive only small painted plaques or *pinakes* of terra cotta, made for votive or funeral purposes; but a vase of the period from Ithaca (Aetos No. 600) does show a temple with

[9] As Kübler, *Kerameikos*, V. 1, 180–81; Matz, *GGK*, I, 135, 202, 344–45.

figures painted on its walls.[1] The forms of the vases, again, may have been influenced by contemporary architectural and sculptural concepts of space, for in these arts notable progress occurred during the age of revolution.

In the field of architecture, historic Greek society did not devote its surplus energy to the erection of great fortress-palaces which would manifest the power of kings. The increasingly tight political ties which were now emerging were of quite different type from those of the Mycenaean age; the functions of the city-state did not yet demand major public secular buildings. The one bond of mankind which required visible architectural commemoration was the worship of a common divine force, under whose protection the population of the incipient city-state grouped itself in aristocratic guidance. As this link grew in potency and as the Greek world became richer, the temple form was correspondingly elaborated from extremely simple roots.

It is unfortunate that we do not have the evidence to examine in detail the resurgence of an architectural spirit in Greece, for the shape in which men cast their buildings always reflects basic attitudes about their views of the world and their own place. The very fact that monumental architecture completely vanished from the Aegean at the end of the Mycenaean stage throws into high relief the collapse of highly organized societies; the Dark ages were not a period in which men dared—or had the strength—to build enduring monuments. What little has been uncovered can be dated only on the basis of accompanying pottery or stratigraphic position; the remains in themselves display no monumental sense and no effort at conscious organization of space. Not until this objective became apparent in sharply defined ground plans and in the formulation of precise building members such as the column can the history of Greek

---

[1] Ithaca vase: Robertson, *BSA*, XLIII (1940), 101–02. Plaques: Boardman, *BSA*, L (1955), 51–66. Large paintings: Benson, *Geschichte der korinthischen Vasen*, 88, 92–93; Payne, *Protokorinthische Vasenmalerei*, 14; Robertson, *BSA*, XLVI (1951), 154–55; Rumpf, *Malerei und Zeichnung*, 29, 37; Kraiker, *Aigina*, 18, who accepts panels but not wall-painting. Cook, *Geras A. Keramopoullou*, 117, does not consider it likely a separate style was used in larger works.

architecture truly begin; but this brings us down virtually to the middle of the seventh century.

From the earlier remains we may elicit some scant light on the building techniques and spatial concepts from which the temple sprang. While the skill which had led to the marvelous stonework of the last phases at Mycenae (Plate 2a) disappeared in the collapse of the Late Bronze age, men of the first millennium inherited their basic techniques of construction. Not all of the earlier buildings were destroyed; human society survived, though barely, in the rude villages huddling on the hillsides of Greece. Houses and other structures were erected on a rough stone foundation laid in a shallow trench; floors were commonly pounded dirt. The upper courses were of stone or of mudbrick with timber posts and other members, which probably were plastered; windows were few and high; roofs, either pitched or flat, were brush, covered with mud and a watertight coat. Buildings found at Siphnos, apparently of the eighth century, were well constructed, but the occasional examples elsewhere in Greece do not suggest great care and conscious premeditation of architectural effects in this "carpenter's work."[2]

The ground plans of houses in the Dark ages reflect, no doubt instinctively, certain aesthetic principles. In the foundations there are two main patterns, one rectangular (or nearly so) and one with curved lines, either entirely oval or with rounded

[2] The phrase is Matz's, *GGK,* I, 350. The nature of the evidence may be seen in *BSA,* XXXVIII (1937–38), 66–68 (Karphi); *BSA,* XLIV (1949), 8–10 (Siphnos); Hutchinson, *BSA,* XLIX (1954), 220 (Cretan model at Khaniale Tekke); Gallet de Santerre, *Délos primitive,* 215–20 (Delos). Ground plan: H. Bagenal in *Perachora,* I, 42–51; Lorimer, *Homer and the Monuments,* 438–39; *Hesperia,* II (1933), 542–51 (Agora); *ILN,* February 28, 1953, 328–29 (Smyrna); *AnatSt,* VIII (1958), 31 (Miletus). *Megaron:* Chap. 5, n. 8 (p. 174), above; Lorimer, *Homer and the Monuments,* 411–12; *ILN,* December 31, 1955, 1144–45 (Chios); the relations between Homeric references and archaeological indications are further discussed by Gray in *Homer and His Critics,* 163–70.

Earlier survivals: Lawrence, *Greek Architecture,* 291–93, who suggests that the Middle Helladic inheritance was greater than that from Mycenaean building; Roland Martin, *Recherches sur l'agora grecque* (Paris, 1951), 105–27, who seeks to find Minoan-Mycenaean survivals. See also William Bell Dinsmoor, *The Architecture of Ancient Greece: An Account of Its Historic Development* (3d ed.; London, 1950), which accepts the Aryan myth.

apse at the back. This latter shape had been common in Middle Helladic days, but not in the Mycenaean world; its reappearance has been argued to reflect the entry of new elements during the age of invasion. Of this I am far from convinced; basically the two main plans reflect major differences in building the super-structure—of rough stone in the rectangular shape, of mudbrick in the rounded—and even at times in roofing techniques.

The rectangular pattern, called the *megaron,* also had an-cient roots; in Chapter 1 we noted its appearance in early Troy. To define more fully the nature of the *megaron,* this type con-sisted of a squarish room with a hearth in the center which was flanked by posts to hold up the roof; a vent lay over the hearth. In a front of the room a porch was supported by two posts or columns. Well-known in the Mycenaean palaces, this form con-tinued across the Dark ages as virtually the only remnant of architectural order. In the pitifully simple root, however, lay apparently the highest sense of disciplined space available to Aegean men; for the earliest architects were to seize upon this plan and evolve from it the new temple pattern.

In Crete, religious sanctuaries seem to have existed all across the Dark ages. The rude settlement at Karphi, which was described in Chapter 4, had a walled, open-air shrine (1100–900). The first roofed temples thus far found in the island scarcely date from before the eighth century, but they fall into a common pattern. The temple at Dreros, which is perhaps of the early seventh century, is 10.9 by 7.2 meters over-all. Its major elements are a pronaos and a cella, the flat roof of which was supported by the walls of brick and by two columns in the center, on either side of the sacred hearth. At the rear were a bank, on the right, for offerings, and an altar on which stood statues of the gods, two female, one male, made of bronze plates by the technique known in Greek sculpture as *sphyrelaton.*[3] Roughly the same type occurs at Prinias and Gortyn; the builders of Crete seem to have clung conservatively to ancient patterns.

The earliest evidence from the mainland of Greece and the

[3] Sp. Marinatos, "Le temple géomé-trique de Dréros," *BCH,* LX (1936), 214–85, who dates this building rather too early *c.* 750; Levi, *Annuario,* XVII–XVIII (1955–56), 237, 239–46, on Gortyn; the new shrine of Hera Limenia *c.* 750 at Perachora is similar, *Perachora,* I, 110–13.

Aegean islands suggests greater poverty but more willingness to experiment. Here the sanctuaries apparently had at first only an altar for sacrifice; but at some undefinable point before 800 simple chapels began to appear behind the altars. At Perachora and at the Argive Heraeum small clay models of the eighth century were discovered which might possibly have been houses but seem more probably to have been temples.[4] These models show a simple building with a foreporch supported by two columns and a peaked roof over the main room; the best-preserved example from Perachora has a rounded apse, that of the Argive Heraeum is rectangular. The first shrine of Artemis Orthia, probably of about 800, was perhaps 9 meters by 4.5; the foundations of the temple of Hera Akraia at Perachora are 8 by 5 meters, with rounded apse.[5] Greek architects did not easily come to sharp, clearly defined structural shapes.

At Samos a relatively large temple of more developed character was erected early in the eighth century, but this Heraeum still lacked the clarity and conscious formulation of space of the next century.[6] Initially it was a narrow, rectangular building on a foundation 33.5 meters by 6.75; a row of thirteen columns ran down the center of the cella and masked the base of the cult statue, hidden behind the last column. As the eighth century wore on, the Samians evidently grew dissatisfied with this architectural expression. First they added, probably late in the century, a colonnade of wooden columns, seven on the front,

---

[4] *Perachora*, I, 34–41; Kurt Müller, "Gebäudemodelle spätgeometrischer Zeit," *AM*, XLVIII (1923), 52–68; Sidney D. Markman, "Building Models and the Architecture of the Geometric Period," *Studies to D. M. Robinson*, I, 259–71.

The date of the model of a Cretan temple published by Alexiou in *Kretika Chronika*, IV (1950), 441–62, is lowered by Brock, *Fortetsa*, 143, to 830–20. Other such huts are known from Crete (Alexiou, p. 450) and from Greece (Young, *Late Geometric Graves*, 186).

[5] *Perachora*, I, 28–31; *Artemis Orthia*, 10–12.

[6] Ernst Buschor, "Heraion von Samos: Frühe Bauten," *AM*, LV (1930), 1–99, esp. 13–15; *AM*, LVIII (1933), 150–52; Hanfmann, *HSCP*, LXI (1953), 29, lowers the date from 800 to later in the eighth century (but cf. Lawrence, *Greek Architecture*, 91–92). On the building below the Oikos of the Naxians at Delos, see F. Courby, *BCH*, XLV (1921), 233, and René Vallois, *L'Architecture hellénique et hellénistique à Délos jusqu'à l'éviction des Déliens (166 av.J.-C.)*, I (Paris, 1944), 18, 115. Matz, *Gnomon*, IX (1933), 467, calls these long, narrow buildings "riesige Bauernhäuser."

six on the back, and seventeen on each side; at this time a shell of ashlar masonry was placed about the altar before the temple. This regularization and embellishment was only a stopgap. Early in the seventh century the Samians seem to have pulled down the temple—there is, at least, no evidence of fire in the excavation reports—and erected a temple of about the same size but with quite different spirit. Two rows of columns now ran down the interior so that the cult statue at the back was visible as the focus of the internal space; around the cella stood a colonnade which was arithmetically uniform, six on front and back and eighteen on each side, with a second row of six columns on the front to add majesty and a sense of depth. The walls of the new structure were of good stonework at the base, then of sun-dried brick and timber.

At this point Greek architects had suddenly stepped over the great divide of their architectural history. On the one side lay simple, essentially unconscious creations in space; on the other, the deliberate manipulation of physical materials to create a three-dimensional structure, solid and firm yet organically alive in its play of light and shadow, of horizontal and vertical lines. The Heraeum at Samos is only one of the new examples, for at Delos and at many other sites large-scale building broke out suddenly about the same time.

The next step, the translation of the colonnaded temple plan into stone throughout, was perhaps technically connected with the development of tile roofs, which required heavier support but permitted a gentler pitch and so a somewhat wider structure. Roof tiles had been known earlier in the Aegean, but, like so many other refinements, had died out in the Dark ages; traditionally their manufacture and use was an invention of Corinth.[7] Yet in architectural history emphasis must never be placed solely on building techniques. The transition to stone arose as well from the greater wealth of some Greek states—

[7] Payne, *Necrocorinthia*, 248–52; Lorimer, *Homer and the Monuments*, 440–41; E. D. Van Buren, *Greek Fictile Revetments in the Archaic Period* (London, 1926). The roof of the temple on the Aetos vase is painted in checks, apparently to suggest tiles; Robertson, *BSA*, XLIII (1948), 101–02, would date this scarcely after 700. The first actual example is the temple of Apollo at Thermum, of the mid-seventh century.

while others were forced to continue to build in wood—from the greater interest of Greek society in housing its gods as magnificently as possible, and from the greater daring of men in cutting and shaping raw stone blocks out of formless nature to express their human aspirations.[8] By the middle of the seventh century the rectangular temple of stone with external and internal colonnades, pediment, terra-cotta revetments and roof was becoming set as the basic religious structure of the Greeks.

In architecture, as in Orientalizing pottery, men had achieved revolution by concentration and by elimination of such variants as oval plans. One root of the new architecture, the *megaron* plan, came from the Mycenaean inheritance. Oriental influence had played a part as well, especially in the formation of the Dorian and Ionian orders, though the precise steps in this development are still hotly debated.[9] The very audacity which led the Greeks to build monumentally owed much, I suspect, to their increasing knowledge of Oriental cities, and the necessary wealth was only attained with the quickening of economic ties to the East. Yet the product is unmistakably Greek and represents a new triumph in architectural sensitivity; from the most primitive of building techniques and simplest of floor plans Greek architects had created true beauty.

Balance and restraint, the harnessing of dynamic action, logical analysis and then synthesis of clearly defined parts—all these are marks of the Greek temple, Greek statue, and Greek vase. The temple, as has often been observed, was essentially a jewel box, set on a platform to encase a statue; the Greek architect, unlike the Gothic, took a part of space and cut it off sharply from the infinite, chaotic world roundabout his structure. Internal space was not his principal concern, but in reducing a small part of the world to perfect order he went far

---

[8] Matz, *GGK*, I, 351–52, whose suggestive remarks are marred only by his compulsion to see a revival of a Mediterranean megalithic spirit.
[9] Among the many recent essays on this problem are A. von Gerkan, "Die Herkunft des dorischen Gebälks," *JdI*, LXIII–IV (1948–49), 1–13; M. L.

Bowen, "Some Observations on the Origin of Triglyphs," *BSA*, XLV (1950), 113–25; R. M. Cook's note, *BSA*, XLVI (1951), 50–52; see also Dinsmoor, *Architecture*, 50–64; C. Weickert, *Typen der archaischen Architektur in Griechenland und Kleinasien* (Augsburg, 1929).

beyond the sprawling beehives of Minoan palaces or the vast but empty colonnades of Egypt. In looking at such a finished example as the Parthenon a sensitive observer can perhaps best feel one of the greatest gifts of Greek thought to subsequent civilization, the concept that man can reduce the physical world to orderly terms comprehensible in rational, human modes of expression. Much remained to be done in sharpening this concept after the age of revolution was over, but the basic step of creating the stone temple had been achieved. The very fact that we cannot tell precisely how the Greeks had evolved their great architectural type is another mark of the suddenness with which development proceeded in the early seventh century.

Beyond the temple it is scarcely possible to discuss Greek architecture in the age of revolution. Houses remained simple structures for the basic needs of life; villages show virtually no trace of planning, save in the provision of an open space for a market and a simple foundation. These rude agglomerations were not yet walled, but the close-packed blocks of houses with common exterior walls, located usually on commanding ground, were fairly defensible. As interstate warfare grew in the seventh and sixth centuries and as states grew richer, the need for walls was to emerge. Thus far even the colonies could do little more than create a fortress refuge, although Smyrna in Asia Minor seems to have flung a mud-brick wall about its fairly small nucleus even so early as the ninth century.[1]

THE EMERGENCE OF SCULPTURE

ANOTHER great artistic triumph of the age of revolution was the wide-scale resumption of sculptural activity. The audacity which led men to the first major steps here is a mark of the intellectual strength of the eighth century; the speed with which

[1] R. V. Nicholls, *BSA*, LIII–IV (1958–59), 35–137, who essays (p. 115) to find other early parallels; most are not convincing. J. K. Brock, *BSA*, XLIV (1949), 9, reports a village wall at Siphnos; see below, Chap. 10, n. 8 (p. 340).

three-dimensional modeling in clay, wood, bronze, and stone developed attests the extraordinary openness of men to experiment in the decades just on either side of 700. The firmly set style which we call Dedalic was under way by at least 680, and the first virtually life-size statue in stone, the Nikandre figure from Delos, is generally dated before the mid-century mark.[2]

As one looks back from Nikandre into the eighth century, it is amazing that so much had been accomplished in so short a time. The Geometric style was not one calculated to encourage three-dimensional reproduction of the real world of man and beast; before 800 the plastic sense of the Greeks had expressed itself mainly in the beautifully integrated but abstract shapes of Protogeometric and Geometric vases. A very thin tradition of sculpture, it is true, had survived throughout the Dark ages. Cult statuettes of human and animal form were made at this time in Crete, largely in imitation of Minoan and Mycenaean prototypes; and a few bronze and hand-molded clay animals have been found at sites in Greece. At times the animals were simplified virtually past identification, but the plumpish horses of the tenth- and ninth-century graves at the Kerameikos are rather engaging, naïve reflections of reality unfettered by any sense of canons (see Plate 9b).[3]

[2] Basic studies of the early figurines are Müller, *Frühe Plastik*, 60–89, which is unfortunately too typological and does not bring out clearly the development in the period here under consideration; Emil Kunze, "Zu den Anfängen der griechischen Plastik," *AM*, LV (1930), 141–62, which is criticized on some dates by Hampe, *Frühe Griechische Sagenbilder*, 32–38; Peter Knoblauch, *Studien zur archaischgriechischen Tonbilderei in Kreta, Rhodos, Athen und Böotien* (Diss. Halle, 1937), esp. pp. 17–38; Homann-Wedeking, *Die Anfänge der griechischen Grossplastik*, 11–41, with W. Kraiker's long review article, *Gnomon*, XXIV (1952), 449–60. Works on sculpture in stone will be noted below insofar as they concern the early period.

Catalogues of terra cottas: Jen-

kins, *Perachora* I, 191–255; Dieter Ohly, "Frühe Tonfiguren aus dem Heraion von Samos," *AM*, LXV (1940), 57–102; *AM*, LXVI (1941), 1–46. Very little on the early period will be found in the Louvre *Catalogue raisonnée des figurines et reliefs en terre-cuite grecs, étrusques et romains,* I (Paris, 1954), and R. A. Higgins, *Catalogue of the Terracottas in the Department of Greek and Roman Antiquities, British Museum,* I (London, 1954).

[3] An example of Cretan work is *BSA*, XXXVIII (1937), pl. XXXI (Karphi); on the mainland, see *Kerameikos*, V. 1, pl. 142, which may be compared to the rigid work on pl. 143 (and *CVA Deutschland* IX, pl. 128, Munich 6597, 7810) of the mid-eighth century.

In the eighth century came new factors which at once encouraged the Greeks to essay sculpture on a broader scale and suggested the patterns to be followed. Among these factors were acquaintance with Oriental art, the increasing crystallization of Greek views of the gods, and the breakdown of Geometric pottery; most important of all was the increasing interest of man in his own nature. To follow in detail the working of these stimuli in the sculpture of the eighth century proper is virtually impossible on the basis of the material now at hand. It is extremely difficult to date the rude, small terra-cotta figurines, handmade until after 700, often artless in intent, and conventional in type over long periods; [4] consecutive series of these figurines which reach back into even the eighth century are very limited (Samos, Perachora, and a few other sites). Bronze statuettes are likewise few until well after 700. Worse yet, we cannot arrange the figurines along a clearly established line of progress. This fact is in itself suggestive. The late eighth century was a period of wide experimentation; from its manifold creations a firm style emerged only in the decades immediately following 700.

Despite these uncertainties we can establish a few important points for evaluating plastic progress. It is clear, in the first place, that the instinct to model was already present in the Aegean world before the onset of Oriental influence. Again, the basic drive which led to the resumption of sculpture was the crystallization of religious and intellectual views, which was Greek in origin.

The dress, however, in which these views were expressed owed as much or more to the Orient than any other art of the era. The five ladies found in a Dipylon grave of shortly after 750 are made of ivory, an Eastern material; and both their naked pose, the *polos* on their heads, and the stiff arrangement of their arms at the side are of Oriental origin (Plate 19a). Many of the details of the relatively advanced modeling smack of Eastern refinement as well, though the general spirit of the

---

[4] Note the conservatism in the series recently published by John H. Young and Suzanne H. Young, *Terracotta Figurines from Kourion in Cyprus* (Philadelphia, 1955). On the other hand, terra-cotta work was often more open than monumental sculpture to free experiment; cf. Kunze, *AM*, LV (1930), 142, and Knoblauch, *Studien*, 9–10.

figurines is Greek.[5] Clay and bronze statuettes of the eighth century (Plate 19b) frequently share wide, deep-set eyes, prominent nose and chin, and upward tilt of the face, all of which are almost surely Syrian in origin.[6] Even more certainly Oriental is the "Etagenperuke" or layered hair, which became very common especially after 700 (Plate 21a). And, as we noted in Chapter 5, the increasing tendency of the Greeks to express their sharper concepts of the gods in plastic form owed much to Oriental prototypes.

The richly elaborated artistic tradition of the East, nonetheless, was not taken over entire by the Aegean. The dominant principles of the Geometric style are clearly pronounced in work of the late eighth century, which was often characterized by a slimming and almost mathematical manipulation of natural forces. This artistic outlook was limited in clay figures by the nature of the material, but could find fuller vent in bronze statuettes of men and horses, which have been found in numbers at Olympia and turn up spottily elsewhere. The rod-like warriors and charioteers who perched on the edges of the great bronze caldrons are first cousins of the solemn abstractions on Dipylon and other Late Geometric vases.[7]

[5] Kunze, *AM*, LV (1930), 148–55, dated this grave to about 800; Kübler, *Kerameikos*, V. 1, 92–93, placed it at *c.* 745 at the earliest (but on p. 179 ascribed the ivories to the later years of the period 775–750). See also Karo, *Greek Personality*, 28–31; Barnett, *JHS*, LXVIII (1948), 4, and Dunbabin, *Greeks and Their Eastern Neighbours*, 39, who are firm on the difference in spirit from Oriental work, against Homann-Wedeking, *Anfänge*, 19, 131.

[6] Syrian influence: Dunbabin, *Greeks and Their Eastern Neighbours*, 36–37; Homann-Wedeking, *Anfänge*, 22; Higgins, *BMC Terracottas*, nos. 575–581 (late eighth-century reliefs from Crete). Layered hair: Poulsen, *Der Orient*, 179; Jenkins, *Dedalica*, 19–20; Müller, *Frühe Plastik*, 87–88, 167–76, on other details; F. R. Grace, "Observations on Seventh-Century Sculp-

ture," *AJA*, XLVI (1942), 341–59. Note that Egyptian influence on Greek sculpture appears only in the late seventh century (Karo, *Greek Personality*, 103; Dunbabin, *AJA*, LVI [1952], 221–22).

[7] Kunze, *Olympia-Bericht*, IV, 105–18; Stanley Casson, "Bronze Work of the Geometric Period and Its Relation to Later Art," *JHS*, XLII (1922), 207–19. A naïve naturalism may still be found in such work as the round dancers of Athens (NM 6236; C. Zervos, *L'Art en Grèce* [2d ed.; Paris, 1936], fig. 68) and Olympia (Berlin 01. 8702; Neugebauer, *Bronzen*, I, pl. 5); but more typical is the centaur battle in New York (Met. Mus. 17. 190. 2072). See Benton, *BSA*, XXXV (1934–35), 116; Ernst Buschor, *Die Plastik der Griechen* (Munich, 1958), 10–14; Hampe, *Die Gleichnisse Homers*, 36–37; Homann-

As the treatment of the human figure by vase painters changed, so too did that of the sculptors. One landmark along the way is the warrior statuette dedicated on the Acropolis, apparently a free-standing figurine of about 720 (Plate 20a); for here perhaps best of all in the surviving works we can sense the release from old bonds which came at the end of the eighth century.[8] Whereas the Dipylon ladies stand stiffly—if indeed they can be said to "stand"—this warrior has broken loose in violent action, with lance in hand. His modeling is loose. The outlines of the body are not sharply defined, but the parts of the figure are beginning to flow together as in the first Protoattic drawings (see Plate 17b). An inner life and tension pulsate especially in the face, the eyes of which stare wide-open out on the world, "a new, open gaze which is still filled with childish amazement." This nude male warrior, too, foreshadows the famous *kouros* type of stone statuary.[9]

Between the Acropolis warrior of the late eighth century and the Mantiklos bronze (Plate 20b), found in Boeotia and commonly dated to the first quarter of the seventh century, we cross as great a divide as that which marks contemporary pottery and architecture. The Mantiklos figurine was sharply conceived and firmly modeled; its master no longer stood in an era when all restraint had been cast aside. The outline is clear, the internal contours are deliberately shaped and more carefully reflect the anatomy of the human body, the head looks at the world with secure, disciplined countenance.[1] Still, there are a Geometric stiffness and lack of proportion which are perhaps in part of pro-

---

Wedeking, *Anfänge*, 17–18; Knoblauch, *Studien*, 19–20; Kunze, *AM*, LV (1930), 143.

[8] Kunze, *AM*, LV (1930), 144; Ohly, *Griechische Goldbleche*, 148; Samian parallels, Ohly, *AM*, LXVI (1941), 23. The quotation below is from Knoblauch, *Studien*, 19, who compares terra cottas, 21–22.

[9] An even earlier forerunner is the terra cotta T. 57 of Samos, Ohly, *AM*, LXVI (1941), 8. See generally G. M. A. Richter, *Kouroi* (New York, 1942).

[1] Grace, *Archaic Sculpture in Boeotia*, 49–50; Homann-Wedeking, *Anfänge*, 36–37, 51.

The Menelaion woman (*BSA*, XV [1908–09], pl. 10) shows the same advance, but Homann-Wedeking, *Anfänge*, 31, is right in feeling that the provincial stiffness of this figure may mislead us as to its date; cf. Kunze, *AM*, LV (1930), 160, and Wace, *BSA*, XV, 146, who gives the accompanying pottery. Other parallels to this stage are given in Ohly, *AM*, LXVI (1941), 25–26, who unfortunately places T. 393 too early (cf. Homann-Wedeking, *Anfänge*, 28).

vincial origin but suggest as well that stubborn survival of earlier ways of thought we have already noted in the pottery. Other bronzes of the period from Olympia and elsewhere attest how difficult was the step forward in sculpture.[2]

In its frontal gaze, triangular face, and modeling of facial features the head of the Mantiklos bronze is not far removed from the style called Dedalic, which emerged in the northeast Peloponnesus by at least 680 and swept over much of Greece; an example of the first stage of this sculptural outlook is given in Plate 21a from the shrine of Artemis Orthia at Sparta. As the leading student of this style, Jenkins, has observed, "the very earliest Dedalic heads are of course primitive in appearance, yet they have in them already much more of the later Dedalic than of the Subgeometric they immediately succeed. The transition was evidently rapid and the break complete, involving not merely a progress in technique but a complete intellectual change of standpoint as well."[3] In his last clause Jenkins goes too far, for the appearance of the taut, geometrically composed faces of Dedalic style, however abrupt, was not a complete denial of earlier artistic attitudes. Yet the Dedalic style in its new treatment of mass reflects a far more conscious conception of human existence in the physical world.

Now, finally, the way was open to "monumental" sculpture, and the step from statuettes of Dedalic type to marble statues was swiftly taken. The Nikandre figure of Delos (Plate 21b), which must be put before 650, is simply unthinkable in the eighth century.[4]

[2] Bronzes showing a Geometric survival are given by Kunze, *Olympia-Bericht*, IV, 119–25.

[3] Jenkins, *Dedalica*, 12. His discussion of the style is very useful; see also his "Laconian Terracottas of the Dedalic Style," *BSA*, XXXIII (1932–33), 66–79, and "Archaic Argive Terracotta Figurines to 525 B.C.," *BSA*, XXXII (1931–32), 23–40.

But his effort to ascribe the style to Dorians will not fit the evidence. It appears early as far as Samos in T. 387, 723, etc. (Ohly, *AM*, LXVI [1941], 28–30) and at Thera; N. M.

Kontoleon, "Κοῦροι ἐκ Θήρας," *Arch. eph.* 1939–41, 1–33, places the Dedalic origins in a better framework and also discusses the creation of the sixth-century "Ionian" style. Levi, *Annuario*, XVII–XVIII (1955–56), 277–88, still essays to demonstrate a Cretan origin for the Dedalic style on the basis of the new Gortyn finds.

[4] Homann-Wedeking, *Anfänge*, 124–26, eliminates the idea that the sanctuary at Samos had a statue before the first temple, though W. Kraiker, *Gnomon*, XXIV (1952), 453, still accepts it. Cf. Franz Willemsen, *Frühe grie-*

Fierce debate still swirls over the precise area where large-scale work on stone first occurred, for students still insist, most unnecessarily, upon trying to localize the major developments of early Greek culture far too minutely. The Dedalic background was shared by the more developed regions of the Aegean as a whole; the very obvious existence of many local styles of large-scale sculpture by the end of the seventh century suggests that plastic development from the earlier figurines proceeded on as many independent lines as did Orientalizing pottery. We simply do not have for sculpture the evidence which exists in the field of vase painting and there permits us to pin down the details of progress. As far as the employment of marble is concerned, the islands of the Aegean, where good marble was easily quarried, may have led the way,[5] but marble, though highly important as a material for the expression of sculptural views in the seventh century, was not the only available medium. Other kinds of stone could be used, statues of hammered bronze plates have been found at Dreros in Crete, and the primitive wooden figures which are recorded in ancient sources probably dated in the main from the seventh century. I seriously doubt that large-size carving in wood preceded much, if at all, large statues in other media.[6]

In the progress of Greek sculpture we can see once again the powerful forces which drove the arts in the age of revolution. By 650 the sculptors of Greece had reached firm ground, from which their pupils progressed steadily; and yet it is impossible to outline in clear, evolutionary stages the rapid advance of their own teachers. A veritable revolution had taken place in the few brief decades between the Acropolis warrior and the first Protodedalic figurines. Though the Oriental contribution was marked in this era and continued to be powerful, the main line of Aegean sculptural progress had driven it further away

---

chische Kultbilder (Diss. München 1939); Matz, *Gnomon*, IX (1933), 467; Knoblauch, *Studien*, 22–23. Contra, Kunze, *AM*, LV (1930), 141–42.
[5] So Homann-Wedeking, *Anfänge*, 94–95; on the progress of the debate, see

Demargne, *La Crète dédalique*, 307–18.
[6] Our earliest wood statuette is that from Samos published by Ohly, *AM*, LXVIII (1953), Beil. 13, *c.* 625–600 B.C.

from the Orient: the rod-like statuettes of Syria and the Aegean in the eighth century had far more in common than did such a head as that of Plate 21a and contemporary seventh-century Oriental work.

In their achievement Greek sculptors had proceeded much as had their confreres in architecture and pottery by limiting the number of types within which they worked and by refining these forms in ever more exquisite detail. From the beginnings of large-scale stone sculpture only three main types, the standing nude male (*kouros*), the standing clothed female (*kore*), and the seated female figure were to busy the workers in stone;[7] and in the minor decorative arts a similar concentration can be found in the marvelous development of such animals as the griffin (Plate 24b) and sphinx, lion and horse.

The life which now pulsated in the products of the sculptors' shops reflected, perhaps more sharply than anywhere else in the arts, a new outlook on the world. Greek sculpture, in truth, came into existence because men needed it as a mode of expression. One quality, however, we must be careful not to ascribe to the new artistic outlook: the Greeks were not simply imitating nature. The vase paintings and the sculpture of the seventh century attest far more careful observation of man and animal, just as the contemporary architecture manifests a more conscious appreciation of space. Men were obviously brooding on their own nature; but what resulted was not "realistic" art. On the contrary, the creation of artistic canons had the effect of eliminating naïve, open observation of the world. "By a sudden and radical change," Jenkins observes, "all naturalism in plastic art is left behind and its place is taken by a rigid mathematical conception of the head which bears no direct relation to nature whatever. . . . The Dedalic head is an Idea: the intellectual has succeeded to the unintellectual, the formula to the naturalis-

---

[7] Cf. Homann-Wedeking, *Anfänge,* 129–30; Matz, *GGK,* I, 183. Animals: see below, Chap. 8, nn. 8–9 (pp. 280–81), 1–2 (282); and on horses, above, Chap. 5, n. 1 (p. 155); Chap. 4, n. 2 (p. 133). Other work, which cannot be considered here, includes the pins (Jacobsthal, *Greek Pins,* 20–24), the fibulae (Blinkenberg, *Fibules grecques et orientales;* Hampe, *Frühe Griechische Sagenbilder*), and jewelry (Giovanni Becatti, *Oreficerie antiche dalle minoiche alle barbariche* [Rome, 1955]).

tic." [8] Thus, too, the Doric column and temple had succeeded to the rude chapel as an intellectual appreciation of space; lions, griffins, the figures of men themselves, all were ordered and refined as men drove to impose their sense of structure upon the chaos of nature.[9]

[8] *Dedalica*, 14; cf. Knoblauch, *Studien*, 32; Gerhart Rodenwaldt, *Die Kunst der Antike* (Berlin, 1927), 33; C. T. Seltman, *Approach to Greek Art* (London, 1948), 30–32; E. Loewy, *Die Naturwiedergabe in der älteren griechischen Kunst* (Rome, 1900). I return to the broader significance of this point below, pp. 294 ff.

[9] Jenkins, *Dedalica*, 41, well notes how similar the ordering of the Dedalic male figure is to that of the Doric column; see the relief figure in *Perachora*, I, pl. 103, n. 187.

CHAPTER 8

THE INTELLECTUAL UPHEAVAL: II

ALONGSIDE THE BURGEONING ARTS of the era from 750 to 650 ran a swelling volume of literature. Unconsciously poet and artist shared the same spirit so well that their works reciprocally illuminate each other. Whereas Ripe Geometric pottery could only hint at much which the *Iliad* makes plain, Orientalizing draftsmen became ever more competent to express in visual form complicated ideas and new points of view. And consciously too there are now clear interconnections between literature and art, for potters and smiths began just before 700 to illustrate scenes from myth and epic. The earlier pictures of leave-taking, battles, and other events in Ripe Geometric art were typical and generalized. Then, quite suddenly, the exploits of Heracles and Trojan heroes became sharp and unmistakable on vases, bronze tripods, *fibulae*, and other artistic products.[1]

[1] Among the many recent treatments see the lists of epic scenes in Hampe, *Frühe Griechische Sagenbilder*, 80–81, and *Die Gleichnisse Homers;* Kirk, *BSA*, XLIV (1949), 148–50; Webster, *BSA*, L (1955), 38–50, *From Mycenae to Homer*, 168–74, and *Greek Art and Literature*, 700–530 B.C., 18–19; Dunbabin, *Greeks and Their Eastern Neighbours*, 77–87. Most of these lists are too inclusive. The eighth-century scenes of leave-taking between ship captain and his wife (e.g., BM 1899, 2–19. 1 from Thebes; Hampe, *Frühe Griechische Sagenbilder*, pl. 22) are not necessarily the abduction of Helen by Paris. Hampe (after Blinkenberg, *Fibules grecques*, 163–69) and Kraiker, *Neue Beiträge*, 46, identify cer-

tain twin figures as the Siamese-twin Molione (Louvre A 519 [*CVA France* XVIII pl. 5]; Agora P 4885 [*Hesperia*, Supp. II, p. 70, fig. 44]; New York 14. 130. 14; Athens NM 11765); but note the just reserve by J. M. Cook, *BSA*, XXXV (1934–35), 206.

The earliest certain examples of myth in art are, I think: (1) the Tiryns shield with Achilles and Penthesilea, or Heracles (cf. Brommer, *Herakles*, 35, 71–72), which I illustrate on Plate 23a—but Dietrich von Bothmer, *Amazons in Greek Art* (Oxford, 1957), 2, lowers its date appreciably; (2) the Boeotian *fibulae* of Heracles and the Lernaean monster (Hampe, 41–42). Against Hampe's dates, however, cf. Cook, *BSA*, XXXV

As between the two fields, we are on safer ground chronologically when we take up the relatively sure sequences of pottery and figurines; but most students will be able to appreciate the new ideas of the age more easily in their literary form. Here are reflected the broadening interests and wealth of the cultured classes in the aristocratic city-states, which furnished a new and ever more consciously appreciative audience to the poets. These men, the more sensitive members of the community, revealed in their verse a twofold drive. On the one side they were spokesmen for common feelings; on the other, they were imperiously impelled by their own personal reactions to the great stresses and changes of the age of revolution. In expressing their views they aided the less articulate and less reflective to establish new patterns of thought. The success of the lyric poets in reaching an advanced plane of social and personal values was a token of the basic confidence of Greek civilization; their polished meters and forms of verse were a mold for later poetry.

The historian who turns to literature cannot entirely avoid the necessity of aesthetic judgment, but this is not his primary aim. Many excellent studies have treated early Greek literature for and in itself.[2] My purpose accordingly must be, first, to determine what sequence and date for the several authors have the best historical justification; and, secondly, to explore the light thrown by literature on the forces at work in the age of revolution. More specifically, the last epic bards and the first lyric poets reflect admirably the views of the age on two basic points, the nature of mankind and its relations to the gods.

(1934–35), 207, and Kirk, *BSA*, XLIV (1949), 147.

Centaurs and centauromachies, which occur in the eighth century, do not necessarily reflect specific myths, though they do show an unreal world. Vase examples: *CVA Copenhagen* II, pl. 73; *Clara Rhodos*, IV (1931), 310 fig. 344 (sketch in *Annuario*, VI–VII [1926], 337 fig. 222; cf. D. Feytmans, *BCH*, LXXIV [1950], 161, 177); *CVA Deutschland* II, pl. 5; Beazley, *Development of Attic Black-figure*, pl. 2. Figurines: Athens NM 12. 504 (*AM*, LV [1930], pl. xxxviii. 2) or

New York 17. 190. 2072 (Buschor, *Plastik der Griechen*, 12). Cf. Demargne, *La Crète dédalique*, 281–84.
[2] The recent discussions in Hermann Fränkel, *Dichtung und Philosophie des frühen Griechentums: Eine Geschichte der griechischen Literatur von Homer bis Pindar* (New York, 1951); Bruno Snell, *The Discovery of the Mind: The Greek Origins of European Thought* (Oxford, 1953); Max Treu, *Von Homer zur Lyrik* (Munich, 1955), will indicate the earlier literature.

THE *ODYSSEY* AND HESIOD

MUCH THAT was composed in the century 750–650 has long since been lost. Archaic literature was still too primitive in form and expression, too much the product of ill-resolved tensions, to command fully the attention of later ages. While this work was written down in the new Greek alphabet, it was composed not to be read but to be heard—either sung or accompanied by the improved lyre and other musical instruments.[3] The trowels of the excavators can bring back, in part, the equally neglected works of early sculptors and potters, but they cannot rescue the corpus of such poets as Eumelus of Corinth, Callinus of Ephesus, and Terpander of Miletus, of whom later anthologies and glossaries preserved at best a fragment or two.[4] The minor poems in the epic cycles were often illustrated on seventh-century vases, their argument was preserved in later summaries and references, but their text has not survived. Modern efforts to restore this lost literature and to evaluate its merits are like the reconstructions of vanished artistic masterpieces from literary descriptions—often ingenious, sometimes suggestive, but never reliable bases for detailed historical argument; and the music which accompanied the literature is hopelessly gone.

The major material which has survived more or less intact consists of the *Odyssey*, the works assigned to Hesiod, and the extensive fragments of Archilochus. The chronological order in

[3] Music was always one of the most important arts; and Damon of Athens was surely right in observing (fragment 10): "Musical modes are nowhere altered without [changes in] the most important laws of the State." While the main course of musical development in early Greece is irretrievably lost, very important steps clearly took place in the age of revolution. The gamut of musical instruments was considerably amplified about 700 (cf. Max Wegner, *Das Musikleben der Griechen* [Berlin, 1949], 138–40); the Greeks themselves felt that their significant music began at that time with Olympus of Phrygia (cf. the evidence in Edmonds, *Lyra Graeca* I, 4–10). For the dance, which was also important, cf. Kunze, *Kretische Bronzereliefs*, 212–15, who gives the physical evidence in addition to August Brinkmann, "Altgriechische Mädchenreigen," *Bonner Jahrbücher*, CXXX (1925), 118–46.

[4] Fragments in Ernest Diehl, *Anthologia lyrica graeca*, fasc. 1–3 (3d ed.; Leipzig, 1949–52). The *Homeric Hymns*, which I shall not consider except in passing, range on down into the sixth century; cf. the edition by T. W. Allen, W. R. Halliday, and E. E. Sikes (Oxford, 1936).

which these three have just been listed is the usual one, and I believe it to be the correct arrangement, historically speaking. When we draw conclusions on this basis, however, we must be judicious. Modern studies of Greek literature sometimes go much too far in postulating that in details of technique and in manipulating motifs each author knew of his predecessors and built deliberately upon their treatments. The early poets hearkened to the voices of the Aegean; they also worked within very local frameworks. A later author might, moreover, reach back and express ideas which were virtually obsolete.

Yet the basic changes in Greek culture must be reflected in its literature, and this fact is not difficult to establish. While the *Odyssey* was formed at the point where Late Geometric art was almost ready to yield to the Orientalizing ware, the poems of Hesiod are just beyond this great divide. Archilochus comes later yet and expresses the same spirit as the artists of the mid-seventh century who created Middle Protocorinthian and Middle Protoattic vases. By this point Greek civilization had emerged onto a new plane.

To judge from the illustration of epic scenes on vases, the *Odyssey* had become widely appreciated through the Greek world by the early seventh century. Two Late Geometric vases which show scenes of shipwreck are too general in import to prove that their artists knew our present poem; and in any case men must long have heard the tale of the seafaring Odysseus in its primitive forms.[5] But the marvelous Middle Protoattic vase from Eleusis, which depicts the blinding of Polyphemus (Plate 23b), and two companion portrayals of the event on Argive and other work begin a continuous chain of specific, graphic scenes which rest upon equally specific literary descriptions.[6] By this

---

[5] Munich 8696 (Hampe, *Die Gleichnisse Homers*, 27–30; R. Lullies, *AA* 1954, cols. 261–64; Kraiker, *Neue Beiträge*, 45) and the vase from Ischia (*Römische Mitteilungen*, LX–LXI [1953–54], pl. 14–16). So, too, the appearance of the hexameter on vases about 700 at Ithaca (*BSA*, XLIII [1948], 82) and Ischia (*Rendiconti della Accademia nazionale dei Lincei*, 8. ser. X [1955], 215 ff.) and Athens (NM 192) does not necessarily mean that the epics had crystallized.

[6] *ILN* November 13, 1954, 841; Courbin, *BCH*, LXXIX (1955), 1–49 (Argos and Aristonothos vases); escape of Odysseus on the Ram Jug (Kraiker, *Aigina*, no. 566). See

point the developed version of the *Odyssey* must have received general acceptance, and the tone of the *Odyssey*, as we shall see shortly, suggests that it had already been fashioned for a few generations.

The *Odyssey* was thus later than the *Iliad* and not composed by the same poet, though it arose by a similar process out of ancestral materials treated in the same fashion of oral poetry. If we set the *Iliad* before 750, then the *Odyssey* will fall about 740–720. Much ingenuity has been exercised by Homeric scholars to prove (or occasionally to disprove) its junior relationship on technical grounds such as differences in vocabulary, in the handling of the hexameter, in the use or absence of similes, and in epic technique generally. Old words and verb forms, to give an example, which are common in the *Iliad* are absent from the *Odyssey*, which in turn has more abstract nouns. Such quasi-mathematical proofs can never quite hit their mark. Both epics have later, interpolated passages, and the *Odyssey* contains its share of old strata—though no student of Homer can convince his peers just which lines in either epic fall into these categories. Much of the poetic contrast, moreover, is not of chronological origin. The two poems tell diverse kinds of tales; they may have been composed in widely separated areas, though not necessarily so; and the younger poet may even not have known the specific formulation of the old tale of Achilles in the *Iliad*.[7]

Hampe, *Frühe Griechische Sagenbilder*, 74–76. The argument by Willy Zschietzschmann, "Homer und die attische Bildkunst um 560," *JdI*, XLVI (1931), 45–60, that Attic illustration of Homer began only with the Panathenaea of 566 will not stand in the light of more recent evidence.

[7] Date: Denys Page, *The Homeric Odyssey* (Oxford, 1955), 148–49, opts apparently for about 800; Rhys Carpenter, *Folk Tale, Fiction and Saga in the Homeric Epics* (Berkeley, 1946), for 625; Lorimer, *Homer and the Monuments*, 493–509, for the last third of the eighth century; Webster, *From Mycenae to Homer*, 282–83,

comes to the dates I prefer. Among the recent studies of the *Odyssey* cf. Reinhold Merkelbach, *Untersuchungen zur Odyssee* (Munich, 1951); Friedrich Focke, *Die Odyssee* (Stuttgart, 1943). On a far fringe are the efforts to derive it from an ancient Mediterranean stock: L. A. Stella, *Il poema di Ulisse* (Florence, 1955); G. Patroni, *Commenti mediterranei all'Odissea di Omero* (Milan, 1950), and "Studi di mitologia mediterranea ed omerico," *Memorie dell'Instituto lombardo*, 3. ser. XXV–XXVI (1951).

Vocabulary: Page, *Odyssey*, 149–56; cf. Webster, *From Mycenae to Homer*, 275–83, W. Diehl, *Die wört-*

The basic chronological relationship nonetheless is clear. If we take the plot of the *Odyssey* as it now runs with the shifts back and forth between Odysseus and his son Telemachus, the pattern is more discursive, less concentrated, less stylized than is that of the *Iliad;* yet the structure is more involved and richer in attendant variety. In artistic terms, the *Odyssey* reminds one of the growing complexity and breakdown of inherited patterns visible in Late Geometric pottery. In its hints, again, of political change, in its picture of that wider geographical and economic horizon which marked the first steps in Greek colonization, and in its archaeological parallels the *Odyssey* also reflects the conditions of Greek society when the age of revolution was just commencing.[8]

Even more significant testimony on the direction of Hellenic development lies in the psychological and religious temper of the *Odyssey*. From their first lines, as Fränkel has well observed, the *Iliad* and *Odyssey* diverge in spirit.[9] Achilles, a man of anger who sacrifices others to his rage, stands over against the thoughtful Odysseus, who tries to save his companions and himself. The physical world about man now begins to appear in real hues—one consequence is the virtual absence of similes from the younger poem. And the figure of man himself is changing. As in incipient Protoattic pottery the human form in the *Odyssey* seems at times to have been conceived as a whole, not as a collection of parts, and an internal force animates the

---

lichen Beziehungen zwischen *Ilias* und *Odyssee* (Greifswalder Beiträge, XXII [1938]); Manu Leumann, *Homerische Wörter* (Basel, 1950), studies specific examples. Note, however, the brief essay of J. A. Scott, "Two Linguistic Tests of the Relative Antiquity of the *Iliad* and the *Odyssey*," *CP*, VI (1911), 156–62, who concludes that the two poems stand in this respect on the same level as against Hesiod.

Relation of the two poets: Page, *Odyssey*, 158–59; but the deliberate effort of the poet to tell the fall of Troy and the fate of the heroes thereafter must be kept in mind. Cf. Alfred Heubeck, *Der Odyssee-Dichter und die*

Ilias (Erlangen, 1954).
[8] Artistic parallel: Whitman, *Homer and the Heroic Tradition*, 287–90, who comes down too far (pp. 290–95) in comparing the *Odyssey* to Early Protoattic and so placing it about 700. Archaeological references: Nilsson, *Homer and Mycenae*, 135–37, 208.
[9] Fränkel, *Dichtung und Philosophie*, 121; his discussion, pp. 120–32, is useful. Note also the developed analysis of the beauty of Calypso's cave, *Odyssey* V. 60–75; no passage in the *Iliad* contains such a vivid, many-sided picture. Human figure: Treu, *Von Homer zur Lyrik*, 13–14, 49, 68, who notes examples (though this study must be analyzed carefully).

physical frame. Though self-consciousness as such does not yet exist, qualities of determination and calculation are the hallmark of the much-enduring Odysseus, who thoughtfully lies and poses, rather than blazing forth in childish wrath. In the *Iliad,* to look only briefly at the religious machinery, fearful events occur at the will of the gods; in the *Odyssey* the folly of the suitors themselves or of the shipmates of Odysseus brings upon their heads their merited punishments. No doubt the gods still rule the world of Odysseus, but they operate not so often *propria persona* as indirectly through men who take their course more into their own hands.

In comparing the divine apparatus of the two epics or in ranking Achilles beside Odysseus, the temptation is great to overpress the divergences, for in the *Odyssey* much which was to characterize men's views of themselves and of the gods during the next century lies almost visible. But only *almost* visible. The *Odyssey* was the last great flowering of the epic tradition. Some of the other poems of the Trojan cycle, pulled together from the old stock of tales by Arctinus, Stasimon, and other lesser men, may come from the seventh century, though not from its later decades.[1] The *Odyssey,* however, will not stand such a date. The individual outpouring of feelings in the lyric poets, the personal appearance of the author which is already obvious in Hesiod—these are still absent, along with much else of the psychological, religious, and political temper of the new Greek outlook of the seventh century. The *Odyssey* is close to the *Iliad,* but a gulf separates it from the next works of Greek literature. Not without some semblance of justice have most men ascribed the two epics to a single author.

In the *Iliad* and *Odyssey* the inheritance of the earlier centuries of Aegean development was summed up and passed on to

[1] Literary remains in T. W. Allen, *Homer,* V (Oxford, 1912). The lists given in n. 1 (p. 261) above show that the *Little Iliad* and *Cypria* were, if anything, more popular sources for vase painters than the greater epics. This remained true later as well; in Kunze's list of Trojan scenes of the sixth century in *Archaische Schild-* *bänder* (Berlin, 1950), 139–73, none are from the *Odyssey.* Cf. the lists of Laconian illustration, Lane, *BSA,* XXXIV (1933–34), 162–68, which has only the Blinding of Polyphemus from the greater epics. Arctinus is said by the Suda (*s.v.*) to have been born *c.* 740 (8th Olympiad).

later ages far more obviously and openly than in the arts, where the Geometric outlook was overridden and outwardly was dismissed. If the epic poems continued to be popular and their influence was so feared by such diverse thinkers as Xenophanes and Plato, the fact illuminates a cardinal theme of this volume, the continuity of that basic pattern of civilization which had been set in the Dark ages. Yet the equally apparent fact that the epic tradition ceased to produce major fruit during the age of revolution shows well that it was no longer adequate to encase men's new thoughts about the complexities of life—in fine, that revolution *was* taking place in the Greek world at this time.

If the *Odyssey* falls before the full onset of the upheaval, the scope and date of which we have already identified in the arts, Hesiod, the author of the didactic poem *Works and Days*, comes after this great event. He is only barely thus to be placed, for his verse form, vocabulary, and general poetic approach owe much to the epic tradition. His cry for justice against the bribe-swallowing *basileis* likewise seems an early outburst in the political unrest which produced the organized city-state. The whirlwind which burst upon Greece at this time was so swift and tempestuous that the pupil of the Heliconian Muses may be dated very close to the author of the *Odyssey;* on the chronology here employed, Hesiod perhaps fits best into the decade or two just on either side of 700. The lines which assert that he once crossed to Chalcis and won a tripod for song at the funeral games of King Archidamus—slain, according to tradition, in the Lelantine war about 705—are thus actually valid, though they have often been rejected as spurious since the days of Plutarch.[2]

---

[2] *Works and Days* 654; Plutarch, *Moralia* 153F; other ancient speculation may be found in Erwin Rohde, *Kleine Schriften*, I (Tübingen, 1901), 39–52. Hesiod: Friedrich Solmsen, *Hesiod and Aeschylus* (Ithaca, 1949); Jula Kerschensteiner, "Zu Aufbau und Gedankenführung von Hesiods Erga," *Hermes*, LXXIX (1944), 149–91, with full references to earlier work; H. T. Wade-Gery, "Hesiod," *Phoenix*, III (1949), 81–93; T. A. Sinclair, *Hesiod, Works and Days* (London, 1932). Whether Hesiod knew the Homeric epics is much debated: Leumann, *Homerische Wörter*, 330; Page, *Odyssey*, 36. Margarete Riemschneider, *Homer: Entwicklung und Stil* (Leipzig, 1950), and others have placed Homer after Hesiod.

(a) Late Geometric vase (K. 1356) which reflects the loosening of Geometric forms (Kerameikos Museum). Photograph courtesy Deutsches Archäologisches Institut in Athens.

(b) Late Geometric amphora with advanced depiction of runners and deer on neck and conservative treatment of chariots below (Ashmolean Museum 1935. 19, Oxford). Photograph courtesy Ashmolean Museum.

PLATE 17 · Decay of the Attic Geometric Spirit

(a) Transitional amphora using an abundance of Orientalizing motifs but still dry in style (Louvre). Photograph courtesy Musée du Louvre.

(b) Early Protoattic vase with huge sphinx (Kerameikos Museum). Photograph courtesy Deutsches Archäologisches Institut in Athens.

PLATE 18 · Emergence of the Protoattic Style

The *Works and Days* is extraordinarily fascinating. It is pungent and blunt; true poetic genius shimmers in its swiftly shifting kaleidoscope; above all, this is the first written illumination of the stresses and changes of the late eighth and early seventh centuries. Many of its lines will concern us when we come to the political and economic aspects of this era; even in treating the general intellectual development of the time I find it difficult to omit any of Hesiod's terse, graphic pictures. For the first time in Greek history a specific individual speaks for himself, and the ethical tone of his outcry rings in one's heart like the contemporary, biting indictments of injustice which welled up in the early prophets of Israel.

As Perses had defrauded his brother of his inheritance, so acted many men, dishonoring their parents, violating their oaths, plotting in envy. "Strength will be right and reverence will cease to be" (lines 192–3). Thrice Hesiod essayed to demonstrate or to explain this wickedness, once by the myth of Pandora, once by the fable of the hawk and the nightingale, and once by a rational picture of the five ages of mankind. For the present day, as Hesiod viewed his era of turmoil, was the fifth period, an iron age after the golden, silver, bronze, and heroic stages of the past; "and men never rest from labour and sorrow by day, and from perishing by night; and the gods shall lay sore trouble upon them . . . there will be no help against evil." [3]

Yet in his myth of Pandora Hesiod had already shown that Hope remained as a blessing among the plagues given to men by the gods. To Hesiod, as to Homer, mighty Zeus still raised and lowered men as he willed—"there is no way to escape the will of Zeus" (line 105). The reiteration of the powers of the deathless gods is an incessant theme from the opening to the closing lines of the *Works and Days,* and betokens a more conscious effort to explain the apparently unjust ways of the world. A phenomenal change was now in progress. Only rarely in the epics did the Olympian deities step past their roles of allotting fates to men and aiding their favorite heroes by gifts of strength

---

[3] 176–78, 201. This scheme is generally taken as Oriental in its four metallic stages, with a Greek addition of the heroic age; cf. T. G. Rosenmeyer, "Hesiod and Historiography," *Hermes,* LXXXV (1957), 257–85.

or good counsel; Hesiod boldly proclaimed a mighty vision of all-seeing Zeus, who "fails not to mark what sort of justice is this that the city keeps within it" (line 269). By him sat, as a deified force, his daughter Justice; to man he had given right (*dike*) and earthly rewards if justice be observed. These lines are our first evidence that the Greeks were coming to conceive their gods as ethical forces, as principles which could restrain that complete overturn of all standards threatened by the innovations which then swept over Aegean society.

The upheaval as such, it is interesting to note, Hesiod did not oppose. Wealth gained by labor brought fame and renown, and honest rivalry in hurrying after wealth he approved early in his poem: "this Strife is wholesome for men" (line 24). Briefly he suggested the dynamic tone of the era in the mutual vying of potters, craftsmen, minstrels, even beggars; and at greater length he described the life of the farmer in tones which were far from pessimistic. Though his home village of Ascra was "bad in winter, sultry in summer, and good at no time" (line 640), yet the peasants in the rich Boeotian plains below evidently could hope to prosper and to heap up Demeter's fruits in their barns by hard work. Only let them beware, burst out Hesiod, of a flaunting woman, for "the man who trusts womankind trusts deceivers" (line 375). His practical, realistic outlook, which stressed a firm-fisted cautious morality, stood far removed from the heroic idealizations of the earlier epics. But here, too, Hesiod reflected his age, as we shall see when we examine the economic spirit of the age of revolution; and in such a succinct line as "observe due measure: and proportion is best in all things" (line 694) a famous axiom of later Greek ethics rings loud and true.

A considerable volume of other poetry, ranging from a description of Heracles' feats to astronomical lore, clusters about the name of Hesiod. Some parts of the collection are surely much later, but one work in particular, the rather inflated and self-conscious *Theogony*, is now commonly assigned to the author of the *Works and Days*. There is little to support this ascription. The very fact that it names Hesiod in the opening lines and refers to his instruction by the Muses of Mount Helicon makes one pause, for the author of the *Works and Days* does not therein call himself Hesiod.[4] Whoever the author of the *Theogony* may be, the poem seems to be a product of the early or mid-seventh century, as is also its companion, the *Eoiae;* and both throw light on Greek mental processes at this time.

The objective of the two works was the conscious ordering of the mass of myth on the origin of the world, then of the gods, and finally of the mortal beings who traced their ancestry to divine seduction or adultery. The primeval substance was Chaos, whence came the ordered parts of nature; the process of development was that of physical generation, which often produced opposed forces, destined in their turn to interact physically. Dynamic action thus found a place in an essentially static scheme. As a fundamental concept of the world the account in the *Theogony* is sometimes picturesque, but basically it appears primitive. Most certainly the view was not a novel fruit of the early seventh century. Hints in Homer, such as the description of earth-circling Oceanus, father of the gods, show that the main scheme had been inherited.[5]

This cosmogony itself was strikingly like that of Mesopotamia and Egypt; but, whether indebtedness existed or not, the important point is that only now did the Greeks feel ready to systematize the framework of creation. Their developed view on the topic, moreover, diverged as markedly from that of the Orient as did the contemporary Hellenic arts. The *Theogony* is an obviously Greek product in its sharply conceived scenes of anthropomorphic gods; in its poetic imagination, which manages to struggle through the mass of names; and in its mental outlook, quite different in tone from the Marduk tale of creation.

While a truly critical, rational approach could not be expected so early in a work of pious intent, the *Theogony* lies in

[4] *Theogony* 22 ff. The identity is accepted by Wade-Gery; Fränkel, *Dichtung und Philosophie,* 136; Diller, *Antike und Abendland,* II (1946), 141; Kurt Latte, ibid. 163. T. W. Allen, *Homer: The Origins and the Transmission* (Oxford, 1924), 78–85, is opposed.

[5] *Iliad* XIV. 201, XIV. 246, XXI. 195;

cf. *Theogony* 776, 787 ff.; Lesky, *Thalatta,* 58–87; P. Walcot, "The Text of Hesiod's *Theogony* and the Hittite *Epic of Kumarbi,*" *CQ,* L (1956), 198–206. On the later effects of the scheme see especially Hans Diller, "Hesiod und die Anfänge der griechischen Philosophie," *Antike und Abendland,* II (1946), 140–51.

the background of Greek speculation in the next century. Eventually the sharp critic Heraclitus was to dismiss the poem as "knowledge without intelligence" (fragment 40, Diels); but the first true philosophers of Western civilization proceeded on much the same lines as the author of the *Theogony*. They, too, placed great weight on the play of opposites, conceived physical substances in divine terms, and personified into real entities such abstract forces as Love and Strife. In terms of the age of revolution itself the *Theogony* suggests a growing search to find order, causation, and unity. The world which lay about the author was no longer simply undifferentiated Chaos; or, as one might put the situation more historically, the traditional, unconscious outlook of the Dark ages was now being overpassed by conscious analysis.

ARCHILOCHUS OF PAROS

THE THIRD great figure in Greek literature of the period, Archilochus, is completely beyond the age of revolution proper; for we can fix his acme rather certainly as just before 650.[6] In his poetry Archilochus spurns the wealth of Lydian Gyges, who died in 652, according to Assyrian records; he mourns the disaster of Magnesia, which was destroyed about the same year; and a third chronological reference, to an eclipse visible at Paros or Thasos, presumably may be connected with the eclipse of

[6] F. Jacoby, "The Date of Archilochos," *CQ*, XXXV (1941), 97–109, against Alan Blakeway's effort, *Greek Poetry and Life* (Oxford, 1936), 34–55, to put him back to 740/30–660. See also François Lasserre and André Bonnard, *Archiloque: Fragments* (Paris, 1958), xxiii–xxix; Lasserre's rather bold reconstruction, *Les Epodes d'Archiloque* (Paris, 1950); Carlo Gallavotti, "Archiloco," *La Parola del Passato*, IV (1949), 130–53.

New materials have appeared in N. M. Kondoleon, *Arch. eph.* 1952, 32–95; Werner Peek, "Neues von Archilochos," *Philologus*, XCIX (1955), 4–50; Kondoleon, "Zu den neuen Archilochosinschriften," *Philologus*, C (1956), 29–39; Werner Peek, "Die Archilochos-Gedichte von Oxyrhynchos," *Philologus*, XCIX (1955), 193–219, and C (1956), 1–28; the same, "Neue Bruchstücke frühgriechischer Dichtung," *Wiss. Zeitschrift Halle Univ.*, V. 2 (1956), 189–207. The Glaucus monument of Thasos: *BCH*, LXXIX (1955), 348–51.

648. The youth of Archilochus probably overlapped the old age of Hesiod.

That so great a change in poetic techniques and intellectual point of view could occur in two generations would be unbelievable, were it not for the testimony of the parallel revolution in the arts. Hesiod, if we may credit the *Theogony* (lines 27–8), learned from the Muses how to utter true things, as against the fictions of the epic, and the spur to his *Works and Days* lay in personal mischance. But his poetic manner was that of the earlier epic tradition, his mental approach remained largely mythical, and the bulk of his long poem was an impersonal summation of farmers' wisdom which he couched in didactic terms. Archilochus, on the other hand, looms up before our startled eyes as a magnificent individual.

All that happened—loves and hates, military mishaps, political strife—he filtered through his poetic genius and hurled forth directly, realistically, hotly, in brief outcries. What mattered was not the specific event, for Archilochus did not narrate in the epic sense but rather gave his own feelings born of the event. And as these might vary, so, too, must his verse. Drawing upon simple, popular verse forms (and perhaps on the experiments of his contemporaries), Archilochus established for later poets a great stock of manifold lyric meters.[7] The epic hexameter was too useful a tool entirely to die, but thenceforth it was only one of many modes of poetic expression.

Alike in his break with old poetic convention and in his fiery vehemence this poet reminds one of the vigorous, almost undisciplined experiments of Protoattic potters. Born to a Parian noble by a slave woman, Archilochus was an aristocrat by Greek rules of descent, albeit poor, and his poetry shows him in the role of leader of men; but his values were not those of the Homeric heroes. He knew the epic poems, and deliberately rejected both their poetic style and their view of man.[8]

[7] Lasserre, *Archiloque*, lxii–lxix. Note the fragments of the *Margites* in Papyri Oxyrhynchi 2309, which Archilochus knew (Lasserre, *Les Epodes d'Archiloque*, 62–63); Peek, *Wiss. Zeitschrift Halle Univ.*, V. 2 (1956), 189–91.

[8] Archilochus, fragment 68, imitates *Odyssey* XVIII. 136, though this is an argued point (Snell, *Discovery of the Mind*, 47 n. 2). Most accounts of Archilochus' background fail to take

The *Iliad* celebrated glory even at the price of death; Archilochus (fragment 217, Lasserre-Bonnard) bluntly asserted that a man dead was a man forgotten. In famous lines he admitted that he ran before the Thracian tribesmen and threw away his shield—"no matter, I can get a better one." [9] The legendary heroes of the past, to judge from our fragments of Archilochus, had completely vanished from his active thought, which concentrated upon his feelings in the bustle of actual life. So, too, the mythical dress was gone, and even the new *genre* of animal fables which he shared with Hesiod and Aesop was simply a piquant device through which he could make concrete his passions.

Here finally, in Greek civilization, is an individual human being, living from day to day, returning hate for hate and love for love (fragments 120 and 35). It is small wonder that later Greeks romanticized Archilochus, and in doing so perhaps selected for survival those quotations and fragments which best expressed his relative modernity.

Enough of the poet's work, however, is extant to show that he was a man who fitted the seventh century, not Hellenistic Alexandria or a modern European metropolis. The individualism which he exhibited had its roots in the magnificent heroes of the *Iliad* and the *Odyssey*—that is to say, in the nascent aristocracy of the eighth century; and Archilochus represents the next step in the development of the aristocratic outlook. Its conscious awareness of human freedom and its liberation from the more superficial bonds of convention are evident in his work. So, too, is the continuity of a basic social unity. The savage abuse and satire of his fellow men must not mislead us; Archilochus was bound more tightly to the fabric of society than a modern individualist could endure.[1] Archilochus' heart, like those of the

---

into account the notable pottery then being produced on Paros; see Plate 16a and O. Rubensohn *s.v.* Paros in PW, col. 1804–09.

[9] Fragment 13; cf. Richard Harden, "Zwei Zeilen von Archilochos," *Hermes,* LXXX (1952), 381–84.

[1] Bonnard, *Archiloque,* xxxi–ii, xliv, xlix; Fränkel, *Dichtung und Philosophie,* 206–07; Snell, *Discovery of the Mind,* 44–46, 61. But see also Webster, *Greek Art and Literature, 700–530* B.C., 28–33.

Lesbian poets Alcaeus and Sappho at the end of the century, beat with simple passions, and his mind saw the events in his life as basically typical, generally applicable to his contemporaries. His lyric verse was meant to communicate the poet's reflection to others, to instruct, and to illuminate scarcely less than were the new elegies written by such men as Callinus.

In Archilochus' view of the place of man in the universe the temper of the seventh century again looms up. Fundamentally Archilochus was confident, as was Hesiod; but he felt no less than did Hesiod and the epic poets that man was a frail creature in an unpredictable world where the gods ruled all. "Such," he advised Glaucus (fragments 115–16), "becomes the mind of mortal man as Zeus may bring him for the day"; so, he deduced, let us take each day as it may come. If ill befall, then Archilochus exhorted his heart (fragment 118), confronted by pains without remedies, to bear up and resist its enemies. "Conqueror, do not overexult; vanquished, do not groan prostrate in your house. Savour your successes, mourn your reverses, but not too much. Learn the rhythm which governs the life of men." [2]

Here lies the idea of law, which we shall see again in many political and religious views of the age; here, too, lies the root of the great Greek concept of later days, *sophrosyne* or balance and due awareness of man's limitations and of the consequent need for moderation. By the end of Archilochus' century these views, which had long been unconscious bases of Greek thought, were to gain conscious expression in the verse of Solon and in the Delphic cult of Apollo.

At the death of Archilochus, not long after 650, Greek poetry had a varied system of elegiac and lyric meters through which authors might express their ideas to their fellow men. These poets were almost entirely aristocrats, and the flavor of their thoughts no doubt reflected to some degree the greater emancipation, the greater security, and the mounting luxury of

[2] Note, too, fragment 296, his observance of the festival of Demeter and Kore; the power of Zeus et al. in fragments 86, 82, 123, 110, 37, 171.

the Greek upper classes. Yet, as I must insist in greater detail later, Aegean society was still fundamentally a unity in which all classes shared a similar outlook and moved in the same direction. The sensitive poets were in the van of a common parade, and it would be a serious mistake to distinguish a "peasant" Hesiod from an "aristocrat" Archilochus.[3]

The views of the poets were now far more individualistic, realistic, and centered on the present day than had been permitted by the epic tradition; in the casting off of old bonds lies a mark of the age of revolution. Driven by the dynamic, pulsating forces of a rapidly expanding society, men looked out on the world afresh, saw things never seen before, and communicated their vision in more supple forms than Aegean society had ever known. But let us make no mistake in our amazement at their vision. Much there was which they did not see—in the poets, for example, the physical hues and shapes of nature made only a halting appearance [4]—much they visualized in ways which were not to continue even to classic days, and much they merely saw in fuller detail than had their forefathers. What had taken place was a process of clarification within an ancestral frame.

Nor was the product of revolution complete anarchy, though at times Archilochus' passion seemed destined to lead him thither. New motifs and new modes of communication no sooner made their appearance than they were consolidated into polished and refined molds of thought. Lyric and elegy stand beside the *kouros* and *kore* of sculpture, the developed temple form, and Middle Corinthian pottery as types which at once confined and promoted expression. Only thus could a collapse of literary order have been avoided; and while the poetic achievement of the age of revolution was amazing, we must remember that it was a hardly bought triumph of which we see only the successes, not the failures. Even in Hesiod and Archilochus, who did survive, the tensions of the age were ap-

---

[3] Nor can the literature of Greece be explained on a dialectal basis; cf. Treu, *Von Homer zur Lyrik*, viii.

[4] Treu, *Von Homer zur Lyrik*, 82–122, on *Odyssey*; 213–15, on Archilochus; 79–80, 193, etc., on color sense.

parent. Fears as well as hopes pervaded both literature and art in the early seventh century.

RELIGIOUS SIGNS OF STRESS

To UNDERSTAND these fears and hopes we must go beyond verses and vases to the hearts of their makers, and in making the effort we come to the most fundamental psychological aspects of the age of revolution. The search must be conducted in the field of religion. Always in early societies religion embraces a very wide gamut of human life; frequently it is the best illuminated subject, thanks to the conservative inclinations of men in sacred matters. Here I shall concentrate on the marks of Greek religious experience which suggest how the stresses of the era affected authors and artists as individuals; the communal aspects of religious change and ethical evolution will fall to the next chapter.

By the eighth century men had quite surely begun to elaborate the primitive structure of Greek religion which we examined in Chapter 4. They were building temples at which rites became more elaborate. Cults of heroes emerged at sacred points. The *Iliad* suggests strongly that Hellenic views of the gods had, at least on one level, advanced far toward the later anthropomorphic patterns.

The gods of Mount Olympus, as depicted by Homer, were sharply defined forces in human form, with human passions, but were largely liberated from the dictates of communal or individual morality. These forces dominated man utterly; in particular they gave to the heroes both superhuman strength and insane folly. Yet the gods, on the one side, had essentially to move in orderly paths; and, on the other, men felt a childish independence to do as they would. Beside and below the Olympian gods stood a world of generalized religious forces which appear to us in the concept of the *daimon,* tales of centaurs and the like, and the first figurines. The earliest plastic representations, from the mid-eighth century on, were of female divine forces (the *potnia theron* et al.); down virtually to 700 none of the clay and bronze figurines can certainly be identified with any specific goddess, god, or hero.

These changes not only suggest that Greek society was beginning to move well before 700 but also indicate the major directions in which religion reflected that movement. Although further developments in the age of revolution did not lead men to reject the basic beliefs of their fathers, the dimensions of evolution were as great in the field of religion as in any other area. The human beings who poured out their energies in a great blaze of action from the end of the eighth century still felt gods and spirits to be close at hand. Fundamentally men were confident of divine support. Not always did their plans mature, but prosperity and success attended human efforts sufficiently often in this age of expansion to attest the favor of the gods. On the communal level the product was the ever more magnificent housing of the gods; individuals, too, embellished the sacred precincts with statues, huge bronze caldrons, and a host of other tokens of gratitude and reverence. The decisive advance in crystallizing divine forces into human shape, which spread from literature to the arts, admirably reflects man's confidence in his own achievements and capabilities.

This confidence at times went far. A heaven-storming audacity, a sense of unfettered experiment, and an almost anarchic outlook are visible alike in the more extreme Protoattic pottery, in the vehemence of Archilochus, and in the oppression of the weaker by the stronger which produced the passionate outcry of Hesiod's *Works and Days*. In their pride men might sometimes dare to forget the gods and to feel—though perhaps only spasmodically and in limited respects—that their future lay in their own hands. In the *Iliad* and in myth the gods came down on earth frequently. In the *Odyssey* celestial visitations were rarer, though divine control remained potent. In the *Works and Days* only the servants of Zeus, "thrice ten thousand spirits, watchers of mortal men," roamed over the world, clothed in mist. And in Archilochus the gods had drawn far away in a physical sense; as an acute critic observes, "d'une façon générale, leur pression sur le monde de l'homme est moins forte.

Ce n'est pas en chaque événement qui l'atteint, en chaque geste qu'il tente, que l'homme rencontre les dieux." [5] While this is a just summation of one major strand in seventh-century thought, it must not lead us too far. Nor was confidence the only characteristic of man's relations with the gods. Fear is never far from pride, and men were growing not only bolder, not only richer, but also more consciously analytical. This meditation resulted among the poets in the poignant realization, as expressed in the *Homeric Hymn to Apollo* (lines 192–3), that "they live witless and helpless and cannot find healing for death or defence against old age." Joy in accomplishment was accompanied by a sense of guilt, by a suspicion that the gods might turn jealous. The conservative reluctance to yield old ways, revealed in the stubborn survival of sub-Geometric pottery, was reflected in religion also, in expressions of anxiety states.

Whether these fears were entirely new cannot be determined, for our evidence on the subject virtually begins with the age of revolution. That they were altogether novel may be doubted; on the other hand their tyranny seems to have swelled abruptly at this point. Neither in the earlier epic nor in literature and art afterward does a sense of anxiety manifest itself as sharply. The epic *Cypria* and the Hesiodic *Catalogue* explain the origin of the Trojan and Theban wars as being efforts by Zeus to meet the complaints of Earth against man's overabundance or overboldness. In myth a common subject is the punishment of man for undue audacity. Some tales of this type may well be ancestral, but the presence of the theme in the early seventh century is attested by the *Theogony*'s recitation of the myth of Prometheus. Magic, too, may have gained new weight in the age of stress. The *Works and Days* has a notably superstitious, magic level, which leads to bans on the use of uncharmed pots or women's bathwater; [6] magic plays a greater role in the *Odyssey* than in the *Iliad*.

[5] Bonnard, *Archiloque,* lii–iii. Hesiod: B. Snell, "Die Welt der Götter bei Hesiod," *La notion du divin depuis Homère jusqu'à Platon* (Bern, 1954), 97–124.

[6] *Works and Days* 748–49, 753–54; the same climate of opinion produced the bell figures of Boeotia (Grace, *Archaic Sculpture in Boeotia,* 10–15). See also Chap. 4, n. 7 (p. 130); and

In the lyric poets man remained as much a puppet of the gods as in the epic; when human consciousness grew more acute, his helplessness (ἀμηχανία) was more keenly felt. Various heroes, said Alcman, had been conquered by Fate (Aisa); and he drew the moral: "Mortal men may not go soaring to the gods," but must live day to day.[7] Yet in essaying to make this theme clear, we must not oversimplify the complex strands of the era. The independence of the individual human being and, with it, individual responsibility were making a first conscious, though timid, entry into the pattern of Greek civilization. Poets and audience still considered the gift of poetry god-inspired; but within at least some realms of human experience the new authors felt themselves self-moved.

The most intriguing evidence of human fears is that of the monsters and wild beasts who appear so swiftly and so abundantly in Late Geometric and Orientalizing art. In their source the figures came largely, though not entirely, from Oriental art; but indebtedness in form does not necessarily connote indebtedness in substance. Only a few monsters were chosen from the huge Oriental stock, and those so drawn were "promptly imbued with Hellenic spiritual forces, transformed into genuine Greek daimonic personalities."[8] Divine forces representing the

in general E. R. Dodds, *The Greeks and the Irrational* (Berkeley, 1951), though most of his analysis bears more directly on the sixth and later centuries. His view, too, of the breakdown of father-control seems doubtful. As he notes (p. 29), the *Iliad* shows little fear of the gods.

[7] Alcman, fragment 1; Fränkel, *Dichtung und Philosophie*, 183–86, 222–23, and "Man's 'Ephemeros' Nature according to Pindar and Others," *Transactions of the American Philological Association*, LXXVII (1946), 131–45; cf. Otfrid Becker, "Das Bild des Weges und Verwandte Vorstellungen im frühgriechischen Denken," *Hermes*, Einzelschr. IV (1937), 23–34, on Poros. Archilochus, fragment 261, which asserts that Tyche and Moira give a man all things, is of doubtful authenticity; R. Pfeiffer, "Gottheit und Indi-

viduum in der frühgriechischen Lyrik," *Philologus*, LXXXIV (1929), 137–52, thinks this is a fourth-century verse. The opposite view (Archilochus, fragment 331) that "all things are made for mortals by human toil and care" is rejected by Bonnard-Lasserre. On man's independence, see also Snell, *Discovery of the Mind*, 69–70.
[8] Karo, *Greek Personality*, 34. These motifs have been studied in detail, but a general interpretation is much to be desired. Nilsson, *GGR*, I, 216–55, gives one of the best sketches of this level of Greek religious thought; see also Hans Herter, "Böse Dämonen im frühgriechischen Volksglauben," *Rheinisches Jahrbuch für Volkskunde*, I (1950), 112–43.

The Gorgon, for example, is not necessarily a Greek effort to explain by myth an Oriental artistic motif, as

wild powers of savage nature, but not conceived sharply in anthropomorphic guise, were a fundamental part of Greek religious beliefs. As Nilsson notes, they outlasted the great gods and passed on into modern Greek folklore; at the other boundary of Greek civilization their origins must go far back into primitive days. What is significant is that men of the late eighth and early seventh centuries felt so pressing a need to *represent* the untamed quality of the world. Since the human form seemed ill-fitting, artists turned to the rich treasure of wild beasts and imaginary figures of the Orient, took what they needed, and remolded the borrowings with a native aesthetic sense.

The force which thus drove men can only be explained if we keep in mind the psychological tensions which accompanied the tremendous upheaval of the era. The griffins, sphinxes, and sirens, for instance, do not illustrate myths; that is, they do not have true histories nor do they do anything. They simply *are*, and by their presence manifest a sense of demonic powers encompassing mankind.[9] The smiths who evolved the marvelous griffin type which adorned votive caldrons by the hundreds in the seventh century poured into this fierce-beaked creature such

argued by Clark Hopkins, "Assyrian Elements in the Perseus-Gorgon Story," *AJA*, XXXVIII (1934), 341–58; and Edouard Will, "La décollation de Méduse," *RA*, XXVII (1947), 60–76. See Matz, *GGK*, I, 142; Nilsson, *GGR*, I, 243–44, 226. More generally note the observation of Schäfer, *Reliefpithoi*, 78, that while battles of animals go back to the fourth millennium B.C., not one Greek example has an exact analogy in Oriental art; on this point cf. Kunze, *Kretische Bronzereliefs*, 165, 199. Dunbabin, *Greeks and Their Eastern Neighbours*, 55–56, points in quite the wrong direction in suggesting that this wave represents a perversion of Greece by the Orient.

Gorgons: H. Besig, *Gorgo und Gorgoneion in der archaischen griechischen Kunst* (Diss. Berlin, 1937); Konstantinos Gerogiannes, "Γοργὼ ἢ Μέδουσα;" *Arch. eph.* 1927–28, 128–76; Thalia P. Howe, "The Origin and Function of the Gorgon-Head," *AJA*,

LVIII (1954), 209–21; Sp. Marinatos, Γοργόνες καὶ Γοργόνεια," *Arch. eph.* 1927–28, 7–37; Payne, *Necrocorinthia*, 79–89, who stresses their Greek character; Karo, *Greek Personality*, 32–35.
[9] Sirens: Emil Kunze, "Sirenen," *AM*, LVII (1942), 124–41 (esp. 131); Matz, *GGK*, I, 141, 317; Ohly, *Griechische Goldbleche*, 80–81. Kunze and Nilsson, *GGR*, I, 228–29, reject the idea that the siren is the soul of the dead.

Sphinx: N. M. Verdelis, "L'Apparition du sphinx dans l'art grec aux VIII° et VII° siècles avant J.-C.," *BCH*, LXXV (1951), 1–37; Kunze, *Kretische Bronzereliefs*, 178–84; Müller, *AM*, L (1925), 54; Schäfer, *Reliefpithoi*, 31–33; A. Dessenne, *Le Sphinx: étude iconographique. I. Des Origines à la fin du second millénaire* (Paris, 1957).

Chimera: Anna Roes, "The Representation of the Chimera," *JHS*, LIV (1934), 21–25.

a spirit (Plate 24b). Even while perverting into a knob the top-knot of hair which the griffin form had had in the Orient, they added to the wicked, almost incomprehensible power of their creation.[1] The unpredictability and the savagery of the physical world which still enfolded the Greeks in the age of revolution rise before us nowhere better than in these creatures of night-mare. Mankind always secretly fears "things that go bump in the night," as the Scotch prayer puts it, but the artistic expression of this uneasiness reached a peak, at least for the Greeks, in the seventh century.

A companion fear of death appears in the plenitude of wild beasts which parallel the monsters. On the surfaces of Late Geometric and Orientalizing vases lions pounce upon unsuspecting, grazing cattle or turn their snarling heads out on the spectator in grim rows; in sculpture they stand alone as bronze statuettes and as larger-scale work in stone. The meaning of these ferocious creatures is suggested by the similes of the *Iliad*, which often evoke the lion as an image of the greatness, power, and fearfulness of the hero who fights and slays his foes;[2] for always in these lion similes with their "toothy jaws, glaring eyes, and bristling mane" lurks the Darkness of Death, "mournful and fearful, pale, shrivelled, shrunk with hunger, swollen-kneed," as he appears on the shield of Heracles.[3] The successive

[1] Jacobsthal, *Greek Pins*, 41. Griffins: Henri Frankfort, "Notes on the Cretan Griffin," *BSA*, XXXVII (1936–37), 106–22, and *Art and Architecture in the Ancient Orient*, 154, 177; Ulf Jantzen, *Griechische Greifenkessel* (Berlin, 1955); Karo, *Greek Personality*, 63–65; Payne, *Perachora*, I, 127–30.

[2] Lions: Dunbabin, *Greeks and Their Eastern Neighbours*, 46–48; Jacobsthal, *Greek Pins*, 76–78; Kunze, *Kretische Bronzereliefs*, 169–70, 184–88; Ohly, *Griechische Goldbleche*, 76–77, 150–51 (Homeric parallels); G. P. Shipp, *Studies in the Language of Homer* (Cambridge, 1953), 79, who argues that the similes are linguistically of Homer's own era. A battle of men and lions appears already in Mycenaean art on the stele of Grave Gamma, Circle B (Mylonas, *Mycenae*,

135–37). In early Chinese art, incidentally, the *t'ao t'ieh* apparently ate man (W. Willetts, *Chinese Art*, I [Penguin, 1958], 162).

[3] Whitman, *Homer and the Heroic Tradition*, 89; *Shield* 264 ff. In the description of the center of Heracles' shield, given over to Fear, "worked in adamant, unspeakable, staring backward with eyes that glowed with fire," horror has risen into a conscious feeling, unlike the shield of Achilles in the *Iliad*. So, too, on the Bellerophon kotyle, the Gorgo and Chimera are the focus (Kraiker, *Aigina*, p. 18).

Man-eating lions: Ohly, *Griechische Goldbleche*, E 3; Copenhagen NM 727 (*CVA Copenhagen* II pl. 73 (74) 5, with bibliography); see also Hahland, *Corolla Curtius*, 130–31, who links the scenes of this vase to-

stages of Attic artistic symbolism make the theme equally clear. First, on gold bands and vases, lions attack animals; then men fall before the wild beasts—remarkably graphic is the brutal composition of two lions at once devouring a man (Plate 22a); then come straight representations of warriors in duels and funeral games.

Throughout Greek art from the middle of the eighth century down well into the seventh century death intrudes frequently, and man responds to the ultimate proof of his weakness not with dignified resignation but with fierce, macabre horror. A similar mood recurs at one later point in Western history, in the fifteenth and sixteenth centuries after Christ; and, as any reader of Huizinga's *Waning of the Middle Ages* will know, this too was a period in which magic, religious tension, and fears bubbled up in men's minds alongside daring advance.

THE EXORCISM OF FEAR

The significance of the monsters and death-dealing beasts in Orientalizing art is not exhausted when one notes that they reflected the terrific stress of the age. Such figures represented men's fears, but they also expressed superbly the power and vitality of a revolutionary era. A fine example of this aspect is the leg of a tripod found at Olympia (Plate 24a), where a scene of two lions fighting each other symbolizes starkly the fierce contention of the two heroes (Apollo and Heracles?) vying in the panel above for a tripod of victory. Men of the era, to repeat an earlier observation, were basically confident. They were also, as we have seen, fearful; but in the end, as Greek civilization reached a new plane of consolidation, hopes

---

gether as showing death and funeral games. The composition appears in Etruria (Hanfmann, *Altetruskische Plastik*, 26–28); cf. Akurgal, *Phrygische Kunst*, 51–52; Kunze, *Kretische Bronzereliefs*, 205–07; Jacobsthal, *JHS*, LXXI (1951), 87.

Even more macabre is the Tenos sherd, Athens NM 2495, showing a warrior with four gaping wounds, whose private parts are being devoured by a bird of prey: Kunze, *Kretische Bronzereliefs*, 250–51, pl. 54b; Schäfer, *Reliefpithoi*, 85.

overcame fears. The victory, however, was not easily bought, and even in the end men could not entirely overcome their knowledge of human frailty.

Among the avenues for exorcising fear, one was its conscious expression. Another was the reinterpretation of the old gods as concerned with earthly justice, and a third resulted from the creation of virtually new cults. In the first of these outlets lies a major reason for the abundant depiction of the monsters in art and for their crystallization in myth.[4] The clay masks of demon heads found at Tiryns, from about 700 on (Plate 22b), and the masks of Artemis Orthia are perhaps testimony to plays or rituals of a propitiatory as well as fertility purpose; temples commonly bore a Gorgon or Medusa, like the magnificent averter of evil on the temple of Artemis at Corcyra; the evolution of sirens, lions, and other figures into canonical types represents the domestication of the unknown. As one advances through the seventh century, the untamed fearful quality of the wild figures slowly fades away until by 600 they had become disciplined, endurable forces. The lions of the ripe archaic period were not tame pets, yet they were no longer simply hideous and frightening. While storms and other evidences of nature's ferocity continued to appear in the lyric poets, the wild, almost uncivilized quality of the similes in the *Iliad* vanished. Animals were thinly disguised reflections of mankind in the fables.

Civilization, in sum, became more certain; and its distinction, incidentally, from barbarism grew more obvious. Both myth and art elaborated markedly the divine and human figures, such as Heracles and Theseus, who had in the past made dis-

---

[4] As Hermann Fränkel, *Gnomon*, XXVIII (1956), 572, notes, some of the gloomiest scenes were on drinking vessels. Are they a mark of the sentiment *memento mori?* The theme of exorcism has occasionally been noted but never fully explored; cf. Karo, *Greek Personality*, 72–73; Beazley, *Development of Attic Black-figure*, 16; Matz, *GGK*, I, 317; Homann-Wede-king, *Anfänge*, 85. Kübler, *Kerameikos*, VI. 1, 151–57, also discusses the sense of death in the seventh-century vases.

Medusa: Gerhard Rodenwaldt, *Altdorische Bildwerke in Korfu* (Berlin, 1938), pl. 12; R. Hampe, "Korfugiebel und frühe Perseusbilder," *AM*, LX–LXI (1935–36), 269–99.

coveries or had eliminated forces of evil.[5] The very theme of the conflict of order and chaos, of civilization and the wild, was cast in the form of centaur battles, the contest of Zeus and Typhon, the battle of the giants (from the sixth century), and so on. Intellectually and aesthetically men thus gained a deeper sense of the meaning of civilization and became more confident of its endurance. How great a mark of the Greek genius was this achievement can easily be appreciated if one compares to it the Etruscan decline into demon-ridden fright.

Another mode by which men could harness unrest was by consolidating moral standards under divine protection. In earthly terms the problems of justice and ethics were still largely communal matters; though men's answers to this range of problems became more internalized and personal, Greeks did not proceed as far on the path as did Hebrews. The ethical reforms of the seventh century, accordingly, will be taken up mainly in the next chapters alongside social and political changes. Yet justice is an individual problem as well, and its preservation in any political system must rest on firm assurance to each man that the ultimate powers of the world are forces which favor righteousness.

The gods could not yet be loved, but already in Homer, and still more in Hesiod, the poets were elaborating and stressing their role as guardians of justice. Some divine figures, alas, continued to serve fallible mankind as mentors of lechery and thievery, but Zeus now blessed the virtuous with earthly prosperity and punished the wicked with plague, drought, and war. The gods, too, were ever more sharply conceived as embodiments of the sense of order in the world. The *potnia theron*, Mistress of Wild Beasts, who was widely depicted in the late

[5] Cf. S. Papaspyridi Karousou, "Un 'ΠΡΩΤΟΣ ΕΥΡΕΤΗΣ' dans quelques monuments archaïques," *Annuario*, n.s. VIII–X (1946–48), 37–46.

Centaurs: Nilsson, *GGR*, I, 229–32, with references; Schachermeyr, *Poseidon*, 86–87, who cautiously considers them possibly Indo-Germanic, a line argued by Georges Dumézil, *Le*

problème des centaures (Paris, 1929; *Annales du musée Guimet*, XLI). See also above, n. 1 (p. 262). Giants: François Vian, *La guerre des Géants: le mythe avant l'epoque hellénistique* (Paris, 1952), and *Repertoire* (Paris, 1951). Typhon: Kunze, *Archaische Schildbänder*, 82–88.

eighth and seventh centuries, stood as a symbolic representation of the domination of chaos by divine order. Beside and out of such figures the divinities already visible in literature were crystallizing in art by the middle of the seventh century. Not every divine representation can yet be identified by this date, nor was the worship of the Greek deities an intellectual feast stripped of all superstition; [6] still, these gods were marching on their path to classic dignity.

Artistic and literary conceptions of the gods had necessarily to follow the lines already marked out in the Homeric epics. This scheme suited some of the deepest needs of Aegean society, but not all of the new psychological and social problems of the age of revolution could thus be met. In consequence the Greek religious machinery was amplified, and new outlets were installed; i.e., virtually new gods of novel stamp arose. The increase in religious temperature, as one is tempted to call this process, was not simply a reaction to alien viruses. Here and there some influence from the Orient or from the barbarians of the Eurasian steppes may perhaps be detected; on the whole the new cults as well as the old became ever more specifically Hellenic in the classical sense. [7]

Throughout the seventh and sixth centuries the elaboration of Greek religion continued as an active process, in reflection of the ceaseless evolution of Hellenic society, which piled stress on stress. Most of our evidence for Orphism, Cretan mystics, seers, mysteries, and the ceremonies for purifying inherited pollution

[6] All excavation reports on temple deposits of this era contain extremely puzzling objects, which we cannot fully understand. *Artemis Orthia,* for example, is rich in grills, wreaths, and other objects made in lead; *Perachora,* in phiales (perhaps for divination); *Excavations at Ephesus,* in sacred bees, hawks, and so on. Yet the pose of epiphany was disappearing (Matz, *GGK,* I, 483–84); gods thenceforth showed their powers internally as well as by external attributes. A good example of the process is traced in Hoenn, *Artemis.*

[7] The clearest field of possible Oriental influence is the cult of Aphrodite; cf.

the Perachora terra-cotta plaque 183 (*c.* 675–650 B.C.), where a bearded Aphrodite (?) emerges from the genitals of Uranus, *Perachora* I, 231–32, and see also P. J. Riis, "The Syrian Astarte Plaques and Their Western Connections," *Berytus,* IX (1949), 69–90. The influence of northern shamans, found by Dodds, *Greeks and the Irrational,* 140–47, after K. Meuli, "Scythica," *Hermes,* LXX (1935), 121–76, can scarcely have appeared before the sixth century—if then. Rohde, *Psyche,* 314–34, gives a full picture of ancient evidence on seers et al.

comes from later than 650—some of it much later. For the period now under consideration, three cults can be shown to have served especially in the role of purging fears or reassuring the individual. These were the worship of Dionysus, of Apollo, and of Heracles. All three have been so often examined in modern studies and remained so powerful on down through classic times that their roles need only be sketched. None was an absolutely new god, but all were suited, in diverse yet complementary ways, to funnel off basic drives and compulsions of mankind in the early seventh century, when great changes were upsetting its ancestral ways of life.

Most obviously suited to this end was Dionysus, already "the joy of mortals" in Homer.[8] He was a god not merely of relaxing wine but of vegetation as a whole, and his worship was conducted at least partly in frenzied revels by women. The wing of modern scholarship which idealizes the Greeks is always shocked by the tales of the demonic dances on the mountains, in which participants devoured raw flesh to unify themselves with a savior; and it would appear from the grim myths of the fate of Pentheus and others that the more sober masculine leaders of early Greek society sometimes resisted Dionysiac mastery over womankind. Their resistance was in vain. Within the dull routine of domestic work the second sex had fewer means of combating the stress of changing social and economic conditions, and so was swept up in this escape from their trials, which perhaps gained new dimensions in the seventh century. Both sexes, however, could unite in daytime festivities of Dionysus, some of which led to the development of drama.

A powerful school of modern thought, embracing Nietzsche,

---

[8] *Iliad* XIV. 325; cf. VI. 132 ff. The most recent of many studies is H. Jeanmaire, *Dionysos: histoire du culte de Bacchus* (Paris, 1951), who brings him from Asia Minor. It now appears that he may be referred to on Mycenaean tablets (Webster, *Bulletin of the Institute of Classical Studies*, University of London, V [1958], 44); de Sanctis, *Storia dei Greci*, I, 296–301, had already given a level-headed account of his antiquity, apart from overstressing his appeal to the poor (note his antiquity on the island of Lesbos [Page, *Sappho and Alcaeus*, 168–69]).

On the release of stress, cf. Ernst Langlotz, "Dionysos," *Die Antike*, VIII (1932), 170–82; and Dodds, *Greeks and the Irrational*, 76–77.

Spengler, and others, has created a neat opposition between Dionysiac and Apolline spirits as reflecting respectively the ecstatic and rational aspects of Greek civilization; some investigators have gone so far as to find racial grounds for this hypothetical opposition.[9] Greek religious thought cannot be so easily schematized. In early days Apollo and Dionysus were not sharply differentiated, and the two drew apart only slowly in their appeal to divergent parts of the manifold human personality. While Apollo was already in the *Iliad* one of the most powerful of the Olympian deities, his great evolution into lawgiver, patron of music and poetry, oracular counselor, and healer of guilty consciences was a long process. By the end of the seventh century he had essentially assumed a role as the embodiment of Greek rationalism, and was thus celebrated in the *Homeric Hymn to Apollo* and by Alcaeus.[1] By then, too, Apollo was master of the Delphic oracle, and this site was becoming a center of more advanced Greek morality. This appears to have been a recent development: Delphi advanced beyond the func-

---

[9] This theme appears even in sensible accounts, as W. K. C. Guthrie, *The Greeks and Their Gods* (London, 1950), 32, 42, 302–04, or Dodds, *Greeks and the Irrational*, 76. Matz, *GGK*, I, 159, notes correctly that the Mantiklos Apollo (see Plate 20b) "ist eine jähe Daimonie, noch nicht das apollinische Wesen, wie wir es zu verstehen pflegen." Athena played as great a role as adviser to men from Homer onward; cf. Levi, *AJA*, XLIX (1945), 297.
[1] Page, *Sappho and Alcaeus*, 244–50. Delphi: Jean Defradas, *Les Thèmes de la propagande delphique* (Paris, 1954), who puts Apollo at Delphi only in the sixth century; Pierre Amandry, *La Mantique apollinienne à Delphes* (Paris, 1950), and "Recherches à Delphes (1938–1953)," *Acta congressu Madvigiani*, I (Copenhagen, 1958), 325–40, who more properly prefers the second half of the eighth century; Dodds, *Greeks and the Irrational*, 70–75; M. P. Nilsson, "Das delphische Orakel in der neuesten Literatur,"

Historia, VII (1958), 237–50. The effort to link Crete and Apollo—e.g., M. Guarducci, "Crete e Delfi," *Studi e materiali di storia delle religioni*, XIX–XX (1943–46), 85–114—does not convince me.

Expansion of Apollo: Y. Béquignon, "De quelques usurpations d'Apollon en Grèce centrale d'après des recherches récentes," *RA*, XXIX–XXX (1948), 61–75; J. Papadimitriou, "Le sanctuaire d'Apollon Maléatas à Epidaure (fouilles de 1948)," *BCH*, LXXIII (1949), 361–83; W. Vollgraff, *Le Sanctuaire d'Apollo Pythéen à Argos* (Paris, 1957); W. S. Barrett, "Bacchylides, Asine, and Apollo Pythaieus," *Hermes*, LXXXII (1954), 421–44; Gallet de Santerre, *Délos primitive*, 135–40.

Apollo in art: Pierre Amandry, "Statuette d'ivoire d'un dompteur de lion découverte à Delphes," *Syria*, XXIV (1944–45), 149–74; Barnett, *JHS*, LXVIII (1948), 16–17; on the lion motif, see also Brock, *Fortetsa*, 198.

tion of serving as local Phocian shrine only with the great wave of western colonization, and Apollo's wresting of its oracle from Ge, Mother Earth, was barely mythicized. At Epidaurus, at the Boeotian Ptoion, and elsewhere Apollo either supplanted earlier deities or was equated with them in the course of the century.

Dionysus scarcely appears in art down to 600. Apollo turns up somewhat more frequently in statues, statuettes, and other forms. Most popular of the three on vases was Heracles. The first absolutely sure scenes of myth are almost entirely of Heracles' deeds (Plates 23a and 24a); most of his labors—though not all—appear frequently from the early seventh century onward.[2] His defense of mankind against the forces of the wild is sometimes cast in an Oriental dress, for Mesopotamian and Syrian art had a rich, ancient repertoire of such events, connected with the heroic efforts of similar figures in the Fertile Crescent (Gilgamesh and others). Yet here, most surely, the Greek borrowing of artistic motifs had little to do with the basic mythical substance.[3] The outline of Heracles' life was long

---

[2] See the lists given in n. 1 above (p. 261), and Frank Brommer, *Herakles: Die zwölf Taten des Helden in antiker Kunst und Literatur* (Münster/Köln, 1953); Pierre Amandry, "Héraklès et l'hydre de Lerne," *Bulletin de la Faculté des Lettres de Strasbourg*, XX (1951–52), 293–322; Kunze, *Archaische Schildbänder*, 93–126; P. Zanconi Montuoro, "Il tipo di Eracle nell'arte arcaica," *Rendiconti della Accademia nazionale dei Lincei*, 8. ser. II (1947), 207–221. The man fighting the lion on K. 407, 2160, cannot be certainly identified with Heracles (on the similar scene from Chios, cf. *BSA*, XXXV [1934–35], pl. 35. 33). The slaying of Nessos is, however, clear on the Attic stand from the Argive Heraeum; the dispatch of the hydra appears on Boeotian *fibulae* (Hampe, pl. 2, 8); the Stymphalian birds are given on Copenhagen 3153.

[3] Contra, G. Rachel Levy, "The Oriental Origin of Herakles," *JHS*, LIV

(1934), 40–53 (but cf. Hetty Goldman, "Sandon and Herakles," *Hesperia*, Supp. VIII [1949], 164–74); cf. R. Dussaud, "Melqart," *Syria*, XXV (1946–48), 205–30; Dunbabin, *Greeks and Their Eastern Neighbours*, 52–53. Webster, *From Mycenae to Homer*, 125, has tried to find Heracles in the Mycenaean age, too, but we need much firmer evidence on this point than yet appears.

J. L. Myres, "Hesiod's 'Shield of Herakles': Its Structure and Workmanship," *JHS*, LXI (1941), 17–38, places this in the late seventh century, as against R. M. Cook's date of 580–570. Archilochus, fragment 298, is the hymn to Heracles *kallinike* (though this is not universally agreed to be Archilochean).

Heracles and Theseus: Nilsson, *Cults and Politics*, 53–56, who notes that Theseus was portrayed as much more civilized than Heracles from the late sixth century onward.

known; in the *Theogony* and elsewhere his place was a major one, quite independent of art.

Heracles, the superman, is the age of revolution incarnate. No other figure, divine or human, so well typifies and so well illustrates its unique characteristics. Theban-born, appropriated by the Dorians, he stood high in popularity above local heroes everywhere; even at Athens he far outranked Theseus in the seventh century. Not only does he thus suggest the interplay of localism and panhellenic unity in this era, but far more than Apollo or Dionysus he expresses its aristocratic spirit. Favored by the gods, he is a man, a human being who strides forth to mighty achievements; in his deeds he is unhampered by the weaknesses or doubts of mortal men. In these respects he is a noble parallel to Achilles, the embodiment of the early eighth century; but in other qualities Heracles marks a great advance. His famous feats were conducted for the benefit of mankind; in spirit he was far more conscious and calculating than Achilles had been. Withal the passionate violence of Heracles' nature must never be forgotten. The marvelous period which he typifies was one of stress and almost anarchic exuberance; the quality of its hero *par excellence* became fixed for all time on a still primitive level—Heracles, it may be remembered, raped fifty maidens in a night. In classic Athens men were to turn, at least for official purposes, to the figure of Theseus, which could be cast as a civilized servant of the developed state.

The frightful end of Heracles is one which Homer does not seem to know, but which underlines the necessity men felt of accepting the law of Zeus.[4] While Heracles' bitter agony in the shirt of Deianira is of a piece with the fearful imagination of the early seventh century, so, too, is the comforting conclusion that he was translated to Olympus and there "lives amongst the undying gods, untroubled and unaging all his days." If the glory of this mortal man, which was in the seventh century

---

[4] Heracles: *Theogony* 954–55, 530–31; Guthrie, *Greeks and Their Gods*, 240. The suicide of Ajax was a popular scene in seventh-century art (e.g., Corinthian vases, *Necrocorinthia*, 137; Spartan ivory, *Artemis Orthia*, pl. cxxx) and in the sixth-century shield bands (Kunze, *Archaische Schildbänder*, 154–57), though this scene may reflect also the sense of honor in the era, which must be bought even at the price of suicide.

"yet greater than it was before over the plenteous earth," rose far beyond the ordinary repute of local heroes, the motive must have been the extraordinary comfort and encouragement he gave to the men, likewise mortal, who worshipped him amid their own efforts and fears.

The deepening concepts of the *psyche* or soul which manifest themselves in the cult of Heracles and of the heroes as a whole reflect significantly the direction of Greek psychological development. Happiness in the hereafter was still reserved for the few, not the many, and that handful which rose to heroic status was mainly the group claimed as ancestors by the great clans.[5] The tendency to individual self-assertion nonetheless was unmistakable, even though it was still hemmed by many group ties.

Through artistic imagination which made the unknown tangible and so endurable, through ethical reconstruction, through new cults and heroes, men went far in the late eighth and early seventh centuries toward restoring their sense of basic security. The new view of the religious world as an orderly structure lay on a higher, more complex plane than had that of the Dark ages, and it was to fructify philosophy, art, and literature greatly. Yet mankind could not quite exorcise its fears; only temporarily can we forget our mortal frame. The feelings of human helplessness, frailty, and "guilt" went on into the sixth century and continued to exercise the thinkers, poets, and artists of that era. Enough religious development, nonetheless, had been achieved to buttress the basic confidence of the Greeks and thus to support them in their day-to-day endurance of human trials.

Most impressive of all was the ability of the Greeks to pass through the great upheaval of the age of revolution and to establish a new religious and psychological basis for life without yielding their dynamic spirit. Fear had been exorcised, not canonized in patterns of grim myth, restrictive taboos, and rigid

---

[5] Rohde, *Psyche*, 117–20, is suggestive; most of our knowledge on this matter is sixth-century or later. See Webster, *Greek Art and Literature, 700–530 B.C.*, 38–41.

social structure. That had been the fate of the early stages of Mesopotamian civilization, but the Aegean world remained free to develop further the new framework of ethics and religion, just as its art and literature continued to progress within clearly conceived forms. Here, once more, Greek civilization had come to a truly Hellenic outlook, as we commonly understand that term. Solon and Jeremiah lived at the same time, about 600, but their ethical and religious views, though equally firmly held, differed tremendously.

THE HELLENIC OUTLOOK

WHENEVER the historian comes to treat the religious views of a society, he must sense how manifold are the forces and qualities which express themselves in mankind at any point of time. If one is to marshal the relevant evidence systematically, it is almost inevitable that one dissect and analyze an era aspect by aspect; yet the spectrum of human activity is an inextricably interjoined flux. In religious institutions and beliefs the character of contemporary (and past) social, political, and economic attitudes are writ large, but in this region, too, intellectual and sub-intellectual forces work a powerful influence independently of class or profession.

Thus far I have examined, each by itself, the progress of art and of literature and have brought this evidence to bear upon a significant but limited aspect of the religious evolution in the century from 750 to 650. My objective has been to measure the intellectual upheaval as a whole and to fix the dimensions of the end toward which men had unwittingly been tending. Before we turn to further fields, it will be well to recapitulate what we have found.

During the age of revolution the Aegean world progressed clearly into the Hellenic outlook of historic times. This system was now in what is termed its archaic phase, from which it developed inevitably into the classic stage of the fifth century B.C. But archaic Greek civilization is not simply an incomplete prelude to the later magnificent glory. The artists and poets of the seventh century expressed a coherent, interlocking pattern. The fruits of this culture—Archilochus, Middle Protocorinthian and Protoattic pottery, the Nikandre of Delos—were already visible by 650, and for the next century archaic civilization was to produce a host of ever more polished and refined achievements, which were quite distinct in flavor from those of the subsequent classical period.

Nor, on the other hand, was the archaic frame a straight-forward elaboration of what had gone before. No one, looking solely at the intellectual patterns of the Aegean in the early eighth century, could have predicted the developed outlook of the later seventh century. The difference was so great quantitatively as to be virtually a matter of qualitative change. True, the foundations of the later age were those which had been laboriously fashioned in the Dark ages; but the superstructure was the product of a great, sudden revolution. Wherever we search for "links" of gradual evolution, we search in vain. Potters jumped from Geometric to Orientalizing pottery; sculptors, from the rude figurines of the eighth century to sharply defined statuettes and then to large-scale sculpture; architects, from simple chapels to temples. In the field of literature, where only solitary masterpieces have survived, each author's advance toward self-comprehension and conscious analysis of the place of man in the world looms up even more sharply.

The resumption of continuous contact with the Orient was more a mark than a cause of this upheaval. The Greeks turned eastward only when their own society was ready to receive outside influences; and, as I have stressed repeatedly, we must explain this readiness if we are to probe to the bottom of the main forces in Greek advance. Yet an effect of a previous development often becomes itself a cause of subsequent change. Many Greek artists and thinkers drew stimuli from the Orient to break more abruptly with the external domination of old molds and thus to speed the tempo of a revolution which would otherwise have proceeded more slowly. For their new ideas they could draw on an abundance of Oriental motifs and techniques.

The historian, even so, must never mistake the incidental for the substantial. Intellectually, the age of revolution witnessed the crystallization of Greek civilization, not the adaptation of Oriental culture to a Greek dress. By the middle of the seventh century the styles of Greek pottery, sculpture, and architecture were further removed in spirit from Oriental arts than had ever before been true. The *Theogony* and the *Works and Days* show some awareness of Oriental ideas, but their main pattern is not Eastern; the verse of Archilochus does not reveal that this poet owed anything of significance to the East. Modern biological theory, interestingly enough, suggests that when two distinct families of animals or plants of common parentage come into contact the product is sometimes yet sharper difference. The present case perhaps illustrates the validity of this principle in human cultures.[6]

Not only was the general product of the intellectual upheaval Hellenic, but also the methods by which its participants had achieved their gains were of true Greek stamp. The processes which marked early archaic civilization included the limitation of variation by the common agreement upon new forms and the interlocking of the individual creative thinker with society. Nonetheless the Hellenic outlook came also to be marked by an ever more dynamic spirit and conscious exploration of man's place.

Repeatedly we have observed the admirable economy and concentration of the artists and authors of the age of revolution. In virtually every field they made their mighty leaps by focusing their experiments within a narrow range of types. For these men the bewildering variety of nature was a handicap to be overcome, not a fact worthy of reproduction. Archaic artists may be termed more realistic inasmuch as they observed more consciously, but their basic aim was not to express their observation. This was incidental to their creation of ideal types. While these patterns were not in every case fully perfected by 650, they had emerged; the story of subsequent development is

---

[6] Carter, *One Hundred Years of Evolution,* 152–54. When Middle Helladic Greece came into contact with the Minoan world, the product (Mycenaean culture) shows rather more fusion.

largely a matter of their polishing. Greek civilization thus received an enduring stamp of concentration on the ideal, the abstract, the non-personal (though not impersonal). Not until the Hellenistic and, still more, the Roman eras was this outlook to be seriously attacked, but even then it held firm as a basic characteristic of Greco-Roman civilization to the point when that framework eventually collapsed in the Late Roman Empire.

The men of the seventh century who thus limited their approach seem to have done so voluntarily. If they restricted their range, they aimed at greater achievement than might otherwise have occurred. One may go even further to suggest that the stern restriction was an absolutely necessary counter to the forces of stress and change; only by harnessing the energies of the age could society avoid collapse into chaos. Men now were conscious of what they were doing. They were surer of themselves after long centuries marked by physical want and socially primitive structures. Still, they dared not abandon all rules in their leap out of tradition. And so artists and authors imposed upon their zeal new, even more firmly determined patterns, and yielded a rude individuality to communal discipline.

Underlying this problem was the crucial question of the relation of the individual to the group. Scholars who worked or were born in the nineteenth century (the height perhaps of resplendent individualism in modern times) have stressed heavily the creative freedom of the individual in ancient Greece; and it is true that our modern concepts of the nature of mankind have here one of their major roots. In the very point of time we have been examining, some of the most basic aspects of Western civilization were formulated. Hesiod and Archilochus speak to us as individuals, driven by their own passions and problems, as no earlier men had ever spoken. In art the signatures of vase painters and sculptors now commence, in testimony to the pride of the artists and also to the willingness of society to permit this individual assertion.[7] Before 600 individual responsibility rather than collective punishment had begun to be accepted in criminal law. Yet individualism, like realism, was an incidental

[7] Homann-Wedeking, *Anfänge*, 143–44, 52–53; M. Lejeune, *REA*, XLVII (1945), 103–06 on the Kallikleas signature.

by-product of the early seventh century rather than its deliberate aim. Neither artist nor poet spoke entirely for himself; as we examine their products, we feel a generalized, idealistic quality and miss a sense of rounded, internal self-sufficiency.[8] The thinker of this age was first a representative of society and only secondarily an individual; it will be time shortly to consider the consolidation of the city-state as a social and political fusion of individuals into collective unity.

The Hellenic outlook, that is, did not rest upon modern concepts of the individual. The social and political groupings of Hellas were successful enough so that this world never came fully even to the level of individual responsibility which the Hebrew prophets evolved in the fire of earthly catastrophe. Nonetheless Greece reached a happy, though always precarious balance in the seventh century which tended to endure through the tension of opposite forces; and in this balance or, to put the reality better, in this bond of rule and freedom was harnessed their dynamic spirit.[9]

For, having made their revolution, the Greeks did not curb too drastically their ability to move and to change within the new framework. In the bold, swirling lines of Orientalizing vases or in the emphasis upon action in the new depiction of the myths,[1] artists largely broke the Geometric restraints upon the dynamic drive of Greek civilization; and pulsating inner life penetrated the new types. Always in revolutionary eras there is the serious problem of preventing change from decaying into anarchy—and this problem the Greeks admirably met. But there is also the equally serious danger that the very restrictions which safeguard order will re-create a static situation—and this danger, too, archaic civilization overpassed. In part its success was due to the expansion of Greek society through colonization, which opened the Aegean to foreign stimuli and set, as we shall see, economic development on a continuing path; in part,

---

[8] This is, I think, what de Sanctis, *Storia dei Greci*, I, 84, saw when he discussed its lack of "intimità."

[9] Matz, *GGK*, I, 113–15, seems to have somewhat the same view, but fails to express it clearly; cf. also Müller, *Frühe Plastik*, 222.

[1] Kunze, *Archaische Schildbänder*, 72–77.

too, the balance between stability and movement was the product of mutual checks of tensions and opposing forces.

Geographically this balance is evident in the tensions between panhellenic and local attachments. The artistic and literary developments of the age of revolution took place on a panhellenic stage. Especially from the beginning of the seventh century the southern districts of the Greek mainland, the Aegean islands, and the coast of Asia Minor seem to have moved together culturally almost in instinctive sympathy. Modern students tend as a result to assume that once a new motif or technique appeared in any corner of the Greek world it automatically passed in a few years to the rest of the Aegean. This assumption is a dangerous simplification, particularly when used in dating schemes for pottery; but the interaction of the Greek world is nonetheless testimony to the freedom with which its leading elements adopted new ideas—and also to the wide network of communication then in existence. The archaic Greeks knew themselves to be Hellenes, distinct from the rest of the world,[2] and were beginning to celebrate their panhellenic unity in games and religious festivals to the great, common gods.

This international unity can too easily be exaggerated. Beside the outward flow lay a force which pulled men inward. The seventh century was the era in which the city-states of Greece crystallized, and these states demanded, for their own egotistical perfection, all the resources of their citizens. Artistically, Greek localism finds its best reflection in the marvelously varied styles of Orientalizing pottery in the seventh century. In literature, the vigor of lyric and elegiac poetry from Archilochus onward drew much from the poets' emotional involvement in the welfare of their individual states. Politically, the bitter divisions of Greece are too well known to need exposition.

Fully to discuss the major characteristics of Greek civilization—for this is in the end what results from an analysis of the

[2] Archilochus, fragment 97; Hesiod, *Works and Days* 528, and fragment 26 (ed. Rzach); in fragment 7 from the *Eoiae* Hellen appears as eponym of the Hellenes, father of Dorus, Xuthus (the father of Ion), and Aiolos.

intellectual upheaval 750–650—is impossible; brevity, on the other hand, must lead to distortion. Yet one final aspect of the method by which the Greeks advanced so rapidly cannot be passed over. By the seventh century the Hellenic outlook had assumed an air of conscious exploration and intentional analysis. Man was cutting himself deliberately loose from the accidental flow of life, and opened his eyes to gaze upon himself.[3] Wherever a comparison is made between products of the eighth and the seventh centuries, the same result obtains in this respect. The clearest example is the treatment of epic and myth on the vases; while the artists of the eighth century created the techniques by which specific scenes *might* be illustrated, their pictures remained generalized duels, lion hunts, and so on. Only in the seventh century did vase paintings turn into the clearly identifiable mythical pictures of Orientalizing ware.

Behind the ability to depict specific scenes and to see human beings as conscious creatures lay a conjoined development of abstract thought. This achievement was not an absolutely fresh discovery of the seventh century. In Homer the Greek language already showed the beginnings of ability at abstraction, conscious reflection, and other characteristics of the later Greek mind.[4] Despite these early beginnings, the quantitative difference between 750 and 650 is so great as to be qualitative. By the later date men knew what they were doing. They recognized the obstacles and felt how little independence men had before the great forces of the world; but with wisdom they could fathom "the rhythm which governs the life of man" and so could act. Thought, true, was not yet as supple as it was to become thereafter; men still sought the ideal in factual and concrete images. Their basic presuppositions strike us, as they did

[3] From Dedalic art on, statues have eyes; W. Deonna, "Les Yeux absents ou clos des statues de la Grèce primitive," *REG*, XLVIII (1935), 219–44.
[4] Abstraction: Fränkel, *Dichtung und Philosophie*, 52, 57–58; Myres, *BSA*, XLV (1950), 258; Webster, *From Mycenae to Homer*, 256–57; Snell, *Discovery of the Mind*, 227–37; Whitman, *Homer and the Heroic Tradi-* *tion*, 13. Concrete images: Fränkel, *Dichtung und Philosophie*, index, 653–59. Opposites: Fränkel, "Eine Stileigenheit der frühgriechischen Literatur," *Wege und Formen*, 40–96. Time sense: Fränkel, "Die Zeitauffassung in der frühgriechischen Literatur," *Wege und Formen*, 1–22; Treu, *Von Homer zur Lyrik*, 123, 224.

also the later Greeks, as frequently naïve. The marshaling of complex masses gave rise not to crystalline unities but to such wandering mazes as Hesiod's *Works and Days* or to simple manipulations of diametrical opposites. The virtually timeless plane of Homer had now yielded to a sense of rapid, almost meaningless change from day to day; a connected sense of the flow of time came only later. Much remained to be done, and when it was achieved the archaic era was over.

Nonetheless the intellectual upheaval 750–650 was one of the most fascinating and most crucial steps in the progress of Western civilization. "In Greece, and only in Greece, did theoretic thought emerge without outside influence; . . . it was only with the help of the unique achievement of the Greeks that the other societies were able to progress beyond their own pace of conceptual development." [5] The Hellenic outlook now existed in conscious, coherent form, and marked off the Greeks who shared it from all other peoples. The speed, sureness, and magnificence of this achievement are amazing, but the bearers of Greek civilization are not solely important for their own accomplishment. No sooner had the new structure arisen than it began to display an amazingly attractive force for other peoples. Whereas the Greek culture of the Dark ages had influenced only the shores of the Aegean, archaic art and literature were to be admired and imitated widely over the Mediterranean. To this end the political and economic expansion of the Aegean world, the subject of the next two chapters, contributed greatly.

[5] Snell, *Discovery of the Mind,* 227 (speaking specifically of science).

CHAPTER 9

SOCIETY AND THE INDIVIDUAL

THE HISTORY of mankind's intellectual development offers
no more fascinating topic than the ever shifting attitudes of men
toward their own nature. The degree to which they feel themselves to be individuals, the consciousness with which they engage in self-analysis, the willingness or reluctance with which
they bear communal burdens—all these are of major importance; and in each Greece witnessed marked evolution during
the age of revolution.

The growing self-consciousness of the era has already been
observed in the mirrors of the arts, of literature, and of religious developments. Individualism, however, is a dangerous
word to employ without qualifications at this juncture. From
the seventh century on—even from the Homeric world onward
—the Hellenic outlook was stamped by a complex, fructifying
tension between human egotism and communal ties.

To understand what occurred in social relationships it is important to remember that the Aegean underwent no fundamental alteration during the century 750–650 in class structure,
economic patterns, or ruling elements. There were no external
invasions nor any major internal upheavals. In particular, new
elements of commercial or industrial stamp remained minor in
size and weight well down into the seventh century. Modern
theories about the rise of the nation-state in European history
tend to assign crucial significance to the emergence of non-
agricultural middle classes; whatever may be the merits of
this conceptual scheme as an explanation of recent political and
intellectual evolution, it will not fit the ancient evidence on the

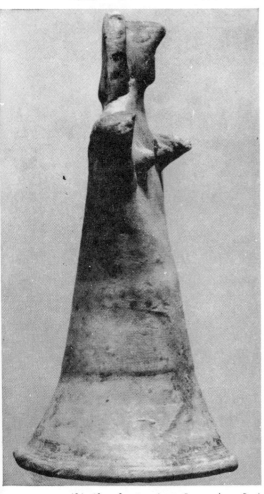

(a) Ivory goddess from Dipylon grave, Oriental in some details but akin to Dipylon pottery figures (National Museum 776, Athens).

(b) Clay figurine from Samos (no. 873) with upturned head common in the era. Photographs courtesy Deutsches Archäologisches Institut in Athens.

PLATE 19 · *Late Geometric Figurines*

(a) Warrior from the Acropolis showing a beginning of inner unity (cf. neck of Plate 17b) (National Museum 6613, Athens). Photograph courtesy Deutsches Archäologisches Institut in Athens.

(b) Statuette dedicated by Mantiklos to Apollo, a provincial Boeotian work but with defined outline (Museum of Fine Arts 03.997, Boston). Photograph courtesy Museum of Fine Arts, Boston.

PLATE 20 · *Emergence of Archaic Sculpture*

early *polis*. The economic advances of the era will be discussed in Chapter 11; but on the whole it is safe to say that the city-state was the fruit of tensions within an agricultural world.[1] The rise of the *polis* may have been much facilitated by the continuing simplicity of economic patterns and by the still almost primitive social structure of the age of revolution.

Within this basic limit, nonetheless, the era did see very significant social alterations. Some of the displacements bore especially on the two main classes, the landlords and the peasants, both separately and also in their relations to one another. Other modifications affected all men, regardless of their social stratum; among these were shifts in the relative position of the sexes and alterations in the strength of various social units.

The fruits of the evolution were many. Men came to visualize far more consciously the problems inherent in the relations between individuals and society. The divine forces governing mankind were increasingly conceived as ethical forces. In this process the Greeks advanced less far than did the Hebrews, but modern morality stems from the ethics of Plato and Aristotle as well as from the fiery words of Israel's prophets. The ethical and religious concepts which thenceforth governed Greek life were partly tailored to suit the individual but also to a marked degree were group-oriented.

For beside conscious individualism came also more conscious ties, both on the level of specific classes and also in the structure of the community. Whereas the earlier, ancestral distinctions between upper and lower levels had existed only on a simple, almost unconscious basis, the upper class now progressed into an aristocratic outlook which has influenced noble patterns ever since. The political system which held together Aegean society underwent marked alteration in the direction of the city-state. Looking back across the course of later Greek history, we can see that social change in the period 750–650, with its attendant results, was so great as to be a veritable revolution.

---

[1] See Johannes Hasebroek, *Trade and Politics in Ancient Greece* (London, 1933), 31–32; and J. M. Cook's recent picture of Old Smyrna as largely agricultural, *BSA*, LIII–IV (1958–59), 16–17.

THE PLACE OF THE ARISTOCRATS

IN THIS SOCIAL REVOLUTION the upper classes must first claim one's attention. These were the most powerful, the most vocal, and the most aggressive part of Greek society; these reacted most obviously and fully to every innovation sweeping over the Aegean. On the upper level, if anywhere, an individual had room to assert his own independence. Yet we shall find, as we proceed, that the noble element did not lose its unity through atomistic, self-seeking drives. Nor did the upper classes stand alone in the Greek world. They were not absolutely dominant; the growing power of the aristocracy as a class and the self-awareness of aristocrats as individuals constituted only one root of the new ethical and political concepts.

By the seventh century the upper classes of Greece were at last clearly evolving the marks of an aristocracy—i.e., a group which manifested social distinctions in an obligatory way of life consciously conceived as more refined, more cultured, and more leisurely than that of the masses.[2] Our greater awareness of distinctions between upper and lower classes may in part simply reflect the greater volume of evidence, but this cannot be all the explanation. The physical remains of the tombs attest a growing separation of rich and poor; the hints of the *Iliad,* when coupled with the continuing evolution of the seventh century, suggest fairly clearly that social alterations were actually occurring.

If an aristocratic outlook thus began to jell, we must look to several factors. The basic economic, religious, and political eminence of the upper classes was an inheritance from earlier centuries; what was now being added was, first, an increase in wealth and, secondly, a more conscious analysis of man's nature and place. The nobles surely gained a large part of the growing

---

[2] Hermann Strasburger, "Der soziologische Aspekt der homerischen Epen," *Gymnasium,* LX (1953), 97–114; G. M. Calhoun, "Classes and Masses in Homer," *CP,* XXIX (1934), 192–208. Webster, *From Mycenae to Homer,* 156, 163, 185, argues that the tracing of genealogies in Homer was a recent step, as was also the formation of families calling themselves "sons of . . ." (*dai*).

economic resources of Greece. They were also the element which mainly consumed the new luxuries brought from the East and which supported local craftsmen in the rapid development of Aegean arts. In one way or another, the upper classes of Greece became increasingly aware of Oriental patterns; but one may doubt whether their knowledge of an alien world, where civilization was grouped about kings and aristocracies, gave any significant model to their own self-assertion.

The creation of a consciously aristocratic pattern was, in the social field, a close parallel to the evolution of new molds for artistic and poetic thought. It came suddenly, after foreshadowings in the *Iliad* and *Odyssey;* by the time of Archilochus, and still more by the end of the seventh century, when Sappho, Alcaeus, and Solon flourished, it was quite apparent. What followed thereafter was refinement of the form, for across the sixth and fifth centuries aristocratic ideals experienced further evolution and polish.

Since our literary evidence becomes relatively abundant only in the later, more advanced stages, it is not altogether easy to trace the intensification of the aristocratic outlook semantically. The famous phrase for aristocrats was to be *kalokagathoi,* as distinguished from the *kakoi* or base; but in the seventh century we cannot be sure that its constituent parts, *kaloi* (beautiful = polished) and *agathoi* (good = pre-eminent), had entirely come to have reference to class position rather than to individual merit.[3] This process does seem to have been under way; and early poetry has an abundance of other phrases— *gennaioi* (noble-born), *eupatridai* (of good father), *diotrephes* (Zeus-nurtured), "daughter of many kings," and so on—which reflected aristocratic pride in lineage. This spirit found other vents as well. The *Catalogue of Women, Eoiae,* and other Hesiodic lists described mortal-divine unions from which great

[3] On the concept of beauty in Homer, cf. Treu, *Von Homer zur Lyrik,* 36–40; the term *kalokagathos* appears only in a comparative form, in *Iliad* XXIV. 52. Bravery and beauty, moreover, do not necessarily go hand in hand either in the *Iliad* (V. 801, 787; the picture of Paris generally) or in Archilochus. Neither Treu (p. 175) nor Julius Gerlach, 'Ανὴρ 'αγαθός (Diss. Munich, 1932), consider *agathos* a class term in the seventh century. Sappho, fragment 155, or Archilochus, fragment 9, give examples of the phrases in the text.

families boasted their origin; the very extensive reworking of
the myths which was under way was in part dictated by the
desire to interlock the major clans of Asia Minor and Greece.
Many of these, such as the Basilidai of Ephesus, the Neleids of
Miletus, as well as the Medontids of Athens, were of royal background; and in general kingly, noble, and priestly families
merged into one unified upper class in the seventh century.[4]

As this social outlook became more developed, the problem of transmitting it to the next generation grew pressing.
Nobles were deliberately educated to proper standards of
life by many modes. Much must have been done within the
family; youths also attended wiser adults, such as the "school"
of Sappho, and hearkened to the more impersonal words of
the poets from Homer onward. Males, in particular, were
trained in gymnasia and attended communal meals of warrior
bands (where these still existed). Homosexuality, ignored by
Homer, became widely accepted both in its more elemental
aspects and as a bond between noble model and noble
aspirant.

Consciously guided into the proper paths in childhood,
nobles were as adults subject to constant scrutiny by their peers.
Upper and lower classes were distinguished primarily as groups,
not as individuals; and the nascent aristocrats must exemplify
the virtues of their class. The character of a hero arose from,
and was embodied in, his actions; his ensuing glory and repute derived from the judgment of his fellow men, which was
expressed in such adjectives as *agathos* or such nouns as *time,
kleos*. In modern terms, Greek society was framed as a shame
culture, rather than a guilt culture. Individual self-perception
and self-expression inevitably arose out of such factors, as
we shall see shortly; but this aspect was not pre-eminent in
seventh-century society. Greek life was intensely communal.
The concepts of upper-class conduct as a distinct pattern, once

---

[4] Louis Gernet, "Les nobles dans la
Grèce antique," *Annales d'histoire
économique et sociale*, X (1938), 36–
43; I am not sure the argument for
distinct priestly families in earlier
times is altogether sound.

Training: H. I. Marrou, *History
of Education in Antiquity* (New York,
1956), 5–13, 43–44; on the system of
communal Cretan meals, see Willetts,
Ancient Crete, 13–17.

consciously appreciated, evolved steadily into that system which eventually abstract thinkers such as Plato and Aristotle codified and teachers such as Isocrates imparted even to foreigners.

The background of upper-class life continued to be agricultural and in part rural. Some aristocratic estates of early Attica can be identified through later topographic nomenclature and by archaeological remains; the countryside of Teos apparently was held in the main by some forty families, each with its *pyrgos* or fortified refuge.[5] Both as a pastime and for more practical reasons, aristocrats delighted in the hunt, and raised horses with no less pride than had their ancestors in the eighth century and earlier. The terms *hippeis, hippobotai,* etc., became in several places virtually titles for the governing classes, and aristocrats compounded their personal names with *Hippo-*. Chariots now were used for racing, not for battle, but horseback riding came into wider practice after the Cimmerians and other nomads had shown the way. In the Lesbian poets, as in Homer, the phenomena of nature were an immediate part of man's environment.

To say this does not mean that the Greeks of the seventh century, whether noble or peasant, lived like savages in full contact with the physical world. The dwellers in Aegean lands, as was pointed out in Chapter 4, were forced to group themselves in clusters both for purposes of defense and for geographical reasons. The nobles did not isolate themselves completely in rural strongholds, like many of the feudal lords of medieval Europe, but preferred as their abode the central *asty* of each tribal area. This site, for reasons of clarity, I shall translate by the

[5] D. W. S. Hunt, "Feudal Survivals in Ionia," *JHS*, LXVII (1947), 48–76; Webster, *From Mycenae to Homer*, 151, notes Mycenaean parallels. On the *gamoroi* of Syracuse, see Dunbabin, *Western Greeks*, 55–57.

Horse riding: Nikolaos Yalouris, *Athena als Herrin der Pferde* (Diss. Basel, 1949; *Museum Helveticum*, VII [1950], 19–101); Edouard Delebecque, *Le Cheval dans l'Iliade* (Paris, 1951); T. Talbot Rice, *The Scythians* (London, 1957), 69–70; see

also the earlier picture in Chap. 4, n. 2 (p. 133); Chap. 5, n. 1 (p. 155). Horseback riding was already known in *Odyssey* V. 371, *Iliad* XV. 679, and on Geometric vases (e.g., Athens NM 810, 13038; cf. Whitman, *Homer and the Heroic Tradition*, 354). The fact that Artemis was especially a huntress in Ionia may lead to diametrically the opposite conclusion from the view of Nilsson, *GGR*, I, 469, that it reflects a survival of delight in the hunt among an *urban* aristocracy.

economically colorless word "town," rather than by the common but dangerous equivalent of "city."

The epics commonly locate the upper classes in the towns and distinguish clearly between rural and *asty* dwellers; in the next century Solon, in speaking of the *astoi,* seems to be thinking primarily of the aristocrats, and Sappho scorns the "countrified" girl.[6] As the greater gods lived together on the peak of Olympus, so the aristocrats dwelt in the hubs of earthly life, where they were kindled by, and in turn promoted, the latest ideas. Here they might enjoy the most recent luxuries produced by wandering and local artisans; for to make our picture complete we must remember that beside the nobles dwelt both peasants and a slowly increasing number of traders and craftsmen.

Architecturally the towns were primitive. Socially they were simple, and the men who inhabited them could step quickly into the world of fields and pastures, of wild animals and elemental forces of nature which lay all about. But the intellectual stimulus of the towns was not thereby limited. While the highly sociable character of Greeks was a vital factor throughout their history, this trait never played a greater role than in the early seventh century. The close personal association of the upper classes at this time was a tremendous force in promoting the lightning swiftness of contemporary change. The aristocratic pattern, true, was rising as a basic mold for social life, but the leaders of the Greek world enjoyed nonetheless a remarkable openness of mind.

The opportunities of the aristocrats, that is to say, were great as old patterns and customs yielded, and they seized the moment avidly, even ruthlessly. In intellectual outlook they seem scarcely to have boggled at any novelty; their basically rational, inquisitive spirit produced within a century the first speculative philosophers of Western civilization. Even more

[6] Town-dwellers: *Iliad* II. 806, XV. 558; *Odyssey* II. 77, II. 154, VI. 262 ff., VII. 131, XIII. 192, XVII. 206. Peasants in town: *Iliad* IX. 154; *Odyssey* XVII. 182, XIV. 372, XXIV. 210. Solon: Meyer, *Forschungen zur alten Geschichte* I, 307; Sappho, fragment 57. Strasburger, *Gymnasium,* LX (1953), 99, and "Der Einzelne und die Gemeinschaft im Denken der Griechen," *Historische Zeitschrift,* CLXXVII (1954), 227–48, from this point of view overemphasizes the rural tone in early Greek society; cf. Bolkestein, *Economic Life,* 18–22.

obviously characteristic of the seventh-century nobility, and of great importance both for good and for evil, was its almost childish joy in the new physical delights of life. "Haughty, adorned with well-dressed hair, steeped in the scent of skilfully-prepared unguents," as Xenophanes (fragment 3) later scornfully indicted the purple-clad lords of Colophon, the aristocrats of Greece everywhere sought ivories, bronzes, the latest wares of Corinth; one great surprise to modern scholars at the excavation of Artemis Orthia was the revelation that early Spartan nobles had followed this common path. Luxury (*abrosyne*) is a leitmotif of the poetry of the seventh and sixth centuries.[7] The concept, to be sure, is always a relative matter: an Assyrian monarch would have scorned a noble Greek house as a hovel. Would Greek painted pottery have developed so far if its purchasers have been able to afford shelves laden with gold and silver vessels?

In other vital respects the leading classes of Greece were as free of narrow restrictions. The geographic framework of the epic world had been the Greek Aegean as a whole; even the distinction between Greek and non-Greek was not yet sharp in the *Iliad*.[8] Aristocrats had wide contacts through guest-friendship and intermarriage. Unfortunate men who murdered their kinfold or otherwise failed to fit into the social structure of their homeland moved as far afield as the minstrels. Once outside their native fold, refugees were desperately insecure unless they gained the protection of an alien *basileus*, but this tie seems easily granted to nobles in the *Iliad*. From the wide range of pottery and bronze motifs one may suspect that similar protection was also accorded to outside artists. "For these men," says Eumaeus, "are bidden all over the boundless earth."

---

[7] Mazzarino, *Fra Oriente e Occidente,* 215 ff., gives a good analysis.

[8] This distinction was, however, beginning to appear, as Gomme, *Greek Attitude,* 43–45, notes.

Movement abroad: *Iliad* XV. 430–32, XVI. 571–74, XXIII. 85–90, XXIV. 480–82, etc. Exiles as outcasts: *Iliad* XXIV. 531 ff., XVI. 59; *Odyssey* XV. 224, 254, XIII. 259. Distrust of strangers: *Odyssey* VII. 32–33, XIII. 201–02 (= VIII. 575–76), XIV. 124–25; these must be placed beside the emphasis that strangers should be well treated in VI. 207–08, I. 119–20, VIII. 546. These exiles are the root of the seventh-century mercenaries (Fanta, *Der Staat,* 65–66). Eumaeus: *Odyssey* XVII. 382–86.

Within the age of revolution the international ties were intensified as movement became more common and safer and as the ken of Hellas was enlarged. The young girls who chirped about Sappho in Lesbos made marriages as far afield as Lydia;[9] wherever we know pedigrees of noble stocks, alien elements commonly can be found. Casual raiding by land and sea probably declined, for the Greek world was becoming more orderly; but aristocrats could serve as mercenaries abroad in the East, found colonies, or perhaps engage in long-distance trade. Archilochus as well as other nobles (and peasants too) felt free to migrate and to travel. By the seventh century the famous shrines and games of later Hellas, centered on such points as Delphi, Olympia, and Delos, had emerged as focal points for the international flow of aristocrats and artists, which at once bound together the more conscious levels of Greece in a sense of common unity and differentiation from the outside world and also fostered the transmission of new ideas and objects.

Politically the upper classes of the earlier, epic stage had not been tied down by abstract bonds of state and community. Hector and others fought for their fatherland, and the Achaeans yearned for home; but when such concepts are concretely described, they resolve themselves into family, estates, and native hearths.[1] Within the seventh century political attitudes began to change. Deep involvement in local struggles makes its first appearance in Archilochus' vehement attacks on his foes; in Sappho and Alcaeus, and even more in Solon and Tyrtaeus, there rise before our eyes aristocratic politics of feuding factions and the ambitions of individual leaders, as well as true patriotic love for one's country. The aristocrats, who had much to gain from political mastery, did not disdain to exploit their opportunities. Even on this level, nonetheless, we must not visualize too sweeping a change. The international ties of family connections, travel, and culture exerted significant influences; the local unit of the *polis* had only just emerged and did not swallow up men's energies *in toto*.

[9] Heuss, *Antike und Abendland*, II (1946), 49–50.
[1] *Iliad* II. 178, II. 454, III. 244, XII. 243, XV. 496–98, cf. IX. 593–94;

Odyssey I. 58–59, V. 220, IX. 34, etc. Cf. Hoffman, *Festschrift B. Snell*, 158–60.

The very forces, finally, which promoted the conscious realization of aristocratic position also impelled individual members
of this class to their own self-assertion. The aristocratic pattern
was not one of personal abnegation. Both the growing prosperity
and the incessant flux of archaic Greek life promoted human
pride. The contention of the epic heroes for glory thus passed
on into fierce political rivalry among noble factions; and insofar
as this vent was narrowed by the consolidation of the city-state
the yearning for repute in the eyes of one's fellows was expressed
in competition at impromptu and organized games.[2] The agonal
or competitive spirit became a major aspect of Greek aristocratic
nature in the eighth and seventh centuries. Socially there was
the same tendency to break all bars which can be observed in
Protoattic pottery and other fields; but the inherited structure
of Greek civilization was able to throw up new forms and molds
which checked social license, while yet permitting individual
human beings a wide field for action. The relations between the
aristocracy as a class and its members as self-seeking individuals
are not simple; the tension which resulted not only caused stress
but also promoted the enduringly dynamic quality of Greek
civilization.

It is time to impose qualifications upon this general picture of the aristocratic class. Historians are much too easily
carried away by the pretensions of the voluble governing circles
to be the font of all desirable change, the arbiters of intellect;
for the great movements in human history are not thus class-
bound. Wherever one turns, the same forces drive rich and poor,
literate and illiterate, toward the same goals. Those who appear to be the leaders in any era are chiefly marked out by
greater sensitivity of spirit or outward stature in a common
procession.[3]

[2] Will, *Doriens et Ioniens*, 30–31.
Strasburger's interesting argument,
Historische Zeitschrift, CLXXVII
(1954), 227–48, that men were coming to feel themselves primarily as individuals and were not conscious of
unity in a Gemeinschaft must be fitted into this framework; the local ties
were, after all, ancestral and were not
so likely to receive direct expression.

[3] I have considered this problem in
another period of history in *Civiliza-
tion and the Caesars*, 262–65, 312–13.
An example of class interpretation of
Greek history is that of Margaret O.
Wason, *Class Struggles in Ancient
Greece* (London, 1947).

To label Greek culture in the age of revolution—or there-after—solely as "aristocratic" is to forgo any possibility of un-derstanding its evolution. It is natural that we tend to call the human-centered, physically active, essentially rational outlook of the Greek world aristocratic, inasmuch as we know that this spirit has been an important force in subsequent noble pat-terns of life. In the later centuries of Greek civilization the Hel-lenic outlook was consciously sharpened and refined as a mark especially of the upper classes; from them it was taken over by the senatorial leaders of Rome; and modern aristocracies have largely been trained within the classical tradition.

In the period we are now considering, when this system first became a conscious possession of Hellas, it was a creation of archaic society as a whole. Only superficially, as in the choice of subjects by vase painters and poets, did the culture of the age of revolution reflect aristocratic interests.[4] The oppositions which have often been drawn between the peasant Hesiod and the aristocratic Archilochus, or on the divine level between Apollo and Dionysus, are made much too sharp. In both pairs new ideas of the age of revolution are evident; if the individual figures at times appear to be incompatible, this is mainly a testimony to the manifold variety of humanity at any time. Only in very small degree can such differences be used to distinguish class atti-tudes.

The power of the Greek upper classes and the individualism of its members, after all, were bounded by two major checks. One was the internal product of their own character; the other was imposed upon the leading elements from outside. In the first place the aristocracy was only recently set apart in ways of life from the rest of the population. Located in a system which was evolving rapidly in every respect, it had a superb oppor-tunity to seize political and economic advantage, often in un-

---

[4] Kübler, *Altattische Malerei*, 29–30, gives examples; I have suggested above, pp. 154–55, a possible connec-tion between noble patronage and Dipylon products. C. A. Robinson, Jr., "The Development of Archaic Greek Sculpture," *AJA*, XLII (1938), 451–
55, and "Observations on Seventh-Century Greek Sculpture," *AJA*, XLVIII (1944), 132–34, essays to find connections between artistic shifts and political changes, particularly in the rise of the tyrants.

just fashion, and thus to capitalize on its inherited position of prominence; yet in social forms, as in the development of Orientalizing pottery, the Hellenic inheritance of the past prevented men from rejecting their sense of communal structure and responsibility. Landlords and peasants had earlier been bound together in a tight web of tribe, phratry, and other social, religious, and political units, the power of which was not broken all at once. The more thoughtful members of the upper classes felt as keenly as those who were oppressed the serious threat that unchecked individual license might result in communal disunity. When such men as Solon rose in opposition to this trend, they could summon within the hearts of their peers powerful forces—the more powerful because the world of the seventh century was still a simple land where rich and poor lived side by side in small clusters.

That justice which depends purely on the self-restraint of the rulers is a fragile blessing. Beside the aristocracy stood, in the second place, an outside check in the form of the rest of society. Individually the masses were powerless and often suffered from aristocratic pressure. Taken together, they had both inherited resources in tribal unity and the spirit of personal leadership and also new strengths resulting from contemporary economic and military changes. While the Greek world could not prevent—and did not try to halt—the consolidation of the aristocracy as its outwardly dominant element, it could—and did—impose a lasting curb upon the degree of that domination. Any assessment of the social changes which underlay the rise of the city-state must take into account not only landlords but also peasants; and some social developments of importance were independent of class.

OTHER SOCIAL CHANGES

THE NON-ARISTOCRATIC part of the population consisted of independent peasants who owned their own fields; landless men who made a living as day laborers on the farms or plied the trades of artisan, merchant, and shipper; and household slaves. The last element, which was beginning to expand into the field of industry, may be ignored in its social role; slaves were still very restricted in numbers and had no perceptible influence on political changes. The landless *thetes,* too, were of scant importance except insofar as their numbers swelled during the age of revolution and emphasized the need for colonization. The commercial and industrial segments of this group did not yet have any independent political role of weight.[5]

While the historian can only guess at the proportions of peasant small holders and landless workers in the late eighth and early seventh centuries, the small farmers were fairly clearly a major part of the population in most areas.[6] What happened to the peasants during the age of revolution must be a thread of importance in Greek social and political development; but unfortunately changes on this level can be measured only in their most basic outlines. The voices of history speak usually in cultured tones. In probing archaic Greece it is a stroke of luck that we have even so partial a reflection of the problems of the ordinary men as Hesiod's *Works and Days;* for the most part conclusions in this field must rest on the dangerous course of arguing back from visible developments to their probable cause.

One underlying factor, thus, must have been a great increase in population, which began by the early eighth century or even before. The archaeological record shows ever wider settlement, ever more numerous cemeteries; when we come to examine the outbreak of colonization at the very beginning of the age of revolution, we shall not be able to avoid the impression that there must have been a surplus of manpower. The causes, however, of the great demographic shifts in history are always difficult to explain.[7] In eighth-century Greece and later there

[5] See above, Chap. 4, n. 1 (p. 131); and below, Chap. 11.
[6] The predominance of small properties, noted in Bolkestein, *Economic Life,* 26–27, 29–30, was not necessarily a later development.
[7] The comments of M. I. Finley, *JRS,* XLVIII (1958), 157–58, are more useful than the essay by J. L. Myres,

"The Causes of Rise and Fall in the Population of the Ancient World," *Geographical History in Greek Lands,* 172–208. J. L. Angel, *Journal of Gerontology,* II (1947), 20, argues an increase of two to three years in life span between the eras 1150–650 and 650–150 B.C., but he has come to doubt his conclusion (*Khirokitia,* 417).

may have been an increase in life span due to more settled and secure life, though our skeletal material is rather scant for firm statistics; but there was also, surely, an actual increase in the birth rate. To account for this mysterious factor, which is not even arithmetically demonstrable, one can say no more than that, by and large, agricultural production, especially of grain, rose and that peasants *could* prosper in the century 750–650.

Another force which affected the peasants' lot was their partial liberation from the unwritten, static rules of life which had at once limited and protected their position in the past. Peasant landholders, whether descended from the primeval stocks or from the invaders, had become firmly entrenched in the social organization of tribal Greece during the Dark ages. To their richer neighbors and to the Zeus-born kings they yielded the mastery of political and religious machinery, and they seem from hints in the epics to have been required to provide not very well defined "gifts" to their leaders; but no consciously organized system of manorial dues had been inherited to curse their lot.

When Greek life began to evolve more freely, the peasants were thus legally able to change their occupation or to move to urban centers and new colonies; Hesiod's father migrated from Cyme to Boeotia. This freedom was not an entire blessing, for as the farmers lost the protective shield of ancestral fixity, they were exposed directly to serious stresses which threatened their economic independence. The rise in population itself brought critical problems in the division of small farms, which Hesiod tried to counter in his advice that a man have only one son.[8] Worse by far must have been the harsh pressure from the aristocrats, increasingly unified and distinguished from the lower orders, increasingly bent on enjoying the material fruits of the new prosperity of Greece. The increase in total production which was occurring must not be conceived in the phenomenal terms of modern industrial development. Generally in history the few can have more goods only if the many have less; or at

[8] *Works and Days* 376–78. The common tendency to stress this passage, however, must take into account his subsequent remark: "Yet Zeus can easily give great wealth to a greater number. More hands mean more work and more increase."

least, in periods when production has actually risen to a considerable degree, the rewards will commonly be divided in very unequal measure.

By ill-seen means, such as exploitation of the requirements of gifts, by loans in time of famine, by distortion of justice, by brutal exercise of superior power, the governing classes assailed their weaker neighbors and at times forced the peasantry down virtually or entirely into serfdom. In Crete, in Sparta, in Thessaly the farming population was in historic times legally bound to the soil and owed payments to the upper classes. While this tendency may have been an inheritance from the age of invasion or a concomitant of later colonization, it was in its final state a product of the growing distinction of the aristocratic elements and their willingness to use their power.[9] In Athens, as we know from the unrest in the days of Solon, the peasantry came close to falling into the same pit.

Hesiod directed his bitter attack on the bribe-swallowing *basileis* against this line of development. The important aspect of the *Works and Days* is too rarely noticed: it is not the specific injustice which occasioned the poem but the fact that Hesiod was able to cry out. To judge from the epic reference to "insolent folk in the *demos*," forces already stood in opposition to noble aggrandizement in the eighth century;[1] Hesiod continued the strain; and eventually the peasantry in most districts was able to save itself from utter dependence economically and politically. That the escape was narrow the events at Athens make clear; but it did occur. The retention of essential independence by the peasantry was one of the most crucial factors in Greek political history.

This victory, which is not what we might expect, was the product of many forces. Colonization provided a safety valve; town markets were appearing where non-agricultural elements

---

[9] Serfdom does not appear in Homer; see Hasebroek, *Griechische Wirtschafts- und Gesellschaftsgeschichte*, 22; Paul Guiraud, *La Propriété foncière en Grèce jusqu'à la conquête romaine* (Paris, 1893), 407–18. Compare the reduction of Polish, Russian, and other East European peasants into serfdom, which occurred only in modern times. Athenaeus VI. 263–272 is our main evidence on Greek serfdom.

[1] *Odyssey* VI. 274–75; note the "base churls" (*kakoi*) of IV. 62–64.

bought rural produce and some farmers could employ commercial and industrial talents; not all of the expanding production necessarily went to the upper classes. The military changes of the era played a part, for the peasantry furnished a vital section of the heavily armored infantry which, as will appear in the next chapter, now safeguarded the independence of each state. Socially, the communal unity of earlier, tribal days lingered on to give the peasants a standard by which to recognize oppression and avenues by which they might express their views. On the other side, the more perceptive aristocrats felt in this bond a limit to their freedom.

In explaining the survival of independent lower classes we must also keep always in mind the very simple framework even of seventh-century Greece. The land was fortunate in its geographical and spiritual separation from the more developed civilization of the Orient. In Palestine a similar aristocratic consolidation was occurring at this very period, and the first prophets were raising their voices against oppression. Unfortunately for the poorer Jews, outside military pressure and foreign models tipped the scales in Israel in favor of the upper classes. The Greek world, on the other hand, could more easily cling to older patterns. The peasants, in the last analysis, stood off the aristocrats; and, as we shall see later, the creation of the city-state reflects a basic compromise between the leaders and the led.

Not all the social forces in seventh-century Greece were products of class evolution or class struggle. A shifting attitude toward women—or, better, a hardening of masculine claims to superiority—is reflected in ugly diatribes by "peasant" Hesiod and by later aristocrats alike.[2] Greek women, to be sure, never

---

[2] *Works and Days* 373–75, *Theogony* 591 ff.; Semonides of Amorgos, fragment 7; Phocylides, fragment 2. The expression of similar attitudes began in *Odyssey* XI. 441 ff., XV. 20–23 (vs. VII. 67 ff.), which is in many ways a story of the relations between men and women, while the *Iliad* concerns itself solely with men. On the actual place of women, see H. D. F. Kitto, *The Greeks* (rev. ed., Penguin, 1957), 219–36. Dress: Lorimer, *Homer and the Monuments*, 358–59. Jewelry: Matz, *GGK*, I, 472–73, and the many studies on Greek jewels. Harlots: Archilochus, fragments 91, 241–42.

lived secluded in harems, and the poetry of Sappho at the end
of the seventh century abundantly testifies that women then
had minds of their own, which were at times deemed worthy of
education. Yet widespread female emancipation was not a prize
which men were willing to yield; the product was a sharpened
distinction between the sexes. Often, at least in the upper classes,
men considered the second sex worthy only of adornment, both
in increasing complexity of dress and in wealth of jewelry; harlots appear in Greek literature from Archilochus. The masculine
tone of public society is evident in the new custom of exercis-
ing and competing in the nude,[3] in the development of specific
areas as gymnasia, and in the acceptance of masculine homosexuality.

In itself the male arrogance of the age is politically significant only insofar as it reflects the more conscious assembly of
men for recreation and public business, though a speculative
anthropologist might enjoy proving that the city-state emerged
to keep womankind under control. The declining power of the
old social units over individuals was more certainly of great social
and political consequence. Phratry, clan, tribe, even family could
not hope to endure unchanged in a changing world. Some units
were doomed to purely conventional roles, and all were to yield
a large part of their powers. The heir was often the individual
human being, who increasingly widened his bounds intellectually and geographically.

While the direction of this current in the long stream of
Greek history is clear, to measure its speed of flow at any point
is extremely difficult.[4] The recent argument by Dodds that the
basic social problem of the archaic age was the rejection of the
omnipotent father image by rebellious sons, who then felt guilt,
smacks far too much of modern psychiatric shibboleths. What
we would term "individualism" was still extremely limited in
the seventh century. Collective responsibility of a clan in cases
of murder was only beginning to weaken by the end of the

---

[3] Hesiod, Loeb ed., p. 164 (scholiast
on Homer, *Iliad* XXIII. 683); cf.
Müller, *Nacktheit und Entblössung*,
92–94.
[4] Dodds, *Greeks and the Irrational*,

45–49; Glotz, *Solidarité de la famille*,
225 ff.; Willetts, *Ancient Crete*, 59–66,
252–53, on the growing independence
of the family (against the clan) in
Crete.

century; [5] the family and clan base of politics remained a serious problem to statesmen seeking public unity throughout the next century; and the powers which these units lost went to the state as a whole, as well as to the individual. Tensions between older and younger generations, between the individual and the group, must always exist in society. In the age of revolution the significant point is that they became sharper, changed in focus, and were more consciously felt as men came to observe their world more carefully.

The social stresses of the age were serious, but their dimensions must be kept in proper focus. The upheaval affected minor aspects, not the major structure, of the Aegean world. The ancient patterns of tight blood groups persisted, but had to yield some ground before the broadening flow of Greek life. Before and after the great upheaval two main classes existed in this world, for neither slaves nor middle class yet played any significant role by 650. Within a fundamentally solid, simple, unified society these classes were becoming more consciously separated, but neither could exist without the other. While the governing groups gained most from the economic expansion of the Greek world, the peasants did not entirely lose their position.

Growth in itself does not eliminate discontent, but rather intensifies social and political problems. "Secular improvement," as an eminent student of modern economics has observed, "that is taken for granted and coupled with individual insecurity that is acutely resented is of course the best recipe for breeding social unrest." [6] Yet violent political revolution could be avoided in the Aegean of the seventh century. The price required was, first, a reinforcement and clarification of the basic spirit of communal unity and, secondly, adjustment of outward forms of political organization.

[5] Rose, *Primitive Culture*, 191–205.
[6] Joseph A. Schumpeter, *Capitalism,* *Socialism, and Democracy* (3d ed.; London, 1950), 145.

CIVIC AND ETHICAL GODS

AT ALL TIMES men's views of Heaven move in basic harmony with their concepts of this world. Nowhere can we hope to gain better testimony on the social changes just noted, or on the political evolution which will next concern us, than in the main lines of religious development 750–650. Those changes which illustrate particularly the growing self-consciousness and fears of the individual have been discussed in the previous chapter, but they are not the most important aspects of the great remodeling of Hellenic religion. In the seventh century the Greeks still came to the worship of their gods primarily in groups. The major religious shifts reflect the growing common unity and a clearer sense of the need for divine endorsement of communal justice; [7] the increasing attention to individual ethical positions was subsidiary, though significant.

By 650 each of the more developed Greek states was well equipped with a variety of public cults, conducted at specific places in accordance with a regular calendar and in a well-defined ritual (though we known little of this last at any stage in Greek religious history). In its external organization the religion of state demonstrates the rising position of the aristocrats. The greatest gods were those of the Olympian pantheon, which had crystallized during the preceding century and was worshipped primarily on the aristocratic level. Aristocratic control, too, of the priesthoods is often demonstrable; and some of the public cults had earlier been private ceremonies of noble clans. The religious machinery, interwoven as it was with political and social structures, had the usual, incidental benefit of assisting to keep down the ignorant masses.

No one considering Greek religion in the seventh century can place first either its individual appeal or its class character; the state cults were, above all, an effort to unite the entire population of the nascent city-states. They emerged out of earlier tribal worship and expanded their sway as far as the

[7] See in general Guthrie, *The Greeks and Their Gods,* and M. P. Nilsson,   *A History of Greek Religion* (Oxford, 1925), 224–62.

boundaries of each local political unit. Some of the gods were drawn from the great panhellenic pantheon, or were local deities absorbed into the major gods; the characteristics of the earlier figure frequently carried over into the new synthesis. Artemis Orthia of Sparta is not quite the same as the Artemis of Attic Brauron. Each state also had a host of unique divinities, some of which rose at this time from purely neighborhood reverence to state-wide cult—one example of this process of generalization is the fertility worship of Eleusis in the Attic state.

Beside the gods stood heroes, who admirably illuminate the new emphasis on public unity.[8] A few heroes, such as Heracles, remained the general property of all Greeks, but by far the majority were symbols of pride to individual states. Theseus, for instance, who had earlier been revered over a wide area, was then appropriated by Athens, at the cost of a very considerable reworking of myth. Chthonian deities sometimes rose to the level of heroes; other cults, as of Agamemnon at Mycenae and of Menelaus at Sparta, appeared in deference to the popularity of the epics; many heroes were spontaneously generated out of the excitement at discovering old tombs. The source of the cult was immaterial; the significant fact was the sudden outburst of this kind of religious creativity, which clearly manifested a well-nigh conscious effort to unite the state. While the gods defended the *polis* against misfortune, a hero was peculiarly qualified, both as erstwhile human warrior and as a purely local patron, to rally the citizens in their phalanx and lead them to victory in war. The miracle by which the Greeks turned back the Persians was due, said later men, to the gods and to the heroes.

Almost anywhere one turns in Greek religion the interweav-

[8] Hero cults: Rohde, *Psyche*, 98–100, 115–55; L. R. Farnell, *Greek Hero Cults and Ideas of Immortality* (Oxford, 1921); Paul Foucart, "Le culte des héros chez les Grecs," *Mémoires de l'Académie des Inscriptions et Belles-Lettres*, XLII (1918); Nilsson, *GGR*, I, 184–91, 378–83, 715–19. Sites: J. M. Cook, "The Agamemnoneion," *BSA*, XLVIII (1953), 30–68, and "The Cult of Agamemnon at Mycenae," *Geras A. Keramopoullou*, 112–18; *Délos*, V, 67–74, and Gallet de Santerre, *Délos primitive*, 93–96, on the tomb of the Hyperborean maidens; Benton, *BSA*, XXXV (1934–35), 45–73, on the cave of Odysseus at Ithaca; see also *Das Kuppelgrab bei Menidi*. Theseus: Nilsson, *Cults and Politics*, 49–65. Persian defeat: Herodotus VIII. 109.

ing of politics and faith is visible, for the ancient world did not
admit the principle of separation of church and state. As the
polis became a more conscious political guardian of man's security, so, too, the religious ceremonies of its calendar, which
safeguarded that *polis*, were refined and interlocked. In at least
one case we can actually see the insertion of the *polis* into local
agricultural rites. An ancient Cretan hymn to Zeus initially bade
his servants, the Curetes, to leap for wine, flocks, fields, and
hives, but by historic times a significant addition had been inserted: "Leap also for our cities, and our sea-faring ships,
and leap for the young citizens, and leap for fair law-abiding-
ness." [9] Most impressive of all the marks of political and social
unity was the swelling number of temples and sacred precincts
in the Greek states from the mid-seventh century onward. These
were not class monuments, but general focuses for state patriotism, the product of communal work and sacrifice, and the object
of communal pride.[1] The most lasting physical testimony to the
economic and cultural growth of Greece is not in noble, private
houses as evidences of individual luxury but in public, religious
dedications.

Another set of human requirements led to a reinterpretation
of the nature of the gods themselves. The basic problem was the
introduction of dynamic change into society, which put heavy
stress on inherited standards of justice. The powerful could
more easily exploit the poor and had obvious incentives to do
so. A growing population, moreover, pressed one man against
another ever more closely and in ever more complex ways.
Murder, for instance, not merely affected small, geographically
separated blood groups with an urge for revenge, but now
imbued a whole interlocked population with a sense of pollution. The re-evaluation of the claims of men on each other and
the provision of means for safeguarding justice were, of course,
earthly matters, and as such will be examined when we come to
the *polis* itself. Yet the success of human ordinances in preserv-

---

[9] Guthrie, *Greeks and Their Gods*, 46–
47; R. C. Bosanquet, "The Palaikastro
Hymn of the Kouretes," *BSA*, XV
(1908–09), 339–56.

[1] Note the emphasis in *Hymn to Demeter* 296 on the joint labor in the
construction of the Eleusinian shrine.

ing the unity of the community depended squarely upon a firm divine foundation.

As men wrestled with this problem, they could develop new gods or elaborate old divinities as specific defenders of right conduct. The increasing role of Apollo as patron of Greek ethics has perhaps been exaggerated for the seventh century, but cannot be entirely dismissed; beside him appeared Themis (Right), Dike (Justice), the Erinyes (Avengers), and other heavenly hosts. These grew in popular credit especially in the next century as public control was increasingly exercised over blood feuds. Another mode was the evolution of mystic rites of expiation; after the failure of Cylon to seize control of Athens, the city expelled the noble clan of the Alcmeonids which was directly responsible for his murder and secured a noted Cretan purifier, Epimenides, to cleanse it of its guilt.[2]

Specific religious machinery of this type as well as the ethical magnification of individualized divine forces could be useful only if the general principle were established that the gods preferred justice and punished the wicked. The way thereto was paved in the epic. "Verily," said the shepherd Eumaeus in the *Odyssey*, "the blessed gods love not reckless deeds, but they honour justice and the righteous deeds of men." In similar vein the *Iliad* put even more bluntly the wrath of Zeus "at men who by violence give crooked judgments in the *agora* and drive out justice, not regarding the vengeance of the gods." For vengeance, though slow at times, was sure, and men paid a heavy price in the end, both themselves, their women, and their children.[3]

Though the theme was clear enough in epic days, there was then still "no systematic morality which the gods sustain."[4] This

[2] Kathleen Freeman, *Companion to the Pre-Socratic Philosophers* (Oxford, 1953), 27–29, gives the evidence; on the need for purification, cf. Dodds, *Greeks and the Irrational*, 35–36, 44.
[3] *Odyssey* XIV. 83–84; *Iliad* XVI. 384 ff. and IV. 158 ff. Cf. *Odyssey* VIII. 575–76, XIII. 214; *Iliad* IX. 497 ff., XIX. 258 ff. The reverse of the die is prosperity in the land of the

good ruler, *Odyssey* XIX. 109–14. I see no justification for the common assumption that such passages must be later interpolations.
[4] A happy phrase of Whitman, *Homer and the Heroic Tradition*, 243. For typical examples of concern with justice down to 650, see Hesiod, *Works and Days* 248–51, 220 ff., 261 ff.; *Theogony* 88–90; Archilochus, fragments 37, 171.

came amid the social and political stresses of the following age of revolution. From Hesiod at the beginning of the seventh century through Archilochus to Solon at its end the problem of justice mounted to be a dominant concern of the gods. As men followed the paths of justice or injustice, so were they rewarded by Zeus in visible, physical terms: in peace, prosperity, health; or in plague, famine, and toppling walls. The theme is so common, so simply put, that it needs no quotation; but its very reiteration, almost fiercely vehement, suggests that poets felt the gravity of the situation.

The one aspect of early Greek ethics which does require emphasis is its conjunction of individual and communal sanctions, of which the latter bulked much the larger. Individual responsibility and individual punishment were only beginning to receive recognition at this time. In the epic man was generally not responsible for his acts, save in a remarkable speech by Phoenix, which contains virtually unique concepts of prayer, transgression, and the freedom of man's choice at the price of divine punishment or reward.[5] During the following century the basic structure of individual Hellenic ethics was first consciously refined out of its primeval matrix on lines which Greek philosophical speculation was to test and burnish for centuries to come. Historic Greek morality stressed on the one side man's awareness of his limitations—"savor your successes, mourn your reverses, but not too much," said Archilochus—and on the other his ability to act, if only he observed "the rhythm which governs the life of man." In its famous formulations, which were fostered by the Delphic oracle, Know Thyself and Nothing Too Much, this pattern sank into the blood of Greece in the seventh century.

Beside this individual aspect stood the new emphasis on communal justice which was embodied in the city-state form

[5] *Iliad* IX. 497 ff.; Page, *History and the Homeric Iliad*, 300–03. Most treatments of Greek ethics stress later developments and more individualized aspects. For the situation in the seventh century, see below, Chap. 10, n. 6 (p. 343); Gerlach, 'Ανὴρ 'αγαθός, 50–58; Frederic Will, "Solon's Consciousness of Himself," *Transactions of the American Philological Association*, LXXXIX (1958), 301–11.

of political organization. If the individualistic attitude of un-tempered, willful passion was never entirely to die in Greek life, it certainly was not the main source of ethical strength from the seventh century onward. The human being was driven to moral-ity by communal pressure rather than by private fears in his own heart before the awful eye of the divine; and his rewards were conceived far more in physical than in spiritual terms.[6]

A strong sense of communal unity, in sum, continued into the age of revolution and was refined in the new religious and ethical structure of historic Greece. The hallmark of the Greek intellectual temper which has already been noted was a happy blend of individual freedom with group loyalty, forces which were balanced against each other in a basically solid yet dynamic system. While the aristocrats sought, and largely ob-tained, a position of pre-eminence, they were not unchecked. Not for the Greek was the pattern of the overweening, lawless Cyclopes of the *Odyssey,* who did not plant or plow, who did not meet in assemblies or council, "but each gave law to his children and wives, and they do not reck of another." [7]

---

[6] Snell, *Discovery of the Mind,* 156–62; efforts toward individualization in this field came from Solon on.

[7] *Odyssey* IX. 106–215. This is one of the most important passages in the epic on actual political beliefs.

CHAPTER 10

THE RISE OF THE CITY-STATE

THE POLITICAL MASTERPIECE of the age of revolution was the creation of the Greek *polis* or city-state. In Mesopotamia city-states had an ancient history, though by 750 they were mostly swallowed up in empire. Along the eastern coast of the Mediterranean small, city-centered units had long been known and were at this time still ruled by Syrian and Phoenician kings. The Aegean world rose from tribal to city-state level only in the century 750–650, largely in response to its own needs, and in doing so eliminated its monarchs.

The *polis* was more than a political solution of political problems. It emerged out of earlier tribal society as an alternative to the principle of personal leadership, but the success of the Greeks in creating so marvelous an institution can be understood only when we appreciate the intellectual upheaval of the era. If men were to enter upon political revolution, the way was paved and the course of development was directed by the parallel shifts in artistic and literary attitudes, by the changes in class relationships and other social tensions, and by the wide range of religious evolution.

The details of political alterations and history are often obscure. Treaties, laws, and other political documents did not appear until virtually 600 B.C.; no contemporary historian chronicled the steps by which the Greeks passed from tribal organization under *basileis* to republican, consciously organized city-states. As commonly described in modern accounts, the *polis* is seen in the democratic practice of Athens from Pericles to Demosthenes and in the theory of Plato and Aristotle—i.e., after three centuries of development; and students are often blinded by generalizations resting on democratic prejudices or Marxist dogma. In its beginning stages of the late eighth and early seventh centuries the *polis* was a simple structure; but we can see the main forces in its emergence if we keep our view wide. The important innovation was not in physical structures nor in machinery of government but in civic spirit.

The enduring effects of the new political world can hardly be overestimated. Once established, the *polis* protected, accelerated, and withal confined the genius of Greek thinkers and artists like a hothouse; Aristotle eventually was to define man as "an animal of the *polis*." [1] The spiritual qualities of the institution will strike a resident of the modern Western world as more akin to his own views than were the ancestral bases of Oriental kingship. In the world of the *polis* there was a local exclusiveness, an effort to translate political independence into economic autarchy, an unreasoning and sensitive pride of the citizens of each state; and internal rivalry could become so intense that factions would traffic with foreign foes for domestic advantage. Yet the city-state also embodied—and made conscious for the first time—truly noble concepts of communal justice. The free citizen had political value in himself as a holder of rights and responsibilities.

THE DECLINE OF PERSONAL LEADERSHIP

How MAGNIFICENT an achievement was the rise of the *polis* is rarely appreciated; for it was not the inevitable solution to the stresses of the age of revolution. When men searched for a more developed political structure, they could have taken either of two paths. The intensification of collective action and the creation of machinery for its expression was one possibility; this was generally preferred. But there was another exit, that of

[1] Aristotle, *Politics* I. 1. 9. 1253a;   (Boston, 1913), chap. 1.
W. S. Ferguson, *Greek Imperialism*

personal leadership. "To obey the will of one man," said the later philosopher Heraclitus, "is also Law." [2]

In the ancient Orient the god-supported or divine king was almost always the dominant political focus. Even the Hebrews had not been able to avoid this mode of unification, albeit they came to it in the days of Saul and David with justified misgivings and never fully yielded themselves to its requirements. The institution of powerful kingship lay in the Greek background, for the *wanakes* of the Mycenaean age had tried to model their bureaucratic economies on the Oriental prototype. So developed a system did not survive the chaos of the Dorian invasion, but the basic principle of personal leadership continued in the form of the *basileus* or chief over the tribal warriors. During the Dark ages collective leadership seems to have been practiced in some areas; but generally, if the epics do not mislead us, each people looked to one single *basileus* and sought his heir within his clan.

During the age of revolution the *basileis* essentially disappeared as political nuclei. In all Greek history this is one of the most mystifying vanishing-acts, and its puzzling aspects do not decrease when one turns to modern treatments of Greek political evolution. These accounts commonly present the *basileis* in ruddy health in the Homeric world; then, in a page or two, the kings abruptly decline—Alcinous, it is pointed out, was only *primus inter pares* in the Phaeacian fairyland—and next they are dead and buried, whisked away impatiently so that the collective unity of the city-state may take up the entire political stage.[3] The realities of the evolution are much more complex and illuminating.

To understand what was taking place, we must begin not with the aristocracy, postulated as self-confident, consolidated, and dominant, but with the *basileus* himself. In the earlier years of the eighth century, when Greek society began to accelerate its development, the range of the *basileus*' power may even have

[2] Fragment 33 (context unknown, and and not necessarily political).
[3] One example, Glotz, *Greek City*, 38–46, 57–62, will suffice. Alcinous: *Odyssey* VIII. 390–91. Those who cite this passage often fail to note that in XI. 353 (cf. VI. 197) Alcinous asserts that the sending of Odysseus rests "most of all with me; for mine is the control in the land."

tended to increase, just as the incipient national states of early modern Europe turned toward their kings as a prime vehicle for improving political unity. Hints in the *Iliad* suffice at least to warn us against throwing entirely out of court the possibility that the Greeks experimented along this line. On the divine plane, which must reflect human realities, Father Zeus assumed in the crystallizing pantheon a role of master against whom the other gods could speak only to a limited degree. On earth the Zeus-born *basileis* vaunted their pre-eminence in terms which need not be taken as pure reminiscence of Mycenaean days, and Odysseus once in the *Iliad* (II. 204) delivers an interesting argument on the necessity for having only *one* chieftain.

Most significant of all was the role of the *basileus* on the battlefield, the arena where we see him most clearly in the *Iliad*. Superficially, epic battle scenes were cast in terms of individual duels for artistic purposes, just as the conflicts were set between heroes in the medieval *chansons de geste*. Homer and medieval bards alike emphasized the ideal of personal bravery as the motivating force to battle and would have us believe that their heroes were independent of outside control.[4] Poets, however, are not field commanders. Military systems in reality must always be built to compensate for and to counter the human instincts of fear and self-preservation. Neither cowardice nor the danger implicit in individual disregard of commands was an unknown phenomenon in the epic world. In Homer, as in the *chansons de geste,* we can see below the artistic requirements to detect that even heroes went into battle in serried ranks and that the chieftains exerted strong discipline to reinforce that scorn of skulkers and violation of orders which was demanded by the military code of the warriors. In an era when abstract ties did not yet exist and conscious self-motivation was rudi-

---

[4] J. P. Verbruggen, *Die Krijgskunst in West-Europe in de Middeleuwen, IXe tot Begin XIVe Eeuw* (Brussels, 1954), affords significant parallels in this matter. Serried ranks: *Iliad* III. 77, IV. 281–82, IV. 297–305, IV. 427–31, V. 93, VII. 61–62, VII. 141, XI. 343, XI. 593–94, XIII. 125 ff., XVI. 214 ff., XVII. 354 ff., XX. 362. These are not interpolations. Punishment: *Iliad* II. 357–59, 391–93. That cowardice was well known is shown in IV. 299–300, XIII. 278–83.

mentary, personal loyalty and obedience to the chieftain were imperative. We must begin the political evolution of the eighth century with the concept that "it is no common honor which belongs to a sceptred king, to whom Zeus gives dignity." [5]

Thereafter, as domestic problems became more complex, the place of personal leadership enjoyed further sources of support. The cult of heroes enshrined the principle in religious terms, and the later tyrants of historic times, who celebrated the beneficent deeds of Heracles or Theseus in art and cult, could draw on the strengths of this pattern of power no less for their own benefit than for purposes of emphasizing patriotic unity. Even more obvious is the need for leaders in the great wave of colonization. The transplantation of small bands of Greeks from the homeland to new abodes was so staggeringly difficult that colonists seem always to have placed themselves under the leadership of forceful men. The earliest colonies apparently were directed by actual *basileis,* but, whatever the title of a founding father, he was virtually worshipped through the later history of a colony as its *oikistes.*[6]

To place the principle of personal leadership in later times in a proper focus, we must keep these early manifestations always in mind as illustrations of its ancient lineage. Here and there the *basileis* kept at least part of their powers—in Sparta, Argos, Thessaly, and elsewhere. Generally they vanished as effective forces, but even city-states could turn back to individual rule and elevate "tyrants." The term *tyrannos* itself is of uncertain origin, and designates a ruler who gained power not, like a *basileus,* by inheritance but through his own resources.[7]

---

[5] *Iliad* I. 278–79.

[6] The doubts of Dunbabin, *Western Greeks,* 93–94, concerning the *basileus* Pollis of Syracuse do not seem well grounded. If Archias were *oikistes,* he may also have been *basileus.* The official decree on the founding of Brea made its leader "autocrat," Marcus N. Tod, *Greek Historical Inscriptions,* I (2d ed.; Oxford, 1946), 44 ll. 8–9.

[7] Mazzarino, *Fra Oriente e Occidente,* 191, 199–202, 222 ff., is full; further bibliography may be found in Hei-

chelheim, *Ancient Economic History,* I, 526. A. Cony, *Revue hittite et asianique,* VII (1945–46), 12, advanced a Semitic origin for the word; though Dunbabin, *Greeks and Their Eastern Neighbours,* 58, approves it, further proof seems desirable. Does Archilochus, incidentally, call Gyges a tyrant (fragment 15) or merely reject tyranny for his carpenter spokesman? He apparently uses the term for a Greek in fragment 35.

The basic spirit, nevertheless, of the tyrants of Corinth and other states, who fall mostly after 650 B.C., was not an importation, nor was it as much a violation of Greek political theory as fourth-century political scientists suggested. As one examines the practical workings of aristocratic factionalism, it may even be proper to conclude that this rivalry always tended in the direction of producing one-man rule, either when the leader of one faction gained the mastery for which he strove or when the non-aristocratic elements (and many nobles, too) grew weary of the fray and yielded themselves to a leader lest chaos ensue.[8]

Yet Greek political practice rarely came to this conclusion, and the *basileis* themselves did fade away during the age of revolution. The myth of the abdication of king Codrus at Athens, though dated much earlier in tradition, might suggest a rather sudden end; not all rulers may have voluntarily placed their heads on the chopping block. Yet the general lack of myths along this line cannot be accidental.[9] By and large the *basileis* quietly disappeared as effective leaders of the community. Like much else in the age of revolution, the change was probably a swift process, but it took place before true history began. The end result, which alone we can see, was, first, the replacement of the hereditary, lifetime leader by a major public official (*prytanis, archon,* etc.), who was elected for one year, often at the outset from one clan. Secondly, specific powers once held in a single pair of hands were parceled out, as to a warleader (*polemarchos*) and a chief priest (*basileus*). Thirdly, the power of the council (*boule*) was greatly enlarged.[1]

The new system did not by any means weaken executive authority, for many powers which previously had been widely distributed among tribal and clan officials were now being

---

[8] Hasebroek, *Griechische Wirtschafts- und Gesellschaftsgeschichte,* 172, and Heuss, *Antike und Abendland,* II (1946), 45–48, emphasize the effect of noble rivalry in throwing up tyrants.

[9] The argument that Ionia led the way (Cassola, *La Ionia nel mondo miceneo,* 33–34; Beloch, *Griechische Geschichte,* I, 211–18) is not solid; cf. R. M. Cook, *JHS,* LXVI (1946), 87.

[1] Corinth: Will, *Korinthiaka,* 295–306. Crete: Willetts, *Ancient Crete,* 254–55 and passim. Athens: Hignett, *Athenian Constitution,* 38–46. I cannot feel that the tradition of the Atthidographers, according to which the kings of Athens declined from life tenure to ten-year terms and then to election for one year, represents more than a schematic reconstruction of the unknown.

grasped by the state and concentrated in the hands of a few officers. But in the change the principle of individual, essentially irresponsible leadership was definitely rejected. The founders of colonies, however powerful at the moment and however much revered later, established states which were *poleis*. Tyrants were, in the last analysis, considered irregular and could not found enduring dynasties. The decision against one-man rule is the more spectacular when one recalls that even among some Greeks—those of Cyprus especially—the place of the kings was enlarged in steadily greater magnificence during the seventh century.[2] But off in the Aegean the main body of the Hellenes took decisive steps during the century 750–650 toward creating the ideal of the free citizen who exercised his powers within the *polis*.

THE CAUSES OF THE DECLINE

THE REASONS for the disappearance of the *basileis* are, in reverse, essentially the causes of the rise of the city-state, but the process may be clearer if we consider it first as a change from the older ways. Fundamentally, the problem from the point of view of the *basileis* was the weakness of their inherited position. Zeus, though master on Olympus, was subject to the dimly felt laws of fate,[3] and earthly *basileis* were checked by the dead weight of age-old tradition and tribal custom. In early modern Europe, when social and economic changes began to offer to the monarchs the possibility of real power, they could appeal for a theoretical justification to the developed, autocratic political system of the Roman Empire, knowledge of which was preserved across centuries of localism by the Catholic Church, by Roman law, and by the survival of writing. In early Greece,

---

[2] Gjerstad, *Swedish Cyprus Expedition*, IV. 2, 449–58.
[3] E. Leitzke, *Moira und Gottheit im alten homerischen Epos* (Göttingen, 1930); W. C. Greene, *Moira, Fate, Good, and Evil in Greek Thought* (Cambridge, Mass., 1944).

Oriental-type monarchy had been shallow-rooted and survived the Mycenaean collapse only by means of the epic tradition, a dim recollection of no practical effect.

As developments accelerated, the *basileis* could not harness the main forces which might have aided them in assuming the central direction of society; neither could they withstand the positive threats to their survival. Politically the Aegean was still in the seventh century so isolated, and the pressures of its peoples on one another were still so spasmodic, that the Greeks could afford the luxury of dispensing with strong personal leadership if they found a satisfactory alternative method of organizing society.

The inherited weaknesses of the tribal chieftains who succeeded the Mycenaean kings have already been noted in Chapter 4. In the abysmal collapse of the Aegean world which marked the early Dark ages, the centralized Mycenaean palace economies and royal administrations disappeared, and the *basileis* were potent only as leaders of the warriors. In religion and in justice they had some not inconsiderable functions, but beside them stood agents of the community as a whole to act as priests or judges; clans, tribes, and other social units had each their functions, safeguarded by custom; financially the royal storehouse was nourished chiefly from the *basileus'* own lands. This latter weakness may have been a main Achilles' heel for the rulers of the eighth century, as the expenses of state and cult rose and luxury spread its temptations. In a similar situation in early modern Europe the far more powerful kings of the new national states, who could impose taxes of some types, had difficulty enough in keeping their exchequers semi-solvent. When the Greek communities turned to erecting temples or needed to improve guarantees of justice, the *basileis* were too feeble to step in as forceful masters and executors of the common will; temples in particular developed their own independent treasuries.

In the basic role as leaders in war, the *basileis* were crippled by the decline in casual border warfare and by the tendency of the community to choose special leaders for the far more serious struggles over bits of farmland.[4] These changes were connected with a major military reorganization which took place in the late eighth century, the elaboration of the phalanx. While bodies of serried infantry had existed in epic days, now they were more consciously and firmly organized, and each warrior or hoplite was equipped with helmet, corselet, greaves, small round shield, thrusting spear, and stabbing sword. The armor itself was mainly of bronze, the weapons of iron; both owed much to Assyrian innovations.

The appearance of these items in the Aegean world can be dated fairly surely to the closing years of the eighth century. A helmet and breastplate of hoplite armor were buried in the grave of an Argive warrior in the decades just before 700; Late Geometric vases begin to show the hoplite shield with its blazon occasionally, alongside heroic equipment; and on such Proto-corinthian pieces as the Chigi vase the phalanx marches firmly into action.[5]

Although the technical advances permit us to date the military reorganization, its basic prerequisite was psychological. Those commoners who, interlaced with nobles, manned the infantry blocks felt able to withstand the attacks of individual heroic warriors either on foot or in chariots. This ability, in turn, required that men have a sense of their own individual

[4] Arms and armor appear less frequently both in the Kerameikos graves of the eighth century (Kübler, *Kerameikos*, V. 1, 198–200) and in those of Fortetsa (Brock, *Fortetsa*, 200–01); cf. the limited evidence of *Tiryns*, I, 135. But does this imply a reduction in warfare, as Tritsch, *Klio*, XXII (1928), 61, suggests? Grave customs were changing; military equipment was more complex; and the scenes of warfare on the Dipylon vases are not fantasy or myth. See Kübler, *Kerameikos*, VI. 1, 84 n. 13.

Phalanx: H. L. Lorimer, "The Hoplite Phalanx," *BSA*, XLII (1947), 76–138, on the artistic evidence for equipment; Webster, *From Mycenae to Homer*, 212–20. One must remember that round shield, corselet, and even greaves were known in Mycenaean times, Ventris and Chadwick, *Documents*, 292–300, 375–81; *AJA*, LVIII (1954), 235. M. P. Nilsson, "Die Hoplitentaktik und das Staatswesen," *Opus. sel.*, II (Lund, 1952), 897–907, is rather slight; Hasebroek, *Griechische Wirtschafts- und Gesellschaftsgeschichte*, 158–59, 164, notes that other than technical factors were at work. F. E. Adcock, *The Greek and Macedonian Art of War* (Berkeley, 1957), 3–6, is much too brief.

[5] Paul Courbin, "Une tombe géométrique d'Argos," *BCH*, LXXXI (1957), 322–86; Benaki 559, before 725 B.C. (Webster, *From Mycenae to Homer*, 214); Payne, *Protokorinthische Vasenmalerei*, pl. 27–29 (Chigi vase).

(a) Clay head from shrine of Artemis Orthia, Sparta, in Protodedalic style. Photograph from BSA, XXXIII (1932–3), pl. VII. 5.
(b) Marble statue dedicated by Nikandre at Delos, the earliest large-scale work in stone (National Museum, Athens). Photograph courtesy Friedrich Hewicker.

PLATE 21 · *Triumph of the New Sculpture*

PLATE 22 · *Fear and Tension*

importance and yet be bound together strongly enough so that they could rely one on another in the phalanx mass.

The logical implications of this development lead us far into the heart of political change during the century 750–650. In modern times a similar spiritual revolution coincided with great technological developments, first in the long bow and then in gunpowder, to permit the rise of a solid infantry after centuries of noble mastery on horseback; but here the results benefited rather than crippled the kings of the period. They alone could afford the relatively complicated arms factories, could provide the accompanying cannon, and could pay mercenary foot-soldiers such as the Swiss or German *landsknechts* for long-protracted campaigns. In early Greece wars were usually brief and were fought close to home, and the new equipment was simpler than the old. Each man of the phalanx required, not two-horse chariots, but a basic set of arms and armor which any smith could make and which even small landowners could pay for.

While Greek armies continued to need leaders,[6] the main role of commanders in succeeding centuries was to act as an agent of the community in carrying out sacrifices to the gods and heroes who would bring victory, to lead the forces of the city-state to the battlefield, and to maintain there a discipline which rested mainly on a collective will. Such leaders could be changed frequently. Their main qualities must be, not so much tactical or strategic skills—which had little place in the straightforward battles on level ground—but rather popular respect and trust. Kingship, in sum, was not needed so long as foreign threats remained minor. By the time external pressure grew critical, in the form of the onrolling Persian Empire, the city-states had become solid enough to withstand the attack.

The appearance of the phalanx is not a purely aristocratic phenomenon.[7] Nobles had been quite at home in the old system,

---

[6] Consider the emphasis on the leader in Tyrtaeus, fragments 1, 5.

[7] The comparison of the hoplite class to that of knights in thirteenth-century England, made by A. Andrewes, *Probouleusis: Sparta's Contribution to the Technique of Government* (Oxford, 1954), 12, will not quite do. Any student of early Greek warfare should consider carefully the changes in early modern times; cf. C. W. C. Oman, *A History of the Art of War: The Middle Ages* (London, 1898); F. L. Taylor, *The Art of War in Italy,*

for they could afford chariots and horses and delighted, as we have seen, in the depiction of both. The aristocrats, again, in any state were too few to furnish the manpower needed for a phalanx and, insofar as they shared a truly aristocratic outlook, were not likely to have favored the evolution of a military structure in which the individual had to sink himself in the mass. The new tactical formations of the age of revolution were manned mainly by the independent peasants, and in that necessity lies one basic reason for the preservation of their independence.[8] Or, to put the matter more correctly, greater and lesser landowners stood together in the files of the phalanx, as they stood together against the domination of personal leadership in the political sphere.

For the disappearance of the *basileis* does owe much to the quality of the upper classes of the Greek states. The aristocrats of that era, we may assume, resembled the nobles of early modern Europe and opposed *as a group* any tendencies for strong individuals to seize mastery. While the feudal lords usually failed in efforts to curb the monarchs of England and France, the nobles of early archaic Greece succeeded in dragging down the *basileis* to their level. The reason for their success lies chiefly in the fact that the Greek upper classes were not sharply separated from the commoners. They took the lead in creating and in staffing the new executive machinery and in so doing could count on the support of the rest of society; but in recompense the aristocrats had to yield to their fellow citizens real guarantees of just treatment. Wherever those guarantees failed, tyrants and other individual leaders reappeared.

1484–1529 (Cambridge, 1921); Theodore Ropp, *War in the Modern World* (Durham, N.C., 1959), 3–9.

[8] From the military point of view the fact that certain areas depressed the peasants into serfdom can be explained. Thessaly relied largely on cavalry; Crete was populated so thickly that a phalanx could be drawn simply from the warrior bands; and Sparta conquered enough outside territories to support its phalanx.

THE EMERGENCE OF THE CITY-STATE

To THE GREEK WORLD in the late eighth and early seventh centuries the benefits of personal leadership seemed less than those which could be derived from a consolidation of communal unity. Where the title of *basileus* survived, it was mainly to designate a public religious official; certain ancient rites, men felt, the gods would accept only from a mortal so entitled.[9] The alternative solution was the *polis*.

Our main interest in the new political form must be directed to its physical and spiritual marks, which greatly affected the subsequent course of Greek civilization; but first of all the place and date of origin of the *polis* need clarification. Quite commonly, but rather oddly, modern opinion has sought the home of the city-state in Ionia.[1] It is, thus, argued that this district first developed true cities in the economic sense of commercial and industrial centers, was closer to the more advanced Orient, and was under greater pressure from the neighboring kings first of Phrygia, then of Lydia.

These factors are either untrue or irrelevant. The crystallization of the city-state had nothing directly to do with the progress of commerce, and in any case Ionia cannot be shown to have produced new economic centers more swiftly than did the area about the Isthmus of Corinth. While the Greeks, again, were not the first to invent the concept of the city-state, we cannot say that they simply took over an Oriental political form; as in all other fields, so politically the Aegean world was far more distinct from the East in 650 than in 750. And, finally, the outside pressures which did bear on Ionia, one might judge, would have inclined the Greeks of that region to cling to personal leadership.

There is no valid reason to doubt that the geographical

[9] Nilsson, *Minoan-Mycenaean Religion*, 485–86.

[1] Pro (for example), de Sanctis, *Storia dei Greci*, I, 176–77, 274–75 (with other arguments); Victor Ehrenberg, *Der Staat der Griechen,* I (Leipzig, 1957), 8, 16. Contra, Hanfmann, *HSCP,* LXI (1953), 15–19; R. M. Cook, *JHS,* LXVI (1946), 87–88; Mazzarino, *Fra Oriente e Occidente,* 234, 237.

cradle of the city-state was the area which led in intellectual advances—the southeastern districts of Greece proper. The earliest wars in which we can witness city-states at rivalry occurred here; the parent states of the first colonies, which were themselves organized as *poleis,* lay in this region. Thence the new style of organization spread outward in the seventh and sixth centuries, but not all of the men who spoke Greek and shared the main attributes of Greek culture were so grouped even at the beginning of the classic era; some still lived in tribal *ethnoi.*

Another common problem is the effort to find gradual, logical stages through which the tribal state evolved into the *polis.* Such stages simply do not exist in our evidence, and for a very good reason. Political as well as intellectual progress was not a matter of slow advance at this time. The *polis* sprang from the old tribal state, but its appearance was almost surely as sudden a step as was the swift refinement of inherited resources in every field of Greek civilization.

Down through Hesiod the *polis* is lacking. In the epic, assemblies and councils meet as tokens of communal unity, but beside them are the Zeus-born kings; the ties of personal loyalty in the epics are quite incompatible with the spirit of the city-state. The *Odyssey* perhaps points more to the future than does the *Iliad.* In the younger epic an interesting distinction appears between "public" and "private," and the hero of its tale was a man who learned the mind "both of those who are cruel and wild and unjust and of those who love strangers and fear the gods in their thoughts." [2] Though civic justice is not far removed from this concept, not even in the next author, Hesiod, had the great step been taken toward conscious public incarnation of the principle. Despite Hesiod's driving insistence that justice was a communal problem, the anxious poet was not sure that the community would base itself on this spirit; the bribe-

[2] Public vs. private: *Odyssey* IV. 314, cf. III. 82, II. 32, II. 44, XX. 264–65. Variety of states: *Odyssey* VIII. 575–76. Note also the choice of a war-leader by the people of Crete to serve beside the king (*Odyssey* XIII. 265); the argument from Phaeacia is much weaker (see above, n. 3 [p. 326]).

Hesiod: Fränkel, *Dichtung und Philosophie,* 180–81; Victor Ehrenberg, *Aspects of the Ancient World* (Oxford, 1946), 71; and many others. On the meaning of the Hesiodic *basileis,* cf. Calhoun, *CP,* XXIX (1934), 312.

swallowing *basileis* still dominated society. In interpreting this famous term, incidentally, we have no justification for thinking that the Hesiodic *basileis* were simple aristocrats; nobles might be *agathoi*, but they never called themselves *basileis*.

Then suddenly, and in Hesiod's own age, the basic qualities of the city-state emerged.[3] The most direct signpost to dating this event is the military reorganization of the late eighth century, for the spiritual strengths implicit in the hoplite phalanx must be connected with the reinforcement of civic unity in the *polis*. The wave of colonization, which began about the same time, also took place in terms of city-states; the Greek outpouring otherwise could scarcely have been so successful. Most suggestive of all is the indirect clue afforded by the sudden increase of tempo in artistic and intellectual change at this time. The city-state is the political reflection of the new Hellenic outlook. If Hesiod failed to show this shift clearly, we must remember how narrowly he stood, as a poet and as a thinker, within the age of revolution; and unfortunately there is no further literary evidence until the next generation. In the verse of Archilochus the patriotic attachment of the citizen of the *polis* manifests itself. By then, too, the first remodeling of political machinery to accommodate the new spirit was under way.

From that point onward the *polis* passed through consecutive stages of evolution down to the fully developed structure of democratic Athens; political theory progressed from Solon's very specific examination of problems to the abstract analysis of Platonic and Aristotelian treatises; and political history became ever more continuous. In its first stages the Greek city-state differed from the political systems of the fifth and fourth centuries very much as Orientalizing pottery differed from the Attic red-figure masterpieces, or as the first stone statue dedicated by Nikandre preceded the serene classic triumphs of the Olympia pediments. The variation, that is to say, is basically one of degree, not of type. If we turn backward, however, rather

[3] This is about a century later than the date advanced by Victor Ehrenberg, "When Did the Polis Rise?" *JHS*, LVII (1937), 147–59; but much earlier than that argued by Helmut Berve, "Fürstliche Herren zur Zeit der Perserkriege," *Die Antike*, XII (1936), 1–28, and *Griechische Geschichte*, I (Freiburg i. B., 1931), 176.

than forward, and compare the *polis* to its source in the tribal state, the change must appear as one of virtual revolution. To establish this significant point, we may look briefly at the qualities of the city-state.[4]

Physically the *polis* was a definite geographical unit, in which public activities were concentrated at one point, the *asty* or *polis* proper. Herein the city-state seems to have differed from the earlier tribal states principally in its citizens' conscious awareness of clear boundaries and, as a companion factor, in the crystallization of the new units on a tiny scale.

During the Dark ages fairly large districts, such as Attica-Boeotia and Corinthia-Argolid (see Map No. 2), had shared cultural patterns, had worshipped together in amphictionies or religious leagues, and probably had had some vague sense of political kinship.[5] Beside these ties new international sanctuaries arose during the age of revolution, and the priests especially of Delphi perhaps sought to promote international harmony. The fact that the Greeks revered such common gods as Zeus and Athena and met in common games and sacrifices has nevertheless often been overemphasized. Culturally such bonds were important; politically they meant no more than has the acceptance of Christianity by modern Europe. As the city-state rose, external ties weakened markedly.

The smallness of the archaic and classical *poleis*, which always impresses modern citizens of vast territorial states, was to some extent a reflection of the geographical fragmentation of Greece; but this deterministic explanation is only a minor part of the phenomenon.[6] The *poleis* flourished most thickly along the

[4] In what follows, I have drawn on my essay "The Early Greek City-State," *La Parola del Passato*, XII (1957), 97–108. Ehrenberg, *Der Staat der Griechen*, I, gives a recent, annotated bibliography; like the manuals on Greek political institutions, he is concerned with the classic form.

[5] Corinthia-Argolid: Payne, *Perachora*, I, 21–22, who may go too far in his suggestions of political unity; Pheidon's state certainly lost much of its control over Sicyon, Epidaurus, and perhaps Corinth (Andrewes, *Greek Tyrants*, 49). Boeotia-Attica: Young, *Late Geometric Graves*, 104–05, 129–30, 159–61, 218.

[6] Geographical influence is better sought in the mildness of the Mediterranean climate, which permitted outdoor life through the year. Cf. Myres, *Geographical History in Greek Lands;* Ernst Kirsten, *Die griechische Polis als historisch-geographisches Problem des Mittelmeerraumes* (Bonn, 1956).

seaboard, not in rugged inland districts, and their boundaries only partially marched with natural topographical divisions. The state of Athens had enough attractive power to draw into it such geographically distinct areas as Eleusis, Oropos, Eleutherae, and Salamis, which might elsewhere have remained independent. The broad, open plain of Boeotia, on the other hand, was divided into several states, which paid their respects to a geographical and earlier tribal unity by remaining grouped in a super-state league. If the *polis* usually measured its land in the tens or hundreds of square miles and its citizens at most in the thousands, the principal reason is the fact that it emerged in a predominantly agricultural era. Once established, the city-state quickly developed internal, spiritual qualities which tended to limit the possibilities of territorial growth.

The other physical mark of this political atom was its nucleus, the *polis* proper or *asty*. When we distinguish a tribal people from a city-state, however, the modern implications of the term "city" must not mislead us. Each area had commonly had a political, military, and religious rallying point, at or below which men dwelt in an *asty*. On the emergence of the city-state the focal point gained a more conscious significance. Political functions, such as the administration of justice, slowly were transferred from local social units to central courts. Clearer evidence exists for a tendency to concentrate the major religious rites of the state. Local cults, for example, were moved to Athens proper from the outlying areas added in the eighth and seventh centuries; quite generally communal resources were concentrated upon the central temples of the state gods.[7] In the more favored regions the towns served increasingly as economic centers which attracted potters, smiths, and traders. But no specific economic change *necessarily* occurred in an *asty*, either at the time when a city-state arose or as a precondition for its appear-

---

[7] Nilsson, *Cults and Politics*, 27–41; cf. Hignett, *Athenian Constitution*, 34–38. Note, however, that temples do appear elsewhere than in the state centers.

Towns as economic and social centers: *Odyssey* VI. 3–10, 259–69, 291–94; VII. 129–30; VIII. 5–8 (on the Phaeacian town). Cf. the simile of *Iliad* XV. 680–82; and note the growth of eighth-century Argos as argued by S. Charitonidis, *BCH*, LXXVIII (1954), 422–23.

ance. The economic background of the era, it can never be over-emphasized, was agricultural, not commercial and industrial.

The archaeological evidence shows clearly that in the age of revolution the central points were nothing more than large agricultural villages below a fortress-refuge. At Athens several villages lay about the Acropolis; their inhabitants buried the dead in cemeteries in intervening open country, which eventually was swallowed by the classic city. The late, casual growth of urban centers is reflected in the lack of orderly street-planning, which remained apparent in the old cities far down into historic times. Unlike Oriental cities, the Greek hamlets were not arranged tidily about palace or temple; the acropolis was only partially a focus; and the *agora* or political center was but slowly distinguished and embellished. Nor were these towns encased and given form by walls. Athens did not have a city wall until the days of Pisistratus, if then. Few places needed or could afford such extensive outpouring of energies, as distinct from small hilltop refuges, until the late sixth or fifth centuries. Then interstate warfare grew more intensive, urban economies both required better protection and could finance it, and city and country tended to become distinct.[8]

The Hellenic city-state could exist without leaving any marked physical remains at its nucleus; Thucydides' comment (I. 10) on the inconspicuous nature of Sparta, "a straggling village like the ancient towns of Hellas," puts the matter well. The rise of the *polis* was not intimately bound with processes of urbanization, and the modern tendency to compare the Greek *polis* with medieval cities, clustered tightly about castle and cathedral, is misleading in every major respect.[9] To say this is not

[8] Roland Martin, *L'Urbanisme dans la Grèce antique* (Paris, 1956), 189–92; Robert L. Scranton, *Greek Walls* (Cambridge, Mass., 1941); I. T. Hill, *The Ancient City of Athens* (London, 1953), 5; see above, Chap. 7, n. 1 (p. 252).

Agora: W. A. McDonald, *The Political Meeting Places of the Greeks* (Baltimore, 1943); Martin, *Recherches sur l'Agora grecque;* among the many publications concerning the Athenian Agora so far, a brief guide is that of Homer A. Thompson, "The Athenian Agora," *Acta congressu Madvigiani,* I (Copenhagen, 1958), 341–52. See also R. E. Wycherley, *How the Greeks Built Cities* (London, 1949).

[9] So notably Carl Schuchhardt, "Hof, Burg und Stadt bei Germanen und Griechen," *Neue Jahrbücher,* XXI (1908), 305–21. Not even the medieval part of the parallel is entirely

to deny that eventually the most advanced towns did become true cities; but such a later step influenced the evolution of the *polis*, not its origin. Even agriculturally based towns can throb to new ideas and can bind their residents in that "purposeful social complexity" which is the real intellectual mark of urban life.[1]

It is within this simple geographical and physical framework that the *polis* emerged, and the revolution which lies in the event is politically a summation of many intercrossing strands of intellectual, social, religious, and economic development. We must look to find the true marks of the *polis* in spiritual, not physical, attributes. "Not houses finely roofed," said Alcaeus, "or the stones of walls well-builded, nay nor canals and dockyards, make the city, but men able to use their opportunity."[2]

One of the underlying forces was the consolidation of the aristocracy. Superficially, at least, the city-state was a potent vehicle for aristocratic self-expression. The upper classes led the way in clipping the powers of the *basileis;* thereafter they furnished the officials of state, both political and religious, down into the fifth century and beyond. The political standards of virtue ran in parallel course to the increasingly clearly defined patterns of aristocratic morality; artistic preferences in public monuments and statuary were virtually those which the aristocrats privately encouraged. All this, however, does not quite prove a favorite modern thesis that the *polis* had a preliminary phase of purely aristocratic expression; or, if one wishes to take the stand of a cynic, that the new political unit was designed as a tool for the hands of oppressors.[3]

Any just assessment of the true spiritual qualities of the city-state must look far beyond noble circles to the general temper of archaic civilization. No less than the new states of Renaissance Italy, the Greek *polis* was a work of art. It translated into political terms the factors which we have examined in

---

sound; for medieval cities were as a rule at least as agricultural as commercial, and long-distance trade largely rose after and from the towns. Cf. Lewis Mumford, *Culture of Cities* (New York, 1938), 17–22.

[1] Mumford, *Culture of Cities*, 4–6.
[2] Fragment Z 103. Thucydides VII. 77. 7 puts the point even more briefly: "men are the *polis*."
[3] Ehrenberg, *Der Staat der Griechen*, I, 16, 35, as an example.

art and literature: the increasingly conscious analysis of problems, the sudden liberation from tradition, and also the contain-
ment of anarchy within new, simple forms and types which
basically were reinterpretations of ancestral forces.

Essentially the city-state was a clarification and consolidation of the fundamental principles of tribal society. In part it
replaced the *basileis;* in part it did express the aristocratic spirit;
through the new machinery which evolved thereafter, it supplanted the narrower claims of clan and phratry; but mainly
the *polis* was a reaction of the citizen body as a whole to the
serious problems of the age.[4] That reaction manifested itself
initially in the feeling of the inhabitants of the more advanced—
and more disturbed—areas of mainland Greece that they must
work together consciously to prevent change from descending
into chaos; and so the *polis* may have crystallized very rapidly
and quite spontaneously in many localities as an effort to impose
political order on a rapidly evolving society. Once the process
was under way, other areas quickly followed the path in order
to tap the new strengths available in the tighter communal
bonds of the *polis;* so, too, the national state spread over
Europe in modern times.

Only if we comprehend that the *polis* reflected the needs of
society as a whole as against those of specific classes do the social and ethical qualities of the institution stand in their
proper light. One example is the effort to guarantee justice.
Neither in the Homeric nor in the Hesiodic world had the
basileis always fostered justice as much as their Zeus-given position demanded.[5] Nor did the upper classes themselves necessarily behave much better; Solon affords us a grimly detailed
portrait of the oppression of the poor in Attica. Yet a constant
thread in the history of city-state theory is the concept that it
must secure the basic rights of the free citizens. Very early the
polis began to improve public judicial and deliberative machinery; written codes of justice were appearing by the middle
of the seventh century; abuse of privilege was also checked by

---

[4] Thomson, *Studies*, II, 205–06, has
stressed this clearly; on the *demos*
as a whole cf. Mazzarino, *Fra Oriente*
e Occidente, 239–40.
[5] *Odyssey* IV. 691–92; Hesiod, *Works*
and Days 38–39.

the ever latent threat to turn back to personal leadership if mistreatment went too far. The rallying cry for this spirit was *dike* (justice), whose sister was *eunomia*—not democracy or social equality, but the maintenance of traditional right.[6] The claims of *eunomia* could be raised equally against *basileis* and tyrants, against aristocratic excess (as in Solon's elegies), or even later against the pretensions of the lower classes if they sought to overthrow the inherited rights of the nobles. The very universality of appeal in the term underlines the breadth of its meaning as a harkening back to earlier order.

The maintenance of *dike* and *eunomia* rested in part upon the preservation of fundamental independence by the small landowners. If one makes the mistake of taking the *polis* purely as an aristocratic phenomenon, then one must conclude that the poorer peasants succeeded in their struggle with all the cards stacked against them. In reality the city-state was created as an ideal structure independent of class and so may have assisted, rather than hobbled, the lower classes. To suggest that this is the proper interpretation we have some hints of early legislation which protected farm ownership.[7]

Another, quite different foundation of *eunomia* was the rapid development of divine and human morality. The beliefs that the gods favored justice, that natural law governed the universe, that social morality was as vital as was heroic valor in battle—all these were virtues not of the aristocracy but of the Greeks as a whole,[8] and the citizens expected their state to

---

[6] *Theogony* 901–02, makes Eunomia, Nike, and Eirene sisters. The main discussion of Eunomia proper is Solon, fragment 3; cf. Ehrenberg, *Aspects of the Ancient World*, 70–93; Werner Jaeger, "Solons Eunomie," *SB Berlin Akademie* 1926, 69–85; Gregory Vlastos, "Solonian Justice," *CP*, XLI (1946), 65–83. This is not the same as *isonomia*, on which cf. Mazzarino, *Fra Oriente e Occidente*, 221–23; J. A. O. Larsen, "Cleisthenes and the Development of the Theory of Democracy at Athens," *Essays in Political Theory Presented to George H. Sabine* (Ithaca, 1948).

[7] Aristotle, *Politics* II. 3. 7. 1265b, II. 9. 7. 1274b. Will, *Korinthiaka*, 510–12, takes the Cypselid law limiting slaves as a protection of freeholders; this is somewhat doubtful, inasmuch as slaves were rarely farmers.

[8] This point is well emphasized by Hoffman, *Festschrift B. Snell*, 164; Snell himself, *Discovery of the Mind*, 69, couples the feeling of the poets that they speak to their fellow men with the rise of the *polis*. While the idealistic basis of the *polis* is often magnified in modern rhapsodies, the lyrical tone of such works must not lead one to reject totally the existence

foster and spread this common base of life. Far more than did the Hebrew prophets, Greek thinkers connected morality with the state. Ideals, it is true, do not always govern the market places, and recurring internal strife was to be the product of the dynamic tempo of Greek civilization. Yet Phocylides (fragment 4, Diehl) put his finger on the main reason why the city-state can be called the source of political values in Western civilization: "The law-abiding town, though small and set on a lofty rock, outranks senseless Nineveh."

An even clearer testimonial to the fact that the *polis* was not designed solely for aristocratic benefit was its restriction upon individual freedom of action. This characteristic was not an accidental, but a fundamental quality of the city-state throughout Greek history. When eventually, in the fourth century, individuals began to assert their autonomy, the *polis* was no longer viable.[9] Nor was the limitation of the individual specifically an aristocratic virtue, even though the upper classes tended then, as always, to confine conduct within certain noble norms. Aristocratic poets themselves, such as Archilochus, are the men who best reveal this limitation to us, for they chafed under the resulting restriction of their self-expression; later poets refer frequently to the prying talk of "pitiless fellow townsmen" grouped closely together in the small social units of the era.[1] Among the legal restrictions, moreover, which checked individual license were limitations on ostentatious display of luxury.[2]

And, finally, the consolidation of the city-state as a conscious political unit was marked in the rise of patriotism, not as a matter of class loyalty but as a force embracing all free

---

of the ideal. Cf. Alfred Zimmern, *The Greek Commonwealth* (4th ed.; Oxford, 1924); Victor Ehrenberg, *Die Rechtsidee im frühen Griechenland* (Leipzig, 1921).

[9] Cf. Starr, *Civilization and the Caesars*, 8 ff.

[1] Archilochus, fragment 10; Mimnermus, fragment 7; Phocylides, fragment 5; Solon, fragments 10, 11, 13, on public opinion.

[2] Max Mühl, "Die Gesetze des Zaleukos und Charondas," *Klio*, XXII

(1928–29), 105–24, 432–63, assembles their material carefully. On Solon's restrictions cf. Kathleen Freeman, *The Work and Life of Solon* (Cardiff, 1926), 134–35; on the Cypselids, Will, *Korinthiaka*, 512–14; and in general, Mazzarino, *Fra Oriente e Occidente*, 192–93, 217–28. According to Athenaeus XII. 525c, Callinus and Archilochus blamed the fall of Magnesia on the Maeander on excessive luxury; Strabo XIV. I. 40, C. 647 does not give quite the same picture.

men independent of their position and wealth. Local attachment was never quite as overpowering a passion in ancient Greece as modern scholars, influenced by recent nationalistic fervor, have sometimes pictured it.[3] Aristocratic circles, in particular, still had wide contacts and could secure *points d'appui* when expelled from home; citizenship seems still to have been obtained by foreigners with relative ease; and Greek civilization was one great, undivided web. Within this qualification political particularism did begin to rise in the seventh century and cast long shadows over other fields as well. When the city-states came to magnify their unique qualities, they felt it necessary to find these distinctions in earlier history—i.e., in the myths of the past, which were reworked to glorify individual states or to justify territorial claims.[4]

GREEK POLITICAL HISTORY

As THE CITY-STATE coalesced, political history in its modern meaning could commence in Greece. Internally the maintenance and guidance of the new spirit required the provision of more precise machinery than tribal society had felt necessary. The details of progress in this matter must concern primarily the constitutional historian and are far from clear. Political docu-

[3] Victor Martin, *La Vie internationale dans la Grèce des cités* (*VI*ᵉ*–IV*ᵉ *s. av. J.-C.*) (Paris, 1940), is a valuable study from this light.

Exile: Alcaeus, fragment G2 (Page, *Sappho and Alcaeus*, 199), Elemer Balogh, *Political Refugees in Ancient Greece from the Period of the Tyrants to Alexander the Great* (Johannesburg, 1943), is not useful on the early era. Citizenship: Hommel *s. v.* Metoikoi in PW 1424 ff.; Thucydides I. 2. 6; Paul Cauer and Eduard Schwyzer, *Dialectorum Graecorum Exempla* (Leipzig, 1923), n. 415.
[4] Nilsson, *GGR*, I, 708–21, takes up briefly the interrelations of politics

and religion; his treatment is fuller in *Cults, Myths, Oracles and Politics in Ancient Greece*, which mostly concerns the sixth century and later. While Homer, fortunately, was sufficiently set so that his text escaped much alteration, the later *Homeric Hymns*, especially those to Demeter and Apollo, reflect local attachments. Eumelus of Corinth is termed by Dunbabin, *JHS*, LXVIII (1948), 66–68, "the first consciously to falsify myth and legend in the interest of the state," though one may doubt if he is as early as usually stated (cf. Will, *Korinthiaka*, 124–29).

ments appear only when the machinery itself evolves; one must not, to repeat an earlier observation, visualize the seventh-century *polis* in terms of Periclean Athens.

First, apparently, the number of public officials tended to increase while the strength of tribal and clan leaders shrank; the powers of the state became more concentrated, but each official's part of those powers was more carefully specified and his enjoyment thereof was temporally limited, often to a single year. Improvement in the operations of the assembly of citizens and council of aristocrats must have followed swiftly. As far as we can now determine, Sparta may have been the first state, about 650, to introduce a probouleutic council—i.e., a body which considered and prepared public business for the assembly.[5] Athens took over this institution in the days of Solon, but much remained to be done here and elsewhere to curb the power of the clans and to improve public central machinery which could deal directly with individual citizens.

In states which were measured in terms of a few square miles, the machinery itself was not vital.[6] What mattered was the spirit in which the government was operated and for whose particular benefit decisions were made—the stuff, in sum, of that internal political history which we begin to see with some continuity in Athens and Sparta during the sixth century. Even then not all the factors of political debate were purely of city-state character. As Geometric motives long influenced Orientalizing pottery and epic inheritances colored the early lyric, so in politics the principle of personal leadership on the one hand and the small, conservative blocks of tribe, phratry, and clan on the other continued to be significant elements.

Externally, too, formal history began when state policies and aims grew clearer. A connected account of Greek international relations is impossible in the seventh century, and not

---

[5] Andrewes, *Probouleusis*, though questioned by Ehrenberg, *Der Staat der Griechen*, I, 108. The reforms at Athens: Hignett, *Athenian Constitution*, 47–85.

[6] Heuss, *Antike und Abendland*, II (1946), 39–43. Would the restriction of the assembly to 1,000, 600, or the like have represented a limitation in early times, or simply reflect the actual manpower? Old Smyrna had at the most 1,000 households, J. M. Cook, *BSA*, LIII–IV (1958–59), 19–22.

alone because written records were still scant. Archaic Greece long remained a congeries of tribal and city units (much like the dynastic and national states of early modern Europe); the many tiny *poleis* which were emerging did not yet rub fiercely on one another.[7] War had long been "common to all," as the *Iliad* (XVIII. 309) put it, in the sense of tribal clashes, but the earliest contests of actual states known from Greek tradition appear in the age of revolution. A clash between Corinth and Megara may be dated by the Megarian leader Orsippus, a victor in the Olympic games of 720 B.C. Not long thereafter the famous Lelantine war threw first the phalanxes and cavalry of Chalcis and Eretria against each other for the possession of a small, lush plain, and then drew into its loose frame the political and economic rivalries of almost all the more developed states of the Aegean.[8] The course of this war, however, is far from clear; modern hypotheses fit it far too much into terms of trade wars.

Nor can we follow in detail the expansion of the frontiers either of Sparta or of Athens.[9] These, which were to be the great powers of mainland Greece in the future, were still evolving internally and externally. The major state at this time was still apparently Argos, which has so dim a history that modern scholars still vary half a century in dating its great leader Pheidon.[1]

In their ever growing external frictions and internal stresses the Greek city-states were eventually to grind themselves into collapse. They had crystallized on so small a scale but with such

---

[7] Kitto, *The Greeks*, 162, justly notes this; the later situation is described by Martin, *La Vie internationale*, 92–93, 95. The same situation existed in early modern Europe.

[8] Full references on the Megara-Corinth clash are given in N. G. L. Hammond, *BSA*, XLIX (1954), 97; on the Lelantine war, see Chap. 11, n. 3 (p. 376). On the Melian war in Ionia, cf. Roebuck, *CP*, L (1955), 32–33, with references.

[9] The Attic conquest of Eleusis, for instance, is far from clear. If the *Hymn to Demeter* was composed before this conquest, as is often asserted, how then can it be of the sixth century, as is also often stated? Or was the

conquest so late? Cf. Guthrie, *Greeks and Their Gods*, 285 n. 1; Nilsson, *Cults and Politics*, 38; Ch. Picard, "Les Luttes primitives d'Athènes et d'Eleusis," *Revue Historique*, CLXVI (1931), 1–76, which relies far too much on myths.

[1] Of the large literature seeking to penetrate the impenetrable, cf. W. L. Brown, "Pheidon's Alleged Aeginetan Coinage," *Numismatic Chronicle*, 6. ser. X (1950), 177–204, and in *Schweizer Münzblätter*, IV (1953) 49–51; Will, *Korinthiaka*, 344–57. Herodotus VI. 127, in my judgment, is decisive in placing Pheidon late in the seventh century.

intensity that they were later not able to change as Greek civilization continued to evolve. Their political solutions, too, of the problems of limiting individualism and of binding men together in a just community did not endure—but will ours?

The *polis* was certainly a marvelous, virtually miraculous creation in men's minds. Its tiny scale and its rejection of personal leadership were possible only because Greece was still a simple land blessedly free from external pressure; its spiritual qualities, as well as its amazing potentialities as a base for subsequent cultural and political expansion, reflect directly the intellectual quality of the age. The underlying, delicate balance between aristocratic self-assertion and communal patriotism, between might and freedom, was not easily maintained even in the areas which first raised themselves to the pinnacle of political unity marked in the *polis*. Greek political history is largely a study in the extension and perfection of this form of organization, the mold of which had been set in the early seventh century as swiftly and surely as architects had thrown up the temple type. From this communal unity the individual human being gained a firm support for intellectual activity. He paid also a price—the restriction of his own individuality and the failure of Greek culture to develop all sides of personality.

CHAPTER 11

ECONOMIC QUICKENING

AND COLONIZATION

꒒Ꚏ꒒Ꚏ꒒Ꚏ꒒Ꚏ꒒Ꚏ꒒Ꚏ꒒Ꚏ꒒Ꚏ꒒Ꚏ꒒Ꚏ꒒Ꚏ꒒Ꚏ꒒Ꚏ꒒Ꚏ꒒Ꚏ꒒Ꚏ꒒Ꚏ꒒Ꚏ꒒

THE LAST AMONG the major aspects of the age of revolution
which will be considered in this volume is its economic development. Changes here were neither inconsiderable nor unimportant. Without the quickening of conscious economic interest
which then took place, without the quantitative and qualitative
improvement of production, the emergence of the *polis* would
be inconceivable. Artists, authors, and aristocrats alike were supported by the expanding economic system of the Aegean and
were invigorated by the fresh currents of physical luxuries and
concepts which poured in from the outside world. The mighty
movement of colonization in return opened wide areas of the
Mediterranean to Greek culture, which was ever more attractive
to alien peoples.

The significance of economic innovations, on the other hand,
must not be overly magnified. The rise of the city-state may
properly be understood only if one places it against a background still predominantly agricultural; commerce and industry
were very limited in extent and minimal in influence by 650.
Despite real technological progress, early Greece moved forward from a very primitive level and advanced only slowly.
The dimensions of technical development and the formation of
new capital were far less than those of early modern Europe.
One notable result was the failure of the ancient Aegean to
produce an independent, self-conscious middle class, though

the economic and social importance of the early modern *bourgeoisie* has, in truth, been much exaggerated for more recent eras. But let us strike to the heart of the matter: the upheaval which produced archaic civilization was the product of many conjoined factors, each facilitating the changes in parallel fields. Of these forces the economic developments were only one element.

This having been said, it is possible to assess with greater sureness the economic alterations which did take place and to measure their significance both for Greek society and for the economic temper of Western civilization. First among the signs of advance must be placed the change in economic attitudes. Landlords and peasants contended more fiercely over the hard-won fruits of the stony soil; an interest in economic gain came to mark all classes even though the economic sphere was not sharply marked off from other aspects of life. Economic mobility grew, for the progress of commerce, industry, and agriculture took place not within the Oriental framework of palace and temple but in a new pattern of small-scale, relatively free enterprise.

Important in this respect was the great geographical expansion of Greece. On the one side trade and travel to the Orient flourished and tied Greece ever more firmly to the course of history in the Fertile Crescent. On the other, Greek colonization, together with Phoenician and Etruscan trade, bound western and eastern Mediterranean together indissolubly. These external ties and the internal dynamic quality of Greek economic life helped to prevent Greek civilization from sinking back into a semi-static, rigidly fixed structure.

The new economic patterns were not entirely perfected by 650 B.C. Coinage, which at once resulted from and also facilitated the great increase in economic mobility, appeared only in the last half of the seventh century. Full guarantees that the small peasants would remain economically independent were achieved at Athens, our best example, even later. True urban centers and non-agricultural classes were equally tardy in appearance. These advanced aspects do not concern us at the moment; the important problem is to sort out the initial marks of change as the old, self-sufficient, tribal economy moved toward a more mobile, more conscious, and more complex economic outlook.

THE ECONOMIC SPIRIT

BEHIND THE specific evidence of development in agriculture, commerce, and industry lies, as impelling force, a revolution in economic attitudes. During the Dark ages, when men struggled to survive and to hold together the tissue of society, the idea of economic gain or profit had small scope. Its major manifestation then was a casual, almost involuntary reaction directed outward against neighboring peoples in the form of tribal raids for cattle, women, and other movables. As the Aegean world grew richer in the eighth century and as its men became more mobile, the conscious effort to gain economic advantage entered Greek life. Thenceforth the economic spirit, as it may be called, was an enduring force of considerable importance in Hellenic history.

The emergence of this outlook seems a truly remarkable step when one reflects how long traditional patterns had had an opportunity to fix themselves. Yet the transition was perhaps easier than was the parallel rise of the capitalistic spirit in early modern Europe. Greek tribal society had been too simple to evolve the fetters of manorial and guild organization; its religious system did not inculcate the other-worldly, moral virtues of Christianity; and the upper class, while long distinguished as a group of landlords, was not bound by the requirements of a developed aristocratic code.

In many respects modern economic students too often misread the nature of early Greece. We must be wary of assuming, on more recent parallels, that the incipient aristocrats of the eighth and seventh centuries were totally disinterested in economic gain. The rounded picture of an upper class which disdained physical labor and economic rivalry was evolved only later in the treatises of Plato and Aristotle and in the pious wishes of other authors; even then it did not entirely reflect reality.

Even more perverse is the concept, born of exaggerated views on ancient slavery, that Greek citizen bodies as a whole were *rentier* in spirit—this in a barren landscape which cannot support a great mass of non-workers! [1]

If we turn to the Homeric epics, we must find that the heroes delighted in idleness—when they could enjoy this blessing—but they also worked. Their great distinction from hired laborers lay in the fact that they could employ their time as they wished. Often the leaders of society were supervisors, leaning on their staffs to watch the tilling of their farms; yet Odysseus knew how to follow a plow, and Paris both tended sheep and helped in the building of his palace. In the simple social and economic world of the epic there appears no real prejudice against physical labor in itself, and the cunning of craftsmen gained the poet's praise. Prestige came from valor on the battlefield; it also was measured in terms of household goods and herds. Odysseus, disguised as a beggar, told Penelope that her husband would long since have been home, "only it seemed to his mind more profitable to gather wealth by roaming over the wide earth; so truly does Odysseus beyond all mortal men known many gainful ways." [2]

The step from the *Odyssey* to Hesiod is no less decisive in economic matters than in other respects already considered, for in the *Works and Days* we can first detect the conscious appearance of true economic competitiveness. Early in his poem Hesiod graphically portrays the contest of potter with potter and endorses rivalry so long as it is conducted fairly; the basic

[1] Hasebroek, *Trade and Politics*, vii and passim; Bolkestein, *Economic Life*, 62–65 (note his qualifications, 70–73, 153); Ehrenberg, *Der Staat der Griechen*, I, 73 (with reserves); and most Marxist historians. But cf. Heichelheim, *Ancient Economic History*, I, 279; Mazzarino, *Fra Oriente e Occidente*, 213–14.

[2] *Odyssey* XIX. 282–86. Labor in epic: *Iliad* VI. 314; *Odyssey* XXIII. 178 ff., V. 243, XV. 320. A view contrary to that of the text will be found in Finley, *World of Odysseus*, 76–79; André Aymard, "L'Idée de travail dans la Grèce archaïque," *Journal de psychologie*, XLI (1948), 29–45, and "Hiérarchie du travail et autarcie individuelle dans la Grèce archaïque," *Revue d'histoire de la philosophie et d'histoire générale de la civilisation*, XI (1943), 124–46. Craftsmen: *Iliad* V. 60 ff., XV. 410–12; *Odyssey* XV. 319–20. Possessions: *Iliad* V. 612–14, 708–10, XIV. 121–24; *Odyssey* XIV. 100–04 and passim. Covetousness: *Iliad* V. 481; *Odyssey* XIII. 215–16. Finley, *World of Odysseus*, 134–37, overstresses the honorific aspect.

aim of life which he holds out to his rural auditors is hard labor. The purpose of this work is not drawn from an idealization of labor as such, nor is it simply to avoid starvation; the objective is gain. "Work is no disgrace, it is idleness which is a disgrace—through work men grow rich in flocks and in substance—both gods and men are angry with a man who lives idle." Again and again Hesiod returns to the necessity of labor to get ahead; in the command to "work with work upon work" he virtually stutters with urgency.[3]

In this emphasis Hesiod was not exhibiting an avarice limited to the peasant class, for the aristocratic poets in the lyric strain who followed him knew well the conscious pursuit of wealth. Poverty remained a curse, a "grievous and restless ill," which was more keenly felt as the possibilities of wealth and luxury grew. A lengthy fragment of Solon's elegies catalogues the ways of making money—overseas trade, agriculture, industry and art, medicine and foretelling the future—and Solon concludes that those who are richest "have twice the eagerness that others have." [4] The very fact that noble poets emphasize so noticeably the theme that wealth in itself is not enough must lead one to suspect that many of their peers failed to live by the Delphic maxim, Nothing Too Much.

Within the inherited framework of an agricultural society divided between landlords and small peasants, the introduction of economic competition must have led at times simply to the exploitation of the poor by the rich. In itself this result was not entirely without social and intellectual profit; the formation of new capital in eras of expansion frequently requires toughness. Those who claimed the surplus of society utilized their gains partly for the construction of temples and the embellishment of festivals, and even the part they devoted to their own pleasure aided the rise of arts and letters. Not all of the advantage, however, came solely to the old upper classes. The more advanced areas were by now developing commercially, industrially, and

[3] *Works and Days* 303–04, 308, 311, 382.
[4] Solon, fragment 11. See also Alcaeus, fragment Z 41; Theognis 384 ff.; Bacchylides I. 171; Alcaeus, fragment Z 37, who quotes the Spartan Aristidemos: "Money makes the man; no pauper can be noble or held in honor."

agriculturally; and the dynamic possibilities which resulted were also seized by basically free artisans, traders, and peasants. While the details escape us, the rise of these lower classes is obvious by the end of the sixth century.

Everywhere, moreover, there were bars to overly ruthless competition. Much of an average Greek's life was still passed within the dictates of an economy directed primarily toward subsistence and governed by old customs of tribal society. Where the protection of these latter was weakening in the more progressive districts, men turned to the city-state, which incorporated in conscious form the principle of communal fair-dealing or *eunomia*. The aristocratic code itself, as it evolved, came to emphasize the concept that gentlemen must seek other things in life *in addition to* wealth. Excessive, exclusive zeal for economic advantage and the unjust use of force to this end were condemned by aristocratic ethics. By the sixth century the view that "wealth without honor" was base had become canonical, but its roots were far older. In the *Odyssey* overconcern for gain had been the subject of taunt when Odysseus was accused of being "one who, faring to and fro with his benched ship, is a captain of sailors who are merchantmen, one who is mindful of his freight, and has charge of a home-borne cargo, and the gains of his greed." [5]

The appearance of the economic spirit during the age of revolution, in sum, was both unmistakable and also restrained. The economic sphere was not sharply marked off from other aspects of human organization and governed by its own laws. Whether aristocrat or peasant, moreover, an ancient Greek had generally the good sense to try to enjoy life as it passed by. To comprehend his outlook, one must not approach it from the point of view of modern, advanced capitalistic endeavor; a healthful corrective is to come to know the delightfully backward ways of modern Hellenes, who refuse to ruin today in a mad scramble to gain the wealth with which to endow tomorrow. The inhabitants of ancient Greece understood quite well

[5] *Odyssey* VIII. 159–64; Sappho, fragment 148; Phocylides, fragment 9, puts the order, first a living, then virtue. On the limited independence of the economic sphere in early times, cf. the critique in *Trade and Market in the Early Empires*, ed. Karl Polanyi et al. (Glencoe, Ill., 1957).

how back-breaking was the hard physical toil of their simple world, and were happy to avoid it if they could—but few were fortunate enough to be able to do so. Economic possibilities were so limited in this age and classes so static that the chances of improving one's social standing by economic advance were always slight. Yet all these factors only limited the exercise of the economic spirit by men who were basically free to change, and it may properly be said that conscious interest in gain became a part of the Greek outlook during the seventh century.

THE AGRICULTURAL WORLD

AGRICULTURE was always the basic mode of life in the ancient Aegean; it simply will not do to label commerce "a master factor in Greek expansion." [6] Today Greece is still essentially rural, though its agricultural sectors are no longer geared to self-sufficiency. Ancient farmers produced even less per acre, so far as we can calculate; they could not have supported more than a very small percentage of non-agricultural population. Not until the fifth century B.C. did such states as Athens have a sufficiently favorable balance of trade, based on industry and for a time on imperialistic profit, to nourish a large urban population by means of grain bought abroad.

The nature of the central settlements in the early *poleis* we have already examined. While men virtually everywhere lived together in tight clumps for the sake of mutual protection and to

[6] Dunbabin, *Greeks and Their Eastern Neighbours*, 19; Glotz, *Greek City*, 101–02; and many others. The distortions which must ensue may be suggested by Young's comment, *Late Geometric Graves*, 230, that the shift to Protoattic pottery reflected "the change from a feudal and agricultural society to an industrial and commercial society." But see Hasebroek, *Trade and Politics in Ancient Greece*, 44–71, though he overstresses limits on trade; Bolkestein, *Economic Life*;

H. Michell, *The Economics of Ancient Greece* (2d ed.; Cambridge, 1957), chap. 2; Heichelheim, *Ancient Economic History*, I, 268 ff., and works listed therein; Cook's picture of Old Smyrna, *BSA*, LIII–IV (1958–59), 16–17.

Greek agriculture: Hasebroek, *Griechische Wirtschafts- und Gesellschaftsgeschichte*, 10–12, 75–77, 217–21; Faucher, *Mélanges de la société toulousaine d'études classiques*, I (1946), 5–22.

secure unfailing water supplies through the dusty summer, these towns were based on agriculture. Solon reflected the realities of the late seventh century when he calculated the requirements for the different classes of Athens in terms of agricultural produce. Attic industrial and commercial elements, as everywhere else, were still very minor fragments of the body politic; one mark of Solon's extraordinary prescience was his deliberate effort to foster their growth.[7]

Any changes in agriculture, then, whether in matters of technique or in landholding tenures, must be subjects of primary importance in Greek history. Even before the age of revolution got fully under way, the countryside was awakening from a long winter's sleep, and a variety of important developments, of which we can see only the bare outlines, affected virtually every aspect of farming in the more advanced areas.

A quantitative increase in production resulted from the growth in population; as Hesiod observed, "More hands mean more work and more increase."[8] That settled village life spread ever more widely over Greece seems clear from the archaeological evidence. Wherever possible, men exploited previously uncultivated land, such as that which Hesiod's father took up in Boeotia, but in this process we cannot measure the extent to which land that previously had supported flocks was now turned over to crops—or could be so converted. A diminution in the place of shepherding may be inferred both from the dietary references of later literature to cereal consumption as against the abundant references to meat in the epic and also from the fact that flocks played a lesser role in historic literature than in the epic; yet on the latter point one must remember that coined money was now substituted as a medium of wealth.

[7] The fact that tyrants extended aid to commercial and industrial elements does not mean that their rule relied primarily on this element (vs. P. N. Ure, *The Greek Renaissance* [London, 1921]); Nilsson, *GGR*, I, 666, notes the dominance of agriculture in religion. The *Shield of Heracles* (286 ff.) describes only farming and hunting, though it contains a city of men; cf. the shield of Achilles, *Iliad* XVIII. 541 ff.; Hesiod, *Works and Days* 232–37.

[8] *Works and Days* 380. Howe, *Transactions of the American Philological Association*, LXXXIX (1958), 44–65, argues that a considerable shift to grain-raising occurred in the eighth century; her reading of the epic and Hesiodic evidence is not completely compelling.

Qualitative improvement must also have occurred. More people can be fed from the same amount of land if it is suitable for cereal crops as well as for grazing animals; quite probably there was also more attention to terracing, drainage, and irrigation. The olive groves and vineyards of Greece, the importance of which we can establish only in the wider evidence of the sixth century, surely went back at least to the seventh century; Greek pots were not often exported empty, and the colonies furnished a market for oil and wine. Noticeable, too, in excavated sites is the great increase in the use of iron. The true Iron age begins not in the late second millennium, when this metal was first worked all across the Near East, but in and after the eighth century. Even in the seventh century iron spits still served as a medium of exchange; Hesiod's peasants did not yet have iron plowshares. Improvements in technology and the opening of wider sources of supply—the details of which are quite unclear —made iron ever more common and useful.[9]

The surpluses of agricultural foodstuffs which resulted from improved quantitative and qualitative factors were not necessarily large, and could quite easily have been gobbled up by the producers.[1] That they did not thus vanish was due partly to the growth of political and religious machinery, which required taxes and sacrifices; partly to the exactions of nobles; and partly to the tempting wares dangled in front of the farmers by the non-agricultural elements. By force and by desire some peasants were lured into production with an eye to market as well as to their own consumption. What I have just defined as the economic spirit made its appearance at least as significantly and as early in the minds of farmers as of traders.

The development toward economic mobility, which is clearly reflected in the *Works and Days,* opened a Pandora's box for the peasantry of Greece. By donkey and by small boat they might transport their tiny surpluses to the larger centers of population and hope to profit from their extra exertions. Hard

---

[9] For examples, see *Perachora*, I, 73–75; *Artemis Orthia*, 196, 391. The Greek sources of iron were Laconia, Euboea, the Cyclades; see Heichelheim, *Ancient Economic History*, I, 193–97.

[1] M. I. Finley, *JRS*, XLVIII (1958), 161–62; H. W. Pearson, "The Economy Has No Surplus," *Trade and Markets in the Early Empires*, 320–41.

work and luck brought real rewards, which enabled the more supple to break out of the old framework of restricted initiative. The rise of the city-state, as we have seen, reflected the ability of the smaller farmers to maintain their position, and this factor rested partly on the presence of open markets in which peasants could operate independently of noble pressures.

Still, those who sought a profit also took the risk of their search. The peasants grew more dependent on non-agricultural elements for iron tools and for other manufactured products. Insofar as old communal patterns of clan and tribe and old economic conventions waned, the way lay open for the richer and more powerful to oppress the poorer, especially since loans at interest became ever more common and necessary in an increasingly fluid world. The concepts of mortgage, transfer of ownership, and so on at this time were not those of modern law, but of two things we may be certain. Not all men held equal quantities of land, and peasants could lose effective control of their own plots (or more accurately, perhaps, their own independence) through unpaid loans and "crooked judgments." [2] In a few areas the small farmers were reduced to serfdom. Agricultural slavery proper remained quite limited; the soil of Greece could rarely support the capital investment required for slaves.

The glacial calm of traditional, clan-controlled agriculture must have broken up very quickly throughout the more developed districts of the Greek countryside. Some men profited thereby, but others became excess baggage. A part of the surplus population which seems evident in the era of colonization may have been simply the product of faulty distribution of land, as in the splitting of small landholdings among many sons; [3] other men were displaced perhaps by the rise of olive

[2] Already in *Odyssey* XI. 489–91 there occurs "a *kleros*-less man whose source of living was not large"; cf. XIV. 199 ff., and Chap. 4, n. 9 (p. 130). On land title, see John V. A. Fine, *Horoi: Studies in Mortgage, Real Security and Land Tenure in Ancient Athens (Hesperia,* Supp. IX, 1951); Will, *REA,* LIX (1957), 12–24. The collectivism of the Greeks on Lipari was essentially a curiosity; cf. Dunbabin, *Western Greeks,* 331–32, and Robert J. Buck, "Communalism on the Lipari Islands (Diod. 5. 9. 4)," *CP,* LIV (1959), 35–39, against Thomson. [3] G. Glotz, *Histoire grecque,* I (Paris, 1925), 154, and others stress this point.

groves and vineyards; but many areas apparently had an absolute excess of population—measured in economic potentialities of the period—throughout the age of revolution.

The agricultural changes which were transforming Greece were perhaps economically desirable. Socially and politically they were dangerous. The political effects we have already seen in the rise of the *polis*, but purely political panaceas were not entirely effective either in curbing the avarice of the rich or in assuaging the problems of the poor. Commerce and industry siphoned off some elements of the surplus population, but this safety valve was not able in the seventh century—or ever later, for that matter—fully to release the pressures of the agricultural countryside.

THE RISE OF INDUSTRY AND COMMERCE

The expansion of industry and commerce in the era 750–650 must be placed within the whole context of contemporary economic life. In this light, advance in the two sectors now to be considered may appear to have been limited. Greece lacked many important raw materials, its markets could not compare in breadth or richness to those of the more developed Oriental monarchies, and previous levels of economic activity in the Aegean had been extremely low. The archaic graves of Attic citizens in the Kerameikos are poverty-stricken interments beside the rich, timbered chambers of contemporary Phrygian kings or the tombs of Saite Egypt.

If we measure the degree of change from earlier Greek standards, nonetheless, Aegean material progress in the age was truly revolutionary. In industry and commerce the new economic spirit could find play most easily; thence the attractive forces of mobility and adventure could penetrate into more conservative sectors. The rise of commerce and industry affected the cultural outburst of the Aegean at the time and laid a base for continuing economic and political changes in subsequent centuries.

In industry there can be no doubt that production increased appreciably, for its results are evident in our archaeological record. Changes in techniques are also physically perceptible. Many of the innovations were imported from the Orient as contact with the East became more widespread and as the Greek world grew more able to afford the products of smiths and artists. The transfer of techniques, such as the use of molds for figurines, had essentially been completed by the late seventh century, though Greek technology continued to develop at a slower rate thereafter.

The vehicle of the transfer is often argued to have been the movement of Eastern artisans to the Aegean, an assumption for which there is no proof.[4] In historic times the physical equipment of Greek life seems to have been made entirely by Greek artisans, apart from direct imports. Much was always produced within the home itself; the rest came from either traveling or local craftsmen. The existence of mobile workers is well shown in the presence of foreign alphabets on the pottery of Corinth and other sites, the transfer of molds for figurines from one center to another, and the many traditions about migrant sculptors and architects.[5] Skilled industrial specialists were not necessarily bound irrevocably to individual masters; wherever they ventured, they could hope for protection and commissions. On this basic fluidity depended in part the cultural unity of Aegean arts during the age of revolution.

Besides itinerant tinkers flourished more sedentary artisans, who probably were far more numerous. Local craftsmen, working in metal, clay, leather, and wood, appear in Homer; by the seventh century true industrial quarters were beginning to emerge in the villages which clustered below Acrocorinth, the Acropolis, and other more advanced sites.[6] These industrial establishments were small and simply organized,[7] and their

[4] See above, Chap. 6, n. 5 (p. 213).
[5] Alphabets: see above, Chap. 7, n. 2 (p. 238). Mold transfer: Ohly, *AM*, LXV (1940), 68 n. 2; Jenkins, *Perachora*, I, 231–32, 242; Karl Lehmann-Hartleben, "Note on the Potnia Tauron," *AJA*, XLIII (1939), 669–71 (bronze mold). Cf. *Od.* XVII. 382–86;

Kentarô Murakawa, "Demiurgos," *Historia*, VI (1957), 385–415.
[6] The best illuminated is the Potters' Quarter at Corinth; see Agnes N. Stillwell, *Corinth*, XV. 1 (Princeton, N.J., 1948), 10–14.
[7] Their smallness was only relative; half of the named black-figure and

proprietors will scarcely have ranked higher in the social scale than their descendants did in later Athens.

The sedentary industrial elements must have been dependent to a large degree upon the nobles who governed the city-states. Insofar as they produced luxury items, their consumers were the aristocrats. The religious sanctuaries, which were centers for the making of figurines and statues and were adorned by increasingly rich homes of the gods, were directed by priests from the upper classes.[8] Often the nascent industries which produced for market may have developed out of the household economies of the well-to-do, whose slaves might turn out surpluses. Yet not all the increasing product of Greek shops went to the wealthy part of the population, and the men who toiled in industry were in root far freer than their counterparts in the Orient.

Artisan and trader must often have been combined in the same person, but the ever wider dispersal of Greek wares argues for the existence of independent commercial channels. Interchange of pottery and other objects had never entirely disappeared in the Aegean during the Dark ages. At least by the early eighth century this local movement began to take on more impressive dimensions and soon reached out eastward to Syria and west to Italy and beyond. Besides the vases and their now vanished contents there is epic evidence. The *Iliad* mentions wine, slaves, raw metals, and finished products as moving into the Achaean camp before Troy or farther afield;[9] trade references of the *Odyssey* are even wider. Thereafter indications of seafaring stud the lyric poets.

The flow of finished wares and raw materials in and out of the Aegean is visible; not so easily determined is the mode of trade itself. Quite evidently this early age did not know such advanced techniques as central markets and warehouses, rigid distinctions between wholesalers and retailers, or the like; but some modern economic historians would go so far as to

---

red-figure vases came from six factories (Beloch, *Griechische Geschichte*, I, 1, 272).

[8] The terra-cotta factory by the sanctuary at Acragas is a good example; cf. Dunbabin, *Western Greeks*, 265.

[9] E.g., *Iliad* VII. 467 ff., IX. 71–72.

deny that interchange of goods took place within any true "trading" patterns. Such views are extreme, as I shall show in a moment; yet the figure of the enterprising, essentially economic entrepreneur must not be expected too early. In the epics trade was a spasmodic matter not far removed from piracy, an adventurous gamble carried on by the upper classes in a style of mutual exchange of gifts.[1] Even in the seventh century the boundary between trade and piracy seems to have been fluid, and the lyric poets treated any form of seafaring as an act of desperation. Nobles such as Solon of Athens or Charaxas, the brother of Sappho, sailed abroad either to market their home-grown produce or to see the world; peasants, if we may trust Hesiod, scurried briefly to sea during the summer to dispose of their own products. Down to 650 it is not easy to find truly professional traders. The first who may perhaps be called so is Colaeus of Samos, who was blown to Spanish Tartessus while on a westward trip and reaped a fortune in opening this new market.[2]

While all this is true, we are not thereby justified in concluding that genuine trading instincts were lacking. Heroes, no less than specialized merchants, may exhibit economic interests beside other motives. Elizabethan seadogs such as Drake traded, looted, and explored with equal enthusiasm; those major expeditions which were intended to defend England against Spain were managed as joint-stock operations, participants in which had a canny expectation of dividends.[3] In the sixteenth-century Atlantic only men of daring and independent status would risk their lives—or could muster the capital and followers to do so. There is no reason to expect less of seventh-century Aegean society. Greek pots did not simply fly by magic about

[1] See generally Finley, *World of Odysseus*, 68–73, 107–08, though he underestimates the purposeful connection of gifts and trade. Seventh century: *Hymn to Apollo* 453–55; *Hymn to Demeter* 126–27; Heichelheim, *Ancient Economic History*, I, 224–26, 245–47; Hasebroek, *Trade and Politics*, 13–14, who minimizes the place of nobles in long-distance trade; Thomson, *Studies in the Ancient*

Aegean, II, 192–93.
[2] Herodotus IV. 152. Demaratus traded with Etruria and settled there (Pliny, *h. n.* XXXV. 16, 152; Livy I. 34, IV. 3; Strabo V. 2.2, C. 219, VIII. 6.20, C. 378; et al.). See H. Knorringa, *Emporos* (Diss. Utrecht, 1926).
[3] Julian S. Corbett, *Drake and the Tudor Navy* (London, 1912), II, 68–69.

the Mediterranean, and the men who took them were, I think, closely interwoven with the already existent upper classes. In particular, we cannot safely treat the disdain for seafaring, as expressed by Hesiod and others, as an aristocratic disdain for the sea. The Aegean and other waters *were* dangerous; the Greeks admitted the fact, as have many other seafarers, and then gambled, if gamble they must.[4]

The date at which wandering merchants as such (*emporoi*) and also settled traders (*kapeloi*) crystallized out of this fluid pattern cannot be fixed, but one may properly guess that it falls within or close to the age of revolution. By this point men of industrial or peasant background were probably learning how to seize the opportunities of trade, if usually only on a more local and humdrum basis; the great innovation in Greek commerce, as Heichelheim has observed, was to be the appearance of settled merchants, who were basically independent of upper classes or kings.[5]

To make commercial operations more supple and to enhance the growing mobility of capital some form of standard means for exchange and for representation of capital became vital. During the age of revolution the standards remained cattle and ingots of metal, the latter measured partly in Oriental weights. In excavations, gold "dumps" or pellets and iron rods ("spits") also turn up. True coins appeared only after 650. The first, which were made of electrum on the coast of Asia Minor, were for large-scale trade and perhaps for payment of mercenaries; then states in Greece proper began to issue smaller silver units. The fact that only Aegina, Athens, and perhaps Corinth thus coined before 600 may suggest how slowly trade developed as an independent sector of economic life; but in evaluating this mighty step it must be remembered that coinage has also serious political and social prerequisites and overtones.[6]

[4] Lesky, *Thalatta*, 26–32, 251 ff.; cf. J. H. Thiel, *Studies on the History of Roman Sea-Power in Republican Times* (Amsterdam, 1946), 1–11.
[5] *Ancient Economic History*, I, 251–53; cf. Polanyi, *Trade and Market in the Early Empires*, 64–67.
[6] Pre-coinage: De Sanctis, *Storia dei Greci*, I, 453–59; Ventris and Chadwick, *Documents*, 57–58; Hutchinson and Boardman, *BSA*, XLIX (1954), 219, on dumps; on spits, Woodward,

The existence of commercial and industrial links helped to unify Aegean culture. Their intensification accelerated the speed of general development. But they did not determine its characteristics: the place of commerce and industry in Greece down to 650 must not be overemphasized. While Protocorinthian vases sold far more widely than had any eighth-century ware, the potters of Corinth hit their stride in international trade only during the Corinthian period proper, well after 650. Attic ware was scarcely exported until the last decades of the seventh century and did not gain wide markets until after 600.[7] Stone temples, large-scale sculpture, and other marks of an increasing surplus of wealth in Greece appear scantily throughout the last half of the seventh century. Public works for the benefit of shipping began, so far as we know, with a quay at Delos which is dated rather insecurely to the eighth century and may have been intended chiefly for the festivals.[8] Moles and other harbor works turn up at Eretria and elsewhere in the next hundred years; but for really major engineering accomplishments we must come down virtually to the era of Polycrates of Samos, in the last half of the sixth century.

Artemis Orthia, 391–93, and Payne and Wade-Gery, *Perachora*, I, 187–89, 258–60. Bernhard Laum, *Heiliges Geld* (Tübingen, 1924), argues their connection with cult and sacrifice and draws wide deductions on the religious aspects of currency.

Coinage: The first known Aegean coins, published by B. V. Head, *Excavations at Ephesus*, 74–93, have often been dated much too early, as by Charles Seltman, *Greek Coins* (2d ed.; London, 1955); Ettore Gabrici, *Tecnica e cronologia delle monete greche dal VII al V sec. a.C.* (Rome, 1951). See R. M. Cook, *JHS*, LXVI (1946), 90–91; E. S. G. Robinson, "The Coins from the Ephesian Artemision Reconsidered," *JHS*, LXXI (1951), 156–67 (and Paul Jacobsthal, ibid. 85–95); W. L. Brown, "Pheidon's Alleged Aeginetan Coinage," *Numismatic Chronicle*, 6. ser. X (1950), 177–204; on Corinth, Benson, *Geschichte der korinthischen Vasen*,

102–04. The values implicit in the idea of money and its effects are noted by E. Will, "De la aspect éthique des origines grecques de la monnaie," *Revue historique*, CCXII (1954), 209–31; Heichelheim, *Ancient Economic History*, I, 213–20, 251–53, 478–81; R. M. Cook, "Speculations on the Origins of Coinage," *Historia*, VII (1958), 257–62.

[7] Payne, *Necrocorinthia*, 24–25, 48, 59, 184; B. L. Bailey, "The Export of Attic Black-Figure Ware," *JHS*, LX (1940), 60–70, though an incomplete survey, shows the general picture.

[8] Karl Lehmann-Hartleben, *Die antiken Hafenanlagen des Mittelmeeres*, *Klio*, Beih. XIV (1923), 50–52; but Gallet de Santerre, *Délos primitive*, 220, is not sure the quay may be placed so early. Roads were designed mainly for pilgrim traffic, as Beloch, *Griechische Geschichte*, I, 1, 277, pointed out.

(a) Clay shield from Tiryns, showing Achilles' defeat of Penthesilea or Heracles and Hippolyte (Nauplia Museum). Photograph courtesy S. S. Weinberg.
(b) Protoattic amphora with the blinding of Polyphemus on the neck (cf. Plate 15a) and the decapitation of Medusa by Perseus on the body; two sister Gorgons are held back by Athena (Eleusis Museum). Photograph courtesy Deutsches Archäologisches Institut in Athens.

PLATE 23 · Depiction of Myth and Epic

(a) Bronze tripod leg with Apollo and Heracles vying for the Delphic tripod above and a battle of lions below (Olympia Museum B 1730).

(b) Bronze griffon head, originally on a caldron (Olympia Museum). Photographs courtesy Deutsches Archäologisches Institut in Athens.

PLATE 24 · Release from Terror

From such simple trade and industry, conducted on so small a scale, new socio-economic groups of non-agricultural character could not yet emerge as self-conscious, potent political forces. The main centers of population in the *poleis* remained throughout the seventh century, as we have seen, primarily rural towns, and there is no evidence that commercial or industrial elements played any part in the consolidation of the city-state. Insofar as urban groups were to exercise a force in Greek history—and that influence must never be overemphasized—their role could scarcely begin to be significant until 600 or later.

Another class in Greek economic life of which far too much is commonly made is that of the slaves. While we have no really valid evidence on slavery in the seventh century, it seems unlikely that this factor was of any great importance. The sale of captives had already been a theme in the epics;[9] and by the seventh century war and overseas trade were probably producing a constant, though surely limited supply of human fodder. Greek agriculture never rested on slavery; bondsmen appeared in this sector chiefly as herders. Even in classic industry and commerce slaves played a subordinate role in the factories and shops of the most developed centers such as Corinth, Chios, and Athens.

COLONIZATION

"A RAVENING BELLY," said Odysseus, "may no man hide, an accursed plague that brings many evils upon men. Because of it are the benched ships also made ready, that bear evil to foemen

[9] *Iliad* VII. 475 (later), XXI. 40 ff., XXI. 79–80, 102, XXIV. 751–53; *Odyssey* I. 430 ff., XIV. 202–03, XIV. 449–52. Evidence for industrial slavery may be found, for Corinth, in Periander's limits on slavery (Ephorus, *Die Fragmente der griechischen Historiker*, 70 F 179; Nicolaus of Damascus, ibid. 2 A 357; Heracleides, *Fragmenta historicorum Graecorum*, II, 213); for Miletus, in Hipponax, fragment 43 (*c.* 550 B.C.); for Chios, in Theopompus (Athenaeus VI. 265b), who claims that it first made large use of slaves. See generally W. L. Westermann, *The Slave Systems of Antiquity* (Philadelphia, 1955); and my essay cited above, Chap. 4, n. 1 (p. 131).

over the unresting sea." [1] Raiding, looting, even trading, however, were too spasmodic and too limited in effects to satisfy the
continuing pressures which were built up in Aegean society.
From the very beginning of the age of revolution on down into
the sixth century the Greek world spun out many strands of
colonies. If one measures this outburst in relation to the size of
the homeland, it is certainly no less impressive than was the
irruption of modern Europe; the effects of the colonizing movement were tremendous for the rest of the Mediterranean, for
Greece itself, and for later civilization.

In dealing with the topic of colonization the modern historian can speak with sureness on some matters, such as the
names and locations of the new cities, their dates of foundation
(despite irking variations in the ancient tradition), and the
main founding cities, Corinth, Chalcis, Eretria, Miletus, and
others. Everything else is remarkably dark. What is the real
meaning of the term "parent city"? How did malcontents as-
semble at a harbor, get on shipboard, and then actually establish their new settlement? The complex tissue of causes and
stimuli which lies behind the network of new Greek states along
the coastal reaches of the Mediterranean and Black seas must be
ferreted out from limited hints.

The wave of expansion outside the Aegean proceeded principally at the outset from the Greek mainland and from the
island of Euboea. In this respect and in others it links onto the
earlier integration of the Aegean proper which was discussed in
Chapter 4, but the new wave differed appreciably in character and in speed. The spread of Greek culture during the Dark
ages had been a slow process, which had rested upon cultural
absorption of ideas from the mainland as well as on actual movements of peoples. Now, on the other hand, a rather abrupt outpouring took place, on the testimony of a detailed, basically
reliable tradition which is corroborated by physical changes in
cultural patterns at colonized sites.

The main vehicle of the expansion of Greek culture over
the Mediterranean was large-scale migration. Greek settlers
created agricultural communities like the parent city-states of

[1] *Odyssey* XVII. 286–89; cf. XVII. 473–74, XV. 343–45.

the Aegean, not in a casual trickle but in a consciously organized, massive movement. From these nuclei other peoples swiftly began to derive new ideas; Hellas was an ideal which men might admire and imitate, not a chromosome. Yet while the coastal population of the Mediterranean had a generally similar inheritance, only rarely could it fully absorb the ever more refined and unique Greek culture of the age of revolution. The Gauls, the Etruscans, and the Romans in the west and the Lydians and Phrygians in the east afford examples of partial absorption; but the sole area which swung fully, if slowly, into Greek patterns purely by cultural processes was Cyprus.[2] And this was already partly Greek by long inheritance.

Seeping or conquering, the Greeks found openings almost all the way around the Mediterranean. On the seaboard of Syria and Egypt more advanced political structures already existed; here, accordingly, the Greeks came either as traders or as mercenaries and lived in trading posts or camps (Tell Defenneh, Al Mina). During the seventh and sixth centuries Egypt especially relied on the vigor of hired Greek mercenaries, but others roamed as far as Babylon.[3] Other Greeks, as we shall see, entered Etruria and probably the Phoenician colonies as traders and artisans. The major objective of migrants, however, was always to found settlements of agricultural type, and for this purpose they needed coastal lands which were held by backward peoples.

Two regions proved most attractive: the coast of the north-

---

[2] Gjerstad, *Swedish Cyprus Expedition*, IV. 2; M. Borda, "Kyprios Charakter. Aspetti della scultura arcaica cypriota," *Rendiconti della Pontifica Accademia di Archeologia*, XXII (1946–47), 87–154. The same phenomenon may have occurred on the north coast of the Aegean; cf. the apparent Greek reinterpretation of native rites on Samothrace (J. M. Cook, *JHS*, LXXI [1951], 246–47). On the interrelations of natives and Greeks in southern Italy cf. Dunbabin, *Western Greeks*, 40–47, 183–88.

[3] Mercenaries: H. W. Parke, *Greek Mercenary Soldiers from the Earliest Times to the Battle of Ipsus* (Oxford, 1933), 3–6; Mazzarino, *Fra Oriente e Occidente*, 139–42, 288–90; Alcaeus, fragment B 16.10–11; *Ancient Near Eastern Texts*, 308; Brunner, *Historia*, III (1954), 118, on Egypt. Naucratis: R. M. Cook, *JHS*, LXVI (1946), 72–73, and "Amasis and the Greeks in Egypt," *JHS*, LVII (1937), 227–37; F. W. van Bissing, "Naucratis," *Bulletin de la Société royale d'archéologie d'Alexandrie*, XXXIX (1951), 33–82; Hasebroek, *Trade and Politics*, 60–66, who overemphasizes the place of mercenaries here.

ern Aegean and the Black Sea, and the tip of Italy and Sicily. The first of these I shall not discuss, for the stream of colonization which flowed north was minor in strength, generally late, and limited in effect. Even in Chalcidice the Greek settlements came no earlier than the start of the westward movement; those elsewhere on the north coast of the Aegean were founded thereafter, and the colonies on the Propontis went back only to about 700; such major Black Sea colonies as Sinope got under way in the seventh century.[4] Down to 650 the main vent for Greek migration was southern Italy and Sicily, which deserve fuller study.

Greek settlement in the West had a complex background. Intermittently the Aegean and the west-central Mediterranean shores had been in contact since daring Early Cycladic traders blazed the way, if indeed they were the first. By the Mycenaean period trade into this area, still spurred from the Aegean, attained quite noticeable dimensions, but toward 1200 direct connections seem to have been broken. While a little Greek Protogeometric ware may have trickled into southern Italy, local potters developed a Geometric-type ware on their own.[5] Not until the eighth century is there firm evidence that Italian craftsmen knew what was happening in Greece; actual Greek vases appear in quantity only in the Orientalizing phase.

By this time other peoples of the eastern Mediterranean

[4] Chalcidice: R. M. Cook, *JHS*, LXVI (1946), 71–73, 77–78, 82. Cyzicus: Akurgal's excavations, *Fasti archaeologici*, IX (1954), no. 118. Sinope: E. Akurgal and L. Budde, *Vorläufiger Bericht über die Ausgrabungen in Sinope* (Ankara, 1956). Rhys Carpenter, "The Greek Penetration of the Black Sea," *AJA*, LII (1948), 1–10, must be checked by Benjamin W. Labaree, "How the Greeks Sailed into the Black Sea," *AJA*, LXI (1957), 29–33; and A. J. Graham, "The Date of the Greek Penetration of the Black Sea," *Bulletin of the Institute of Classical Studies*, University of London, V (1958), 25–42. A. A. Iessen, *The Greek Colonization of South Russia* (Leningrad, 1947; Prague, 1951), seems to stress commercial motives for that area. Will, *Korinthiaka*, 127–28, surveys the most recent interpretations of the Argonauts.

[5] Protogeometric: Taylour, *Mycenaean Pottery*, 159–68. Local Geometric: Åkeström, *Der geometrische Stil in Italien*, who dates the style too late; F. Villard and G. Vallet, "Géométrique grec, géométrique siceliote, géométrique sicule: étude sur les premiers contacts entre Grecs et indigènes sur la côte orientale de la Sicile," *Mélanges d'archéologie et d'histoire*, LXVIII (1956), 7–27; Benton, *BSA*, XLVIII (1953), 264–65.

were also active in the West. Phoenician traditions, as filtered through Greek and Roman sources, would put traders of Sidon and Tyre at Utica in North Africa about 1100, at Gades in Spain soon thereafter, and at Carthage (Qart-hadast, New Town) in 814. These dates have been accorded rather blind respect by modern scholars, though they are in themselves no more valid than is the variant Greek tradition which placed the foundation of Cumae as early as 1150. Not only is there no sure archaeological evidence for Phoenician activity in the western Mediterranean until the eighth century, but even in neighboring Cyprus firm Phoenician footholds seem to have come only about 800. If we are to date Greek colonies largely on the basis of their graves and other deposits, the same principle must be applied to the Phoenicians; on this reasoning it must be concluded that significant Phoenician and Greek activity in the West began at the same time. The earliest datable pottery at Carthage, amazingly enough, is a deposit of Punic and of sub-Geometric Corinthian and Cycladic ware at the Tanit shrine, which cannot be put much back of 750.[6] From the physical evidence one might be justified in deciding that the Greeks were the first to reach Sicily and possibly even Spain.[7]

Whether and when the Etruscan lords came from the eastern Mediterranean to the lovely rolling lands north of Rome are problems which need not be examined here. The important

---

[6] Pierre Cintas, *La céramique punique* (Paris, 1950); P. Demargne, *RA*, 6. ser. XXXVIII (1951), 44–52; Jean Vercoutter, *Les Objets égyptiens et égyptisants du mobilier funéraire carthaginois* (Paris, 1945); Edmond Frézouls, "Une nouvelle hypothèse sur la fondation de Carthage," *BCH*, LXXIX (1955), 153–76; Rhys Carpenter, "Phoenicians in the West," *AJA*, LXII (1958), 35–53; Emil O. Forrer, "Karthago wurde erst 673–663 v. Chr. gegründet," *Festschrift Franz Dornseiff* (Leipzig, 1953), 85–93.

Cintas found nothing at Utica before the eighth century, but his excavation was checked by ground water (Carpenter, *AJA*, LXII [1958], 42). W. F. Albright, "Some Oriental

Glosses on the Homeric Problem," *AJA*, LIV (1950), 162–76, and *Studies in the History of Culture*, 37–45, argues for a tenth-century beginning. See generally the bibliography in Heichelheim, *Ancient Economic History*, I, 482–85; and on Cyprus, Gjerstad, *Swedish Cyprus Expedition*, IV. 2, 436–41.

[7] Sicily: Dunbabin, *Western Greeks*, 20–22 (after Beloch). Spain: Carpenter, *AJA*, LXII (1958), 49–51; Antonio García y Bellido, *Hispania Graeca* (Barcelona, 1948); Pedro Bosch-Gimpera, "La Formazione dei popoli della Spagna," *La Parola del Passato*, IV (1949), 97–129, and elsewhere gives an earlier date for the Phoenicians (the tenth-ninth centuries).

point is that Etruria, more than any other part of Italy, was ready to receive Oriental influences by about 750–725, and thus was opened to Greek artistic achievements which were colored by the same Eastern dye. Even before 700 the Etruscans had taken over and mangled the Greek alphabet for their own mysterious language; Greek pottery became ever more popular; very soon after the Greeks had launched into full-size stone sculpture Etruscan artists began to follow the same molds, first alongside the Oriental mode and then in lieu of it. Etruscan bronze work and bucchero vases, in return, appeared in Greece occasionally thenceforth.[8] Once the Greek sun had emerged over the eastern horizon, it never thereafter set so far as Italian culture was concerned.

Into Etruria Greek influence came not through colonies but through the medium of traders and artisans, drawn by the native ores of the area and by the riches of its lords.[9] Had we better evidence, I suspect that we might find that the Greeks played similar roles in the early stages of the western Phoenician colonies. The attractive forces of the expanding Hellenic civilization, however, would never have had so potent an effect on the West if there had not also been extensive settlement.

The immediate precursor to the wave of colonization was apparently a thin but bold sortie by men of Odyssean stamp who were adventurers, even pirates, but also knew more honest "gainful ways." Their origins, if we may rely on the pottery found in the West, were chiefly in the Cyclades. Beside island wares Rhodian and Cretan vases turn up early but in lesser degree, and Corinthian ware either appears or influences native types along the Greek coastal islands of the western route.[1] Ithacan

---

[8] Emil Kunze, "Etruskische Bronzen in Griechenland," *Studies to D. M. Robinson*, I, 736–46; Georg Karo, "Etruskisches in Griechenland," *Arch. eph.* 1937, 316–20; Robertson, *BSA*, XLIII (1948), 103.

[9] Riis, *Tyrrhenika*, 194, 200; Blakeway, *JRS*, XXV (1935), 147–49, on Demaratus; Margherita Guarducci, "Iscrizioni greche su vasi locali di Caere," *Archeologica classica*, IV (1952), 241–44.

[1] Will, *Korinthiaka*, 38–45; Paolo Enrico Arias, "Geometrico insulare," *BCH*, LX (1936), 144–51; Demargne, *La Crète dédalique*, 321–25. Though Alan Blakeway, "Prolegomena to the Study of Greek Commerce with Italy, Sicily, and France in the Eighth and Seventh Centuries B.C.," *BSA*, XXXIII (1932–33), 170–208, and "Demaratus," *JRS*, XXV (1935), 129–49, dated Greek pottery too early, the priority of trade over settlement cannot be en-

pottery reflected Corinthian styles well back into the ninth century. Cycladic motifs can also be found on Ithacan vases of the late ninth century, but most of the insular influence here, along with Cretan and East Greek pots, must be placed late in the eighth century. At Corcyra, which in later days was often but not necessarily the next stop westward, Greek vases do not appear earlier than in Italy itself. In Italy and Sicily proper we cannot on the basis of present evidence detect the presence of Greeks until the mid-mark of the eighth century. Even the scattered traders who brought west the first vases seem to have sought temporary *points d'appui* along the coast; the journey out and back was long, and the processes of trade or mutual exchange of presents probably formal and time-consuming. Both tradition and archaeological evidence suggest pre-colonial settlements of Greeks at such western sites as Ischia off Cumae.[2]

This stage lasted only a brief, if necessary moment. Political, economic, and social conditions in the Greek homeland were at a rare conjunction of propitious development, and large quantities of men were ready to enter the dangerous search for new homes. The reports brought back from western shores en-

tirely discarded. Contra: Cook, *JHS*, LXVI (1946), 80–81; Villard, *Gnomon*, XXV (1953), 11, and *Mélanges d'archéologie et d'histoire*, LXVIII (1956), 9–10, 19–20. Hugo Hencken, "Herzsprung Shields and Greek Grade," *AJA*, LIV (1950), 295–309, finds evidence in shield designs of the renewal of Aegean trade westward by the early eighth century; see also his essay "Syracuse, Etruria and the North," *AJA*, LXII (1958), 259–72. Cf. generally Dunbabin, *Western Greeks*.

Ithaca: Robertson, *BSA*, XLIII (1948), 121–24; see above, Chap. 4, n. 7 (p. 116).

Corcyra: Excavations of B. Kallipolitis in 1955, *JHS*, Suppl. LXXVI (1956), 20; on the role of Corcyra, Dunbabin, *Western Greeks*, 194–95; Benton, *BSA*, XLVIII (1953), 340.

[2] P. Zancani Montuoro and U. Zanotti-Bianco, *Heraion alla Foce del Sele*, I

(Rome, 1951), 22–24; G. Buchner, *Rendiconti della Accademia nazionale dei Lincei*, 8. ser. X (1955), 215–34 (Ischia); Dunbabin, *Western Greeks*, 6. Jean Bérard, *La colonisation grecque de l'Italie méridionale et de la Sicule dans l'antiquité* (2d ed.; Paris, 1957), is often fantastic (summary in *REG*, LIV [1941], 198–217). On the legends, see E. Wikén, *Die Kunde der Hellenen von dem Lande und den Völkern der Apenninenhalbinsel bis 300 v. Chr.* (Diss. Lund, 1937); E. D. Phillips, "Odysseus in Italy," *JHS*, LXXIII (1953), 53–67, who agrees with Blakeway and Dunbabin that detailed passages of the *Odyssey* reflecting trade in slaves with Sicily (XXIV. 307, 211, XX. 383) may be of the eighth century. Stesichorus of Himera elaborated the tale of Heracles in his *Geryoneis* early in the sixth century (Dunbabin, *Western Greeks*, 330).

couraged them to gamble in this direction; by about 730–725 the first organized group of settlers, from Chalcis and Eretria combined, had pushed out westward to Cumae, as far apparently along the Etruscan trade route as geography and other factors permitted. Another group of farmers from an inland Corinthian village soon colonized Syracuse in Sicily. Thereafter new settlements followed rapidly under the auspices of Corinth, Chalcis, and other advanced centers of mainland and insular Greece.

The causes of the outpouring and the reasons for its success alike are linked with the new forces at play in the age of revolution. In the fact that colonization was predominantly agricultural in purpose we can see that the Greek world was still essentially a rural one. Yet major stimuli were stirring men to break away. Some districts solved the rural problem internally (Boeotia, Attica); some conquered their neighbors (Sparta); a few, such as Aegina, were already turning to commerce on a large scale. All these took no part in the wave of colonization; but many restless districts were ready to disgorge malcontents who were landless or were starving on tiny acres. Only desperation, one must always remember, drove men to the labors and terrors of overseas settlement. Fortunately, ample plains lay open along western shores, better watered than those of Greece but sharing essentially the same climate; in site selection agricultural advantages were generally preferred over commercial possibilities.[3]

Leadership was equally important. This was furnished by members of the upper classes who had been ejected in the factional strife of the homeland states or were uneasy under the pressure for conformity in the new *polis* patterns; many, no doubt, were simply adventurous. Neither leaders nor followers, however, could have won footholds in the West so swiftly and so widely if they had still acted within the old tribal frame-

---

[3] Aubrey Gwynn, "The Character of Greek Colonization," *JHS*, XXXVIII (1918), 88–123; other bibliography in Heichelheim, *Ancient Economic History*, I, 494–97; R. M. Cook, *JHS*, LXVI (1946), 84–86, a balanced survey; Roebuck, *Ionian Trade and Col-* onization, 87–137. The agricultural aspect can be overemphasized; in the very first colony (Cumae) the choice of site seems to reflect an eye to commercial opportunities at least as much as to agricultural exploitation of its sandy environs.

work of life. A prerequisite for Greek colonization, taken by and large, was the emergence of the tight bonds of communal loyalty and willingness to co-operate which marked the city-state.

The outward token of this unity, which guaranteed success, was the new phalanx form of military organization; for, like the small bands of Europeans who boldly penetrated Old and New Worlds in the early modern period, the Greek colonists had a superior military technique. Led by an *oikistes*, the settlers were able to fight and win, and then to maintain their dominance over far larger masses of native tribesmen. In doing so, the Greeks of each colony had to rely mainly on their own resources. Most of the new settlements were independent city-states unto themselves,[4] and colonies rarely received (or welcomed) extensive reinforcements once they had divided up their lands.

Behind and implicit in all these factors is the general spirit of the age of revolution. Its dynamic force impelled the colonists in the first place. Its conscious analysis of problems led men to conceive the possibilities of plunging overseas. Its sense of order and structure gave them the forms in which they could succeed.

EFFECTS OF GREEK EXPANSION

So GREAT a movement as that which occurred in the age of colonization must feed the forces by which it was nourished. Inasmuch as the reciprocal effects of colonization on the homeland fell largely after 650, they cannot be considered at length here; but we must note at least their tendency to intensify earlier economic and social tendencies. The results of colonization, moreover, underwrote the dynamic quality of Greek civilization.

Economic interest and personal mobility had been preconditions of the colonizing spirit; both in turn were enhanced by the movement of large numbers of Greeks overseas. Such

[4] Note the qualifications of Gwynn, JHS, XXXVIII (1918), 115–17; Dun- babin, *Western Greeks,* 56.

specialized products of home agriculture as olive oil and wine gained ever wider markets. Incense, fine and cheap vases, metal wares, textile products, and other processed items went to the colonies, which sent back largely raw materials; Greek trade began to assume an air of mass interchange for the first time in Mediterranean history.[5] The great swell of Aegean industry and commerce came after the colonies were abundant and well established, and was at least partly connected with this source of demand. The colonies, too, though initially agricultural, inevitably served as focuses of trade with the natives roundabout. In this function the Greeks seem, to judge from our knowledge of southern Russia, to have remained passive;[6] native traders came to acquire the new wares and passed these tempting items far inland. With the wares went, at least in more advanced areas, ideas as well. Rome had become a city-state and was taking over Greek cults by about 600; inland Segesta in northern Sicily had turned itself into a virtually Greek city by 500; and the native Sikel cultures in eastern Sicily were yielding by this date.[7]

Politically, the wave of colonization produced double-edged effects at home and in the new Hellas. On the one hand the recognition of Hellenic unity was greatly fostered. Though each colony, as a rule, went out from one home state, with its blessings (expressed in a permission to take its sacred flame and gods), with leaders drawn from its aristocracy, and perhaps with its material support, some bands of settlers were drawn from several areas. More important, the coastal strips of settlement were a crazy-quilt intermixture of Chalcidian, Corinthian, and other origin, and their harbors seem to have been open equally to any traders. By the late seventh century Corinthian pottery was dominant everywhere in the West, but in the sixth century Corinth had to yield to Attic competition, which perhaps made its way largely via Ionian trade channels.[8] While

[5] This has often been treated; the details may be found in Dunbabin, *Western Greeks*, 211–58. See Cook, *JHS*, LXVI (1946), 86.

[6] A. I. Tjumenev, "Chersonesskie étjudy V," *Vestnik Drevnej Istroii*, 1950/4, 11–25 (summarized in *Historia*, II [1953], 120).

[7] Brea, *Sicily*, 159–60; Dunbabin, *Western Greeks*, 95–112, 171–93.

[8] Blakeway, *BSA*, XXXIII (1932–33), 204–07; Dunbabin, *Western Greeks*,

colonists felt some reverence toward a parent state as they looked homeward, they were far more attracted to the international festivals which were emerging in the period. The prominence of the Olympic games owed much to the fact that Olympia could easily be reached from the western settlements. So, too, the easy access to Delphi from the Corinthian Gulf fostered the glory of Apollo's oracle among the western states, which lined its Sacred Way with their treasuries. Both of these shrines attracted even non-Greek dedications by Etruscans and Romans.[9]

Although a sense of international unity, particularly on cultural and religious matters, was intensified by the process of colonization, the other tendency of political activity in the seventh century was also fortified. Political localism grew, and the rivalry of the city-states became more conscious. Abroad, the colonies were independent of each other and grew rich swiftly. Mutual suspicion and envy had abundant opportunity to become so irreversibly fixed in the new states that they fell to interstate warfare as fiercely as did the homeland in the sixth and fifth centuries. Against the relatively powerless natives, even against the more developed Phoenicians and Etruscans, they could maintain themselves though divided; but in the end the internecine struggles of the western Greeks paved the way for their conquest by the simpler, more solid power of Rome.

At home, too, the seventh and sixth centuries witnessed ever sharper antagonisms, and international relations sloped downward toward that status of continual tension reflected in Plato's observation (*Laws* 626a): "Every city is in a natural state of war with every other, not indeed proclaimed by heralds, but everlasting." In this dismal development the role of overseas spheres of influence and trading interests was quite sec-

226–27; Riis, *Tyrrhenika*, 201, based on inscriptions on Attic vases. Yet a possible Etruscan trader turns up at Athens, AA 1940, 338 ff., and Dunbabin, *Western Greeks*, 242–43, postulates Corinthian shipment of Attic ware westward.

[9] Kunze, *Studies to D. M. Robinson*, I, 742; Dunbabin, *Western Greeks*, 39–40. The role of Delphi in directing early colonization is debatable. Defradas, *Les Thèmes de la propagande delphique*, cuts it down even more than does W. G. Forrest, "Colonisation and the Rise of Delphi," *Historia*, VI (1957), 160–75.

ondary. As the *poleis* crystallized out of tribal society, their edges, metaphorically speaking, became sharper, and sparks resulted more easily when such states clashed. The increase in population, moreover, made each arable acre ever more vital; the bloody, long-protracted Lelantine war between Chalcis and Eretria was fought over a tiny plain. The interest of Thucydides and other later writers in sea-based empires must not lead us into the mistake of interpreting early Greek history in terms of thalassocracies.[1]

Nonetheless, the new factors implicit in commerce and colonization were not utterly unimportant, nor was the policy of the city-states determined solely on agricultural bases. If Corinthian trade dominated the West eventually, political as well as commercial and artistic factors may have played their part.[2] Herodotus and Thucydides both indicate that many states far afield from Euboea were drawn into the Lelantine war. While the distant powers, such as Samos and Miletus, or Corinth and Megara, had local reasons for antagonism, their rivalries would scarcely have meshed in the Lelantine war had commercial ties and hostilities not exerted significant influence in the later seventh-century Aegean.[3] As commercial connections between colonies and homeland intensified, every event, internal or external, thenceforth reverberated throughout the Mediterranean; every pressure or intrusion from outside affected in some degree the whole of the Greek world. "Greece lies scattered in many regions," rightly observed a later Hellene.[4]

Even more powerful than the economic, political, and social pressures which resulted from colonization were its effects on the course of Greek civilization. Geographically the Hellenic outlook expanded from its initial cradle—a tiny area embracing no more than the southeastern districts of Greece proper and the adjacent islands—to an astoundingly broad stage which reached

[1] See my "Myth of the Minoan Thalassocracy," *Historia*, III (1954–55), 282–91.
[2] Dunbabin, *Western Greeks*, 16–17, 227. Others disagree strongly.
[3] Herodotus V. 99, Thucydides I. 15; A. R. Burn, "The So-called 'Trade-Leagues' in Early Greek History and the Lelantine War," *JHS*, XLIX (1929), 14–37; Blakeway, *Greek Poetry and Life*, 34–55; Forrest, *Historia*, VI (1957), 161–64.
[4] Dio Chrysostom, *Orations* XXXVI. 5.

from the Tyrrhenian to the Black Sea. The earlier kernel, the Greek mainland, remained dominant; but the historian of archaic Greek culture must keep his eye on developments in eastern and western outliers. The Ionian settlements, already under way, grew rich and powerful; in Sicily and Italy Greek civilization struck firm roots. From the sixth century onward both fringe districts added intriguingly different variations to archaic culture in philosophy, art, literature, religion, and even political concepts.[5]

From the wave of colonization, finally, Greek civilization derived one of its most important stimuli to continuing evolution. Not only physical bodies but also historical societies tend to remain at rest, or to follow constant courses; the explanation of variable velocity in human development is one of the most serious problems in historical mechanics. For centuries Greek life had moved slowly, and the forces of tradition had full opportunity to harden their control over men's ways. Then men broke out of inherited patterns in the late eighth and the seventh centuries; and, while establishing a basically solid new foundation for their culture, continued to advance with remarkable rapidity. The process was neither easy nor automatically successful; a factor of major importance lay in the shocks and the breaks from old ways implicit in the movement of relatively large numbers of Greeks about the Mediterranean. Thereafter Greece lay open to spurs from every direction, and in return could transmit its achievements to many foreign regions.

The archaic pattern of life was not to last forever, for organized forces of change had been built into its structure. In part these forces derived from ancestral stimuli, which had been set free by the age of revolution, but in part they were new products of the economic forces we have considered in this chapter. Greek colonization emphasized the dynamic elements in Aegean society; the major Greek states, moreover, gained resources for an ever richer cultural life in the interchange of finished products and raw materials with the colonies. The eco-

---

[5] Mazzarino, *Fra Oriente e Occidente*, 18–20, adumbrates an interesting concept of poles. See on the West especially Ernst Langlotz, "Wesenszüge der bildenden Kunst Grossgriechenlands," *Antike und Abendland,* II (1946), 114–39.

nomic spirit flourished in this clime. Commercial and industrial classes were not in themselves significant forces during the great changes of the age of revolution proper, but eventually the growth of these elements made them powerful enough to demand political, religious, and cultural recognition. At that point the marvelous synthesis we know in classic, democratic Athens was ready to dawn.

CHAPTER 12

EPILOGUE

THE GREAT WAVE of overseas expansion is a fitting terminus
for a study on the origins of Greek civilization. Hellenic culture
was by now a seaworthy bark, able to sail anywhere; in most of
the ports to which it came it was highly welcome.

This was not the first movement which had set inhabitants
of the Aegean into restless endeavor. From Neolithic days, if not
before, the area had seen migrations, though most of these had
pushed into, rather than out of, the Aegean basin and had perhaps been more productive in terms of ideas than of ethnic shifts;
the most notable precursor of the historic colonization was rather
the widely ranging excursions of Mycenaean folk. But the expansion of the fourteenth and thirteenth centuries B.C. had been an
abortive experiment, cut short by the upheavals at the end of
the Bronze age. The outliers which had been scattered abroad
largely lost contact with the Aegean, which in turn sank into
isolation.

If the swarming which now occurred was greater and more
enduringly influential, its causes must be sought abroad and at
home. The areas of western Europe to which the Greeks came in
the eighth century had advanced remarkably during the Late
Bronze and Early Iron ages. They were ready to accept outside
influences more continuously as well as on a higher plane. The
Greek impetus in this direction was reinforced by other avenues of Eastern influence such as the Phoenicians and perhaps
also the Etruscans.

Native Greek development during the dim centuries from
1100 to 750 also played a major part in ensuring that the historic

wave produced greater effects than had the Mycenaean expansion. That earlier process moved from a land which had itself but recently attempted to graft the Minoan achievements onto its poverty-stricken inheritance from the Middle Helladic period; the Mycenaean economic and political structure rested, superficially at least, upon an effort to ape Oriental monarchy. Historic colonization, on the other hand, was the outpouring of a unified Aegean world, which had built by unconscious evolution a strong cultural and social system and which was itself ready to absorb new stimuli from east and west. In the establishment of the new colonies are summed up the economic development, social stability, and political progress of the age in which Greek colonization emerged; through this vehicle the culture of Hellas, steadily advancing in quality, could be spread outward. If Greece was now, as earlier, a mediator between the Orient and Europe, it had refined its inheritance into a noble structure of virtually new stamp.

From this period forward Greek history entered upon ever more complex ways. Italy, Greece proper, Asia Minor, and the Orient all interacted politically. Internally, economic and social development continued; the resulting tensions and forces affected many aspects of life. The cultural evolution of the Aegean had been well and truly launched on an ever more conscious road, aspects of which we have examined in the rise of Orientalizing pottery, stone sculpture, the temple, and the lyric; in these areas refinement and complexity proceeded apace into the manifold achievements of the late archaic and classic eras. Our information, as a result, becomes ever more abundant, though never so full as historians of these later ages might desire.

The subsequent development has often been discussed, and its main outlines at least are reasonably secure. Here I need not carry the story of Greek civilization further; even to sketch the fascinating history of the sixth century would be both presumptuous and of little utility. Let us turn back to see exactly what had occurred, first and primarily in the age of revolution and then more briefly in the era when Greek civilization was founded.

The preceding chapters have examined analytically the

many aspects of the miracle which I have termed the age of revolution; but at the end of the account a sensitive student may well feel that the explosion is tinged with the incredible. During the century from 750 to 650—or, to hazard greater precision, principally in the brief decades from 720 to 680—the Greek world was galvanized into an interlocked revolution which affected every aspect of its structure. Nowhere, true, were the new patterns fully fashioned by 680; but by that date their basic outline was clearly visible.

The revolution was of many parts, but all expressed a common intellectual change. Accordingly the same major forces appear whether we turn to the arts, to letters, to religion, or to political, social, and economic institutions. This fact is fortunate, for often the evidence for a single aspect is weak. The period lies on the first fringe of historic times; but the hints which emerge in any field bear striking resemblances to those in adjacent areas.

The underlying event was a crystallization of the still inchoate promise of Greek culture in the Dark ages. This event took place on simple lines. Archaic Greece was still not far removed from barbarism, and in any case its geographical endowment was not one of material riches; but would the miracle have occurred amid opulence? In literature, in the arts, even in politics, the Greeks refined very limited forms which their genius selected as vehicles for almost limitless achievements. Selection and refinement were now virtually conscious processes.

The men who achieved so much were clear and logical in thought, but they were not passionless monsters. Only by imposing upon themselves the tyranny of form and type and by restricting individual license for the communal good were the Greeks able to master the threats of anarchy. The victory was barely won. Whether we turn to the physical testimony of Protoattic pottery or open our ears to the outcries against aristocratic exploitation, we can see that men came close to shattering all the bounds of earlier customs. Had they done so, the capabilities of Aegean civilization would have been blasted.

The achievement of the age of revolution, measured in the deepest historical terms, was twofold. On the one side the Greeks evolved a sense of individual, conscious meditation; and there emerged a concept of the political importance of the individual, which was safeguarded by the justice of the political system. Yet also men agreed to subordinate individual passions and aims within a commonly accepted structure of life and thought. Greece was deeply fortunate in that its greatest revolution took place, first, in a period when its internal system was still simple; and, secondly, at a time when the Aegean was not yet under severe external pressures.

Wherever we turn in the age, we must sense its decisive importance in spurring the Greeks to enduring creativity; yet more, the achievements of the era were a firm foundation for many basic qualities of Western civilization. One example may suffice, which has been admirably sketched in Sir Kenneth Clark's *The Nude: A Study in Ideal Form*; the Greek artistic concept of the nude human figure which was created in the seventh century B.C. has dominated European artistic thought down to the present generation. When even a sober historian generalizes about the age of revolution, his pen unconsciously moves into a range of forceful terms not always approved in Clio's trade—"genius," "miracle," and "achievement" have inevitably crept into the preceding paragraphs.

For their use I do not apologize—the significance of the age of revolution in human history requires no less—and yet such words can be dangerous. Too often they have been used to mask an unwillingness, or inability, to penetrate to the hidden springs which drove the Greek world. These springs, nonetheless, can be found; or, at the least, the search conducted in this volume has been devoted to that end.

In explaining the age of revolution one must pay due attention to Oriental stimuli. By the eighth century the East, no less than the western Mediterranean or Hellas itself, had progressed far beyond the level of the Late Bronze age; development there had been far greater, partly because civilization was more deeply rooted and had bent rather than broken in the upheavals of the late second millennium. The lure of Oriental culture, always tempting to less civilized areas, had been much enhanced by the cosmopolitan, graceful form it had assumed in the ninth and eighth centuries. That Eastern influences actually had a continuing effect on the Greek world from 800 onward is abundantly testified in the history of the alphabet, the appearance of Oriental-type monsters and mythical creatures, and many other artistic changes during the eighth and seventh centuries.

These forces, however, are not primary. Change was already under way in the Aegean before Eastern contacts were resumed on a significant scale. This basic point can be shown both from the Dipylon pottery and from the *Iliad*; Oriental stimuli can at best be used to account for the degree of speed with which development took place and for some of the avenues in which native enthusiasm spilled out. The Aegean down to this point had been an enclave, which turned outward to the Orient and gained inspiration thence because *it* so desired. Never again was the situation to be true in Greek civilization. After the resumption of ties with the Orient and the sowing of colonies over the western Mediterranean and Black seas the Aegean homeland was inextricably bound up with the rest of the ancient world and endured now Persian, now Roman onslaughts. The favorable stars which shone down on Greece at the end of the eighth century were a unique constellation. And the Greeks were amazingly able to use their light.

The sources of Greek progress lay within Hellas itself. By the latter decades of the eighth century these forces had gathered enough momentum to break forth in a volcanic, awe-inspiring rush; but before this event lay centuries of slow evolution, which have here been called the Dark ages. These years, like many dim eras, must exercise one's imagination—what mighty energies must have lain, coiled in outward sloth, in the men of the early Greek world! Later centuries, indeed, made of this age a period of mythical fantasy, and so it still often appears in historical works. But myths and folklore are poor tools to employ in the search for the true quality of the Dark ages; we are now, at last, fortunate in having surer guides in the outwardly dull pages of archaeological reports. Vases themselves can feed that imagination which must be part of the historian's equipment, provided always that we make use of the ceramic evidence with judicious understanding.

In the second section of this volume an attempt has been made to elicit the meaning of the physical material which has survived from the era 1100–750 and, secondarily, to fit within this framework whatever evidence of value may be drawn from the survivals of religious, social, and political customs and from the Homeric *Iliad*. The historian must consider everything else first and only then may venture to form tentative deductions from the timeless world of the epic.

The picture which results for the Dark ages is one of very slow change after the terrific upheaval at the end of the Late Bronze era. In the evolution of Protogeometric and then Geometric pottery we have the surest guide to the tempo of development and can detect the drawing together of the Aegean basin into a common frame of culture, albeit marked by local differentiations which became ever more clear. Linguistic and traditional evidence, however, tends to corroborate the general picture presented by the pottery.

In studying the Dark ages I have drawn attention not only to the main lines of evolution but also to the highly interesting problems involved in the tempo of development and its sources. Periodization is always a difficult problem in history, for the men of any age do not suddenly and casually decide that they will live in different fashion from their fathers. Yet there are true watersheds.

The greatest of these was the deeply significant change which can be dated approximately to the eleventh century. Then Protogeometric pottery appeared, rather suddenly and rather broadly over several mainland districts of Greece. More was involved in the change of potters' outlooks than might appear at first sight: this is the point at which Greek civilization emerged. The men who took the crucial steps did so largely out of the sheer necessity of establishing a new order of life, if their society was to continue to exist as a viable form. They drew almost entirely on the past in doing so; there are no signs of external influence at this point of time. But let us be perfectly clear: neither the Mycenaean world nor the earlier stages, which were sketched in the first two chapters, are in themselves Greek, in the sense in which we apply that term to historic

Aegean culture. When we probe back from classic and archaic aspects of that culture, we find uninterrupted continuity as far as the beginnings of Protogeometric style, but no further; the turning point was the eleventh century. What then occurred was a veritable "jump," unpredictable in one sense, yet explicable in rational terms once it had occurred.

The historian who studies the progress of early Greece may justly feel that it is a story which makes sense and that it can now be surveyed in its main lines. Much remains to be discovered; and the efforts which may be made today on the basis of evidence now at hand will prove faulty ere long. Still, the student may hope to put his fingers on some of the basic forces which directed the story, or in the search to stimulate others to think more deeply. The emergence of Greek civilization is a subject which will endlessly fascinate its modern heirs who live within the stream of Western culture; an outlook which could already by the eighth century produce the *Iliad* or so marvelous a vase as the Dipylon amphora illustrated in Plate 11 was one of amazing potentialities. Anyone who is aware of the difficulties involved in its rise may justly marvel the more at its results.

INDEX

Index